Spain 1812–2004

Second Edition

Spain
1812–2004

Second Edition

MODERN HISTORY FOR MODERN LANGUAGES

Christopher J. Ross

Hodder Education

www.hoddereducation.co.uk

First published in Great Britain in 2004 by
Hodder Education, part of Hachette Livre UK,
338 Euston Road, London NW1 3BH

www.hoddereducation.co.uk

© 2004 Christopher J. Ross

The advice and information in this book are believed to be true and
accurate at the date of going to press, but neither the author nor the publisher
can accept any legal responsibility or liability for any errors or omissions.

British Library Cataloguing in Publication Data
A catalogue record for this book is available from the British Library

Library of Congress Cataloging-in-Publication Data
A catalog record for this book is available from the Library of Congress

ISBN 978 0 340 81506 9

6 7 8 9 10

Typeset in 9.25 on 13pt Lucida by Phoenix Photosetting, Chatham, Kent
Printed and bound in India by Replika Press Pvt. Ltd

What do you think about this book? Or any other Hodder Education title?
Please send your comments to www.hoddereducation.co.uk

Contents

Preface to First Edition

It is perhaps easiest, and best, to begin by saying what this book is not. It is neither a detailed, chronological account of events in Spain, nor an attempt to provide new insights into their historical significance. The latter, in particular, it could not be, because I am not a trained historian. Nor is the book aimed primarily at students of history. Instead, its intention is to help students, in the widest sense, of contemporary Spain to recognise and understand the historical references that come up so frequently in contacts with the country and in reading about it. It is also intended to be accessible to them, regardless of whether they are currently studying other aspects of modern history, or have done so in the past.

One obvious prerequisite for understanding is information. However, I have taken the view that the provision of facts – stating dates, describing events, naming names – should not be the book's main concern. I have tried to concentrate instead on giving an overview of developments and the relationships between them. In doing so, I am well aware of laying myself open to charges of superficiality and over-simplification. All the more so as the book's focus is almost entirely on politics and on one of its major components, economics; social and cultural aspects are touched on only in passing. I can but hope that the generalisations involved are on balance more enlightening than misleading and, above all, that the book might encourage and allow readers to go more deeply into subjects which, inevitably, are covered only briefly here.

Any history book of finite length faces the problem of limits – of where to begin and where to end. Many courses on modern Spanish history, I know, concentrate mainly or wholly on the twentieth century. However, I felt that the best way of grasping the country's political development in the modern era was to consider the last two centuries as a unit, bound together by a single theme: the arduous but ultimately successful struggle to establish democratic institutions and practices. In that sense, the year 1812 provides an obvious starting point, with the appearance of Spain's first constitution. As the endpoint I have chosen 1996, because the general election held in that year completed a full cycle of alternation in power from Right to Left and back again, under free democratic conditions, for the first time in the country's history.

The book begins with a prologue which gives an outline picture of what Spain was like in 1812, and why. The main text consists of ten chapters, arranged chronologically, with the level of detail increasing significantly as time progresses. Internally, the chapters are divided into thematic sections. Each begins with a paragraph outlining the main contemporary developments in the wider world which impinged on those in Spain, for the benefit of readers who have not previously studied modern western history. Each is followed by one or more 'exhibits', contemporary Spanish texts relating to the themes covered in the chapter, and accompanied by a number of questions designed to raise discussion on them. Following the last chapter, an 'afterword' attempts to draw out some themes of relevance to current events.

The overview approach notwithstanding, some concepts and institutions either crop up recurrently or are particularly important during a particular period. A brief summary of their main features and complete evolution, not restricted to the period of the particular chapter in which they are included, have been highlighted in special 'inserts'. They are given in their Spanish form, with an English equivalent. Throughout I have tried to use natural English terminology; where reference is made to specifically Spanish concepts I have tried to render them in a way which transmits the meaning rather than the appearance of the words (e.g. 'clans' rather than 'families' for the groups that jostled for influence under the Franco regime, and were known in Spanish as *familias*). Where words appear in single inverted commas they are a direct literal translation of the Spanish (e.g. 'social concertation' for *concertación social*). Bracketed Spanish terms are intended to give an indication of usage in context; there is no suggestion that they are the sole Spanish equivalent to the preceding English word or phrase.

I have included relatively frequent cross-references, of the form '(pxxx)', since otherwise the thematic structure would require an unreasonable amount of repetition. No direct references to other works are included in the text, however, as I believe they serve little purpose in a book of this sort. I make no claims of originality, and any given statement could be checked or followed up in a number of the sources cited in the 'Further Reading' section. Here, again, I have only attempted to scratch the surface, and to indicate works that should be reasonably accessible to non-historians. Anyone who subsequently takes a serious academic interest in some aspect of the period discussed will find them a useful starting point for further bibliographic searching.

I owe a number of debts of gratitude to the various authors whose works I have consulted. I should also like to thank Elena Seymenliyska for coming up with the original idea for the book, and for her advice during its gestation, and to thank Mag. Rafael de la Dueña, of the Instituto Cervantes in Vienna, for his help in locating appropriate exhibits. I am deeply grateful to my parents and brother, who in their various ways planted and nurtured an interest in history that has given me enormous pleasure, and ultimately allowed me to undertake the task of writing this book. Most of all, though, I am indebted to my wife Ulli for her encouragement and support, and for putting up with the emotional ups and downs of the book's production while living through an altogether more fundamental and demanding type of gestation period.

Christopher J. Ross, Vienna, December 1999

Preface to Second Edition

In addition to those expressed previously, I should like to offer my thanks to Eva Martinez of Arnolds for her advice and support, and to Ann McFall for pointing out a number of errors in the First Edition; the responsibility for those that remain and for any new ones is, of course, entirely my own. The translations of the various Exhibits now included are my own; since the purpose of them is to make the texts more accessible I have opted for fairly free renderings in places, although hopefully without altogether destroying the 'flavour' of the originals. Finally, while it cannot be anything but an inadequate gesture, I would wish to place on record my sorrow for the victims of the terrorist attack in Madrid on 11 March 2004, and my respect for the way in which the Spanish people and their new leaders have responded to the atrocity.

Christopher J. Ross, Vienna, April 2004

Chronology of main events

1812   Constitution of Cadiz proclaimed
1814   Ferdinand VII restores absolute rule
1820   Riego's declaration forces Ferdinand to recognise Constitution
1823   Absolute rule re-imposed
1828   Colonies on American mainland lost
1833   Outbreak of First Carlist War; moderate liberals called to government
1840   Carlist War ends; Progressives stage revolution
1843   Moderate rule restored
1854   Progressives stage revolution
1856   Liberal Union assumes power
1868   'Glorious Revolution' deposes Isabella II
1873   First Republic declared
1874   Monarchy restored in the person of Alfonso XII
1895   Formation of Basque Nationalist Party (PNV)
1898   Defeat in war with US leads to loss of most remaining colonies, including Cuba
1906   Jurisdictions Act confirms *de facto* Army supremacy over civilian politicians
1909   Unrest in Barcelona culminates in the 'Tragic Week'
1914   Catalan regional government established
1917   Protests by various groups lead to severe crisis
1918   Formation and collapse of National Government
1923   General Primo de Rivera seizes power
1930   Primo de Rivera resigns
1931   King Alfonso XIII flees the country; Second Republic declared
1933   Right-wing government elected
1934   Attempted left-wing revolution fails disastrously
1936   Popular Front government elected; attempted right-wing coup leads to outbreak of civil war
1939   General Franco wins civil war, establishes dictatorship
1946   UN recommends international boycott of Spain
1953   Agreements signed with Vatican and US, end of Spain's isolation
1959   Stabilisation Plan marks change of economic strategy
1962   Spain refused admission to European Economic Community
1968   ETA begins campaign of violence
1973   ETA assassinates Admiral Carrero Blanco
1975   Franco dies, Juan Carlos I crowned king

1977   Democratic general election is held, won by centrist UCD
1978   Adoption of new constitution
1979   Devolution granted to Catalonia and the Basque Country
1981   Military extremists attempt coup
1982   Socialist government elected
1983   Initial devolution process completed, with creation of 17 regions
1986   Spain enters European Community; Socialist government re-elected
1988   Main trade unions stage general strike
1989   Socialist government re-elected
1992   Government adopts convergence plan to meet Maastricht criteria
1993   Socialist government re-elected, but requires support from Catalan CiU
1994   Further round of devolution completed
1995   GAL affair results in arrest of former Interior Minister
1996   People's Party wins election, forms government with support of Catalan CiU
1998   Basque nationalists sign Lizarra Pact, ETA announces ceasefire
1999   ETA ceasefire ends
2000   PP re-elected with overall majority
2001   Further round of devolution; Basque government launches 'Ibarretxe Plan'
2003   Spain takes part in invasion of Iraq
2004   Terrorist attack on Madrid; Socialists return to office

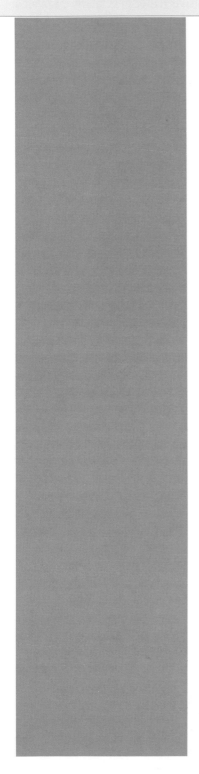

Prologue

To an astonishing degree, the course of Spain's history was determined by one, brief period. In little over 50 years, the country was transformed from a collection of rather insignificant statelets into Europe's leading power, and the centre of a transcontinental empire. The gross mismatch between this new status and Spain's limited resources meant that her imperial glory was short-lived, and followed by a rapid decline – relative to her European neighbours – that was not reversed until the recent past. Hence the crucial importance of that fateful half century and of its key moment, the most famous date in Spanish history.

The first significance of 1492 is that it marks the end of the 'Reconquest' (*Reconquista*), the almost eight-centuries-long process of expelling the Moors from the Iberian Peninsula. For much of that time large tracts of what is now Spain were under Muslim rule, especially in the south. Yet the lasting impact of Arab occupation was relatively slight. More important were the effects of the Reconquest itself on the various kingdoms of the gradually expanding Christian north: Portugal, Castile, Navarre and Aragon.

One enduring effect of occupation was the high value accorded in Spain, as in other societies frequently at war, to military activities and prowess; another was the tendency to grant extensive rights over newly recovered territory to local communities or powerful nobles. Perhaps most important of all, as it progressed the Reconquest became less a matter of regaining land and more a religious affair, a Crusade comparable – and explicitly compared – to the attempts to recover the Holy Land from Muslim rule. As a result, the inhabitants and rulers of Christian Spain came to see themselves as having a particularly close relationship with the Catholic Church.

These features were most marked in Castile, which by the fifteenth century was the only Christian kingdom with a Moorish frontier. Already the strongest Iberian power, Castile's influence was further extended when Ferdinand, husband of its reigning Queen Isabella I, succeeded to the throne of Aragon, thus uniting the two kingdoms under Castilian leadership. From this strengthened base the 'Catholic Monarchs' launched the campaign that enabled them, in January 1492, to capture the last Moorish stronghold of Granada. With the exception of Navarre, which was not incorporated until 1515, a united Spain had been established within its modern boundaries.

Before the momentous year was out the young kingdom was presented with a dazzling challenge and opportunity. In December, Columbus returned from his first voyage under Isabella's sponsorship to announce the discovery of the 'Indies', which as it transpired were, in fact, the Americas. Over the next half century he and his successors were to establish a vast Spanish Empire whose mineral riches – above all, silver – were shipped in vast quantities to the motherland.

Spain's imperial power was by no means limited to the New World. In 1519, Ferdinand's grandson and successor as King of Spain, Charles I, inherited from his other grandfather a collection of territories sprawling from the Netherlands to Italy – the family possessions of the Hapsburgs. While these made him the most powerful man in Christian Europe, they also brought him numerous and powerful enemies. Charles was engaged in almost constant struggle throughout his reign: as defender of Christendom against the Turks, of Catholicism against the newly emerged threat of Protestantism, and of the Hapsburg lands against the rising power of France.

On Charles's death the Hapsburg inheritance was divided. Yet Spain's position as Europe's leading power, and her sense of a special link with the Church, meant that there was no reduction in the commitments faced by Philip II, his son and successor on its throne. The effects on what was essentially a poor country, with few natural resources, were devastating. The costs of constant war soaked up the flow of American treasure, saddling Spain with debts that were to burden it for centuries, and leaving nothing over for the country's development.

The primacy of foreign affairs also prevented much-needed reform at home, where the former kingdoms of Castile, Aragon and Navarre, like the colonies and the European possessions, were governed as distinct entities. Moreover, the various Aragonese territories (Catalonia, Valencia and Aragon itself) and also the Basque provinces, including Navarre, were effectively exempted from taxation and military service, so that the burden of these fell almost entirely on Castile. Conversely, the merchants of Barcelona and Valencia were excluded from trade with the Americas, which remained the preserve of Castile. However, since that region was lacking in commercial expertise, the main beneficiaries of the American treasure were Italian and German bankers.

These conditions precipitated a rapid decline in Spanish fortunes during the seventeenth century, a process paralleled by the degeneration of the Hapsburg line, whose last representative – Charles II – died childless in 1700. His death triggered off the War of Succession, in which Spain was reduced to the status of battleground and booty for the European powers. It was ended in 1713 by the Treaty of Utrecht, under which Gibraltar was ceded to Britain. The Treaty's main effect, however, was to place a representative of the French Bourbon dynasty on the vacant Spanish throne, in the person of Philip V.

Although Spain was permitted to retain her American Empire, she was stripped of all her European possessions. By removing the temptation to play the role of European power that had so overstretched its limited resources, these provisions contributed to a modest revival in the country's fortunes. This process was helped along by Philip's reforms, brought together in the New Structure (*Nueva Planta*) decrees, which abolished the privileges of the former Aragonese territories, and of Catalonia in particular. Henceforth the whole of Spain was to be run on the King's behalf by a single council of ministers: the 'Council of Castile'.

These measures were a foretaste of the Spanish Bourbons' intention to install the system of absolute monarchy (*absolutismo*) already established by their French cousins. This differed from earlier, feudal forms of rule in that the King's authority was un-trammelled by the rights of particular social groups, institutions or regions. However, the Bourbons enjoyed limited success in Spain. This was partly due to the country's terrain, which made it much harder to centralise administration. But their plans also met stubborn resistance from those who stood to lose power and influence, especially the nobles and the Church. Above all, the royal authorities' chronic poverty severely limited the Bourbons' capacity to impose their rule.

Later in the century Spain was touched by another form of French influence, the intellectual revolution known as the Enlightenment (*Ilustración*). Its main impact was felt after 1759, when Charles III came to the throne. Able and energetic, he was strongly influenced by the enlightened despotism (*absolutismo ilustrado*) then in vogue among Europe's monarchs, and attempted to apply its lessons in Spain. He encouraged agri-cultural improvement, through irrigation programmes and the settlement of sparsely populated areas. Crafts and primitive industry were promoted by government funding and the relaxation of restrictions to trade, such as internal customs duties.

Yet, once again, a lack of resources restricted the impact of Charles' measures. He was not helped by the fact that the new thinking was associated with a country against which Spain had spent the better part of two centuries at war; its adherents were widely despised as 'Frenchified' (*afrancesados*). Moreover, despite taking steps to restrict the power of the Catholic Church – most controversially, by expelling the Jesuits from Spain and her colonies in 1767 – he could not break its hold over much of the population. Controlling most of what passed for an education system, the Church was well placed to resist tooth and nail the new philosophical and scientific ideas with which Europe was abuzz.

antiguo régimen

old order

The name *ancien régime*, associated above all with France, was given in retrospect to the structures characteristic of late eighteenth-century Europe. Its main features were: politically, the system of absolute monarchy, under which individuals were subjects without rights of their own; socially, a strict hierarchy dominated by the court and aristocracy; and economically, extensive intervention by the royal authorities into the workings of an embryonic market. In Spain it also encompassed a number of features left over from earlier periods, including the nobles' rights of jurisdiction over their tenants (*señoríos*), the system of entail, which meant that much land could not be bought or sold (p8) and the traditional privileges (p12) still retained by a number of areas.

Thus, as the eighteenth century drew to a close, the '**old order**' that was about to be shaken by the French Revolution was far from fully developed in Spain. Not only the Church but most of the landowning aristocracy and the mass of the people were deeply conservative, and tied firmly to traditional ideas and practices. The state apparatus was weak and there were few signs of the modern economic development that was starting to take place elsewhere in western Europe. Militarily insignificant, Spain became more and more of a backwater, cut off from events to the north.

Spain's isolation was abruptly interrupted by the 1789 Revolution and the subsequent wars between France's new rulers and their enemies. Too weak to resist her neighbour, she was drawn into a series of costly campaigns on France's side; in 1805 almost her entire fleet was destroyed at Trafalgar. Three years later Napoleon Bonaparte, by now Emperor of France, decided he needed direct control over Spain in order to invade Britain's ally, Portugal. His troops occupied much of northern Spain, and in May 1808 he forced King Charles IV and his son Ferdinand to renounce their claims to the Spanish throne, which he awarded to his brother Joseph, thereby triggering the 'War of Independence' (known to English-speakers as the Peninsular War).

The War lasted until 1813, when the last French troops were driven out of Spain. During the intervening years they controlled much of the country, or at least the larger towns, the main routes and the surrounding districts. In the occupied areas they imposed the changes of their own Revolution, removing restrictions on the use of land and property, and the privileges enjoyed by Church and aristocracy. Such reforms earned the French a degree of support, especially from government officials influenced by Enlightenment ideas. But only a tiny minority were 'Frenchified' in that way; the vast majority of Spaniards bitterly opposed French occupation. To a considerable extent, the War was the first genuinely national experience in Spanish history.

The mass of the people saw the War in very traditional terms, as a struggle to place their rightful King, Ferdinand – 'Our Heart's Desire' (*El Deseado*), as he became known – on his father's throne. As well as monarchism, however, the War also served to reinforce support for the Church, whose clergy often played a leading role in organising and sustaining resistance. At the same time, there was a redoubled hatred of all things French – a not unnatural response to the occupiers' sometimes gruesome methods, which were often repaid in kind. These three factors – Church, King and visceral anti-French feeling – came to form the basis of a primitive and deeply conservative patriotism.

Another important aspect of the War was the nature of the fighting. After their regular army had suffered several crushing defeats, the Spaniards wisely left conventional warfare to the British forces that had landed in Portugal. They concentrated instead on guerrilla warfare (*guerra de guerrillas*), with irregular, locally based bands using their knowledge of the terrain to harry the superior French forces, one effect of which was to establish a tradition and experience of such techniques among the civilian population.

Another was to reconfirm the strong local loyalties to individual regions, districts and even villages, which Spain's geography and history had always encouraged, and which received a further boost from a second feature of the War. For, with their master gone, most local representatives of the old royal authorities held back from organising resistance to the French. The task fell instead to *ad hoc* local committees (*juntas*), which, with the French in control of most main roads, operated more or less autonomously, under the leadership of prominent figures in local society.

To the extent that this role fell to the landowning nobility, the emergence of the committees served to reinforce not only local loyalties but also the status of traditional institutions. In some cases, however, precisely the opposite occurred. In many towns in the south and south-east, where the French presence was weakest, direction of the committees was seized by merchants and early manufacturers, who represented the newer commercial forces in society. As such they were especially susceptible to the revolutionary ideas brought by the French, including the notion that a country should not be governed by the whim of a hereditary monarch but by the will of its people, of the nation as a whole. Indeed that idea had a wider appeal among a populace that had been left largely to fight for its own liberation, with little help from established authorities.

In 1810 this idea of national sovereignty inspired local committees around the country to send representatives to an assembly. It met in Cadiz, which, protected by a British fleet, had become the effective capital of unoccupied Spain. Two years later the impromptu Parliament completed drawing up a blueprint for the country's future government. Spain had acquired its first Constitution.

Summary of main points

- After dominating Europe for a century, from about 1660 Spain fell into sharp decline and became increasingly isolated from its neighbours.
- The War of Independence had a profound impact on Spain, strengthening traditional and local loyalties, but also allowing revolutionary ideas of national sovereignty to find expression.

Throughout continental Europe the final defeat of revolutionary France in 1815 led to re-establishment of the old order, the key features of which were the absolute power of the monarch and his chosen ministers, and wide-ranging legal restrictions on economic activity. As a result, absolute rule conflicted with the interests of the growing commercial middle classes, who regarded with envy the political and economic freedoms enjoyed by their British counterparts, and in particular the right to own and enclose land. This *bourgeoisie* formed the core of the movement for change known as liberalism, whose most dramatic moments came in the various revolutions of 1830 and 1848. Its progress was halting but real, and by the 1860s most western European states had in place constitutions formally limiting absolute rule, and establishing some democratic rights as well as economic freedoms. These developments went hand-in-hand with the beginnings of industrialisation similar to that already experienced in Britain. Having thus largely achieved their main, economic aims, liberals tended to lose their reformist zeal and increasingly allied with more conservative forces in society, in order to resist destabilising pressures for further political change.

Liberals, reactionaries and generals (1812–1868)

The early date and radical provisions of the Constitution approved at Cadiz in 1812 placed Spain in the vanguard of European liberalism. Indeed its architects were the first men to be dubbed liberals. From the 1930s on, again relatively early, the country was run by governments that were liberal, at least in name. Yet little progress was made in terms of real reform, whether political, economic or social. In reality, Spanish liberalism was both weak and divided, while the forces opposing change were relatively strong and well-entrenched. The resultant stalemate allowed the army and its leaders to play an exceptionally important role in public life.

The liberal movement

In the event the Cadiz Constitution was overturned within two years (p11); thereafter it was in force only between 1820 and 1823 (*trienio constitucional*) (p15). Moreover, once liberals came to power permanently they backtracked from its provisions, a retreat that was the logical consequence of Spain's condition and their own division into two antagonistic factions. The result was that by the 1860s it had still proved impossible to establish a stable liberal regime, far less implant the principles laid out in 1812.

On paper these marked a complete break with the old order (p4). While the monarch was to remain head of state, effective power would pass to the Parliament (*Cortes*), which was to consist of a single elected chamber. Admittedly the right to vote for some of its members would be restricted to property holders, but the remainder were to be elected by universal (male) suffrage. The right of nobility and the Church to hold land in perpetuity was abolished, along with other privileges enjoyed by these institutions and by particular localities. Barriers to trade within Spain, such as internal customs barriers, were removed. Finally, the Constitution established a range of freedoms, in particular that of expression, one result being the emergence of a lively and highly partisan press.

These provisions were very radical for their time, but above all for Spain, a country that had fallen steadily behind most of western Europe. It had generated very little commerce or industry, elsewhere the breeding ground of liberal ideas, whose triumph in 1812 was possible only because of the exceptional circumstances of the War of Independence (pp4–5). Meanwhile, the vast bulk of the population continued to eke an uncertain living from the land, in a state of ignorance and illiteracy. Famines and epidemics remained common until the nineteenth century was almost over. Repeated wars, first in the vain attempt to retain the American colonies mostly lost in 1828, later also within Spain itself (pp12–13), imposed the further burdens of taxation and conscription. The result was a constant mood of popular grievance, exploitable not just by those anxious for change but also by those who wished to prevent or reverse it.

To add to these problems, the liberal movement (*liberalismo*) was divided over the extent of reform that was needed. Gradually the split gave rise to two broad groupings, often described as 'parties', but in reality much looser entities than would today be understood by this term. Neither had a clearly defined structure; both were constantly rent by squabbles among the factions that formed behind their various leading figures. Their membership was tiny and constantly changing. What is more, both persistently breached the basic principles of constitutionalism they supposedly espoused.

The movement's more conservative wing was concerned chiefly with economic liberalisation: removing the innumerable restrictions which then constrained business activity. In practice its concern focused heavily on creating a free market in land, through the process of disentailment (*desamortización*), on which a tentative start had been made in the previous century. This involved abolishing the ban on trading certain types of land; common lands, aristocratic estates and those owned by

Moderados

Moderates

Emerging as a distinct grouping around 1833, the Moderates included the most conservative elements of the Spanish liberal movement – the wealthiest of the new commercial and industrial classes – together with some more enlightened supporters of the **old order** (p4); 'Frenchified' bureaucrats (p3) and the landowning aristocracy. Their main concern was economic liberalisation; politically, they favoured a form of democracy so limited as barely to merit the name, and in many ways their unbroken rule from 1843 to 1854 resembled a military dictatorship (pp15–16). Thereafter they broke up into factions before disappearing altogether in the 1860s.
See also: **Partido Conservador** (p26)

the Church. In the last case, the government also forcibly acquired some lands and sold them on the open market. The main gainers from these sales, the first round of which took place in 1820–23, were the already well-off, including leading representatives of the more right-wing liberals.

By the time some of them were recalled to power in 1833 (p12), the chief aim of these **Moderates** had become to preserve the gains they had made. But they also knew that stability would only be possible if changes were made in the way Spain was run. Between 1843 and 1854 they therefore introduced substantial reforms to the administration of justice and government. Most importantly, the entire tax system was overhauled and placed on a more rational footing. These measures, while causing resentment among those who had previously enjoyed special fiscal privileges, at last provided Spain's rulers with an assured income.

However, the Moderates took their concern with stability to extremes. Twice they introduced new constitutions blatantly designed to keep themselves in power, and reducing the liberties of 1812 to a mockery. The second, adopted in 1845, restricted press freedom, brought local government under central control and gave the monarch the right to appoint the Senate, the upper house of parliament introduced in 1834. By tightening the property qualifications for voting, it restricted the franchise to a tiny clique of the very wealthiest males. Yet, even with such a reduced franchise, the Moderates routinely resorted to **election-rigging**. Elections became a means of keeping up democratic appearances – their rivals were always allowed enough seats to play the part of parliamentary opposition – rather than a way of attaining office. For that the Moderates relied on the favour of a monarch implacably opposed to their opponents (p13) or, *in extremis*, a military uprising (p15).

The Moderates' sparring partners, the **Progressives**, were more radical, their goals extending to elements of political and social reform. In particular they favoured a greatly extended franchise. The Progressives' following was correspondingly broader, both socially and geographically. Perhaps their archetypical supporters were the post-seekers (*pretendientes*) of Madrid and the various provincial capitals, frustrated by their failure to obtain one of the government posts that, in the general absence of industry, were the main source of urban employment.

This somewhat broader base, and the Moderates' refusal to relinquish office, encouraged Progressives to espouse the idea of a 'lawful revolution', supposedly justified by

> ### *fraude electoral*
> ### election-rigging
>
> First perfected by the **Moderates** between 1843 and 1854, when the electorate was tiny, election-rigging was later used by all parties (p10) and involved a range of fraudulent activities. Electoral rolls would be published late, so that those omitted had no time to complain. Since votes were cast publicly, patronage and intimidation could be used to influence electors. By contrast, scrutiny of the votes was secret, so that as a last resort results could simply be falsified. The whole operation was controlled by the Interior Ministry in Madrid, which allowed the government to determine the composition of Parliament down to the identity of individual members. After the Restoration of 1876 election-rigging became part of the wider system of **political clientilism** (p29), and remained widespread as late as 1923.

Progresistas

Progressives

From around 1836 'Progressives' was the name given to the liberal movement's more radical wing. The loose grouping's main popular support came from the lower middle classes of the provincial towns, especially in the south and east. They aimed to establish a relatively democratic form of rule, with a large electorate (although not universal suffrage, even for males) and the elimination of aristocratic privileges and Church influence. They were only in power for brief periods in the late 1830s and following the Revolutions of 1840, 1854 and 1868, but during their time in office they were responsible for much reforming legislation. After 1870 they split into two factions, neither of which survived the First Republic of 1873–74 (p23).

See also: **Partido Liberal** (p26)

---

the despotic behaviour of those in power. Such popular uprisings were frequent, and tended to follow a pattern. Discontent would break out in one or more provincial capitals. Then leading local radicals would form revolutionary committees (*juntas*) to control and channel the unrest. Often the civilian uprising would be connected with a military declaration (p14). In 1840 (p15), and again in 1854 (p16), events reached truly revolutionary dimensions, sweeping the Progressives to power. But these were exceptions; most 'revolutions' amounted merely to minor insurrections that were soon quashed. Their main effect was to create a dread of disorder among the better-off, whose property and sometimes lives they placed at risk.

In any case, the Progressives' own leaders were generally cool towards the idea of overthrowing their rivals by force, preferring to play out the comfortable role of parliamentary opposition. In 1849 this inactivity drove some of the most radical Progressives to break away and form a separate 'Democratic Party'. Moreover, during their brief periods in office, Progressive leaders seemed intent on aping the Moderates' worst faults, such as rigging elections. Twice, in 1837 and 1856, they too adopted constitutions tailored to their own interests. Both, albeit more radical than those they replaced, backtracked considerably on the Cadiz provisions: significant powers were retained by the monarch and the franchise, although widened, remained restricted to a relatively small group.

More positively, between 1854 and 1856 (*bienio progresista*) they enacted a broad swathe of legislation that provided Spain with a legal framework for modern business activity. At the same time a third major tranche of disentailment took place, the Progressives having already pushed through the second in 1837. Yet they took no concrete steps to ensure a more equitable distribution of disentailed land, as they had always preached. By now many of their own leaders had acquired such estates, which along with their parliamentary seats and a measure of social prominence, gave them a stake in the existing system. Significantly, the conspiracies that overthrew the Progressive governments installed in 1840 and 1854 were both supported by many of the party's own leaders, who now had more in common with the Moderates than with their own followers.

After 1856 an attempt was made to recognise this reality by bringing together all but the most conservative Moderates with most of the Progressive leadership, in a single 'Liberal Union'. Meanwhile, although the 1845 Constitution was reinstated, relatively broad freedom was allowed to those Progressives who remained outside the Union. Along with signs of economic advance, notably a railway boom, these arrangements briefly offered some hope of real progress. However, the boom soon petered out, having done little other than widen still further the gulf between rich and poor.

Even in the economic sphere, then, liberals had not managed to lay the basis for lasting progress. Politically their failure was still greater, in that even they remained unprepared to abide by the basic principles of their own doctrine, the Union's supporters (*unionistas*) being no more prepared to relinquish power than the Moderates had been. Eventually, they were ousted from office not by an election but by the monarch (pp13–14), a step that was fully in accordance with the Constitution in force more than fifty years after the first liberals had sought to abolish such traces of absolutism.

The forces of reaction

To be fair, as well as their own divisions, Spanish liberals also had to face stiff opposition. Significant sections of society remained suspicious of, if not downright opposed to, reform and the slow pace of economic and social change meant that this opposition suffered much less erosion than in other parts of western Europe. At its heart were the monarchy, and above all the Catholic Church, but as time went on sections of the liberal movement itself also drifted towards the conservative camp.

The strength of opposition to liberal reforms was made clear as early as 1814, when a virtually unopposed military coup restored the absolute monarchy in the person of Ferdinand VII (p4). Events under his rule revealed just how reactionary some Spanish opinion was. For the parlous state of the country's finances meant that Ferdinand had no option but to allow his ministers to pursue policies similar to the enlightened despotism of the previous century (p3). These involved a certain rationalisation of the country's administration and economy, to the detriment of the privileges traditionally enjoyed by the nobility and by certain areas. Moreover, a number of his ministers had served the French occupiers during the War of Independence. That, like their reforms, was anathema to the particular type of patriotism bred by the War (p4).

As a result, restoration of the monarchy in itself was not enough to satisfy the most conservative elements of Spanish society. Their anger boiled over in a series of minor uprisings, which often enjoyed the backing of local priests. The Church as a whole warmly welcomed the French invasion that, in 1823, put an end to the next brief period of liberal government – an operation joined by numerous Spanish volunteers, which again met with negligible resistance. Indeed, and notwithstanding the fact that some more enlightened clergymen had been among the 1812 Constitution's architects, it was the Church that formed the main focus of resistance to reform.

On the one hand, its stance reflected the threat to its status and material well-being represented by various liberal measures: abolition of tithes, restriction of the jurisdiction of Church courts, expulsion or restriction of the monastic orders who were its most effective propagandists, and disentailment of its lands (pp8–9). On the other, the spread of liberal ideas menaced the hold exercised by the deeply conservative

Carlistas

Carlists

Advocates of a return to the **old order** (p4), the Carlists came together in 1833 to support the claim of 'Charles V', as they called him, to the throne of his dead brother, Ferdinand VII. Their main support came from the Church, the rural parts of the Basque Country, Navarre, Aragon and inland Catalonia. The Carlists staged three armed rebellions, in 1833–40, 1846–49 and 1872–76, but were unsuccessful on each occasion. After the third defeat their movement split, with a faction known as the 'Integralists', abandoning the claim of Charles's heirs to the throne in favour of even more reactionary demands in other areas, especially regarding the Church's status. The movement was later reunited as **Traditionalism** (p84).
See also: **monarquistas** (p74)

Spanish Church on its flock. For those reasons, it wanted to reverse not just the reforms introduced since 1812, but also some measures taken by absolute monarchs before the War of Independence.

Such was the cause taken up by the King's younger brother. When Ferdinand died in 1833, leaving the throne to his infant daughter Isabella, Carlos and his followers rose in armed revolt, ironically giving the royal authorities no option but to hand over the government to the liberals, their bitter enemies (p9). The battle cry of the **Carlists**, 'God, King and the **old laws**' (*Dios, rey y fueros*), invoked the three main pillars of the old order in Spain – with the religious one in the place of honour. They enjoyed the backing of the Pope, and had considerable support in the north, where liberal attacks on local privileges were often fiercely resented. But the rebels found little backing in the south and east, from the aristocracy, who were among the main beneficiaries of disentailment (pp8–9), or in the towns.

Even so, and despite the military assistance the government received from France and Britain, the Carlists proved hard to defeat. Establishing what amounted to a mini-state centred on the small Navarrese town of Estella, they held out for seven years. One reason for the duration of this First Carlist War was the difficult terrain in the rebels' northern heartlands, which favoured the guerrilla tactics learnt during the War of Independence (p5). Others were the incompetence of the government's generals, and the poor pay and equipment of its conscript forces. But neither were the Carlists in a position to score a decisive victory. Once the more methodical General Espartero took charge of the government forces they were steadily worn down, and in 1839 the bulk of their forces surrendered. In return, their officers were permitted to join the regular army

fueros

traditional local privileges; old laws

Under the **old order** (p4), many towns and districts in Spain enjoyed traditional privileges, such as exemption from taxes or military service. By the 1830s most had been abolished, as much in the interests of administrative efficiency as from liberal principles. However, the Basque provinces and Navarre retained substantial rights, including the freedom to levy their own customs duty. This effectively excluded them from the single market which the rest of Spain now composed. Partially suppressed in 1841, these 'old laws' – as they were known in Basque – were abolished after the final defeat of the **Carlists** in 1876.
See also: **concierto económico** (p28)

without loss of rank, and Basque and Navarrese privileges were guaranteed. The main concerns of the Carlist rank and file having been met, resistance rapidly crumbled.

The Carlist movement survived this defeat, but it was severely weakened. It lived on in Navarre and the Basque provinces, which were stripped of some privileges in 1841 for supporting another conservative uprising, and in inland Catalonia, where fighting broke out again between 1846 and 1849. But, although this is sometimes dubbed the 'Second Carlist War', it was really just glorified banditry. By then, too, gradual social and economic progress had cost Carlism most of what little influential backing it had enjoyed, and the movement split into a number of factions.

Nevertheless, opposition to liberal reforms remained strong, above all from the Church, whose wealth and influence were further threatened by the Progressive Constitution of 1837. For, while this reaffirmed Catholicism's privileged status *vis-à-vis* all other creeds, it also asserted the state's authority over the Church in all temporal matters. Soon after, the Revolution of 1840 (p15) featured a number of attacks on Church personnel and property. Henceforth, such anticlerical violence would be a consistent feature of Progressive uprisings, and the breach between Catholics and liberalism's radical wing became irreperable.

Conversely, from 1840 relations gradually improved with the conservative wing. For the stability these Moderates craved would hardly be served by the Church's destruction as a social institution. Yet, with its resources and income so greatly reduced, that now seemed a genuine possibility, hence the various measures taken by the Moderates to safeguard the Church's position. As well as declaring Catholicism Spain's sole religion, their 1845 Constitution restored tithes, halted disentailment and confirmed the Church in the possession of its remaining lands.

The rapprochement was taken a step further in 1851, when the Moderate government signed a Concordat with the Vatican. Under its terms, the Pope recognised Isabella as Spain's Queen, and the Church retrospectively approved sales of disentailed land. In return, the Spanish state agreed to pay parish priests. Moreover, the Concordat's unclear wording allowed monastic orders to be re-established in Spain, their resumed teaching activities providing a further boost to the Church's resurgent social influence.

Among those associated with this trend was Queen Isabella, as ostentatiously pious as she was notoriously promiscuous. Her closest confidants were extreme conservative religious figures, and her court a stronghold of the most reactionary of Catholic thinking. Her equally religious, and oft cuckolded, husband openly sympathised with the idea of reuniting their family with the Carlist branch through marriage, in order to present a united front against liberalism.

All this would have mattered less had the Moderates not returned to the crown a number of important powers, including the right to dismiss and appoint prime ministers at will. From 1852 Isabella made use of this privilege to elevate a succession of extreme conservatives linked to the Church, alienating not just the Progressives, but even most Moderates in the process. By her obstinacy she triggered off the Revolution of 1854 (p16), the main effect of which was to destroy the Moderates as a political force.

A dozen years later events repeated themselves. Again Isabella dismissed from office the liberal grouping closest to her own views, this time the Liberal Union (p10).

Again she turned to figures on the far right of the political spectrum, ignoring even the remnants of the Moderates. Again she pushed the Progressive leaders to rebellion by refusing to call them to power, even though it had become clear that they represented no real threat to her position, or to that of the propertied classes in general (p10). And again the result was to be intervention by what had become the true arbiter of Spanish politics: the Army.

The role of the Army

Under the old order (p4), armies had been officered almost exclusively by aristocrats and were the unquestioning servants of absolute monarchs. In most of continental Europe, the defeat of revolutionary France brought a return to that situation. In Spain, however, both the anti-French struggle and the post-war context were rather different from else-where, differences which were reflected in the military's composition and understand-ing of its own role. Combined with the extreme instability of the next half century, these factors were to give the Spanish army a unique political significance.

pronunciamiento

(military) declaration

A characteristically Spanish form of military revolt, declarations tended to follow a pattern. A typical declaration began with the action that gave it its name; the reading of a statement of grievances by officers to their troops, as an appeal for support. If successful, this would be followed by risings at other barracks, and by a march on Madrid to force a change of government. Senior officers who did not support a declaration but refused to suppress it were said to have carried out a 'negative declaration'. In time, declarations came to be seen within the Army as a legitimate form of protest, with their own etiquette; for instance, that those involved in an unsuccessful revolt should be dealt with leniently. During the period 1812–68 most declarations were made in support of liberal reforms. Thereafter they gradually became more reactionary, a process that culminated in the revolts of 1923 (p57) and 1936 (pp84–5), both of which imposed right-wing military dictatorships.

The War of Independence had a profound impact on the Army. Its officer corps was broadened by incorporating the leaders of many of the guerrilla bands that had sprung up during the conflict. They, even more than the regulars, had become accustomed to operating with no royal, and little other authority. Consequently, there was a strong sense among officers that they were the true representatives of Spain, with a duty to act in the country's defence as they saw fit. In some cases, too, this feeling was linked to the idea that ultimate authority lay with the people rather than any monarch. Moreover, during the War and the confused events that pre-ceded it, the Army had already intervened in political affairs on several occasions; a precedent had been set.

It is against that background that the typically Spanish tradition of the **military declaration** emerged. It began with the coup that, in 1814, put an end to the first brief period of liberal government. Fears that the Army would always be an agent of reaction led liberals, especially the more radical of them, to espouse the idea of a national militia, a volunteer force drawn from their own supporters, which they duly established when returned to power in 1820. But that interlude was actually brought about by the pro-liberal declaration of Major Rafael Riego, and for some time ahead most such interventions were to come from the left.

The reason lay partly in the legacy of the War, but also in the fact that many declarations were prompted essentially by grievances that had little to do with politics. Riego's support, for example, came from disgruntled troops waiting to embark for the colonial war in South America. Moreover, like his, a number of the early declarations were led by relatively junior officers, the most famous being the sergeants' mutiny which, in 1836, forced the royal authorities to reinstate a Progressive government they had removed.

By this time, however, new factors were entering the equation, largely owing to the civil war that raged for much of the 1830s (p12). Although the conflict brought the liberals back to power, given liberalism's inherent weakness it also placed the new government's survival in the hands of the army. The Carlist War, therefore, led to a further increase in the self-esteem and sense of mission felt by much of the military, and in particular by the individual generals to whom its conduct was effectively handed over. At the same time, they and other officers were confirmed in a growing sense of contempt for civilian politicians. In addition, with the government facing bankruptcy, its troops were paid irregularly at best, so that discontent in the ranks became endemic. Meanwhile the quarrels of Moderates and Progressives (pp9–10), in which neither side was able to establish a decisive advantage, encouraged both groupings to seek military assistance against the other.

These various influences were to be seen at work in the Revolution of 1840, which began as a typical Progressive insurrection (p10). But it became something more when General Baldomero Espartero rejected an appeal from the royal authorities to crush the rebellion. Instead, placing himself at its head, he forced them to appoint him regent, making him the country's effective ruler. This step marked a new departure, since previous declarations had aimed at replacing one civilian government by another. It was possible only thanks to Espartero's rank and the prestige he had won in the Carlist War (p12), which allowed him to expect obedience from the army as a whole.

By assuming power himself, Espartero also took on full responsibility for the always-tricky final task of a successful revolutionary: the re-establishment of order and central authority over the provinces he had himself helped to inflame. He botched it. By failing immediately to crush continuing radical unrest he alarmed the Progressive leadership: by the brutal way he eventually did so he enraged much of the party rank and file. He then antagonised the Army by doing little to improve its pay and conditions. In 1843, these various discontented groups came together with the Moderates to stage another rising, and Espartero was driven into exile.

The Moderates' 'sword', as the generals identified with particular groupings became known, was Ramón Narváez, Spain's effective ruler for the next decade. Throughout that time he took great pains to avoid the sort of military rumblings that had helped to unseat his predecessor. The end of the Carlist War, and the terms on which it was achieved (pp12–13), had made this danger more acute by creating a gross oversupply of officers.

To assure them of posts, Narváez maintained both the army's complement and its budget at inflated levels, brooking no interference in these matters by civilian politicians. He also returned to it powers over local administration and justice removed in 1812. In these various ways he entrenched the army's position as a key institution in the Spanish state, and also reinforced officers' growing sense of themselves as a caste apart from, and superior to, civil society.

Indeed, this period was the closest approximation to a military dictatorship in nineteenth-century Spain. Narváez displayed none of Espartero's reluctance to crush opposition. He imposed martial law at the least sign of unrest, and subjected radicals to a range of repressive legislation – with such effect that the Europe-wide outburst of liberal revolutions in 1848 was barely felt in liberalism's homeland. Yet even so, he regarded himself as a constitutional liberal, and not without justification. Admittedly elections were little more than a farce, but his governments also undertook significant reforms (p9). Furthermore, Narváez resisted growing pressure to restore the influence over public life of liberalism's chief enemy, the Church, not least from the court (p13).

The Queen's meddling, combined with perennial popular dissatisfaction and splits among his own supporters, eventually put an end to Narváez's dominance. However, the decisive factor in the Revolution of 1854 was, once again, the participation of large sections of the army. The uprising followed a broadly similar course to that of 1840: an initial Progressive insurrection, this time augmented by fierce street-fighting in Madrid, where barricades were erected and entire districts lost to government control; the assumption of power by a recalled Espartero, who then proved unable to restore order while retaining Progressive support; and his subsequent removal, this time without the need for a further coup.

His wily replacement was the ex-Moderate General Leopoldo O'Donnell, who had established himself as the Queen's most trusted adviser despite having been a prime mover in the recent Revolution. O'Donnell confirmed his authority by crushing both the Madrid populace and the Progressive militia, which he subsequently abolished. In that sense he was following in Narváez's footsteps, but in other respects he broke new ground. As well as creating the Liberal Union (p10), he sought to reduce the army's ability and propensity to intervene in political life. Largely to that end he undertook Spain's first military expeditions abroad since the loss of the mainland American colonies in 1828, in Mexico and in Morocco.

At the same time, he continued and expanded the practice of having generals appointed to the upper house of parliament. During the economic advance that marked his first years in power (p11), army leaders also became involved with the nascent world of business, a development which bound them even more closely into the country's establishment. Meanwhile, lower down the ranks, the army's considerable administrative role ensured comfortable careers for many. Slowly but surely these developments were making the Army more conservative. But for the present, as the circumstances of O'Donnell's fall showed (pp13–14), the main threat to stability came from the right, and from the Queen in particular. The consequence was to be one final military intervention in the cause of reform.

Summary of main points

Liberalism

- Although liberal ideas gained a foothold in Spain relatively early, the Spanish liberal movement was actually weak and divided.
- As a result, little progress was made in modernising Spain either politically or economically up to 1868. Liberals' most significant reform was to disentail and sell large quantities of Church land, a measure that served to slow down and block other changes.

Reaction

- The most extreme opposition to change was the Carlist revolt of the 1830s, whose main support came from the Church and small farmers in the Basque Country and Navarre.
- After the Carlists' defeat the Church continued to be the main bastion of reactionary feeling, but from the 1840s it enjoyed increasing support from some right-wing liberals, and from the court.

The Army

- The War of Independence left the Spanish army peculiarly prone to intervening in politics. Initially it did so mainly in support of civilian politicians, and particularly the more extreme liberals.
- By about 1840 the military was the most powerful force in Spain, which for the next three decades was effectively ruled by a succession of generals. Meanwhile the Army, especially its senior officers, was integrated into the country's establishment, and its feelings turned gradually more conservative.

Exhibit 1.1: Manifesto issued by the Saragossa Junta *provisional* (1840)

A typical statement issued by civilian revolutionaries

La ciudad de Zaragoza acaba de levantar el pendón de la resistencia legal contra un poder que ha quebrantado la Constitución política del Estado, y que ha sometido la España a la dirección de manos extranjeras.

[... E]l Ayuntamiento de Zaragoza se reunió ayer tarde en sesión extraordinaria y acordó [...] que una Junta provisional reasumiese en sus manos la autoridad pública y la dirección de los negocios de gobierno. Con este objeto, y a fin de que la madurez de la liberación correspondiera más ostensiblemente a la grandiosidad de la empresa, creyó oportuno el cuerpo municipal convocar a su sesión de este día una reunión de ciudadanos que, por su posición personal y por la confianza que mereciesen al país, contribuyeran con sus consejos al acierto que para casos tan graves conviene procurar a toda costa. [...]

De esperar es que la justa ansiedad del público calme con una determinación de esta naturaleza, que bastará por sí sola para poner al abrigo de cualquier conflicto las personas y los bienes de todos los ciudadanos pacíficos; de creer es, asimismo, que la confianza que le inspiran a todos los buenos patricios del Aragón las personas que componen la Junta de gobierno proporcione en breve el restablecimiento de la Constitución política del Estado en todas sus partes y con todas sus leales y legítimas consecuencias.

The city of Saragossa has newly raised the banner of lawful resistance to a government that has infringed the country's political constitution, and subjected Spain to the rule of foreigners.

[... Y]esterday afternoon, the City Council of Saragossa met in extraordinary session and agreed [...] that a provisional Committee should assume the role of public authority with responsibility for running the city's affairs. To that end, and in order that the city's liberation might take a mature form more obviously in keeping with the grandeur of such an enterprise, the Council considered it appropriate to summon to its session today a group of citizens who, because of their personal standing and the confidence they evoke among their countrymen, are in a position to contribute with their advice to achieving the successful outcome which, in such a serious situation, should be sought at all cost.

It is to be hoped that the public's justified concern will be relieved by this decision, which by its very nature will suffice to safeguard the persons and property of all peaceful citizens against any unrest. Similarly, the confidence which the Committee's members inspire in every good Aragonese of rank and worth will surely mean that, in the near future, the country's political constitution is re-established, in full and with all its fair and legitimate consequences.

Source: Fernández Clemente, E. (1975) *Aragón contemporánea (1833–1936)*. Madrid: Siglo XXI.

Exhibit 1.2: General O'Donnell's *Manifiesto de Manzanares* (1854)

One of the most famous military declarations

Españoles: La entusiasta acogida que va encontrando en los pueblos el Ejército liberal; el esfuerzo de los soldados que le componen, tan heróicamente mostrado en los campos de Vicálvaro; el aplauso con que en todas partes ha sido recibida la noticia de nuestro patriótico alzamiento, aseguran desde ahora el triunfo de la libertad y de las leyes que hemos jurado defender. Dentro de pocos días, la mayor parte de las provincias habrán sacudido el yugo de los tiranos; el Ejército entero habrá venido a ponerse bajo nuestras banderas, que son las leales; la nación disfrutará los beneficios del régimen representativo, por el cual ha derramado hasta ahora tanta sangre inútil y ha soportado tan costosos sacrificios. Día es, pues, de decir lo que estamos resueltos a hacer en el de la victoria. Nosotros queremos la conservación del trono, pero sin camarilla que lo deshonre; queremos la práctica rigurosa de las leyes fundamentales, mejorándolas, sobre todo la electoral y la de imprenta; queremos la rebaja de los impuestos, fundada en una estricta economía; queremos que se respeten en los empleos militares y civiles la antigüedad y los merecimientos; queremos arrancar los pueblos a la centralización que los devora, dándoles la independencia local necesaria para que conserven y aumenten sus intereses propios, y como garantía de todo esto queremos y plantearemos, bajo sólidas bases, la Milicia Nacional. Tales son nuestros intentos, que expresamos francamente, sin imponerlos por eso a la nación. Las Juntas de gobierno que deben irse constituyendo en las provincias libres; las Cortes generales que luego se reúnan; la misma nación, en fin, fijará las bases definitivas de la regeneración liberal a que aspiramos. Nosotros tenemos consagradas a la voluntad nacional nuestras espadas, y no las envainaremos hasta que ella esté cumplida.

Spaniards: the enthusiastic reception which the Liberal army has been receiving throughout the country; the commitment of its soldiers, demonstrated so heroically on the field of Vicálvaro; and the applause which, on every side, has greeted the news of our patriotic rising; all these things ensure the triumph, from this day on, of freedom and of the laws we have sworn to defend. Within the next few days, most of Spain's provinces will have thrown off the yoke of tyranny, the entire Army will have come over to ours, the one true cause, and the nation will enjoy the benefits of representative government, for which it has spilt so much blood in vain and made so many costly sacrifices. The time has come, then, to state what we intend to do once victory is ours. We wish to see the monarchy preserved, but without a clique of courtiers to dishonour it; we wish to see basic laws enforced rigorously but also improved, especially those relating to elections and publishing; we wish to see taxes reduced, based on the practice of strict economy; we wish to see proper respect paid, in both civilian and military professions, to seniority and merit; we wish to see our communities freed from the centralism which is destroying them, by giving them the local autonomy they need to protect and promote their own interests, and in order to guarantee this we wish to see the National Militia re-established on a proper basis. These are our aims, which we state openly, but without any intention of imposing them on the nation. The liberal regeneration to which we aspire will be given its definitive form by the governing Committees to be set up as each province is liberated, and by the national Parliament which will meet thereafter – in other words, by the nation itself. We have dedicated our swords to the will of the nation, and we shall not sheathe them until it has been asserted.

Source: Artola, M. (1991) *Partidos y programas políticos 1808–1936: Tomo II.* Madrid: Alianza.

Topics
FOR DISCUSSION

■ What notion of legality and legitimacy emerges from Exhibits 1.1 and 1.2? In other words, how do the revolutionaries justify their actions, and what conception do they appear to have of the role and status of laws?

■ What, judging by Exhibit 1.1, appear to be the main concerns of the Saragossa revolutionaries?

■ What social and political interests are reflected in the demands set out in O'Donnell's declaration (Exhibit 1.2)? How compatible are they with each other? How do they relate to O'Donnell's later career?

■ Why was Spain so unstable for so much of the period 1812–68?

■ What was 'politics' in Spain at that time? Who did it involve? With what issues was it concerned?

CHAPTER 2

Out of chaos, stability? (1868–1898)

Beginning with the creation of modern Italy and Germany, the nineteenth century's final third represented a golden age for European liberalism. In alliance with elements of the old ruling classes, especially the landowning nobility, continental liberals succeeded in establishing a framework for capitalist economic activity and in harnessing the state's power to promote economic development. The result was a second wave of industrialisation in which steel, chemicals and electricity replaced coal and textiles as the key sectors. Meanwhile discontent among the lower classes was dampened down by growing prosperity and by the absence of wars, other than the campaigns involved in extending colonial rule to Africa, the cost of which in terms of European lives was considered acceptable. As a result, governments felt sufficiently confident to extend parliamentary government and the – male – franchise, thereby incorporating a growing proportion of the population into political life. Education, too, was massively expanded, so that by the end of the century universal schooling, to primary level at least, had become the norm.

The Revolution of 1868 was an attempt to restore the relative calm of the century's middle years by removing the element that had disrupted it: the Queen. However, it soon transpired that the monarch had been crucial to the strange form of militarised liberalism that Spain had developed. Consequently, far from restoring normality, the Revolution set Spain on a downward slide into the worst disorder for half a century, culminating in two further military interventions. The experience had a salutary effect on Spain's political elite. Appalled at the chaos they had triggered off, they devised new political arrangements that not only brought a lengthy period without overt unrest but seemingly also embodied liberal ideas in a relatively advanced form. But appearances were deceptive; the country's many problems had merely been swept under the carpet and, left unattended, were becoming steadily more serious.

Revolution and Republic

Although the 'Glorious Revolution' itself was a rapid affair, it was only the beginning of what are commonly termed the 'six revolutionary years' (*sexenio revolucionario*). Its victorious leaders faced not only the usual task of suppressing their more radical followers, but also that of filling the vacant throne. Their disagreements over how to do so compounded unrest in the country. They also rendered the new king's position untenable, thereby making a republic inevitable – and with it yet more chaos.

The speedy success of the 'September Revolution', as the 1868 Revolution was also known, reflected almost universal discontent at a time when economic downturn had hit the profits of the rich and the always precarious living standards of the poor alike. Virtually the entire political elite had been utterly alienated by Queen Isabella's behaviour. Not only Progressives but even the more moderate Liberal Unionists (p10) had resorted to a boycott of official politics (*retraimiento*), refusing to take part in rigged elections or play their part in the charade of parliamentary politics. It was therefore possible to build a broad alliance incorporating both these groups, as well as many Democrats (p10), with the objective of deposing the Queen.

The architect of this 'September Coalition' was General Juan Prim, a leading Progressive. On 19 September, at Cadiz, he organised a military declaration (p14), which was soon followed by other uprisings across the south and east. Before the month was out the meagre forces loyal to Isabella had been defeated by General Serrano at Alcolea, and the Queen herself forced into exile. The Revolution had triumphed and, with Prim installed as Prime Minister, the coalition set about drawing up a new Constitution.

The 1869 Constitution incorporated a number of long-cherished Progressive aims. Known as the 'liberal conquests', they included universal male suffrage, religious freedom, trial by jury, and freedom of association and the press. However, the new Constitution also stipulated that Spain should remain a monarchy, a decision that infuriated the Coalition's more radical supporters. They promptly established a Republican Party, and set about channelling the popular discontent that was already growing against Prim's government.

One cause of dissatisfaction was the suppression of the local 'revolutionary committees' (*junta*s *revolucionarias*) which had as usual sprung up in the uprising's wake (p10). But the main cause lay on the other side of the Atlantic, in Cuba, where a revolt against Spanish rule had broken out within a month of the 1868 Revolution itself. The poorly trained and equipped Spanish forces sent to suppress the revolt suffered severe casualties, mainly from tropical disease. The Cuban War also made it impossible to abolish the *quinta* system of conscription, as Prim had promised, or to fulfil his other main pledge, which was to reduce taxation. All these effects fell disproportionately on the poor who, understandably, directed their anger against their new masters.

Cuba also increased the tensions within the September Coalition. The Progressives who led the government were broadly sympathetic to the revolt, and sought to end it by concessions. This policy enraged the Unionists, who regarded Cuba as the last precious remnant of Spain's imperial past. But what really undermined Unionist backing for Prim was the question of a new king. For the 1869 Constitution retained not only the monarchy but also its considerable privileges, including the right to appoint the prime minister. Mindful of previous experience, both the main coalition parties were anxious for a king with views close to their own.

The Unionists had a candidate to hand; Isabella's brother-in-law, the French Duke of Montpensier. But the Progressives feared that crowning another Bourbon would mean a return to the system which had locked them out of power. They accordingly scoured Europe for a willing alternative of suitably aristocratic lineage – a process which did nothing for Spain's prestige, or that of its new rulers. It ended when Prim secured the agreement of Amadeus, Duke of Savoy, and pushed through his appointment as Spain's new king in December 1870.

Prim's protégé worried Unionists for the same reasons that made him attractive to Progressives. Amadeus's father was the first king of a newly united Italy, whose constitution was much too democratic for Unionists' tastes. Furthermore, as staunch Catholics, many were gravely affronted by the new kingdom's takeover of the Papal States, which had long been ruled by the Church. Once events confirmed their fear that Amadeus would favour the Progressives, the Unionists turned their exclusion into a self-fulfilling prophecy by once again boycotting politics. Despairing of returning to power while Amadeus remained on the throne, their thoughts turned increasingly to deposing him.

Crucially, the King was left to face these difficulties without his mentor, who was assassinated in Madrid on the very day Amadeus arrived in Spain. Prim's death removed the only figure capable of imposing authority on an increasingly restless populace, and of holding together a government sufficiently broad-based to be stable. Without him even his own Progressives split, their left wing breaking away to form a separate Radical Party. The factions spent the next two years squabbling with each other in Parliament, seemingly oblivious to the popular discontent being fanned by Republican agitators. Their behaviour so disillusioned Amadeus that on 11 February 1873 he abdicated.

That same day Parliament voted to abolish the monarchy, and proclaimed Spain a republic. Only a small proportion of its members genuinely supported the step, partly because the Republican Party remained a small, if vocal, minority in the country, and partly because it continued to suffer the effects of election-rigging (p9). But there was simply no viable alternative left. In the event, as the only party wholeheartedly committed to the new form of state, the **Republicans** were voted into power, with Figueras, one of their leaders, becoming Spain's first President.

Thus was the country's fate placed in the hands of a grouping that was peculiarly volatile, due largely to its insistence on federalism as the solution to Spain's problems.

Republicanismo

Republicanism; Republican movement

Republicanism grew out of the liberal movement, the first officially republican party being founded in 1869 by dissidents from the Democratic Party (p10). It was notable for its fervent belief in federalism as the necessary accompaniment to abolition of the monarchy. These Federal Republicans, whose support came mainly from the small-town lower middle classes (shopkeepers, teachers, etc.), governed Spain during the first phase of the First Republic. After the restoration of the monarchy the movement was long in the political doldrums, until in 1908 it split into two factions: the **Radical Republicans** (p48) and the **Reformists** (p39). See also: *Pacto de San Sebastián* (p63)

In the provinces, where grievances against central government taxes were rife, the idea of devolving power struck a chord with many, especially in the lower middle classes. But it also meant that such supporters were constantly suspicious of the party's Madrid-based leadership. At the same time, the implacable opposition of many provincial Republicans to all parties loyal to the monarchy – an attitude that earned them the name of 'intransigents' – clashed with the leadership's policy of maintaining good relations with the Radicals.

It was thus a bitter blow for these compromisers (*benévolos*) when, in April, the Radicals attempted a military coup and, on its discovery, followed all the other monarchist parties in boycotting politics altogether (p22). The upshot was that the Republicans won an overwhelming victory at the May general election, on a turnout of under 40 per cent. But the lack of an opposition merely strengthened the intransigents' demands that the Republic's constitution should include very extensive devolution to the regions. Here, too, the Republican leaders took a more moderate line, conscious of the need for a viable central government. In July Pi y Margall, who had replaced Figueras as President, presented their draft constitution to Parliament. It provoked the intransigents into insurrection.

This '**cantonalist**' revolt forced Pi to resign as President. He was replaced by Salmerón, and the movement was quickly defeated. However, that was not the case of another uprising, this time in the North. There, given renewed hope by Isabella's removal, the Carlist movement had risen again. Although the Carlists' support was no longer what it had been (pp12–13), amidst the confusion of events they were able, as in the 1830s, to take control of much of the Basque Country and Navarre. Like his grand-father, the new pretender to the throne – also called Carlos – established a mini-state with its capital at Estella; over the winter of 1873–74 his forces laid siege to Bilbao.

cantonalismo

'cantonalist' movement

The 'cantonalists', who made up the extreme federalist wing of **Republicanism** in the 1870s, believed that provinces and their subdivisions should be allowed virtually to run their own affairs. In the summer of 1873 they attempted to set up several such 'cantons' in southern and eastern Spain, but being poorly co-ordinated, and lacking any military resources, they were soon suppressed by the Army. Only in Cartagena was the 'canton' able to hold out for any significant time. The term became a byword for the chaos of the 'six revolutionary years', and of the First Republic in particular.

Politically isolated as they were, these events left the Republican leaders totally dependent on an Army increasingly disillusioned by their failure to maintain order. To retain its loyalty the government was obliged to adopt ever more authoritarian policies. These, in turn, only increased the dissatisfaction of those parts of society who had to provide the fighting men and tax revenue for the Carlist and cantonalist conflicts, as well as for the continuing Cuban War. As a result, the government was subject to constant attacks in Parliament which first forced Salmerón to resign, and then, in January 1874, defeated his replacement, Castelar.

At that point the Army stepped in. General Pavía forcibly dissolved Parliament, and a unitary – i.e. centralist – republic was established, with Serrano as President. On paper, its governments were attempts to revive the September Coalition; in practice they were drawn from the remains of the Radicals. Ruling mainly by decree, their practice made a mockery of the 'liberal conquests' of 1869. Isolated and unpopular, their fate was sealed by failure to defeat the Carlists despite the relief of Bilbao.

As the war entered another winter, the Army's patience again gave out. On 29 December 1874, at Sagunto, Brigadier-General Martínez Campos staged a declaration (p14) in favour of Isabella II's son, Alfonso. Within days the government had collapsed, and the First Republic with it, after less than two years of existence. Yet, despite its brief span, the Republic remained imprinted on popular memory as a time of chaos and suffering, an image exploited by those opposed not merely to Republicanism but to change in any form.

The Restoration settlement

The Sagunto declaration was no rogue affair. For some time civilian politicians – relics of the old Liberal Union, Moderate and Progressive parties – had been plotting to restore the monarchy. Indeed, by the end of 1874 no one, civilian or soldier, was prepared to resist such a step. The universal desire was for peace and stability, which over the next quarter-century was to be met to a very considerable degree by the arrangements known as the Restoration settlement.

Their architect was Antonio Cánovas del Castillo, whose efforts over the previous few years had persuaded almost all Spaniards of any influence not only that the monarchy must be restored, but that Alfonso was the legitimate and only realistic candidate. Furthermore, the settlement as a whole closely reflected his ideas. Their model was Britain, whose prosperity and freedom from internal strife seemed the antithesis of Spain's experience.

To Cánovas' mind the foundations of British success were, firstly, that a broad spectrum of the country's political and economic leaders had regular access to government and, secondly, that power could change hands between sections of this elite without military involvement. He noted, too, that while Britain had achieved both without having a written constitution, Spain had not, despite producing five such documents since 1812. Accordingly, although the formal basis of his settlement was a new Constitution, what it really depended on was a new style of political practice.

That in turn rested on two pillars. The first of these, initially regarded by Cánovas as the more crucial, was the King. Under the 1876 Constitution Alfonso retained the power to appoint and dismiss prime ministers, his mother's abuse of which had triggered off disaster in 1868 (pp13–14). So Cánovas devoted great efforts to imbuing in Alfonso the notion that the price of retaining his theoretically wide powers was to abstain from using them in practice. Hence his deep concern when Alfonso died suddenly in 1885. Yet Cánovas' worries turned out to be groundless. Alfonso's widow, Maria Cristina, acting as regent for her infant son, proved willing and able to apply his teaching as well as her husband had done.

In practice, the settlement's second pillar, the existence of two well-disciplined political parties, proved more fundamental to Cánovas' arrangements. These 'dynastic

Partido Conservador

Conservative Party

Founded in 1875 by Antonio Cánovas del Castillo, the party's original name of 'Liberal–Conservative' reflected its roots in the liberal movement, specifically the Liberal Unionists (p10) and the **Moderates** (p8). However, its philosophy was truly conservative, in the sense of opposing any challenge to traditional institutions – the monarchy, the landowning aristocracy and the Catholic Church – and the established order in general. From the 1890s the party was increasingly rent by disputes between followers of Cánovas' pragmatic approach to politics and critics of the corruption which pervaded Restoration politics. After 1909 these led to the Party's effectively splitting over the 'puritan' policies of its leader, Antonio Maura (p40). Greatly weakened, it was finally destroyed by the 1923 coup.
See also: **turno pacífico** (p29)

parties' – so-called from their allegiance to the Bourbon line – were in a sense heirs of the mid-century Moderates and Progressives (pp8,10). But essentially they were Cánovas' creation, modelled consciously on the two great British parties of the period, whose leaders' speeches he was reputed to learn by heart.

Thus, bizarrely, as well as founding his own **Conservative Party**, Cánovas also played an important role in creating its sparring-partner, the **Liberals**. In truth the two were more allies than rivals, since the key to peaceful alternation lay in their agreement voluntarily to abandon power to each other at regular intervals. Moreover, while out of government, each agreed to act out the part of parliamentary opposition, rather than turning to conspiracy or exposing the charade by boycotting politics (p22). The necessary discipline among the party rank and file was maintained partly by the knowledge of eventual return to office, and partly by the

personal authority and political skills of Cánovas and his Liberal counterpart, Práxedes Sagasta.

These arrangements finally allowed governments to operate without the constant threat of insurrection. Thus the Conservatives, who held power for much of the Restoration's first decade, were able to reverse a number of the 'liberal conquests' of 1869 without any return to disorder. Once the Liberals had enjoyed a sustained period of office after 1885, universal – male – suffrage and other reforms were reintroduced, again without any threat to stability. More broadly, one of the settlement's unquestionable achievements was to create a more relaxed climate, not just in political but also in social and cultural terms.

Partido Liberal

Liberal Party

Founded in 1875 by Práxedes Sagasta, originally under the name of 'Fusionist Liberals', the party was broadly the successor of the **Progressives** (p10) as the more radical wing of the liberal movement (p7). However, its commitment to reform was strictly limited by its participation in the undemocratic arrangements to ensure **peaceful alternation in power** (p29). After 1900, except during the brief leadership of José Canalejas (p40), its main concern became to halt the resurgent influence of the Church, especially in the field of education. Although it was in government for long periods the party became increasingly factionalised, and was effectively destroyed by the 1923 coup.

The more settled atmosphere was illustrated by the way in which the thorny issue of the Church's status was handled. Although the 1876 Constitution made Catholicism the official state religion, it explicitly permitted the private practice of other faiths. Yet even that compromise proved unacceptable to a significant sector of right-wing opinion, including some in Cánovas' own party. To mollify it, he consolidated the Church's virtual monopoly over school education. Typically, he did so not through new legislation but simply by failing to raise the tax income necessary to provide the state schooling required by law.

Cánovas' inaction helped to maintain the revival of the Church's social influence among the better-off (p13), which had been further boosted by the strongly anticlerical nature of much unrest during the 'six revolutionary years'. The Liberals accepted this with surprising equanimity, partly thanks to the Constitution's guarantee of a private sphere of religious freedom, but mainly because their opponents were prepared to compromise. Thus the Conservatives made no attempt to block the establishment of private lay schools, among them the influential 'Institute of Free Education', which provided an education system outside Church influence to those who were able to pay. They also refused to accept the Church's demands to be allowed to set up its own universities.

The religious issue also demonstrated the dynastic parties' ability to neutralise potentially disruptive elements on their fringes by incorporating them. For Cánovas' pragmatic approach reconciled all but the most reactionary right-wingers, and in 1883 the small but influential Catholic Union party joined his Conservatives. On the Left, the Liberals exercised a similar capacity for the assimilation of potentially disruptive elements (*atraccionismo*), luring disillusioned and dispirited Republicans (p23) with the prospect of access to power and influence. Even the Republican leaders forswore any attempt to overthrow the new regime by force, and accepted its existence as a fact; some, most notably ex-President Castelar, came close to giving it their positive endorsement.

The only significant figure who refused to accept the new disposition was the former Radical leader (p23), Ruiz Zorrilla. After going into exile he launched several abortive coup attempts, but their pitiful failure served only to underline the solidity of Cánovas' arrangements. On the Right, too, any remaining military threat was extinguished when the Carlist uprising was finally crushed in 1876. Splintering into traditionalist and reformist factions, Carlism virtually disappeared for 60 years (p13). Its defeat was followed by the abolition of Basque and Navarrese traditional privileges, thus finally making Spain one single economic entity (p12). The price paid, apparently minor, was a **special financial arrangement** which effectively devolved tax-raising powers to the two areas.

Two years after the Carlists' defeat, the Cuban War also came to an end, thus removing the principal cause of popular resentment. The change in popular mood was further boosted by a marked improvement in Spain's economic situation during the first decade of the Restoration period. The initial stimulus came from foreign investment in mining, itself the result of the free trade and other liberalising legislation brought in during the 'revolutionary years' – one of their few lasting, positive effects.

concierto económico

special (Basque and Navarrese) financial accord

In compensation for the suppression of their **traditional privileges** (p12) in 1876, special accords were concluded with the Basque provinces and Navarre, under which the provincial authorities collected taxes in their area and paid the central government a lump sum for the services it provided. Franco suppressed the arrangements relating to Vizcaya and Guipúzcoa – but not those of Alava or Navarre – in 1937 (p100), but under the devolution arrangements introduced after his death (p142) they were re-instated in full.

Thereafter a number of factors combined to sustain the upturn: a phylloxera epidemic decimated the French wine sector; the Bessemer process was discovered, making Basque iron ore potentially profitable for the first time; and the railways experienced a second boom.

These developments relieved to some extent the precarious conditions of the poor, and gave the small but growing middle class a strong stake in the existing order, symbolised by the aristocratic titles granted to a number of industrialists. They also gave the appearance that Spain was, at last, catching up on its neighbours socially and economically, just as the political arrangements that contributed to them were leading to advances in the political sphere. Indeed, one supporter of the Restoration settlement, pointing to the fact that Spain had universal male suffrage while only around one-fifth of British adults had the vote, dubbed Spain 'Europe's most modern monarchy'.

Towards 'disaster'

Such a grandiose claim may have had some basis in constitutional theory. But, as Cánovas had recognised, what mattered was political practice, and there, any advances made in his settlement were more than cancelled out by other, retrograde aspects. Not only that; political backwardness had social and economic effects, which tended to hold Spain back in those spheres, too. Far from leading the field in modernisation, Spain had missed out on most of its key aspects; it was, in effect, a disaster waiting to happen.

The Restoration settlement's fundamental weakness was that its apparently liberal, even democratic political arrangements were a sham. That was true first and foremost of Cánovas' boast that he had taken the Army out of politics. He always insisted that the Restoration had been the result of civilian plotting, and played down the military contribution. But in reality, Alfonso's coronation had been secured by the refusal of other generals to put down Martínez Campos' revolt (p25).

Nor thereafter did the Army cease to be the ultimate arbiter of events; it merely refrained from exercising that role, because civilian politicians were careful to observe its sensibilities. They respected the tradition established by Narváez, and kept strictly out of its internal affairs (pp15–16). However, at the same time they left responsibility for law and order in its hands and those of the militarised Civil Guard. Crucially, coming on top of the unnerving 'revolutionary years' the Army's pampered treatment extinguished what remained of its reforming ardour. From now on its influence was conservative, if not downright reactionary.

For the moment, though, that change was less damaging than the corruption at the settlement's core, the arrangements which ensured the **peaceful alternation in power** of the two dynastic parties. Just as earlier in the century, elections were a sham, with the results determined in advance by the government of the day. What was new was the scale of **political clientilism** required to ensure that outcome, with an electorate so much larger than before (p26).

The key to the operation of clientilism was local government. Mayors of individual towns and villages, and the civil governors responsible for an entire province, wielded very extensive powers that were the main source of the patronage and sanctions needed to make clientilism work. They were also named by the central government in Madrid, which could thus keep tight control over the whole system. Its model was the one that had long been used in France, where abuses were kept in check by independent district courts. But in Spain the magistrates were also government appointees, and themselves integrated into the apparatus of clientilism.

---

turno pacífico

peaceful alternation in power

The practice of peaceful alternation, established after the Restoration of 1876, enabled the **Conservative** and **Liberal Parties** (p26) to monopolise and exchange government office without the **military declarations** (p14) common before 1868, while avoiding the need to hold genuine elections. The success of this strategy depended on the prime minister at the time voluntarily resigning and advising the king to appoint a figure from the opposing party in his place. An election would then be held, allowing the new government to obtain a majority by the use of **clientilism**. Initially based on tacit agreement, the arrangement was formalised in 1885 by the secret Pact of El Pardo between the party leaders, Cánovas and Sagasta.

---

caciquismo

political clientilism

Particularly prevalent during the Restoration period, when it became a byword for corruption in general, clientilism was a system that allowed election results to be influenced by governments once the electorate had become too large for **election-rigging** (p9) alone to achieve that end. Its agents were local party bosses (*caciques*), drawn from the influential members of local society, such as landowners, mayors and even priests, who dispensed favours and official jobs on orders from their leaders in Madrid, as well as resorting to straightforward bribery and intimidation.

Nor did the Conservative and Liberal Parties (p26) who ran this system bear any real resemblance to their British namesakes, whose rivalry was the political expression of the conflicting economic interests of industrialists and commercially minded large landowners. In Spain, where industrialists remained scarce, and few landowners were interested in their estates' commercial potential, the parties remained mere cliques of politicians, concerned with no interests except their own. Rather than providing a means of transforming programmes into action they acted as channels for distributing the favours of office – jobs, contracts, honours – to their supporters whenever the system brought them back to power. In some areas a single local boss might even serve both parties at once.

The parties were the first part of Cánovas' construction in which cracks appeared. Ironically, they came from within his own Conservatives, with the emergence of a faction who regarded the corruption involved in alternation as a threat to the country's moral fibre. The leader of these 'puritans', Francisco Silvela, proposed ending the practice by loosening central control over local councils, and making them subject to genuine elections. Yet he too believed in control by the elite, and so planned an element of corporate suffrage. This gave the owners of businesses the right to have votes in that capacity, in addition to those they were entitled to as citizens. Fearing that this change in the voting system would exclude them permanently from local, and thus from national power, the Liberals rejected the plan out of hand. Silvela then pressed his leader to abandon alternation.

Cánovas' refusal to do so split the Conservative Party. But the division was only temporary, and normality – in Restoration terms – soon returned. Despite fading memories of the 'revolutionary years' (p25), despite Cánovas' murder (p46) and Sagasta's retirement around the turn of the century, the Liberals and Conservatives continued to be held together by the promise of regular booty. Any challenge to them continued to be smothered by the clientilist system, by widespread apathy and cynicism, and, when the need arose, by military repression, as with the upsurge of anarchist activity in the 1880s (p46). However, if the political cracks could be papered over, the settlement's other damaging effects could not.

Some of the difficulties resulted from Cánovas' religious compromise (p27), whose terms were devised to cement the alliance between the Church and the better-off, among whom the upsurge in Church attendance was concentrated. Apart from the peasant farmers of Old Castile, the poor abandoned the Church in droves, disillusioned by its failure to denounce the appalling living and working conditions in the southern countryside and the embryonic northern industrial areas. It is hardly surprising that bitter anticlericalism should have become a major aspect of social division in Spain. More immediately, those unable to afford a private lay education were forced to rely – at best – on hopelessly antiquated Church-run establishments.

The lack of a proper education system did not merely blight the lives of millions; it also severely constrained the country's economic development. Similarly, the centralisation of local government had worse effects than the spreading of dubious moral values: with even the most minor of decisions requiring approval from Madrid, the operation of the councils was painfully slow. Worst of all, under a fiscal system unchanged since the 1850s, taxes were ludicrously low, and their application little better than arbitrary. But reforming the system would have meant taking on influential sectors of opinion – something no government would risk. As a result, both central and local administration were starved of the funds they urgently needed to improve the country's physical and social infrastructure.

Inadequate infrastructure caused major problems for Castile's important wheat farming sector. So antiquated was Spain's transport system that, since the 1869 free trade legislation, American imports had been able to undercut domestic wheat in the vital Catalan and Basque markets. In 1885 the other mainstay of the rural economy suffered a devastating blow, when Spanish vines, too, were hit by phylloxera. Economic growth (pp27–8), based on rising rural incomes which were in turn founded on the wine trade's rapid expansion, was reversed. For the masses, in particular, the accompanying rise in prosperity was brought to an abrupt halt.

If agriculture remained so important to the economy it was because industrialisation was so limited. Apart from the mines and railways, almost all of which were foreign-controlled, industry was confined to two sectors: textile manufacture in Catalonia, and iron and steel production in the Basque Country. Yet even in those centres the picture was less rosy than it seemed, because the technology used in both industries was outdated – a problem compounded in the Catalan case by the small size of the firms involved. As a result, both regions were threatened by more competitive European rivals.

The response of the Basque and Catalan industrialists was to join the Castilian cereal farmers in lobbying for an end to free trade. In 1891 their efforts bore fruit when the government introduced prohibitive tariffs on imported goods and produce. However, while such protectionism safeguarded the short-term profits of the three powerful groups concerned, it was extremely bad for their customers, who now had no alternative sources of supply. In the longer term protection was also disastrous for the three sectors themselves, since it removed any incentive to increase productivity or to innovate, causing Spain to fall still further behind the leading industrial countries.

That fact was brought brutally home by events in Cuba. Indeed, the country's last important colony was itself a prime example of how Spain was out of phase with the industrialised world. Even at the zenith of commercially driven colonialism, Spain was still drawing little benefit from Cuba's economy, since it was largely controlled by American interests. When a fresh rebellion broke out on the island in 1895 the same interests orchestrated an outcry in favour of US intervention, as a result of which the battleship *Maine* was sent to the island. When it exploded in Havana harbour in February 1898, although the cause was probably an accident, public reaction left President McKinley with no option but to declare war.

Spain was hopelessly outmatched. Its fleet – as opposed to the bloated naval bureaucracy, filled on the basis of political favours – had suffered gravely from the general lack of public funds. The ships' guns were antiquated, the crew had not been trained to use them, and the vessels themselves had insufficient coal to steam at full speed. The results would have been comic, had they not been so tragic. In the summer of 1898 the entire navy was destroyed in a few engagements lasting a matter of hours; in the decisive one, which took place off Santiago de Cuba, only one American sailor died. The Philippines and Puerto Rico were lost to the USA, and Cuba, while nominally independent, became a *de facto* American dependency.

Reaction in Spain to 'the disaster', as these events soon came to be known, was as revealing as the events themselves. Conservative politicians and much of public opinion – the former blind to reality, the latter hopelessly ill-informed – went from the assumption of easy victory to numbed shock. And while the Liberals were generally quicker to foresee the appalling outcome, they cynically chose to keep their insight to themselves, for fear of losing popularity. Material backwardness, while bad enough in itself, was far from the full price of what was presented as stability but was really stagnation.

Summary of main points

Revolution and Republic

- The 1868 Revolution quickly achieved its main objective of overthrowing Queen Isabella. But it failed to bring stability, since its mass support was soon disillusioned by the relative conservatism of its leaders, who were themselves split over who should succeed to the throne.
- In 1873, even though Republicans remained a minority, these disagreements led to the declaration of a Republic. Its chaotic life was marked by two civil wars, as well as the continuing conflict in Cuba, and within two years it was brought down by a military coup.

Restoration settlement

- The settlement put in place by Cánovas in 1875 was designed to avoid such military intervention, and other types of unrest that might threaten the established classes.
- It was based on the restoration of the Bourbon monarch and, above all, on the creation of two political parties (Conservative and Liberal), which were more cohesive than their forerunners and willing to hand over power to each other.
- Further important factors were a partial reconciliation between the Church and the political elite, and a – temporary – economic upswing.

Towards 'disaster'

- The progress achieved under the restoration settlement was almost entirely superficial.
- Politically, it was based on corrupt clientilism and on the authority of particular individuals; the 'dynastic parties' remained weak and represented no interests other than their own.
- Economically, advance came to a halt as soon as external circumstances changed. Real progress was hamstrung by the lack of proper education and taxation systems, and by the protectionist policies imposed by large landowners and the small group of industrialists.

Exhibit 2.1: A voice of radical Republicanism (1870)

Extracts from an edition of a Republican paper which appeared two days before the arrival of King Amadeus in Spain, and the assassination of his mentor, General Prim

> […]No le bastaba a ese grande reo de lesa-revolución, que se llama *gobierno septembrista*, haber negado los derechos individuales, disputar la Soberanía del pueblo con la soberanía de un tirano extranjero, inviolable, indiscutible, inamovible y hereditario; desmoralizar la administración, desangrar a todas las clases de la sociedad, oprimir al pueblo y amordazar la prensa; era necesario algo más, y para que nada faltara a sus traiciones, a sus crímenes y perjurios, ha concluido por sancionarlos con el voto de una [Asamblea] Constituyente facciosa, que con la vergüenza y el vilipendio de la nación española, ha votado su muerte, que está reclamando su más pronta e inmediata ejecución. […]
>
> Ciudadanos españoles sin distinción de clases ni de partidos políticos: el rostro de nuestra madre la patria ha sido escupido y abofeteado, su altivez humillada y su honor difamado por un intruso, por un TIRANO EXTRANJERO. ¿Qué hacemos? ¿A qué aguardamos? ¿Consentiremos que un tirano de Italia esclavice al valeroso pueblo español, a la España con honra, libre e INDEPENDIENTE? […]
>
> Ciudadanos españoles: la patria está en peligro. Cuando el tirano extranjero coloque su inmunda planta en tierra española, que esta afrenta sea para todos la señal de exclamar con el coraje de los pueblos ultrajados:
>
> ¡AL combate!
> ¡ABAJO LO EXISTENTE!
> ¡VIVA EL EJÉRCITO ESPAÑOL HONRADO!
> ¡VIVA LA SOBERANÍA NACIONAL!
> ¡VIVA LA REVOLUCIÓN!

> […]For that bunch of counterrevolutionaries, the so-called 'Septembrist'[1] government, it was not enough to have denied individual rights, or to have replaced the sovereignty of the people by that of a hereditary foreign tyrant, inviolable, unquestionable and irremovable, or to have demoralized the public service, bled white all classes of society, oppressed the people or gagged the

press; it had to go further and, so that its treachery, its crimes and its falsehoods should lack nothing, it has finally sanctioned them with the votes of a faction-ridden Constituent Assembly that, to the Spanish nation's shame and humiliation, has voted for its own extinction, which is crying out to be effected as quickly as possible. […]

Citizens of Spain, of every class and political party: our beloved fatherland has been spat upon and insulted, its pride humbled and its honour impugned by an outsider, by a FOREIGN TYRANT. What shall we do? What are we waiting for? Are we going to allow an Italian tyrant to enslave the valiant Spanish people, and honourable, free, independent Spain itself? […]

Citizens of Spain, the fatherland is in danger. When the foreign tyrant places his vile foot on Spanish soil, let that affront be the signal for all to cry with the spirit of an offended people:

TO combat![2]

DOWN WITH THE EXISTING SYSTEM!

LONG LIVE THE HONOURABLE SPANISH ARMY!

LONG LIVE NATIONAL SOVEREIGNTY!

LONG LIVE THE REVOLUTION!

[1] From the September Revolution of 1868.
[2] A play on the name of the publication in which the text appeared.

Source: *El Combate*, Madrid (25 December 1870).

Exhibit 2.2: Cánovas on the monarchy (1886)

Extracts from a speech to Parliament

La idea de todos los monárquicos y en todas partes, es que la monarquía, que para eso es hereditaria, porque de otra suerte sería una irrisión que hereditaria se llamase, es, por su naturaleza, perpetua. [...]

No hay que pensar, pues, que con esta convicción nosotros podamos aceptar ni poco ni mucho, ni de cerca ni de lejos, el principio de una evolución pacífica y falsamente apellidada legal, detrás de la cual pudiera estar la supresión de la monarquía. Nosotros concebimos una monarquía que puede errar, que puede caer; pero nosotros no podemos admitir que eso se prevea por las leyes de un país; no podemos admitir que, en las circunstancias normales de la nación, se tenga por sobreentendida en las leyes y en el régimen político, que el rey pueda ser a cada instante separado por un funcionario cualquiera, sin los beneficios siquiera de la inamovilidad, ni de los reglamentos. [...]

Para nosotros jamás, por ningún camino se puede llegar, por medio de la legalidad, a la supresión de la monarquía, a causa de que no hay legalidad sin la monarquìa, a causa de que sin la monarquía puede haber hechos, puede haber fuerza, puede haber batallas, pero no hay, ni puede haber, legalidad. [...]

For monarchists everywhere, the monarchy – and this is why it is hereditary, since otherwise it would be ludicrous to call it so – is, by its very nature, eternal. [...]

So nobody should think that, believing this as we do, we could ever accept, to any extent or in any form, the idea of a peaceful process of evolution, allegedly legal but in reality not so, at the end of which might lie the monarchy's abolition. We can conceive of a monarchy that is fallible, or overthrown. But we cannot allow that the law of the land provide for such an eventuality. We cannot allow that, under the country's normal circumstances, it is somehow assumed in legislation and political practice that the King could be deposed by a mere public servant, lacking even the protection of his irremovable status, or the disciplinary code. [...]

In our view, there can be no way that leads, within the ambit of legality, to the monarchy's abolition, since without the monarchy there can be deeds, there can be power, there can be battles, but there is not, and there never can be, any such thing as legality. [...]

Source: Diario de Sesiones (3 July 1886).

Topics
FOR DISCUSSION

- How would you describe the tone of Exhibit 2.1? What sort of political climate does it conjure up?
- What do its authors appear to want? What ideas seem to lie behind the text?
- How does Cánovas conceive the notion of legality (Exhibit 2.2)? Are there any similarities with the conceptions illustrated in Exhibits 1.1 and 1.2?

- Bearing in mind that it enjoyed very widespread support, why did the 1868 Revolution turn out so disastrously?
- In a sense, the Restoration period represents the 'golden age' of the Spanish liberal movement. How do its arrangements relate to the aspirations embodied in the Cadiz Constitution?

CHAPTER 3

Change frustrated (1898–1923)

As the new century began and industrialisation continued in Europe, the workers' movement formed in the old one gathered strength. It was divided into various branches. The largest, Marxist socialism, held that economic advance would lead inevitably to the fall of capitalism and social revolution, a process some socialists sought to accelerate by working for political reform. Anarchists thought such activity pointless, believing that revolution must come spontaneously; their main strength was in Russia, the great power where industrialisation had made least headway. Common to all these groups, however, was the belief that workers' loyalties were to their class, rather than to their country. A major factor in holding them in check was thus the rise of nationalism, which in 1914 culminated in the outbreak of the First World War. In most countries, ideas of international class solidarity were forgotten as workers flocked to join up. Russia took a different path, and the communist revolution of 1917 gave renewed heart to militant workers across the world. It also provoked a virulent reaction from their opponents, the first sign of which came with Mussolini's seizure of power in Italy, in 1922.

Although its direct impact was limited – the framework of the Restoration settlement remained in place for a further quarter-century – the 'disaster' of 1898 had a profound effect on Spain. By setting off a process of national self-examination, it stimulated various forces which sought to bring about far-reaching change in the way the country was run, including a vague but widely-felt urge to 'regenerate' it. Another was the feeling of distinctiveness in certain regions which led to demands for some form of self-government. Yet a third was the workers' movement, which believed in a quite different form of salvation, through social revolution. The three were very different from each other; they were also far from homogeneous, and divided into a number of often antagonistic strands. The result was their common frustration.

The 'Regenerationists'

Some Spaniards had long been aware of their country's failure to keep pace with its neighbours, politically, socially and above all economically. But the events of 1898 brought that failure into sharp relief for many, and crystallised a belief that drastic action was needed. Such 'regenerationist' thinking emanated from all the better-informed sections of society, from both within and without

regeneracionismo

'regenerationist' ideas/thinking

Although the term had already been in use before (see, e.g., Exhibit 1.2), the events of 1898 brought the notion of regeneration to the forefront of public debate in Spain. Indeed, the literary and philosophical strand of regenerationist thinking is associated with the group known as the '1898 generation' (generación del 98), whose most significant members were Miguel de Unamuno, José Ortega y Gasset and Ramón Maeztu. The group's ideas were diverse, and also varied over time, so that it is impossible to speak of a coherent 'movement'. The same is even more true of the wide range of regenerationist proposals put forward for changes in political, economic and social structures. However, what they all had in common was a concern about Spain's general backwardness (atraso), and a desire to eliminate it.

the elite which had access to power under the Restoration settlement.

'Regenerationists' were not just a diverse crew; they were sometimes each other's enemies. They included Republicans, for whom regeneration meant abolishing the monarchy, but also the young King, Alfonso XIII, who came of age in 1902, with his keen interest in new technology and plans for Army reform. In fact, the closest thing to a coherent statement of **regenerationist ideas** was to be found in the life and works of one man: Joaquín Costa. At the core of his work were extensive proposals for agricultural reform through technical improvements, and especially for more and better irrigation, which he attempted with some success to implement in his native Aragon. To complement them Costa advocated drastic land reform (p70). He also argued that the large estates of the south, notoriously underused and thus unable to provide adequate employment, should be broken up and sold off to create the class of small farmers of which some early liberals had dreamt.

These changes would, Costa felt, release the 'live forces' in Spanish society that were excluded from influence by the practice of political clientilism (p29). To try and break its hold, in 1899 he set up a party-cum-business association, the National League of Producers. This soon received support from the Chambers of Commerce, who were the representatives of small business in Spain's provincial towns. However, larger industrialists showed no desire to break their alliance with the large landowners (p31), and without their help the League made no electoral headway. Its main achievement was to organise a non-payment campaign against what the government of the day understood by regeneration, tax reform, which was also the prerequisite for implementation of Costa's own plans. In the face of such contradictions, and its powerful opponents, the League soon collapsed.

This failure convinced Costa that clientilism could not be defeated under the existing system. To achieve that, he felt that Spain needed an 'iron surgeon' (cirujano de hierro), a charismatic leader who would enjoy virtually unlimited powers for a brief period, before returning the country to parliamentary rule. An early candidate for this role was General Polavieja, who had commanded Spanish forces in the Philippines in the run-up to the 1898 'disaster'. On his return he took up Costa's attacks on the political system, quickly attracting such a substantial following that the government was forced to appoint him Minister of War. But Polavieja's plans to modernise the Army

– for him the key to regeneration – were also blocked by the government's budget reform plans. Polavieja resigned in protest, and his support faded away.

Costa's other hope lay with the **Reformist Republicans**, who agreed with his emphasis on concrete, viable proposals rather than dogma. Thus, instead of just railing against Church control over the school system, as Republicans had tended to do in the past, the Reformists drew up detailed plans to change the content of education, and in particular to introduce an element of vocational training. However, they too ran up against clientilism (p29), and remained a small minority, albeit one with a degree of influence.

Given the workings of the Restoration settlement (pp25–6), the only feasible vehicles for regenerationist ideas at this time were the two 'dynastic parties'. Ironically, it was among the Conservatives that their influence was more evident, as had already been shown in Francisco Silvela's unsuccessful attempt to reform local government (p30). Now, as leader of his party, Silvela became Prime Minister in the wake of the 1898 'disaster'. Once confronted with the appalling state of public finances which had made that inevitable (p31), their reform became his top priority.

> ### *Partido Republicano Reformista*
> ....
> Reformist Republican Party
> ---
> The Reformists were one of the two factions into which the **Republican movement** (p23) divided in 1908. They subsequently abandoned their almost exclusive concern with constitutional reform (abolition of the monarchy, federalism) in favour of formulating practical proposals for change in specific fields, particularly education. The party enjoyed little electoral success, and disappeared under the Primo dictatorship, but from it emerged many of the **Left Republicans** (p68) responsible for major reforms during the Second Republic.

The plans of his Finance Minister, Villaverde, met widespread opposition, not least from Costa's League, because they included an element of tax reform, although in fact taxation remained very low. Their principal aim, which was to bring spending under control, was achieved by the cuts that provoked Polavieja's departure. Once they had been implemented, Villaverde's changes set the tone of Spanish budget policy for the next 70 years, making it even harder for governments to stimulate economic development.

Economics were a minor concern for Silvela's protégé and successor, the greatest and most controversial of Conservative regenerationists. Like his mentor, Antonio Maura was a 'puritan' (p30); he believed that Spain's problems were essentially moral, and that he could solve them by 'dignifying' politics. He talked of a 'revolution from above', by which he meant that the steps necessary to eliminate corruption should be taken by the existing elite, to which he belonged. What he could not, or would not see was that its position depended on the very corruption he sought to eliminate.

In 1902 Maura received an early warning of the contradictions inherent in his ideas. As Interior Minister, he insisted on reducing the government's use of clientilist tactics (p29) in that year's election, which resulted in significant Republican gains in the larger cities. He was undeterred, and three years later, on becoming Prime Minister, he renewed his efforts to clean up politics with a fresh attempt at local government reform. However, like Silvela, he did not intend that free local elections should break the hold of the better-off on local politics, and therefore repeated his proposal for a form of corporate suffrage (p30). Once again the plans were frustrated by the Liberals, who could see more clearly than Maura the danger they posed to the two parties' common interests (p26).

Not that Maura was blind to the threat of the new forces emerging in society. Indeed, he made no secret of the fact that his 'revolution from above' was intended primarily to pre-empt one 'from below', by the workers' movement. In 1908 his fears of such an outcome led him to introduce a number of repressive measures, including restrictions on the right of free association. The Liberals saw their chance, and joined the Republicans in a 'Bloc of the Left' to run a campaign against the new measures, under the slogan 'Maura, No!'

To Maura, the Liberals' abandonment of the tacit alliance between the 'dynastic parties' was tantamount to treason. He offered his resignation to the King, demanding the chance to manufacture a vote of confidence in fresh elections. But Alfonso, worried by the re-entry of Republicanism into mainstream politics, now saw Maura as the biggest threat to stability. He accordingly accepted the resignation offer, and handed power over to the Liberals. Many of Maura's Conservative colleagues backed the King's action, leaving their former leader an embittered and isolated figure (p49).

Up to this time the Liberal Party, which now returned to power, had shown little interest in regeneration. As the heir of the liberal movement's radical wing, its theoretical priority had been the constitutional reforms of the 1880s (p26) – although by that time the arrangements which allowed the party to carry them out had rendered them meaningless! Since then, preserving those arrangements intact had been the Liberals' over-riding concern. Their differences with the Conservatives had been reduced to hysterical attacks on the revival of Church influence – partly because the Church posed a minor threat to the relative tolerance of Restoration society, but mainly because anticlericalism was an easy means of attracting popular support (p30).

This situation only began to change under the leadership of José Canalejas. After he was appointed Prime Minister in 1910, Canalejas sidelined the religious issue by introducing the 'Padlock Act' (*Ley del Candado*), which, while seeming to place restrictions on the monastic orders that were the main focus of popular concern, effectively left their situation unchanged. That opened the way for him to push through a second, more progressive tax reform, which for the first time hit rental incomes, and so acted as an incentive to more productive investments. He also overhauled local government finance and abolished the rich's right to buy themselves out of military service. His further plans included a scheme for rural land reform that would allow underused estates to be expropriated from their owners.

Canalejas fell victim to an assassin in 1912 (p46), before much of his programme could be implemented. After his death some further efforts were made to put regenerationist ideas into practice. Eduardo Dato, Maura's successor as Conservative leader, brought in Spain's first industrial relations and social security legislation, before he too was assassinated in 1921 (p47). The Liberal governments of the early 1920s were influenced by the ideas of the Reformist Republicans. However, with Canalejas gone and Maura isolated, the only concerted attempt at regenerating Spain lasted for just a few months in 1918 (p50). Meanwhile, as the country continued to stagnate, the backwardness against which the regenerationists railed was increasing all the time.

Regionalists and nationalists

The extent of economic backwardness was far from uniform across Spain. By the 1890s Catalonia and the Basque Country, in particular, had undergone a considerable degree of industrialisation. In both regions, each of which was already distinctive in its own way, the experience gave rise to demands for self-government. But, just as the industrialisation processes and the historical backgrounds were very different, so too were Basque and Catalan regionalists – or, as many would see themselves, nationalists.

Regionalism first made its appearance in Catalonia. There, feelings of distinctive identity had deep roots, since for two centuries after the creation of a united Spain the region had enjoyed extensive self-government. Even after the loss of autonomy in 1714 (p3), when Catalan ceased to be used officially, the language remained strong in daily use and literature, and in the latter part of the nineteenth century it experienced a renaissance (*renaixença*). Its leading figure, Valentí Almirall, was also the first man to give Catalan regionalism (*catalanismo*) a political dimension.

In 1892 Almirall's ideas were set out by his disciple, Enric Prat de la Riba, in what effectively became the movement's programme. These Manresa Principles (*Bases de Manresa*) were steeped in Catalan history, and showed the influence of federal republicanism in the region (pp23–4). As well as calls for Catalan to become the region's official language there were demands for devolution within a federal Spain. The Principles also reflected a newer concern: that Catalonia's development had been delayed by the backwardness of Spain as a whole, and by having to provide a disproportionate share of taxes from which it saw little return. The appearance of this grievance indicated how regionalism and economic development were closely connected.

Industrialisation in Catalonia was a gradual process, and a natural extension of Barcelona's tradition as a major port and commercial centre. It was founded on the textile industry, whose leaders' great concern in the later nineteenth century was to mount a successful campaign for import protection (p31). Although Catalan culture was important to the textile magnates, it did not spur them to political action. However, the events of 1898 persuaded them that their longer-term interests could only be protected by a fundamental change in the way Spain was run.

The industrialists' turned first to General Polavieja (pp38–9), who had expressed sympathy for their views. When this hope proved vain, they decided to take up Almirall's strategy of a separate Catalan party, and sponsored the foundation of the **Regionalist League**. Their financial and political clout enabled them to break the shackles of clientilism (p29), and within a few months the party had made sweeping gains at the 1901 general election. Five years later the League brought together a broad alliance of political forces, known as Catalan Solidarity, which in 1907 won an even more dramatic victory.

Lliga Regionalista

(Catalan) Regionalist League

Formed in 1901 with the support of local business interests, the League demanded home rule for Catalonia, while also seeking to influence the policies pursued by central governments through lobbying. Françesc Cambó, a leading industrialist, was responsible for fostering the necessary contacts in Madrid; the League's other main figure, Enric Prat de la Riba, was its head within Catalonia. Until the 1920s it was by far the largest Catalan regionalist party, but thereafter it was overtaken by other, more radical groupings (p61), and ceased to be a significant force after 1923.

These electoral successes further increased the magnates' leverage over Madrid, and helped them to persuade the government to impose yet higher import tariffs. In 1914 they obtained another concession when a Catalan regional government, the *Mancomunitat*, was established. Its powers may have been strictly limited but, run by the League and with Prat as its first head, it enabled the industrialists to implement what amounted to a form of conservative economic regeneration in Catalonia, with considerable success.

To a large extent the League had now achieved its aims. Its demands for self-government went no further than devolution, partly for historical reasons but above all because it responded to the industrialists' present needs. They wanted to control their own affairs, but they knew that their businesses depended on the Spanish market. They also realised that the home market would grow only if the country as a whole prospered. Hence their desire not just to remain a part of Spain, but to influence its development, and hence their rejection of any thought of independence.

Such moderation and rationality sat oddly with another aspect of the Manresa Principles, which Prat in particular tended to play up during election campaigns: their stress on a fundamental clash of interests between the 'artificial' Spanish state and the Catalan fatherland (*patria*). Yet the indirectly elected *Mancomunitat* scarcely looked like a national assembly, while its existence also served to accentuate the contradiction between the League's policies in power and its claim to represent Catalonia as a whole.

It became clear that, as on Barcelona city council, the League's first priority in regional government was to protect the textile magnates' commercial interests. Little attention was paid to social policy or the conditions of the poor, and the result, especially in Barcelona, was an increase in the already high level of social tension. Yet when this tension erupted in unrest, the League's leaders saw only a threat to their own property, and consistently backed a policy of outright repression. As a result, they alienated much of the mass support for regionalism which their early successes had first tapped, then further encouraged.

The lack of popular backing for regionalism in the Basque Country was one difference between the situations in the two regions. A more fundamental one was that, while Catalan regionalism represented an attempt to seize the benefits of economic advance for Catalonia – or for some Catalans – its Basque counterpart was essentially a rejection of such development. It was also a reaction to a very different experience, since in the Basque Country – or more precisely, in and around Bilbao – industrialisation was anything but gradual. Instead it was a rapid and traumatic process, which transformed what was essentially an administrative and market town and its rural hinterland into a centre of large-scale heavy industry in a little over 20 years.

The historical and cultural background to these changes was also quite different from the Catalan case. By the 1890s the Basque language (*euskera*), whose literary tradition was minimal, had died out in much of the region, particularly in the Bilbao area. Nor had the Basque Country ever formed an administrative unit, though it is true that many Basques had a strong sense of local loyalty, as they had shown in their support for the Carlist movement (p12). But their feelings focused mainly on the area's constituent provinces, with which its traditional privileges were associated (p12).

These factors strongly influenced early Basque regionalism, whose followers shared the fiercely conservative Catholicism typical of the Carlists, and regarded cultural issues as strictly secondary. As members of Bilbao's traditional social elite, they resented the tide of industrial development that had under-mined their status, and, Canute-like, they dreamed of turning it back. Their bitterness found expression in a political philosophy that often seemed more like a religious creed.

Their leader was Sabino Arana, to whom the very concept of a 'Basque Country' can be attributed. Initially he was only concerned with Bilbao and its province, Vizcaya, but under the influence of Catalan ideas he conceived the idea of a Basque nation. This was defined, according to Arana, not by cultural but by racial distinctiveness, and its 'homeland' of *Euzkadi* (now usually written *Euskadi*) took in Alava, Guipuzcoa, Navarre and parts of south-western France, as well as Vizcaya.

Around these dubious notions Arana wove a complex web of nationalist mythology. Its main themes were Basques' unique relationship to the Church and their tradition of primitive democracy, embodied in the provincial privileges abolished in 1876 (p27). Restoration of these 'old laws' was the platform of another of Arana's creations, the **Basque Nationalist Party** (PNV). As a national goal it sounded modest, but since it

Partido Nacionalista Vasco (PNV)

Basque Nationalist Party

Founded in 1895 by Sabino Arana, the PNV's main aim has always been Basque self-government, although it was traditionally ambivalent as to whether by that it meant complete independence. Heavily influenced by traditional Catholicism, for a long time the party's programme was socially conservative, with a strong egalitarian streak; it has close links with the trade union Basque Workers' Solidarity (STV). By the 1920s it had established deep roots throughout Basque society, symbolised by the network of local PNV clubs (*batzokis*). This enabled it to survive attempts by Primo de Rivera and, above all, Franco to stamp out Basque national feeling (p100); indeed, it emerged from the Franco period greatly strengthened. Since the restoration of democracy it has been the Basque Country's largest party, running the regional government set up in 1980, first on its own, later as the dominant partner in coalitions. After suffering a grave crisis and split in 1986 (p162), the PNV went through a moderate phase during which it retreated from talk of independence. More recently, however, it has taken a more radical turn, and its differences with the Spanish government and parties have come to dominate the country's politics (pp173–6). See also: **Frente Popular** (p76); **Euskadi ta Askatasuna** (p123); **Pacto de Lizarra** (p174) would have meant separating the Basque Country from Spain economically (p12), it was quite unacceptable to any Madrid administration. To its own followers the PNV talked openly of 'independence', an aim much more in tune with its diatribes against the Spanish 'immigrants' (*maketos*) who flocked to the industries it hated.

Up to 1923 the PNV had minimal impact on Spanish politics. Its ideas held scant attraction for most Basque industrialists and financiers, the most powerful of whom had good links with politicians in Madrid and controlled the provincial councils which, under the 1876 settlement, enjoyed considerable financial autonomy (p28). More broadly, the party's quasi-racist rhetoric alienated industrial workers, including most indigenous ones, and the region's intellectuals. Outside Bilbao regionalists remained a small and isolated minority.

Yet, arguably, isolation – from immigrants, from the modern world in general – was precisely what they sought. It allowed them to create a 'community', bound together by a dense network of associations, some social, others designed to provide mutual support for particular groups, especially the small farmers who became the move-ment's bedrock. At the heart of this society-within-a-society was the PNV, giving it deeper roots across a wider social spectrum than any other party in Spain. That, together with the backing of some industrialists who wished to break the grip of the existing economic 'oligarchy', gave Basque regionalism its deceptive strength.

Like its Catalan cousin, it was helped considerably by the fact that Spain had missed out on developments which served elsewhere to fuel national feeling, especially universal education and mass participation in the political system. Economically, Spain did not become a single market until 1876. Instead of engaging in the race for new colonies, it lost the remnants of Empire. Furthermore, for all the benefits, neutrality in the First World War also meant that it never experienced the surge of social solidarity felt by belligerent nations. For these various reasons, Spaniards largely lacked a strong sense of common identity to counter the competing claims, not just of regionalism but also of class loyalty.

The workers' movement

If Spain's economic backwardness was partly responsible for regionalism, it also meant that the country's industrial working class was small, and its workers' movement corre-spondingly weak. Particularly affected was the movement's Marxist branch. As in Russia, socialism was surpassed in both support and activity by anarchism, whose ideas were better suited to a country where poverty was concentrated on the land, and which also established a strong presence in Spain's premier industrial centre.

Marxism was represented in Spain by the **Spanish Socialist Party** (PSOE), and its sister trade union, the General Workers' Union (p59). Both were founded by Pablo Iglesias, who dominated the Spanish socialist movement (*socialismo español*) until his death in 1925. He also embodied its strengths and weaknesses. A tireless organiser, he was renowned for a strict rectitude very different from the morally relaxed attitudes of most politicians. But he was no original thinker and his party did not have the intellectual wing common elsewhere. As a result, the PSOE's ideas remained a mere rehash of basic Marxist theory, taken almost entirely from the work of French socialists without due allowance for the massive differences between the two countries.

Iglesias defined his party's task as building up class loyalty among industrial workers in preparation for a revolution that would come only once Spain had properly modernised. This pessimistic philosophy met with an understandably limited response. It was best received among those who enjoyed some status and security: Madrid printers like Iglesias himself, and workers in the mines and factories of Asturias and the Basque Country where trade union activity gave a focus for socialist organisation. In Catalonia, on the other hand, where its Madrid-centred leadership was resented, the PSOE made little headway, while the potential for rural or middle-class support was almost entirely ignored.

Admittedly some intellectuals, including Unamuno (p38), joined the party in the wake of 1898, but the main reason for the influx of members at this time was workers' resentment against the Cuban War (p31). Once that was over, support fell away again, leading Iglesias to relax his refusal to co-operate with any middle-class party (*indiferencia*). In 1909 he formed a loose alliance (*conjunción*) with the Reformist Republicans (p39), thanks to which – and to opposition to the new war in Morocco (p58) – he was elected the party's first MP. In the crisis year of 1917 the PSOE even joined the broad campaign for political reform (p49). But its failure led to the Socialists becoming disillusioned with co-operation, and in 1919 they broke off the Republican alliance. Iglesias promptly lost his seat, and the PSOE was left with the loyalty of its core supporters and a sturdy, but very patchy, organisation as its only assets.

> ### *Partido Socialista Obrero Español (PSOE)*
>
> Spanish Socialist Party
>
> Founded in 1879, initially under the title *Partido Democrático Socialista Español*, the PSOE was long typified by a cautious approach to its declared aim of social revolution – which it held could only come after Spain had experienced industrialisation and genuine political reform – and by the belief that socialism was a matter purely for the working class (*obrerismo*). Prior to 1923 the party enjoyed very little electoral success; its main achievement was to build up, in its strongholds of Madrid, Asturias and the Basque Country, a party organisation based on the local socialist clubs (*casas del pueblo*). Under the Second Republic, however, despite being plagued by disputes between advocates of continuing moderation and supporters of immediate revolution (pp75–6), the PSOE became Spain's largest party. Banned by the Franco regime, the PSOE took little part in opposing it. Even so, on the restoration of democracy in 1975 it re-emerged as the largest party of the Left, winning power at the general election of 1982 and dominating Spanish politics for the rest of the 1980s and the early 1990s. During that time the party's policies continued the trend begun in opposition towards the political centre, while latterly it was involved in a succession of financial and other scandals (pp159,181). It was finally ousted from office in 1996 but regained power, somewhat surprisingly, in 2004 (p187).
> See also: *Frente Popular* (p76); *Partido Comunista de España* (p88); *felipismo* (p159)

All this time Spanish **anarchism** had been playing hare to the Socialist tortoise, its mercurial progress reflecting the power and naivety of its ideas. They had greatest

anarquismo

anarchism; (Spanish) anarchist movement

Based on the idea that humans' natural habitat is an economically self-sufficient community modelled on a traditional rural village, pure anarchism – or primitive communism – holds that all decisions should be taken by direct and equal participation. All forms of imposed authority, internal or external to the commune, are anathema to anarchists, and they reject any idea of political organisation, such as parties. The revolution that ushers in the anarchist utopia will, they believe, occur spontaneously, the only form of preparation countenanced by some anarchists being 'propaganda by deed', that is, acts of violence against established institutions and the rich. In Spain, such ideas were particularly associated with the landless rural labourers of Andalusia, and with the workers of Barcelona, among whom they tended to take the form of anarcho-syndicalism.
See also: **CNT** (p47); *colectivización* (p87); *milicia* (p86)

impact in the impoverished rural south, where day-labourers scraped a precarious existence on vast estates (*latifundios*), as well as in Aragon and the east. The dominant concern of this rural anarchism was that the land should be handed over to, and divided up among, those who worked it (*reparto de la tierra*), and the early 1880s saw regular incidents of estates being violently seized from their owners. The authorities' brutal response dampened down that expression of anarchist unrest. When it resurfaced in the 1890s it took the form of terrorism, whose victims included Prime Minister Cánovas. But without an organised structure its capabilities did not extend beyond acts of random violence.

Where anarchism acquired greater significance was in and around Spain's largest and most dynamic city, Barcelona. As a great port, it was the entry point for new ideas, including more sophisticated versions of the anarchist creed. At the same time, its industrial growth attracted a steady stream of workers from rural areas where anarchism had already established a hold. The region's textile firms were often small enough to make their operation as communes seem feasible, and, at the same time, the confrontational attitudes of Catalan employers meant that workers desperately needed some means of defending their interests.

These factors meant that in Catalonia anarchist ideas had far more impact than Socialist ones, particularly in the variant known as anarcho-syndicalism. This holds that workers should organise in trade unions (*sindicatos*) and engage in industrial agitation as the means of bringing about social revolution, in the form of a general strike. In 1907 its supporters set up an organisation known as Workers' Solidarity (*Solidaridad Obrera*). Four years later this was succeeded by the **National Labour Confederation (CNT)**, which quickly became by far the largest workers' organisation in Spain. The CNT's ranks included rural anarchists, although they were often suspicious of its tendency to focus on industrial issues rather than land redistribution. Equally some of its supporters, both urban and rural, placed less faith in trade union activity than in terrorism; in 1912 they assassinated a second Prime Minister, Canalejas (p40). Not surprisingly, splits were endemic in the CNT.

The CNT's relations with the Socialists were also stormy, even though the two movements did sometimes co-operate, as during the crisis of 1917 (p49). Generally, though, the PSOE's emphasis on organisation seemed too 'Prussian' (i.e. authoritarian) to anarcho-syndicalists, who also rejected the Socialists' readiness to negotiate with employers; for them, every industrial dispute was a potential revolution. For their part, the Socialists tended to regard anarchists of all types as irresponsible woolly-thinkers whose activities only served to hold back Spain's development, and thus its revolution too. The failure of a general strike to spark such an uprising in 1909 (pp48–9) seemed to confirm their analysis.

In Spain, as elsewhere, the Russian Revolution led to a further split in the already divided workers' movement, with the creation of a Spanish Communist Party (p88). But its initial impact was small, since the new party attracted few recruits. Much more influential was the impression the Revolution's dramatic success made on Spanish workers in general. For, coming in a country every bit as backward as Spain, and in the wake of another failed general strike (p50), it undermined the arguments of both Socialists and anarcho-syndicalists. Conversely, it gave a boost to the advocates of direct action, who launched a new offensive. In 1921 the anarchists claimed a third prime ministerial victim in Dato (p40). But their main targets were the rich of Barcelona, the main setting for what was to be the final act in the drama of Spanish liberalism.

> ### Confederación Nacional del Trabajo (CNT)
> National Labour Confederation
>
> Founded in 1911 as the umbrella organisation of Spanish anarco-sindicalismo (p46), the CNT effectively operated as the political representative of Spanish **anarchism** (p46) in general. Its history was a series of dramatic fluctuations, influxes of support and outbursts of activity alternating with savage repression and declining membership. The CNT reached its greatest strength around 1919, but thereafter suffered defeat in its 'social war' with Catalan employers (p50), and persecution under Primo's dictatorship (p59). During the Second Republic and the Civil War it again achieved mass support, but its loose structure was incapable of surviving more severe repression under the Franco regime, and only fragments survived into the post-1975 democratic era.
> See also: **Frente Popular** (p76); **Partido Comunista de España** (p88)

The end of liberal Spain

Given that none of the ideas on how to improve Spain's condition in the wake of 1898 could be properly realised, the Restoration settlement remained in place. But its key mechanisms had ceased to function, and the country was stagnating. It was also wracked by tensions, not just between the opponents of change and its proponents, but also among the latter. The differences were most intense in Barcelona, where they repeatedly burst into the open. But although they shook the crumbling institutions built by the Spanish liberal movement, they did not bring it down; that was left, once again, to the Army.

Indeed, as early as 1905 it became clear that politicians remained effectively subordinate to the military. In that year, irate officers sacked the premises of a Catalan satirical magazine ¡Cu-Cut! after it had published material that allegedly defamed the Army. They and their fellows then demanded that such behaviour be made an offence subject to military law (and also that spending on the military be increased). That their case should have received the tacit backing of the King was no great surprise (p38). More alarming was the fact that virtually the entire political elite should cave in. Even Canalejas (p40) did not openly oppose the Jurisdictions Act of 1906, whose provisions allowed the Army to silence press criticism and to crush opposition to the Moroccan war. The idea of civilian primacy, so central to the Restoration settlement (p25), was revealed as the myth it had always been.

The next stage in the settlement's breakdown came in 1909, with Maura's rejection of the alternation mechanism on which it was founded (p40). Thereafter it never operated consistently. Governments lasted only months on average, and in the absence of agreement within and between the parties, the King's right to designate a prime minister became decisive. Maura himself, although still nominally a Conservative, used his formidable appeal to build up a personal following, chiefly among the better-off young. This 'Maurist movement' (*maurismo*) was the first mass organisation of the Spanish Right. Yet its leader refused either to turn it into a political party, or to use it as a base to seize power as Costa's 'iron surgeon' (p38), and so remained impotent.

In 1909, too, trouble first flared in Barcelona. The city's status as the cockpit of Spain derived from the fact that it was the point where the country's most dynamic political forces converged and clashed. It was the home of the Regionalist League (p42), which was both the representative of Catalan regionalism and the most effective vehicle of conservative regenerationist ideas (p38). It was also the stronghold of the anarcho-syndicalist CNT (p47), and of the **Radical Republican Party**, whose leader Alejandro Lerroux was a formidable populist and rabble-rouser with a strong following among the city's lower middle classes and the poorest of its poor. In 1909 the tensions between the three exploded.

Violence was triggered – while the political elite was still in turmoil following Maura's bombshell – by the call-up of reservists to fight in the colonial campaign in Morocco (p58). Agitation against the war had already brought together a Republican–Socialist alliance (p45), which now began preparations for a massive protest. But its plans were pre-empted by the anarcho-syndicalists of Workers' Solidarity (p46), who on 26 July declared a general strike in Barcelona. Thus began the notorious 'Tragic Week'.

Partido Republicano Radical
Radical Republican Party

Not to be confused with the Radicals of the 1870s (p23), the Radical Republican Party was one of the two factions into which the **Republican movement** (p23) divided in 1908. Offering no programme as such, its supporters concentrated on vague references to revolution and on virulent attacks against Catalan regionalism, the rich and existing institutions – the Church even more than the monarchy. Their main asset was the following for their leader, Alejandro Lerroux, in Barcelona. The party ran the city council several times, demonstrating a capacity for corruption to match that of the dominant dynastic parties (p26). During the Second Republic it emerged as a national political force (p68), heading a number of governments (pp72–3) before suddenly collapsing in 1935 (p74). See also: **Pacto de San Sebastián** (p63)

For days the city was in chaos, effectively cut off. Inflamed by the anticlerical rhetoric of Lerroux and the anarchists, mobs sacked Church buildings and attacked priests and nuns. After initial hesitation, the authorities' restored order by force. Many of the rioters received long prison sentences but Lerroux, their main instigator, escaped in time to avoid punishment. Five men were executed for their part in the events, including – quite without justification – Francisco Ferrer, the organiser of the 'Modern Schools' which provided free education heavily influenced by anarchist and other libertarian ideas. His death provoked widespread protests at home and abroad, and became a potent symbol of government repression.

Eight years on came a graver crisis. The background was the First World War, which affected Spain considerably, even though it remained neutral. One reason for this was that the country's sympathies were broadly divided, between a pro-German Right and pro-French Left. Another was that neutrality allowed some industrialists to make massive profits by exporting to the combatant countries. This grossly distorted the economy; prices soared, and outside the boom sectors wages failed hopelessly to keep pace.

One group badly hit were the middle ranks of the home-based Army, already disgruntled at the quicker promotion of colleagues serving in Morocco. In the summer of 1917 some officers set up local Defence Committees (*Juntas de Defensa*). Their demands were parochial but, couched in the language of 'regeneration' (p38), with talk of army 'reform' and 'modernisation', they struck a chord with the public and turned the Committees' supporters (*junteros*) into standard-bearers of its discontent.

While the government was struggling to deal with what had become a tricky problem, it stirred up another. In trying to assuage popular resentment by a tax on war profits, it provoked the ire of industrialists, prominent among them a number of Catalans. Cambó, effective leader of the Regionalist League (p42), decided that the time had come for Catalonia to take the lead in changing Spain as a whole. He called an unofficial 'National Assembly' to draw up a new constitution, which he hoped to impose on the Madrid politicians.

Surprisingly, his idea was backed by both socialists and anarcho-syndicalists, who had already been pushed by the economic situation into co-operation with each other. But Maura refused to back the pro-Assembly movement (*movimiento asambleísta*), and the Committees' supporters also kept their distance, unwilling to co-operate with Catalan regionalists. Cambó's plan thus rested on an uneasy alliance between the conservative League and the revolutionary Left.

On 19 July the Assembly met in Barcelona, only to be broken up by the police. The following month the frustration of ordinary trade unionists forced their unwilling leaders into another general strike. This time there was much more violence than in 1909, and before it was crushed there were pitched battles between strikers and police and attacks on employers' property. These, in particular, seemed to make a profound impression on Cambó, since when the government predictably rejected the proposals finally drawn up by his Assembly, he caved in at once. Abandoning his allies and their demands for far-reaching democratic reform, he agreed to join a makeshift coalition with second-rank Liberal and Conservative leaders instead.

The new government only lasted into the early months of 1918, its collapse provoking the King to threaten abdication. This prospect forced the dynastic parties to close ranks. Even Maura was called in from the cold, as the only politician the Defence Committees trusted, to head a 'National Government'. For a short time this looked like a real vehicle for 'regenerationist' ideas (p38). Its driving force was Cambó who, as Minister for Development (*Fomento*), applied the economic policies pioneered by his party in regional government (p42), with considerable success. But, as in Catalonia, he ignored social problems, with fatal results.

In October the coalition's Liberal members, always suspicious of regionalism, used that omission as the excuse to withdraw support for Cambó's policies. Shortly after-wards, their intrigues forced Maura to resign, and the National Government was dead. None of its successors was remotely capable of taking the decisive measures that were so badly needed. Moreover, in their weakness they repeatedly ignored Parliament and passed legislation by decree; censorship was also widespread. The democratic facade of Spanish liberalism was ripped away to reveal the authoritarian reality beneath.

Meanwhile, the end of the First World War brought Spain's uneven boom to a juddering halt. Mismanaged by both government and industrialists, who paid no heed to much-needed investment, it left the economy in a worse state than ever. Unable to compete despite high tariffs, many firms were forced to close, making thousands of workers redundant. The Asturian coal mines and the shipbuilding industry suffered greatly, although once again it was in Barcelona that the resultant desperation took most extreme form. In 1919 workers at the *La Canadiense* electricity company went on strike over a wage dispute. It was soon settled by government arbitration, but when the Army refused to release some arrested strikers the anarcho-syndicalists called a general strike, which was only broken after further massive arrests and the declaration of a state of war.

With industrial action now illegal, the terrorist wing of anarchism stepped up the attacks it had already begun on the Catalan business community. No longer repre-sented by Cambó in government, the industrialists lost faith in the central authorities to protect their lives and property. Taking matters into their own hands they set up so-called 'Free Trade Unions' – a cover for hired gunmen – and a private, paramilitary police force, the *Somatén*. They also collaborated with the local army commander, General Martínez Anido, who ignored instructions from Madrid to tread warily and cracked down ruthlessly on anarchist violence and strikers alike.

For the next four years Barcelona was outside government control, engulfed in a 'social war'. The result was never in doubt. Apart from their inferior resources, the anarchists were handicapped by internal divisions. The CNT leadership had been drawn reluctantly into the 1919 strike, and thereafter its supporters were in constant and sometimes violent dispute with the terrorists. Moreover, after their brief rapprochement, the anarchists and Socialists renewed their usual antagonism (pp46–7).

By 1923 the anarchists had patently lost. But by then, too, the victorious Catalan elite had run into other troubles, since its political influence had been undermined by the events of 1918. In 1922 the Madrid government tried to reverse the policy of protectionist tariffs (pp31,42). Moreover, Cambó's betrayal of the Assembly movement had been the last straw for many supporters of his Regionalist League (p42), who deserted in droves to set up organisations of their own. The largest of these was 'Catalan Action', which demanded a Catalan republic in a loosely federal Spain. Its leader, Francesc Macià, soon became Catalonia's most popular politician, his support outstripping that of the League.

It thus became clear that, however much the Catalan magnates were disillusioned with the existing system, they could expect little to come from its democratic reform either. Their disillusion was shared by some 'regenerationist' intellectuals, notably Maeztu (p38), who had come to see Spain's salvation in the rediscovery of its supposed 'real essence': Castilian, Catholic, and Conservative. He and others linked this reactionary, authoritarian nationalism to Costa's concept of an 'iron surgeon' (p38), taking Mussolini as a model.

Meantime, in July 1921, Spain had again been shaken by disaster abroad when its forces suffered a humiliating defeat at the hands of Moroccan tribesmen (p58). A parliamentary committee was set up to investigate the causes. In summer 1923 the committee completed its report, which would become public once Parliament reconvened. Many had good reason to fear its findings: politicians, who had ignored warnings of inadequate equipment and low morale; the King, who had allegedly encouraged the ill-fated operation; above all, the Army, of whose incompetence and even corruption rumours abounded but whose leaders liked to portray themselves as the helpless victims of political inaction. Appropriately enough it was to be a general who, at long last, would put liberal Spain out of its misery.

Summary of main points

The 'regenerationists'

- The desire to 'regenerate' Spain came in many forms; common to all was their failure.
- The most typical 'regenerationist' was Costa, a political outsider who advocated technological advance and an end to clientilism, whose workings prevented him from exercising real influence.
- The leading regenerationists within the establishment were Maura (Conservative) and Canalejas (Liberal); while the former focused on the need to clean up politics, the latter's ideas centred on social reform. Neither achieved more than minor successes, and Maura's policies split his own party.

Regionalists and nationalists

- In Catalonia, regionalism had deep historical and cultural roots, and was moderate in its political demands. From 1898 the Regionalist League was backed by the region's industrialists and became an important factor in Spanish politics, but after 1918 it lost support to more radical groupings.

- In the Basque Country, regionalism was a more immediate product of rapid industrialisation. The Basque Nationalist Party (PNV) was traditionalist, inward-looking, unwilling to compromise and relatively weak, but its supporters formed a tightly knit and resilient 'community'.
- National feeling in Spain as a whole was much weaker than in neighbouring countries.

Workers' movement

- Before 1923 Spain's workers' movement was relatively small, and was split between socialists, anarchists and – latterly – communists.
- The Socialist Party (PSOE) had strongholds in Madrid, Asturias and the Basque Country. Between 1909 and 1919 it co-operated with Republicans and enjoyed some electoral success, but otherwise Socialists were a small and isolated minority, albeit a committed and cohesive one.
- Anarchism attracted considerable but volatile support in the countryside, especially in Andalusia, but its impact was limited to periodic terrorist attacks. Around Barcelona it developed into anarcho-syndicalism, whose trade union, the CNT, became Spain's largest worker organisation.

End of liberal Spain

- The tensions associated with Spain's failure to reform were especially severe in Barcelona, where Catalan regionalists, anarcho-syndicalists and the populist Radical Republicans all had strong support. Major outbursts of unrest occurred in 1909 (Tragic Week) and 1917.
- On the second occasion unrest coincided with a broader campaign for change. After its failure, attempts at reform were effectively abandoned. Meanwhile, Barcelona was wracked by a 'social war' between anarchists and the Army, which had long since shown itself to be outside civilian control.

Exhibit 3.1: Maura's political philosophy (1917)

Extract from the Conservative politician's memoirs

Como es menester despertar a la opinión dormida, a la opinión desviada, a la opinión descreída y recelosa, hay un error que está muy en boga y que acaso sea lo más íntimo y transcendental del pensamiento del señor Cánovas del Castillo: el error de que las reformas que lastiman intereses colectivos, clases respetables, fuerzas del Estado se han de mirar con mucha circunspección y que no se puede tocar a las cosas. Si no se da con obras a la opinión algo de lo que pide, si no se ve que se la lleva por buen camino, no es fácil que se la despierte, ni se la atraiga por los organismos políticos que engendran los partidos. Por esto yo creo que algo de violencia necesitan las reformas: se trata de una operación de cirugía, y cuando de operar se trata el cirujano no va quitando el miembro muerto o corrompido parte por parte, sino que de una vez lo corta por donde es necesario. [...]

[...M]ás que nunca es ahora necesario restablecer aquella ya casi olvidada [...] confianza entre gobernantes y gobernados; y ya no hay más que un camino, que es la revolución audaz, la revolución temeraria desde el Gobierno, porque la temeridad es, no obra de nuestro albedrío, sino imposición histórica de los ajenos desaciertos. Nunca habría sido fácil la revolución desde el Gobierno, nunca habría sido recomendable, si hubiera podido dividirse la facultad y esparcirse la obra en el curso del tiempo; pero cada día que pasa, desde 1898, es mucho más escabrosa, mucho más difícil, y el éxito feliz mucho más incierto; y no está lejano el día en que ya no quede ni ese remedio.

[...W]e must stir up a public opinion that is sleeping, disorientated, sceptical and suspicious. We must alert it to a fashionable misconception, perhaps the most fundamental and significant error in Canovas' thinking: the idea that changes which threaten the interests of certain groups, or the better-off classes or the institutions of the state, must be approached with the utmost circumspection, and that it is best to let sleeping dogs lie. But if nothing concrete is done to meet the public's demands, if it does not believe that things are moving generally in the right direction, then it cannot easily be stirred or attracted by the organisations set up by political parties. That is why I believe that reform must include an element of violence. It is essentially a surgical operation, and when a surgeon operates he does not remove the lifeless or infected organ gradually, a piece at a time: he cuts out, once and for all, as much of it as is necessary.

[...N]ow, more than ever, we must re-establish that mutual confidence between rulers and ruled that has been almost forgotten. The only way to do that is by means of an audacious revolution, a bold revolution initiated by the government For daring is no longer a matter of choice but has been forced on us by the failures of others. Such a government-led revolution would never have been easy. It would never have been advisable if the task could have been spread out over time and the responsibility for carrying it out divided up. But with every day that has passed since 1898 it has become ever trickier, ever more difficult, and its happy and successful conclusion ever more uncertain. Now the day is not far off when even this solution will have become impossible.

Source: Maura, A. (1917) *Treinta y cinco años de vida pública, 1902–1913*. Madrid: Biblioteca Nueva.

Exhibit 3.2: The Tragic Week (1909)

Statement approved at a public meeting organised by the anarcho-syndicalist Workers' Solidarity (*Solidaridad Obrera*) immediately before the events in Barcelona

Considerando que la guerra es una consecuencia fatal del régimen de producción capitalista;

Considerando, además, que, dado el sistema español de reclutamiento del ejército, sólo los obreros hacen la guerra que los burgueses declaran.

La asamblea protesta enérgicamente:

1. Contra la acción del gobierno español en Marruecos;
2. Contra los procedimientos de ciertas damas de la aristocracia, que insultaron el dolor de los reservistas, de sus mujeres y de sus hijos, dándoles medallas y escapularios, en vez de proporcionarles los medios de subsistencia que les arrebatan con la marcha del jefe de familia;
3. Contra el envío a la guerra de ciudadanos útiles a la producción y, en general, indiferentes al triunfo de la cruz sobre la media luna, cuando se podrían formar regimentos de curas y de frailes que, además de estar directamente interesados en el éxito de la religión católica, no tienen familia, ni hogar, ni son de utilidad alguna al país; y
4. Contra la actitud de los diputados republicanos que ostentando un mandato del pueblo no han aprovechado su inmunidad parlamentaria para ponerse al frente de las masas en su protesta contra la guerra.

Y compromete a la clase obrera a concentrar todas sus fuerzas, por si se hubiera de declarar la huelga general para obligar al gobierno a respetar los derechos que tienen los marroquíes a conservar intacta la independencia de su país.

Considering that the war [in Morocco] is a fatal consequence of the capitalist mode of production:

Considering also that, given the Spanish system of army recruitment, it is the workers who must fight a war declared by the middle classes:

This meeting expresses its vehement protest:

1. Against the government's actions in Morocco;
2. Against the behaviour of certain aristocratic ladies who have insulted the suffering of the reservists, their wives and children, by presenting them with religious medallions and scapulars,[1] rather than with the means of subsistence of which they have been deprived by the absence of the family's head;

[1] The distinctive strip of cloth worn by monks over their habits.

3. Against the dispatch to the front of productive citizens to whom the triumph of Christianity over Islam is a matter of indifference, when it would be possible to form whole regiments of priests and monks who, as well as having a direct interest in the Catholic Church's fate, have no home or family, and are of no material use to the country; and
4. Against the attitude of Republican MPs who, although elected by the people, have failed to take advantage of their parliamentary immunity to place themselves at the head of the masses in their protest against the war.

The meeting also calls on the working class to unite should a general strike be called to force the government to respect the rights of Moroccans to defend their country's independence.

Source: Ullman, J. (1972) *La semana trágica.* Barcelona: Ariel.

Topics
FOR DISCUSSION

- What impression does Exhibit 3.1 give of Maura as a person?
- What typical 'regenerationist' themes are identifiable in it? Which of them were to reappear in Spain's history, and in which periods?
- What are the main grievances expressed in Exhibit 3.2? Other than Spanish workers, with whom do its authors appear to feel solidarity?
- Are there any points of similarity between Exhibits 3.1 and 3.2?

- What did the various forces working for change in Spain – 'regenerationists', regionalists, the workers' movement – have in common, in terms of their following and their aims? What role did Spain play in the thinking of each?
- Why was it so hard to achieve meaningful change in Spain up to 1923?

CHAPTER 4

Change imposed (1923–1931)

Throughout Europe, the 1920s were dominated by the after-effects of World War I, and reaction against the Russian Revolution. The most dramatic consequences were seen in Italy, where the Fascist Party seized power in 1922. Fascism had much in common with traditional conservatism; it was nationalist, authoritarian and anti-democratic. But there were also important differences: fascism's enthusiasm for economic development and concern with the situation of industrial workers; the cult of its leader, Mussolini; and the importance it laid on the Fascist Party itself as a means of controlling society. To not a few foreign observers these ideas seemed like interesting new departures, especially given their positive impact on Italy's backward economy. In that respect Mussolini benefited from the world economy's recovery after its post-war slump, which turned out to be brief. Indeed, it had petered out well before the 1929 Wall Street crash triggered the worst depression of modern times.

The uneasy calm which settled over Spain in the summer of 1923 was broken by a familiar sort of storm. On 13 September, General Miguel Primo de Rivera staged a coup, and assumed power. His declared intentions – to restore order, and bring about the reforms so widely discussed for the last 25 years – meant that his action was generally welcomed by an exhausted country. But he failed to establish a political structure for his dictatorship and, when his reforms ran into difficulties, it fell almost as swiftly as it had risen.

The 'iron surgeon'

Given the almost complete absence of opposition, Primo's coup was a virtually bloodless affair. Though his government suspended democratic freedoms, its authority was established with little need for active repression. As a result, Primo was able to embark almost immediately on the task he had set himself – that of the 'iron surgeon' envisioned by Costa (p38), administering drastic, emergency treatment to save his country.

Although Primo's revolt received no direct backing, it met with negligible resistance. Two factors were crucial to its success. One was the Army's anxiety about the forthcoming results of investigations into the Moroccan War (p51). In time-honoured fashion, it staged its own 'negative declaration' and stood aside (p14). That left matters in the hands of the King. Alfonso also had cause to fear the forthcoming revelations. Additionally, he may have seen a royal dictatorship as the means finally to apply 'regenerationist' ideas (p38). Whatever the reason, he exercised his constitutional prerogative to appoint Primo his Prime Minister.

Spain's new ruler was a man of simple but rather confused beliefs. The strongest was his sense of Spanish nationalism; the 'fatherland' (*patria*) outranked even the traditional institutions of Church and Crown in his scale of loyalties. His modernising tendencies were apparent in his regard for Mussolini. Yet Primo's basically conservative interpretation of his role as 'surgeon' was equally evident in the way he fostered Church influence, and in his admiration for Maura, whose concept of 'revolution from above' (p40) he espoused.

Impulsive, with a strong sense of fairness that bordered on sentimentality, Primo approached his task in a highly personalised manner. He issued constant explanations of his actions and motives, and travelled feverishly round the country to address his people. Such direct contact with public opinion, he felt, allowed him to 'rectify' policies based on his own 'intuition' in the light of popular response. For politicians he had only contempt, sharing the increasingly prevalent Army view that they – along with 'separatism' and 'communism' – were the root of Spain's ills, which it was soldiers' mission to cure.

Given this background, it came as no surprise that Primo's regime, at least initially, took the form of an outright military dictatorship, with the government formed by a 'Military Directorate'. Even at provincial and municipal level civilian authorities were replaced by Army officers. The 1876 Constitution was suspended, a state of siege declared and the press subjected to censorship. Although political parties were not formally banned, all senior civil servants and politicians who had previously held office were debarred, not just from administrative posts but also from directorships in firms awarded government contracts – a key source of business for many large companies.

The most serious problem facing the Directorate was the situation in **Morocco**. Here Primo showed his pragmatic streak. He did not belong to the tightly knit group of officers involved in the fighting there and passionately committed to Spain's role in Africa (*africanistas*). Believing the Spanish positions to be militarily indefensible, he ordered a withdrawal to the coast. However, in

Marruecos

Morocco

Previously confined to the garrison towns of Ceuta and Melilla, Spanish involvement in Morocco as a whole began in 1904, due to pressure to protect mining interests and the desire to prevent French control over the southern shore of the Straits of Gibraltar. Under the Franco–Moroccan Treaty of 1912 Spain was allocated a 'zone' in northern Morocco as a Protectorate, but her hold was constantly threatened by the inhospitable terrain and the resistance of local tribes. In 1921, under the leadership of Abd el Krim, they inflicted an overwhelming defeat on the Spanish 'Army of Africa' at Annual. By 1927, however, the Protectorate had been fully recovered, and it remained in Spanish hands until 1956 (p110). The strategically less valuable colony of Spanish Sahara, further to the south, was finally abandoned in 1975.

1925 the threat to its own Moroccan interests led France to join in operations against the local tribes, giving Primo the chance to 'rectify' his policy. He grasped it through a dramatic amphibious operation at the Bay of Alhucemas, which opened the way to complete victory.

With his internal enemies, Primo dealt more swiftly. The radical wing of Catalan regionalism (pp50–1), which offered token resistance to his takeover, was crushed with ease. However, given his deep suspicion of anything that might threaten Spain's unity, Primo did not stop there. He banned all political expressions of regionalist feeling in both Catalonia and the Basque Country, and abolished the Catalan regional government established in 1914 (p42). The anarcho-syndicalist CNT represented a more formidable foe. But General Martínez Anido, who had been appointed Interior Minister, was given a free hand to extend the repressive policies he had used to win the 'social war' on Barcelona's streets (p50), and during 1924 the CNT's remnants were driven underground. The country was more orderly than it had been for years, if not decades.

The Socialist wing of the workers' movement offered no opposition to Primo, whom it regarded as no worse than the middle-class politicians he had ousted. Indeed, when he showed himself willing, and able, to push through reforms, the Socialists came to see him as a means of speeding capitalist development, and so the approach of their own revolution (p45). This view was especially strong in the Socialist trade union federation, the **UGT**, which enthusiastically backed reforms designed to improve working-class conditions, in particular subsidised housing and medical assistance.

But it was Primo's attempts to reduce the level of industrial conflict that led the UGT to co-operate actively with him. It not only agreed to take part in compulsory arbitration to settle labour disputes, but even became a sort of government agency responsible for operating the statutory code of practice introduced in 1926. Under it, arbitration powers were exercised by joint boards with equal employer and employee representation (*comités paritarios*). The latter was provided by UGT officials, while the union's leader, Francisco Largo Caballero, became a sort of *de facto* labour minister.

The UGT's collaborationist line brought the union considerable dividends, allowing it to consolidate its industrial membership and establish a significant presence in the rural south. At the same time, the policy also provoked tensions within the Socialist move-

Unión General de Trabajadores (UGT)

General Workers' Union

The UGT was founded in 1888 as a federation of Socialist trade unions. Unlike the anarcho-syndicalist **CNT** (p47), it long saw its role as the improvement of workers' material conditions through strictly industrial activity, an attitude reflected in its co-operation with the Primo dictatorship. Under the Second Republic, when it acquired considerable influence (p75), the UGT took an increasingly militant political line that culminated in its participation in the uprising of 1934 (p76) and its revolutionary attitudes during the Civil War. Banned by Franco, the UGT briefly regained an important – and moderating – role in the transition that followed his death (p139). Ironically, after its sister **Socialist Party** (p45) came to power in 1982 its stance again turned more radical (p158), but – like that of unions in general – its influence is now much reduced.

ment as a whole, and deepened the rifts with the fledgling Communist Party (p38) and anarcho-syndicalists. However, the CNT was itself rent by feuds between moderates and extremists, who in 1927 set up the 'Iberian Anarchist Federation' (FAI) as a pure revolutionary organisation, unconcerned with trade union activity. On balance, then, one ironic result of Primo's regime was to strengthen the Socialists' position, both within the working-class movement and in the country.

The measures that the UGT helped to implement enjoyed considerable success, reducing sharply the days lost to industrial conflict. They reflected the dictator's sense of social justice, also apparent in his plans for a single income tax that would hit earnings from capital as well as wages; that proposal, however, met with strong opposition from the banks, and had to be abandoned. The other factor behind Primo's economic policy was his nationalism, which led him to see issues essentially in terms of national prestige. Hence his reintroduction of import tariffs at a higher level than ever before. He saw imports as a slight on Spain's own economic capabilities, to improve which he instigated the country's first large-scale programme of state intervention.

The government's development projects took various forms. The most visible was a massive programme of infrastructure, especially roads, dams and irrigation schemes; electricity was brought to many rural areas for the first time. A number of state-run monopolies were established, sometimes in association with private interests, including the CAMPSA oil and petrol company, the national telephone company (*Telefónica*) and the powerful Water Boards (*Confederaciones Hidráulicas*), as well as a plethora of regulatory bodies to advise on, promote and control activity in a wide range of industries. Finally, to assist in financing development, Primo founded various semi-public banks, covering fields such as overseas trade, house-building and new industries.

Between 1923 and 1928 the Spanish economy showed distinct signs of improvement. Admittedly, that was partly thanks to the favourable international climate. Yet, even so, Primo's measures, social as well as economic, deserve credit for the upswing. Equally, when it was rudely reversed in 1928/29, some of the blame could be ascribed to the first effects of the coming worldwide depression. But the sudden and extreme nature of downturn in Spain was to a large extent caused by grave flaws inherent in those same measures.

The collapse of dictatorship – and monarchy

The fact is that Primo's entire 'revolution from above' contained the seeds of its own failure. In trying to tackle the grievances of so many different groups simultaneously, he finished up by satisfying none and arousing the animosity of most. Since his attempts at political reform were an unmitigated failure, he never gave his regime a solid basis. When the heat was turned up it simply melted away – and the King with it.

Among the first to be alienated by Primo were those intellectuals who had seen in him the realisation of their ideas (p51). One reason for this was the continuing press censorship, another Primo's tendency to intervene 'intuitively' in individual court cases, using his effectively absolute powers to right specific wrongs without thought for the wider consequences. Especially in a country with such a strong legalistic tradition, this approach soon turned admiration to scorn among the intelligentsia, and large sections of the educated classes in general.

Their indignation was heightened by Primo's effective banishment of Unamuno (p38), for protesting against one of his arbitrary interventions. Students, too, were outraged by this treatment of a highly respected professor. They were already protesting against Primo's proposals to extend Church influence into the higher education sphere, by giving state recognition to the degrees awarded by private, Catholic universities. After Unamuno's exile their demonstrations became a permanent feature of Madrid life, and a minor but persistent irritant to the regime.

Another group whose support Primo soon lost was the Catalan business community. Its gratitude at his restoration of law and order turned to anger when he banned the use of Catalan in Church and, especially, at the suppression of devolution (p59). That step was doubly damaging to the industrialists, since it completed the swing of Catalan opinion behind demands for more far-reaching self-government (pp50–1). Along with consolidating Socialism (p60), the other main political effect of the dictatorship was thus to seal the conversion of Catalan regionalism from a conservative monarchist force into a radical, republican one.

Although Catalonia was a much more serious enemy than the intellectuals, or the old politicians who had never accepted Primo – even Maura, his acknowledged inspiration, refused to back him – it was not strong enough by itself to shake the dictator's hold on power. What did eventually have that effect was Primo's scatter-gun approach to reform, which meant that every section of society that had initially backed him was sooner or later offended by one of his measures. For example, while devout Catholics welcomed his concessions to the Church, they deplored his co-operation with 'godless' socialists (p59). In the Basque Country, that worked to the benefit of regionalists (p43); elsewhere it merged with a broader conservative reaction against his regime.

Thus employers were never reconciled to Primo's labour legislation (p59), and those who failed to profit from the creation of state monopolies were antagonised further, as was much of the financial world. Landowners, the very bastion of conservative opinion, were outraged by Primo's attempt to introduce the mildest of land reforms (p70). Both these groups, who tended to share Primo's brand of Spanish nationalism, were disappointed by his inability to achieve either of his foreign-policy aims: the incorporation of Tangiers into Spanish Morocco (p58) and the granting of a seat on the League of Nations' Security Council.

The resultant spreading disillusion formed the background to Primo's attempts at political reform, which began in 1924 with the establishment of the Patriotic Union (UP). Partly modelled on Mussolini's Fascist Party, the UP promoted a cult of the leader, and rejected representative democracy in favour of a direct relationship between the leader and the people, for instance through the rigged referendums which were a feature of the regime. Yet Primo never intended the UP to be a genuine party, never mind a fascist one. Instead he conceived it as a 'Citizens' League', a social organisation that would allow him to tap into opinion but have no political role.

At heart Primo was a traditionalist, out of tune with fascism's modernising tendencies, and the UP's philosophy was influenced chiefly by Spanish conservatism. Only among Carlists (p12), and the personal following built up by Maura (p48), did it find a faint echo. Instead, the bulk of UP's small membership was made up of those who benefited directly from the regime, such as journalists, hangers-on and public servants – many of whom, especially at local level, had been in post before 1923. Their vested interests put paid to the 1925 Municipal Statute which had been intended to clean up local government along the lines originally proposed by Maura (pp39–40). More generally, too, the UP acted not as an instrument of change but as a brake on it.

At national level 1925 did bring some change with the establishment of a new government, in the form of a Civilian Directorate (*Directorio Civil*). Its members were appointed by Primo, largely from the ranks of UP. They were professional experts (*tecnócratas*), chiefly lawyers and economists, usually civil servants; their star was the young Finance Minister, José Calvo Sotelo. These new arrangements were prompted by necessity – military government having become impractical – and were intended to be temporary, pending completion of what was now Primo's main project: a new constitution.

The task of drafting the new text was given to an Advisory National Assembly (*Asamblea Nacional Consultiva*) which differed substantially from earlier constituent bodies. Whereas in the past they had been elected, albeit usually under less than free conditions, the members of Primo's Assembly were appointed by him. Moreover, its powers were limited to producing proposals for the dictator's consideration, which it did in 1928. Unsurprisingly, they pandered to his views, in particular granting the prime minister extensive new powers, including the right to nominate half the members of Parliament.

At a time when the regime's popularity was waning fast, the Assembly's proposals were met by a barrage of criticism. Primo showed his political naivety, first by proposing another of his discredited referendums, and then by appointing a number of his critics to the Assembly. Naturally enough, they used their new position mainly to restate their objections, reinforcing Primo's distrust of anything that smacked of politics. His enthusiasm for a constitution rapidly faded, and the question of how Spain should be governed was left in mid-air.

In this situation of political vacuum the weaknesses in Primo's expansionist economic policies came home to roost. The original intention had been to finance them by extending the scope of income tax. When that idea was blocked by the banks (p60), Primo resorted to increased public borrowing, concealing the additional interest payments in a separate 'Extraordinary Budget'. In effect, he gambled on an economic take-off generating more revenue from existing taxes. When Spain became a victim of world depression – because of its commercial links with Latin America, one of the first areas affected – Primo lost his bet.

At home recession, combined with the inflation inevitably caused by so much public spending, had disastrous effects, especially for low earners. Abroad, the peseta came under intense pressure. For Primo the currency's value was above all a matter of national pride, and he instructed Calvo Sotelo to defend it at what was now a totally unrealistic level. That strategy merely aggravated speculation and made eventual devaluation all the more drastic, forcing the resignation of Primo's most able lieutenant.

The recession had even graver political repercussions. Primo's Socialist allies (p59) grew restive at the plight of their own supporters, and devaluation was a further blow to Primo's prestige among the nationalist Right that his own rhetoric had helped to create. It was a Conservative politician, Sánchez Guerra, who first tried to channel dissent, in January 1929. Although his amateurish conspiracy was easily put down, it had an important knock-on effect. Coming on top of the proposal by the Assembly to cut his powers, its Republican overtones convinced the King that Primo had become the biggest danger to his throne, and he began to distance himself from his Prime Minister.

The last nail in the dictator's coffin was the loss of Army backing. Again it was induced by reforms that, in themselves, were perfectly sensible. To improve military efficiency Primo had insisted that promotion to the rank of general should be based not on seniority but on merit, an attack on military tradition that was bound to ruffle important feathers. On the other hand, his abolition of the Artillery Corps' special privileges was not unpopular in the rest of the Army. But any sympathy evaporated when he reacted to opposition from within the Corps by dissolving it altogether.

Primo's response to the rising tide of discontent was typically impulsive. In January 1930 he spontaneously sought the views of the various Army regional commanders (*Capitanes Generales*). When they evinced a clear lack of enthusiasm for his continuation, he resigned and left the country; he died a few months later. His departure did not immediately threaten the monarchy, since although the King was tainted by his part in Primo's ascent to power (pp57–8), and by having willingly played the dictatorship's figurehead, the continuing use of repression meant that resentment against him was so far unfocused and disorganised. But Alfonso soon contrived to change that.

Ignoring popular and even Army opinion, the King appointed another soldier to replace Primo. His choice, the aged and infirm General Berenguer, proved hopelessly indecisive, first promising to hold a general election, then failing to call it for over a year. While he maintained Primo's legal restrictions on political activity, little or no attempt was made to impose them in practice. His so-called soft dictatorship (*dictablanda*) was to provide perfect conditions for opposition to flourish.

It was channelled mainly by the Republican movement (p23), which had been revived by a new generation of leaders. During 1930 they conducted a campaign that destroyed the King's remaining prestige, at least among the educated classes, and in August they signed a secret agreement with other opposition groups. This **San Sebastion Pact** had some backing from the Army, which

Pacto de San Sebastián

San Sebastian Pact

The Pact agreed in August 1930 in the Basque resort was a secret agreement to overthrow the monarchy. It was joined by various groups which later became known as the **Left Republicans** (p68); the **Radical Republicans** (p48); the radical Catalan regionalist *Estat Català* set up by Francesc Macià (p51); and several prominent defectors from the old 'dynastic parties' (p26), including Miguel Maura, son of Antonio (p39), and the ex-Liberal Niceto Alcalá Zamora.

blamed Alfonso for failing to save the Artillery Corps. A military declaration was planned for 15 December, but Colonel Galán, its commander in the Aragonese garrison-town of Jaca, jumped the gun and the conspiracy was revealed. The setback proved temporary. Galán's execution gave Republicanism a martyr and the trial of the Pact's leaders was a farce, ending in their virtual absolution. Coming from a military court, the verdict indicated how little control the royal authorities now exercised over events.

As their last throw they finally called municipal elections, for 12 April 1931. While supporters of the monarchy won most votes, they were concentrated on the land where clientilism still reigned supreme (p29). The provincial capitals, where elections had some meaning, voted massively for Republican candidates. The more responsible of the remaining monarchist politicians realised that the game was up. One of them, Count Romanones, took it upon himself to act as intermediary between the King and the opposition leaders. As a result of the contacts, Alfonso left Spain on 14 April.

Summary of main points

The 'iron surgeon'

- Primo de Rivera's notion of 'modernisation' was confused, simplistic and authoritarian.
- As well as crushing his opponents, who were in any case initially few and weak, he introduced significant social security and employment regulation measures that won him the support of the Socialist trade union, the UGT.
- His policy of spending heavily on infrastructure projects contributed to strong, if short-lived, economic growth.

The collapse of dictatorship – and monarchy

- Primo's 'revolution from above' contained the seeds of its own failure. Economically, excessive spending contributed to a sharp economic collapse after 1928; politically, Primo was unable to create any alternative to the discredited structures of the restoration system.
- Meanwhile, his haphazard approach to reform alienated a succession of groups and institutions that had initially backed him, including intellectuals, moderate Catalan regionalists, industrialists, the King and, most importantly, the Army itself.
- His abrupt departure left a political vacuum that was effectively filled by the resurgent Republican movement.

Exhibit 4.1: Primo de Rivera's manifesto (1923)

Opening of Primo's 'declaration' on the morning of his coup

AL PAÍS Y AL EJÉRCITO ESPAÑOLES

Ha llegado para nosotros el momento más temido que esperado (porque hubiéramos querido vivir siempre en la legalidad y que ella rigiera sin interrupción la vida española) de recoger las ansias, de atender el clamoroso requerimiento de cuantos amando la Patria no ven para ella otra salvación que libertarla de los profesionales de la política, de los hombres que por una u otra razón nos ofrecen el cuadro de desdichas e inmoralidades que empezaron el año 98 y amenazan a España con un próximo fin trágico y deshonroso. La tupida red de la política de concupiscencias ha cogido en sus mallas, secuestrándola, hasta la voluntad real. Con frecuencia parecen pedir que gobiernen los que ellos dicen no dejan gobernar, aludiendo a los que han sido su único, aunque débil freno, y llevaron a las leyes y costumbres la poca ética sana, el tenue tinte de moral y equidad que aún tienen; pero en la realidad se avienen fáciles y contentos al turno y al reparto y entre ellos mismos designan la sucesión.

Pues bien, ahora vamos a recabar todas las responsabilidades y a gobernar nosotros u hombres civiles que representan nuestra moral y doctrina. Basta ya de rebeldías mansas, que sin poner remedio a nada, dañan tanto y más a la disciplina que está recia y viril a que nos lanzamos por España y por el Rey.

Este movimiento es de hombres: el que no sienta la masculinidad completamente caracterizada, que espere en un rincón, sin perturbar los días buenos que para la patria preparamos. Españoles: ¡Viva España y viva el Rey! […]

TO THE SPANISH PEOPLE AND ARMY

For us has arrived the moment we have not so much awaited as dreaded – for we would have wished always to abide by the law, and for its rule over Spaniards' lives to have remained unbroken. It is the moment to take up the concerns, to obey the clamorous desire, of those Spanish patriots who see no other salvation for their fatherland than to free it from the professional politicians, from those men that, for one reason or another, have been responsible for the sorry tale of misfortune and immorality which began in 1898 and which threatens Spain with an imminent end, as tragic as it would be dishonourable. Even the King's will has been ensnared and trapped in the web woven by these lustful politicians. Often they appear to wish that government be taken over by those they accuse of making it impossible – meaning those who have been the only restraint, albeit a weak one, on their activities, and who have lent to the law and political practice that small element of ethical health, that vague tinge of morality and equity which they still retain. But in reality the politicians are only too happy to succeed each other in rotation, carving up power and deciding the succession amongst themselves.

Very well, now we are going to assume the full responsibility of government ourselves, together with civilians who share our morality and our ideas. There will be no more half-hearted rebellions that solve nothing, while doing so much damage to the robust and manly discipline which urges us to rise now for Spain and for the King.

Ours is a masculine movement. Let him who does not feel himself the complete embodiment of manhood stand aside and do nothing to cloud the bright future we are building for our fatherland. Spaniards: long live Spain and long live the King! [...]

Source: La Vanguardia (Barcelona), 13 September 1923.

Topics
FOR DISCUSSION

■ What insights does Exhibit 4.1 give into Primo's worldview?

■ How does Primo appear to see the role of the Army in Spain's public life? How does his view compare to that of O'Donnell (Exhibit 1.2)?

■ Could Primo have succeeded?

■ How did his situation and approach to government differ from those of Franco?

CHAPTER 5

A troubled democracy (1931–1936)

The 1930s were the decade of depression in Europe. Millions were plunged into poverty, which the political and economic structures of liberal democracy seemed powerless to relieve. Many looked to the authoritarian regimes, which as it appeared from the outside, were enjoying greater success in the Soviet Union, and in Italy under fascism. In their different ways, communism and fascism were both international movements, and both strove to undermine other, democratic regimes by propaganda and by the street violence of their paramilitary gangs. Germany was especially affected, and in 1933 its conservatives attempted to forestall the threat from the Left by taking German fascism into government. Hitler and his Nazis exploited this foothold to establish their own dictatorship, eliminating democratic institutions and cracking down ruthlessly on political opponents. His rise confirmed the Left's suspicions not just of fascism but of the traditional Right, particularly given that conservatives close to the Catholic Church had imposed their own brand of authoritarian regime in Austria. By 1936 Soviet leader Stalin was sufficiently worried to instruct communists worldwide to change tack and co-operate with socialists and middle-class liberals in an all-out bid to halt fascism.

Even before King Alfonso left the country, Spain's Second Republic had been declared by popular acclaim. The country's first attempt at genuine democracy was born in very difficult circumstances, in the midst of world depression and with democracy under growing pressure throughout Europe. Insofar as it shielded Spain from the worst effects of depression, economic backwardness was now, ironically, an asset. But it could not prevent the political tension round about from seeping into Spanish affairs, especially when it resonated so strongly with internal events. For, after a period when its fate lay in the hands of its truest supporters, the Republic's politics were dominated increasingly by two aggressive and antagonistic forces whose commitment to it was questionable at best: a resurgent Right and a newly reunited Left.

The reforming years

In the confusion following the King's departure, a Provisional Government was formed. It was composed mainly of the Republicans who had plotted the monarchy's fall, a heterogeneous group who now became the decisive factor in determining the character of the new Republic. They were also the main driving force behind the many and wide-ranging changes of the 'two reforming years' (*bienio de reformas*) that followed.

The Provisional Government's composition was based on the Pact agreed at San Sebastian in 1930 (p63). Even the one, crucial addition – the Socialist PSOE (p45) – had been represented there by two of its leading figures. All the parties involved in the Pact itself were relatively new, with the exception of the Radical Republicans (p48) – now known merely as Radicals. Their leader, Alejandro Lerroux, had been an important secondary player in sham democratic politics before 1923 and it showed, in corruption and in opportunistic attempts to exploit changes in public mood (p72). So, while his party theoretically formed the centre of the Republican bloc, it differed fundamentally from both wings, each of which was genuinely concerned with meaningful reform.

The 'Republican Right' was a party recently formed by ex-members of the old 'dynastic parties' (p26) who had recently converted to Republicanism. Their main interest was political reform, and they had only limited support. The party's main value to its allies was to reassure the middle classes that the Republic would not damage their interests – hence the choice of its leader, Niceto Alcalá Zamora (p63), to head the new government.

The real core of Republicanism was therefore what, in ideological terms, constituted its left wing. The leader, and archetype, of these **Left Republicans** was Manuel Azaña. As much an intellectual as a politician, he had close links to the '1927 generation' – the new wave of literary and artistic talent whose leading figure was Federico García Lorca. For Azaña and his colleagues, cultural considerations were of prime importance. They believed strongly in the fundamental importance of education as the basis of social change, and were almost fanatically opposed to the social influence of the Church, which they regarded as the main reason for Spain's intellectual and cultural stagnation.

The first task facing the Provisional Government was to draw up a constitution for the Republic. It was assigned to the constituent parliament (*Cortes constituyentes*) elected in June, in which the PSOE and the Radicals led the field and the government parties in conjunction won an overwhelming victory. As a result, most major issues were settled without great dispute. Spain was formally declared a Republic, its citizens were constitutionally assured of a long list of rights and freedoms, and sovereignty was placed in the hands of their representatives: a single-chamber parliament to be elected by universal adult suffrage, both male and female. This house would, in turn, elect the president, whose mainly ceremonial powers would

---

Republicanos de izquierdas

Left Republicans

The Left Republicans were a loose grouping of several small parties during the Second Republic. They inherited the concern for practical reform of the **Reformist Republicans** (p39), from which most had emerged, but also the anticlericalism associated with the historic **Republican movement** (p23). The group's main components were the Radical Socialists (*Partido Republicano Radical Socialista*) led by Marcelino Domingo, the Galician Republicans (ORGA) of Casares Quiroga, and Manuel Azaña's short-lived 'Republican Action', later replaced by the confusingly named 'Republican Left' (p76), also led by Azaña.
See also: **Frente Popular** (p76)

include that of formally appointing a prime minister – now assumed, wrongly as it turned out (p72), to be a formality.

Where compromise proved impossible was over the religious issue, since the Left Republicans, the third largest grouping in Parliament, joined the Socialists in taking a hard anticlerical line. Consequently Article 26 of the new Constitution not only decreed freedom of worship for all creeds, but also broke all links between Church and state, including government funding of clerical salaries (p13). The Catholic Church's position became that of a voluntary association, subject to the law and to taxation but also to certain special restrictions, including a ban on involvement in education.

Article 26 was to become the focus of widespread conservative opposition to the government (p71). For the moment, however, its main impact was within the government itself, whose more right-wing members, including Alcalá Zamora, resigned in protest at its provisions. Yet the differences were patched up and, once the Constitution had been approved in December, Alcalá Zamora was elected the Republic's first president. He was replaced as Prime Minister by Azaña, under whom the government set about implementing a series of ambitious reforms.

In some areas the government built on measures introduced by Primo de Rivera, whose system of joint industrial relations boards (p59) was retained and extended, albeit under a new name (*jurados mixtos*). Similarly, the Socialist Prieto continued Primo's programme of infrastructure investment (p60), to good effect. He could do so thanks to an overhaul of public finances that massively increased government income by tightening up tax collection and administration – and incidentally showed how inefficient they had been previously. Taxes themselves remained very low, with the top rate on income under eight per cent. This approach had the benefit of avoiding offence to the better-off, but also meant that funds for reform were restricted.

In other respects, such as social policy, the Republic made a sharp break with the past, notably in the legalisation of divorce. The most significant initiatives, though, came in the education field. A large-scale school-building programme was begun, aimed at bringing education to the masses for the first time. Teacher training was also greatly expanded. In line with Left Republican ideas, too, was the attempt to bring cultural experience to impoverished rural areas, through such initiatives as the establishment of libraries, and the provision of subsidies for Lorca's travelling theatre company, 'La Barraca'.

Another innovation was the government's policy towards the regions, or more precisely Catalonia, where the regionalist leader Macià (p51) had declared an independent republic on Alfonso's departure, and had to be persuaded to back down by the Provisional Government. His payoff came in 1932, when a regional government (*Generalitat*) was established with much wider powers than its predecessor (p42). Regional autonomy was now underpinned by a Catalan parliament, and at the first election Macià's new party, **Catalan Republican Left**, won an easy victory. While this sealed Catalonia's support for the Republic, at the same time it awakened concerns among Spanish conservatives that their country was starting to break up.

Right-wing concern was also aroused by Azaña's military reforms. These were designed to create a modern Army, which inevitably meant reducing the excessive

---

Esquerra Republicana de Catalunya (ERC)

Catalan Republican Left

Formed in 1931, immediately before the declaration of the Second Republic, ERC was an alliance of left-leaning regionalist groupings. It was led by the charismatic Francesc Macià (p51) until his death in 1933, when he was replaced by Lluis Companys, the man largely responsible for ERC's creation. Despite its talk of independence, ERC was content to settle for the devolution granted by the Republic, under which it dominated Catalan politics and ran the regional government. It was suppressed by the Franco regime and, although it re-emerged thereafter, lost its leadership of the regionalist movement to the newly formed **CiU** (p164). Around the turn of the twenty-first century, however, it enjoyed a strong revival, and in 2003 became an important partner in the regional government (p176).

See also: **Frente Popular** (76)

---

number of officers and making promotion more dependent on ability. They were also supposed to involve modernising outdated equipment, but in the absence of a true tax reform there was no money for that. Inevitably, this aggravated the dissatisfaction caused by the other changes, and by rumours that promotion was now dependent on pro-Republican views. In August 1932 a group of right-wing officers led by General Sanjurjo attempted a coup, but it was quickly suppressed by loyal troops.

The coup attempt came while the government was struggling to pass legislation not only on Catalan devolution but also on an even more controversial issue. Although the need for **land reform** was recognised in principle by all the government parties, its details were another matter. In the summer of 1932 discussions had reached deadlock, but the coup attempt gave them renewed impetus, and measures were agreed soon after. Unfortunately they were badly flawed.

Part of the problem was that Socialist support had to be bought by allowing estates owned by the aristocracy to be expropriated.

As a vindictive reaction against the coup's suspected supporters, the move set an unhappy precedent (p73). It was also a meaningless gesture since, while estate owners were eligible for compensation, the government had no funds with which to pay them. In addition, the understandable emphasis on the plight of landless labourers in the south meant that the problems of northern smallholders were largely ignored. Most important of all, the extent of reform was modest in the extreme.

The land reform fiasco turned discontent on the left of the political spectrum into a major problem for the government (p75). Throughout 1932 it repeatedly had to dispatch the security forces to deal with those who attempted, in a long-standing anarchist

---

reforma agraria

land reform

While referring, as elsewhere, to changes in the pattern of landownership and to landholding in general, in Spain land reform is especially associated with the break-up of the large estates (*latifundios*) commonly found in poorer parts of the country's centre and south, many of which were notoriously underused for agricultural purposes. As a result, land reform became an extremely emotive issue for both wings of the workers' movement, as well as a particular aim of many 'regenerationists' (p38).

See also: **colectivización** (p87)

tradition, to take land redistribution into their own hands (p46). The clashes reached a tragic climax in January 1933 at the Andalusian hamlet of Casas Viejas, when 25 villagers were shot dead after they had killed several Civil Guards.

Azaña's coalition was fatally weakened, and the Socialists increasingly distanced themselves from it under pressure from their left (p75). With utter hypocrisy, the Right – which previously had criticised it for being too mild in dealing with such outbreaks – also used the incident to berate the government as authoritarian. Lerroux, sensing he was aboard a sinking ship, joined in their attacks. In November, unable to command a majority in Parliament, Azaña resigned and a general election was called. Abandoned by the Republican Right, the Socialists and the Radicals, the Left Republicans also fell victim to the electoral system, which effectively ensured that only the two largest groupings in each provincial constituency could win seats. They were decimated, Azaña's own party obtaining just five seats. The reforming years were over.

The rise of the Right

The main feature of the 1933 election was a strong swing to the Right. This reflected the extent to which the government's various reforms, and above all its religious legislation, had provoked a fierce backlash among the more traditionalist sections of Spanish society. As a result, the parties that now took over the Republic's government were concerned to undo the work of their predecessors. Indeed, there was widespread suspicion that the largest of them wished to overthrow the democratic regime itself.

In 1931 the Spanish Right barely existed as a political force. Primo de Rivera's single party (pp61–2) had melted away with its creator. The old 'dynastic' parties had withered under his rule, a process completed by the discredit of their *raison d'être*, the monarchy. Nor was the Church the bulwark it had been. The Papacy's depression-inspired concern with social issues sat uneasily with the reactionary views of the Spanish Right. Within the country many parish priests, finding that their own financial circumstances were precarious, were sympathetic to social reform. When the head of Spain's Church, Cardinal Segura, viciously attacked the newly proclaimed Republic, and was banned from the country as a result, the support he received from Catholics was lukewarm.

This decline in the Right's fortunes was abruptly reversed by the adoption of the new Constitution, whose strongly anticlerical provisions (p69) alienated all shades of Catholic opinion and gave a target against which conservatives could campaign. Further steps in the same direction, including a ban on the Jesuits, only increased their indignation and resolve. For the first time, the Right was able to mobilise supporters *en masse* at rallies over large areas of the country, something which only the workers' parties had previously managed, and then only in particular urban areas.

The catalyst for this transformation was a new political organisation, the **CEDA**, intended by its leader, José-María Gil-Robles, to become a mass party capable of defeating the Left in a free election. Its philosophy was also new to the Spanish Right, reflecting as it did the Christian Social ideas now in favour with the Vatican, which emphasised the state's role in providing for the less well-off. However, the CEDA had

Confederación Española de Derechas Autónomas (CEDA)

Confederation of the Right

An alliance of various right-wing parties, the most important of which was José-María Gil-Robles' People's Action (*Acción Popular*), the CEDA was set up in 1933. Under Gil-Robles's leadership it grew rapidly, and topped the poll at the next year's general election. However, the dubious compatibility of its ideas with democracy made even conservative Republicans distrustful. As a result it was excluded from power until October 1934, when its admission to government sparked off an attempted left-wing revolution (p76). Defeated at the 1936 election, the CEDA disintegrated once Civil War broke out later that year.

other features that made it the object of deep distrust among its opponents.

Part of the problem was Gil-Robles's refusal to make clear his attitude to the Republican form of government. His own fervent monarchism, and the fact that he had rich backers hostile to the Republic, was well-known. Yet he refused to say whether he wanted to restore the monarchy, declaring his policy to be one of adapting to circumstances (*accidentalismo*). Even more worryingly, he displayed open sympathy with developments in Austria, where his fellow Christian Socials had imposed a virtual dictatorship. The government's alarm at the CEDA's rise is thus understandable. But attempting to have the party banned and its meetings broken up represented a clumsy over-reaction that only increased the CEDA's appeal to the swelling ranks of those unhappy with the course of reform.

By 1933 these included employers resentful at the extension of labour regulation (p69), and much of the middle class, concerned that even limited land reform (p70) might herald a threat to their own property. By no means all were particularly conservative; many were convinced Republicans, and suspicious of the Church. Their unease, along with the antagonism evoked in Castile by Catalan devolution, was picked up by the sensitive antennae of Lerroux, who swiftly positioned his Radicals to exploit it by ratting on his government colleagues (p71).

For the 1933 election the Radicals and CEDA formed an alliance which also included smaller right-wing groups, notably the Agrarians, who enjoyed strong support among the smallholders of Old Castile. With the help of the electoral system (p71) the allies won a solid parliamentary majority. The CEDA was the biggest winner of all, and became the largest single party. However, President Alcalá Zamora shared the widespread suspicions of its intentions, and declined to appoint Gil-Robles as Prime Minister. As a result, during its second phase the Republic was run mainly by weak coalitions of centre parties, Radical-led but dependent on the CEDA's parliamentary support.

Known to the Left as the 'two black years' (*bienio negro*), from the colour associated with the Church, this period saw a concerted attempt to reverse the Azaña government's policies, in particular its anticlerical legislation. Thus, as well as repealing some social measures, such as wage regulation, and some aspects of land reform, the Radicals also reintroduced government support for the clergy's salaries – ironically, given that the Church was one of their traditional bogeys (p48).

Another, regionalism, was anathema also to the CEDA's fierce Spanish nationalism, and became a further target for the programme of counter-reform. In the Basque Country, that involved blocking proposals put forward by the Basque Nationalist Party (PNV), previously a firm supporter of the Right. In fact, on many issues the PNV's ideas were very similar to those of the CEDA (p43), but now, on the promise of devolution from a future government of the Left, it began campaigning alongside its traditional Socialist enemies against the central government. And in Catalonia, too, the Right was driven onto the defensive.

There, the old Regionalist League (p42) had recovered some of its former strength in 1933, but at the subsequent regional election it was again crushed by the more radical ERC (p70), this time for good. Emboldened by its triumph, the regional govern ment moved to help one of its key constituencies, the small tenant farmers who had been hit by the effects of economic depression. The Smallholdings Act (*Ley de Cultivos*) was designed to give them greater security by bolstering their rights *vis-à-vis* landowners, but its implications for property rights in general alarmed both the Catalan *bourgeoisie* and the Madrid government, which referred the Act to the Constitutional Court. By doing so it turned a class issue into something much more emotive; a national conflict between Spain and Catalonia. When the Court threw out the Act in autumn 1934, the ERC reacted in correspondingly heated terms.

The ERC's anger was directed chiefly at the Radicals, who had already been weak- ened by the defection of a faction, led by deputy leader Martínez Barrio, which objected to the party's U-turn on religious policy. Sensing an opportunity, Gil-Robles brought the government down, and made the CEDA's entry into its successor the price of his contin- uing support. It was a fateful decision, being used by the Left to justify an attempted revolution (p76). That in turn set off a spiral of increasingly undemocratic behaviour on both sides of the political spectrum, which ended in war.

Already Lerroux had set a bad example. Pardoning former Primo supporters banned from politics by the Azaña government could be interpreted as a gesture of reconciliation; his amnesty for those involved in the 1932 coup attempt could not (p70). But the new, CEDA-dominated administration's reaction to the 1934 'revolution' plumbed new depths of vindictiveness and bias. Thousands of ordinary workers were put on trial, many for relatively minor offences, while the left-wing press was censored and Catalan autonomy suspended. Efforts were even made to implicate Azaña in the rising, when in fact he had tried to calm the situation. Yet the many, and manifestly well-founded claims of Army brutality were not even investigated.

The CEDA's performance in other areas of government was initially less partisan. In some – public works, the status of leaseholders, provision of low-cost rented housing – its Christian Social ideas inspired policies that were little different from those of the Azaña era. However, as the effects of depression, and Gil-Robles's insistence on maintaining military spending, made budget cuts inevitable, his party's line hardened, with education suffering badly. But it was above all the complete reversal of land policy, which now blatantly favoured big landowners that made the CEDA look downright reactionary. Indeed, Gil-Robles's promotion of extreme right- wing generals, and his talk of a 'revolution' to return Spain to its roots, gave weight to

---

monarquistas
....

monarchists

While technically it also included
Carlists (p12), the term
'monarchists' was usually
understood to mean those who
supported the abolition of the
Second Republic and the
restoration of Alfonso XIII
(*alfonsistas*). For the most part
strongly Catholic, some
supported the **CEDA** (p72), while
others joined the smaller, more
reactionary Spanish Renewal
(*Renovación Española*); later they
all gravitated towards the
'Nationalist Bloc' set up by José
Calvo Sotelo. During the Franco
era monarchists were among
the regime's most prominent
supporters (pp104–5), but they
also formed part of the 'legal'
opposition (p124).
See also: **familias** (p104),
aperturistas (p126)

---

the Left's argument that it did not merit treatment as a democratic party.

For some on the Right, though, the CEDA was too cautious. Nominally they were **monarchists** but, for most, the real issue was not so much the Republic's lack of a king as its reformist nature. Their feelings lacked a vehicle until, in May 1934, the charismatic José Calvo Sotelo returned from exile (p62). He gave the far Right a new impetus with his vicious verbal attacks not just on the Republic but on Gil-Robles for 'treacherously' propping it up. Like his contacts with seditious generals, they made the undemocratic nature of his intentions plain to all, supporters and opponents.

Gil-Robles's plans were now approaching fulfilment. The four-year moratorium imposed by the Constitution on amendments to its text would soon be up, and he could move to repeal Article 26. But his moment never came. In late 1935 Lerroux's political career was ended by financial scandal; without their leader the Radicals fragmented and the government fell. Again, President Alcalá refused to countenance a CEDA-led administration, and called an election for February 1936. In total, the Right obtained more votes than in 1933, but its parliamentary strength was decimated, since the enmity between Gil-Robles and Calvo Sotelo prevented the close co-operation between their parties that the electoral system made essential (p71). For the Radicals, such technicalities were irrelevant; in common with the rest of the centre, their support in the country simply vanished.

The reunification of the Left

In 1936 the Right's opponents reaped the reward of standing as a united bloc, in contrast to their fragmentation in 1933. That had been caused by the workers' disillusion with Republican reforms, and its increasingly radical expression. The process of radicalisation was accelerated by the election of a right-wing government, and culminated in an attempted revolution. Its failure, and the government's brutal reaction to it, opened the way for a reunification of the Left as a whole.

In the changing pattern of relations within the Left the Socialists played a crucial role. Given the absence of an anarchist party (p46), they were the only means by which the Left's working-class support was represented in the Parliament, which had become the centre of political life. They were also the link between the workers' movement as a whole and the Republicans, with whom anarchists mainly refused to talk. The main channel for such contacts was the Basque Socialist leader Indalecio Prieto, one of those who attended the signing of the San Sebastian Pact (p63). Thereafter he persuaded the PSOE to drop its policy of non-co-operation with middle-class parties (p45) – over coming the reservations of party leader Julián Besteiro among others – and to join the Republic's Provisional Government (p68).

While he argued that the Republic would bring in the reforms the PSOE had always seen as the prerequisite for a revolution (p45), Prieto's real reason for co-operating with it was pragmatic: that the alternative was much worse. Pragmatism also weighed heavily with the Socialist movement's trade union wing, the UGT (p59), which found that state-sponsored labour regulation brought the same advantages as under the Primo regime, only in greater measure; civil service jobs for union officials, and the title as well as the functions of Labour Minister for the UGT leader, Francisco Largo Caballero. As a bonus, it was able to secure a further rise in membership by offering workers access to – often favourable – arbitration procedures.

Such access remained the preserve of the UGT because Spain's other large labour organisation, the anarcho-syndicalist CNT (p47), continued to boycott arbitration. Its attitude was dictated by the traditional anarchist view that all governments, dictatorial or democratic, were equally bad (p46). Even so, amidst the euphoria of 1931 many anarchists forgot their disdain for '*bourgeois*' elections and voted, mainly for the PSOE. In the same year a group of prominent anarcho-syndicalists led by Angel Pestaña issued a manifesto in which they argued against an immediate revolution. But they and their supporters (*treintistas*) were overwhelmingly defeated, and expelled from the CNT.

For the next two years, anarchism was in thrall to its terrorist tradition, represented by the Iberian Anarchist Federation (p60). Attacks on property were common, often accompanied by waves of political strikes; Barcelona, Seville and Saragossa were especially affected. With the government's failure to legislate an effective programme of land reform, the focus of violence shifted to the countryside (p70). In 1932 the Alto Llobregat area of Catalonia was briefly 'liberated' from government control. Andalusia was another hotbed, with the tragic incident at Casas Viejas merely the worst of many (p71).

Its attitude hardened by the government's tough response to such activities, in 1933 the CNT urged its followers 'Don't vote', an injunction most were happy to obey. In theory, the right-wing government their abstention helped to elect was meant to provoke a spontaneous revolution. In practice, its effect on most anarchists was another bout of the periodic disillusion to which their movement had always been prone.

In the meantime, the failure of land reform had affected Socialists as well, provoking the PSOE to leave the government. The UGT, terrified of losing rural members to the CNT, changed its line even more dramatically. Abandoning his habitual caution, Largo Caballero began to talk of an imminent workers' revolution. After the Right's election victory he set up a semi-secret Workers' Alliance (*Alianza Obrera*), with the aim of uniting militants from both wings of the workers' movement under UGT leadership. He also stepped up his inflammatory rhetoric, warning that he would regard the CEDA's admission to government as a fascist takeover. When it occurred (p73), he was forced to back his words with deeds.

Largo Caballero's call for a 'revolutionary strike' was catastrophic. Dispirited anarchists mainly ignored it, with particularly damaging effects in Catalonia. There, the ERC regional government had also boxed itself into a corner with intemperate attacks on the Madrid authorities (p73), and was dragged along in Largo's wake. The regional premier, Lluis Companys, reluctantly declared Catalonia a free Republic within federal Spain, but few workers rallied to his support and, even worse, the Catalan police controlled by his own party helped to crush those who did. 'Free' Catalonia survived less than a day; in most of Spain the uprising was over even more quickly.

Only in Asturias did the 'October revolution' get off the ground. There anarchists, and Communists, who were well represented among the local miners, backed Largo's Alliance. For a week they controlled the coalfield area. Even when the government sent in hardened units of the Moroccan army, the miners put up determined resistance which ended only after several thousand had been killed or wounded. Their resistance gave the Left a powerful symbol. But it derived more concrete benefit from the government's over-reaction to events (p73), which not only drew workers together but also unleashed a wave of sympathy for them among Left Republicans (p68).

The 1934 uprising thus provided a foundation on which to rebuild the unity of 1931, a process initiated by Azaña. Founding a new party, 'Republican Left', he toured the country speaking in favour of a renewed alliance. He found a willing ally in Prieto, who swung chastened Socialists behind the notion of a **Popular Front** to fight the 1936 election. Its programme was simple: resumption of reforms, release of imprisoned strikers and an amnesty for those involved in the 'October revolution'. On that platform the Front won a narrow lead in votes, which was converted by the electoral system (p71) into a large parliamentary majority.

Although the Front as a whole was broader than the alliance that had formed the 1931 Provisional Government (p68), its Republican component was markedly depleted. Its real strength lay in the working-class support that the CNT had, unprecedentedly, helped to mobilise by calling on its supporters to vote. But, as before, that backing was represented almost exclusively by the PSOE. It was therefore disastrous that pressure from Largo Caballero prevented his party from entering the new government.

Without the Socialists it looked like a minority administration, its only parliamen-

---

Frente Popular

Popular Front

Based on the notion of a broad alliance of all progressive forces to oppose fascism, or the far Right in general, the Spanish Popular Front (more correctly, People's Front) was formed in late 1935. It was made up of: middle-class Republican parties – the **Left Republicans** (p68) and Martínez Barrio's dissident Radicals (p73), renamed Republican Union; regionalist parties – the Catalan **ERC** (p70) and the Basque **PNV** (p43); and elements of the workers' movement – the Socialist **PSOE** (p45), the **Communist Party** (p88) and the 'Syndicalist Party' founded by the renegade anarcho-syndicalist, Angel Pestaña (p75). Once the Civil War started it was extended by the inclusion of the anarcho-syndicalist **CNT** (p47) and FAI (p60).

tary base being that of the Republican MPs, whose meagre numbers actually over-represented their popular support. Even worse, its main law and order instrument was the Assault Guards (*Guardias de Asalto*). Set up in 1931 because of doubts about the existing security forces' loyalty to the Republic, they had since fallen under the control of the Socialists, becoming a sort of party militia. As a result, a succession of weak cabinets were constantly attacked by the Right as unrepresentative and partisan.

The new government provided grounds for such charges by following the bad example of their right-wing predecessors (p73). The 'revolutionaries' of 1934 were not just pardoned but feted, and press censorship was aimed almost exclusively at the conservative press. As well as allowing such actions Azaña succumbed to the mood of hysteria, talking of radical reform in terms calculated to alarm even moderate conservatives. But he remained the Republicans' greatest asset, and when they appointed him President in place of the officious Alcalá Zamora they only worsened their plight. Day-to-day government was left in the charge of Santiago Casares Quiroga (p68), who was quite inadequate for the task.

By this time, in any case, the government was no longer in control of events. Admittedly Catalan autonomy was restored, and work began on similar devolution for Basques and also Galicians; even land reform (p70) was reintroduced and pursued with some vigour. But the real force for change on the land now was the seizure of estates by farmworkers convinced that the Front's victory meant that revolution had come. The Socialists made little attempt to disabuse them. In the cities, too, politics was becoming a spiral of street violence between organised gangs, including those of the openly fascist Falange (p84). Their appearance indicated how the division into two camps apparent in 1933 had been widened and polarised.

On the Left this could be seen in the growing strength of the Communists, to whom the Socialist youth organisation defected *en bloc*. Largo Caballero was speaking of revolution in fiercer terms than ever; on May Day he presided over a massive parade whose banners demanded a workers' government and lauded the Soviet Red Army. Meanwhile, on the Right, Gil-Robles's gradualist strategy (p72) was in ruins; his own party's youth wing defected to the Falange and his leader's mantle passed to the more extremist Calvo Sotelo (p74), who had plans in place for a military-backed coup. On 13 July 1936 they were pre-empted when Calvo Sotelo was murdered by Assault Guards avenging a colleague killed by the Falange. It was the spark that set the country alight.

Summary of main points

The reforming years

- The Republic's 1931 Constitution was mostly uncontroversial and impeccably democratic, but its religious provisions (Article 26) imposed significant restrictions on the Catholic Church that were, at best, ill-judged.
- Like the Constitution, the next two years of the Republic's course were effectively determined by an alliance between Left Republicans and the Socialists, under the leadership of Azaña.

- During this time a range of significant reforms were carried out, most notably a massive expansion of the education system and the granting of devolution to Catalonia. However, neither military nor land reform was carried through successfully; while the first alarmed the Right in principle, the disastrous failure of the second alienated much of the Left, and led to the government's fall.

The rise of the Right

- The Right, moribund at the Republic's outset, was revived by opposition to the Constitution's anticlerical provisions. As a result, the CEDA became the first Spanish right-wing party to attract a mass support.
- Despite winning the 1933 election, the CEDA initially remained outside government because of – justifiable – suspicions that it was anti-democratic. But for the next two years it was the driving force behind attempts to dismantle and reverse many of the earlier reforms, and behind reprisals after the failed 1934 'revolution'.
- Even so, many 'monarchists' considered the CEDA to be too moderate; the resultant split led to the Right being defeated at the 1936 election.

The reunification of the Left

- In 1931 the Socialist PSOE joined the new government, while even some anarchists supported it. However, both groups were alienated by the failure of land reform and split with their Republican allies.
- The Right's 1933 victory led to a further radicalisation; the following year the Socialists, along with Catalan regionalists, staged the disastrous 'October revolution', which was brutally crushed.
- The failure of this uprising, and the government's vicious reaction to it, laid the basis for a renewed and broadened alliance between the workers' movement as a whole, regionalists and Republicans.
- This Popular Front won the 1936 election, but once in power proved unable to stem either anarchist land seizures or street-fighting fomented by extremists on both sides.

Exhibit 5.1: Programme of the CEDA (1933)

Extracts from the first two sections

I. RELIGIÓN

1. La Confederación Española de Derechas Autónomas declara que en el orden político-religioso no puede ni quiere tener otro programa que el que representa la incorporación al suyo de toda la doctrina de la Iglesia católica sobre este punto. Las reivindicaciones de carácter religioso deben ocupar, y ocuparán siempre, el primer lugar de su programa, de su propaganda y de su acción. [...]
2. CEDA formula su más enérgica protesta contra el laicismo del Estado y contra las leyes de excepción y de la persecución de que se ha hecho víctima la Iglesia católica en España. [...]
3. La CEDA [...] se atendrá siempre a las normas que en cada momento dicte para España la Jerarquía eclesiástica en el orden político-religioso.

II. RÉGIMEN POLÍTICO GENERAL

[...]

3. Se ha de organizar la representación nacional de modo que las Cortes reflejen el verdadero sentir del pueblo español, tanto en los estados de opinión política manifestados por los individuos, cuanto en la organización corporativa que responda al carácter orgánico de la sociedad.
4. Robustecimiento del Poder ejecutivo, en la medida que sea necesario, para que desenvuelva eficazmente la función que le corresponde dentro de la organización fundamental del Estado. [...]

I RELIGION

1. The Spanish Confederation of the Right (CEDA) declares that, as regards the relationship between politics and religion, the only course that it can, or wishes to follow is to adopt as its own all the Catholic Church's teaching on this issue. Demands of a religious nature must, and always will, take pride of place in its programme, in its communication with the voters and in its actions.
2. The CEDA opposes, with its utmost strength, the separation of Church and State, and those exceptional and discriminatory measures of which the Catholic Church in Spain has been the victim.
3. The CEDA [...] will, at all times, obey whatever instructions may be issued by the Church authorities with regard to the relationship between politics and religion in Spain.

II POLITICAL SYSTEM
[…]

3. The nation's political representation shall be organised in such a way as to ensure that Parliament reflects the true feelings of the Spanish people, in terms both of the political opinions expressed by individual Spaniards and of the associations that embody the organic nature of society.
4. Strengthening of the executive branch of government, as far as is necessary to ensure that it can effectively discharge the functions that correspond to it within the basic structure of the State. […]

Source: Artola, M. (1991) *Partidos y programas políticos 1808–1936: Tomo II.* Madrid: Alianza.

Exhibit 5.2: The '1934 Revolution' in Asturias (1934)

Statement issued by one of the 'provisional revolutionary committees' established in the province

COMITÉ REVOLUCIONARIO DE ALIANZA OBRERA Y CAMPESINA DE ASTURIAS A TODOS LOS TRABAJADORES

Compañeros: Ante la marcha victoriosa de nuestra revolución, ya gloriosa, los enemigos de los intereses de nuestra clase utilizan todas sus malas artes e intentan desmoralizar a los trabajadores asturianos que en magnífico esfuerzo se han colocado a la cabeza de la Revolución proletaria española.

Mientras en el resto de las provincias se dan noticias de que en Asturias está sofocado el movimiento, el Gobierno contrarrevolucionario dice en sus proclamas a los trabajadores de nuestra región que en el resto de España no ocurre nada y nos invita a entregarnos a nuestros verdugos.

Hoy podemos decir que la base aérea de León ha caído en poder de los obreros revolucionarios leoneses y que éstos se disponen a enviarnos fuerzas en nuestra ayuda. Contra la voluntad indomable del proletariado asturiano, nada podrán las fuerzas del fascismo.

Estamos dispuestos, antes de ser vencidos, a vender cara nuestra existencia. Tras nosotros, el enemigo sólo encontrará un montón de ruinas. Por cada uno de los nuestros que caiga por la metralla de los aviones, haremos justicia con los centenares de rehenes que tenemos prisioneros.

Sépanlo nuestros enemigos. ¡Camaradas: un último esfuerzo por el triunfo de la revolución! ¡Viva la revolución obrera y campesina!

MESSAGE FROM THE REVOLUTIONARY COMMITTEE OF THE ASTURIAN WORKERS' AND PEASANTS' ALLIANCE, TO ALL WORKERS

Brothers: Faced with the victorious advance of our glorious revolution, the enemies of our class interests are using all their evil ploys and attempting to undermine the spirit of the Asturian workers, whose magnificent efforts have placed them in the vanguard of Spain's proletarian revolution.

Thus in the rest of the country reports are circulating that here in Asturias the uprising has been suppressed, while at the same time the counter-revolutionary government announces to the workers of our region that elsewhere in Spain all is quiet, and invites us to hand ourselves over to our executioners.

Today, though, we can report to you that the airbase at Leon has fallen to the revolutionary workers of that region, who are preparing to send forces to assist us. Against the unbreakable will of the Asturian working class the forces of Fascism are powerless.

Rather than be defeated we are ready to sell our lives dearly. To the enemy we will leave only a heap of ruins. For each of us who falls, cut down by the machine guns of their planes, we will exact justice on the hundreds of hostages we hold captive.

Let our enemies beware. Comrades: one last effort for the triumph of the revolution! Long live the workers' and peasants' revolution!

Source: Ruiz, D. (1975) *Asturias contemporánea (1808–1936)*. Madrid: Siglo XXI.

Topics
FOR DISCUSSION

- What does the CEDA appear to regard as the ultimate political authority (Exhibit 5.1)? Does its view have any precedents in modern Spanish history?
- What sort of political regime does the CEDA appear to want? What does it have in mind when it refers to the *'verdadero sentir del pueblo español'*? Do its views in this respect presage any future developments?

- What sense does Exhibit 5.2 give of the political climate in Spain in 1934?
- What, if anything, do the views expressed there have in common with those of the CEDA?
- Was the Republic doomed to failure?
- Why were the various Republican parties so easily marginalised over the course of the Republic?

CHAPTER 6

An unequal struggle (1936–1939)

In the late 1930s European affairs were dominated by the rise of the extreme Right, whose grip on several countries, including Portugal, tightened. There was concern, above all, at the growing strength and aggressiveness of Nazi Germany, which in November 1936 signed the 'Axis' agreement with Italy. This fascist alliance was seen by Stalin as a grave threat not only to Russia's own security but to communism worldwide. In response, he intensified his efforts to form an anti-fascist alliance, confirming communist backing for Popular Fronts such as that which briefly ruled France in 1936 and again in 1938, and seeking international allies. In that regard, too, France offered his best hope. But the French were held back from a Soviet alliance by pressure from their own Right and from their fellow western power, Britain, which regarded communism as a greater threat than fascism. The British policy of appeasing Hitler's territorial demands reached its peak in 1938, when the Munich Agreement effectively handed him Czechoslovakia. Its terms convinced Stalin of the futility of seeking security in the West; instead he began to think in terms of accommodation with Germany.

In July 1936 Spain was shaken yet again by a military revolt. This time, however, the uprising met with fierce opposition, and triggered off a three-year civil war. The conflict's course reflected a shifting balance of advantage, as the initial edge afforded the Republic's defenders by superior popular support was first eroded and then reversed by their own divisions and the rebels' growing cohesion. Foreign intervention from various sources also played a decisive part. For, while it helped to stiffen the Republican authorities' resistance, it crucially enabled the insurgents to survive the failure of their coup attempt. It also contributed to their grinding progress to victory, which went hand-in-hand with the rise to supreme power of General Franco.

The 'Nationalist' rebels

The 1936 rebellion was the result of planning by both soldiers and civilians. But circumstances dictated that it was essentially another old-style military declaration, with no clear leader. Like most of its forerunners the coup failed, but the rebels were rescued by a new factor in such situations: outside intervention. Thanks to this help the Nationalists, as they had become known, were soon in control of a large part of Spain, in which they established what amounted to a separate state.

Comunión Tradicionalista

Traditionalist Party

Formed in 1932, the Traditionalist Party brought together the two divided branches of the **Carlist movement** (p12). Although its nominal aim was to restore the monarchy in the person of the Carlist claimant, the Traditionalists were in reality more concerned about Carlism's broader principles: authoritarian rule in a highly personalised form, extreme social conservatism, and subjugation to the tenets of the Catholic Church. In 1937 the party was forcibly amalgamated with the **Falange** to form the Francoist single party (p92).
See also: *familias* (p104)

In the increasingly tense and polarised conditions of 1936 (p77), various right-wing groups abandoned all notion of regaining power by democratic means and began conspiring to overthrow the Republic's government. Notable by its absence was the CEDA, the party that had spearheaded the Right's recent political rise, since the ambivalent attitude of its leader made it as suspect to the plotters as to democrats (p72). Instead, the principal civilian conspirator was José Calvo Sotelo, who was backed by most of those anxious to see Alfonso XII return to the throne. These monarchists (p74) controlled considerable wealth and influence but as a political force they were heavily dependent on their leader, and so were effectively neutralised by his assassination (p77).

Also involved in the plot were the **Traditionalists**, the heirs of the old Carlist movement. Unlike Alfonso's supporters, they could call on an element of mass support in the Carlist heartland of Navarre where, well before war broke out, drilling of Traditionalist volunteers (*requetés*) was under way. Yet, while they represented an important fighting resource for the rebels, in other respects the Traditionalists' value to the uprising was limited; outside Navarre the extreme reactionary nature of their ideas was as likely to frighten off supporters as attract them.

The **Falange** party's main assets were its charismatic leader, José Antonio Primo de Rivera, and the street-fighting experience of its student gangs (p77). But at the February election it had failed to win a single seat, and despite having grown since, its popular backing remained tiny. Moreover, it was an uneasy alliance between the well-off young (*señoritos*) and a limited number of the workers and peasants to which its leader's romanticised brand of fascism was intended to appeal. Doubts concerning the compatibility of this new approach with the traditional conservatism of the Right in general led to the young Primo only agreeing to join the conspirators at the last minute.

Falange

Falange

Founded by José Antonio Primo de Rivera, son of ex-dictator Miguel (p57), the Falange was composed chiefly of upper-class young men, many of them students. After merging with two other small groupings on the far Right, its membership widened and its official title became *Falange Española y de las Juntas de Ofensiva Nacional-Sindicalista (FE y de las JONS)*. The Falange's ideas were basically fascist; its members embraced technical and economic progress and notions of social justice, while being aggressively opposed to the Left. In 1937 it was forcibly amalgamated with the **Traditionalists** to form the Francoist single party (p92), also known colloquially as the Falange.
See also: *familias* (p104); ***Movimiento Nacional*** (p109)

Given the weakness and diversity of these civilian elements, the uprising became in essence a matter for disgruntled generals among whom each had its sympathisers, even the Falange. Along with a desire for minimal political interference in Army affairs, the military plotters shared two grievances against the Republic. One was the collapse of law and order, for which they held it responsible. The other was a nebulous but powerful conviction that it was destroying a 'true Spain' whose foundation was not 'artificial' democracy but respect for authority, and which made no concessions to equally 'artificial' regionalist claims. Their beliefs led the rebellion's leaders to style their enterprise a 'National Movement', and in the war that followed their side became known as Nationalists (*nacionales*).

The rebels' nominal head was General Sanjurjo, who had been exiled in Lisbon since the failure of his 1932 coup attempt (p70). But even before his death in an air crash on 20 July 1936, age meant that his authority was far from uncontested. Thereafter a number of generals harboured ambitions to replace him, the most obvious candidates being Emilio Mola, who had been responsible for organising the uprising inside Spain, and Francisco Franco, whose task was to assume command in Morocco (p58), where he had served with great distinction. The issue was a touchy one and, given that all the generals expected a quick victory, they tacitly agreed to shelve any decision until it had been achieved.

Their expectations were shattered as soon as the revolt got under way, prematurely, on 17 July in Morocco, and one day later, as planned, elsewhere. In terms of popular backing it suffered from the fact that most barracks were located in towns, while mass support for the Right was concentrated in the northern countryside, above all in Old Castile, where the coup met with little resistance. In other regions its success was limited to a few larger cities where individual commanders acted decisively and rode their luck, most spectacularly General Queipo de Llano in Seville. Elsewhere, and crucially in Madrid and Barcelona, the revolt was crushed (p87).

Even within the armed forces support was patchy. The paramilitary Civil Guard proved much less enthusiastic than anticipated, while the bulk of the fledgling Air Force remained loyal to the government. Within the Army itself reactions were mixed, though most of the lower ranks – mainly conscripts drawn from the social groups that were most solidly behind the Popular Front government elected earlier in the year – were hostile. In Morocco, the elite troops of the Army of Africa rebelled and quickly established control. However, since the naval uprising had been a complete failure – those officers who did attempt to rebel were soon overwhelmed – there was no immediate way the North African forces could be brought into action in mainland Spain.

As a result, the coup's leaders were staring defeat in the face, until they were saved by the first outside intervention of the war. Both Hitler and Mussolini responded to Franco's pleas by sending airforce units to Morocco to airlift his troops across the Straits of Gibraltar to Andalusia. There they linked up with Queipo de Llano's forces to advance on Madrid from the south-west, while other columns under Mola's command approached the capital from the north. Whereas Mola's inexperienced soldiers and Traditionalist militiamen were halted with relative ease, the battle-hardened Army of

Africa advanced inexorably through Extremadura, so that soon all rebel-held territory was joined in a single 'zone' stretching in an arc from Cadiz to the Pyrenees.

At this point the problems of coordinating action on several fronts spurred the Nationalist generals into establishing a single command structure. Franco's control of the Moroccan Army now gave him an unanswerable claim to primacy, and at a meeting in Salamanca on 21 September the generals appointed him to be their Supreme Commander (*Generalísimo*). They also gave him the title of 'Head of the State', for the duration of the war as they thought, although this restriction was omitted from the official announcement on 1 October. For the rebels' purpose was more than military. They were claiming, above all to foreign observers (p90), that the territory they had overrun had the same status as the legitimate Spanish state, whose resistance had turned out to be stronger than expected.

The Republic's defenders

From the moment of the uprising, the term 'Republicans' was used to denote all those involved in resisting it. This involved not only the old Republican parties but also their allies in the workers' movement. Indeed, the workers bore the brunt of the war effort although they were sharply divided on what the war was about, and how it should be fought. The key role in this debate was played by the Communists, whose growing influence was the main reason why unity among the Republic's defenders inexorably crumbled.

Despite persistent rumours of a right-wing plot, the July uprising caught the government off-guard and almost entirely unprepared. The Republicans – in the pre-war sense – of which the government was made up were demoralised by the course of events since the Popular Front's election victory (pp76–7), as was evident in their reactions to the coup. Casares Quiroga, the weak and ailing Prime Minister, simply resigned; his successor, the more conservative Martínez Barrio (p73), sought to negotiate with the rebels; only when he was replaced by José Giral did the government opt unambiguously for resistance.

While its supposed guardians dithered, the Republic was saved by three factors. The first was the indecisiveness shown by the insurgents in a number of centres, the second the loyalty of many Army and Civil Guard commanders (p85), without which their rebel colleagues might well have succeeded. The third was a massive display of opposition to the coup from ordinary Spaniards, especially urban workers, who took to the streets and demanded that the

milicia
....

militia

Groups of volunteers raised to defend the interests of a particular group or party, militias were a feature of Spanish politics from the first half of the nineteenth century (pp14–15). During the Civil War they fought on both sides, but for the Republicans the term acquired special overtones. It implied the absence of conventional military hierarchy and discipline, both within units and in their relations with others and with the overall Republican command; in that sense it was associated with **anarchist** influence (p46).

government give them arms to defend it, as Giral eventually agreed to do. His action allowed the hasty formation of **militia** units by the various workers' organisations, which in several places, including Madrid and Barcelona, played an important part in suppressing the rising.

Spontaneous resistance to the coup was part of a wider phenomenon: the belief among many on the Left that it offered an unparalleled opportunity to stage their own revolution. Their conviction had a variety of effects, including a wave of violence directed against the rich and, especially, against the Church's buildings and personnel. This reaction was largely the work of so-called mavericks (*incontrolados*) acting on their own initiative, and soon died down. Altogether more important was the open debating of revolutionary ideas as to how the country should be run, ideas shared at least in part by some leading figures not just in the anarcho-syndicalist CNT (p47), but also in the Socialist trade union, the UGT (p59).

In a number of towns and cities revolutionary committees (*juntas revolucionarias*), composed of workers' representatives, were set up to administer public services instead of, or alongside the official authorities. At the same time, widespread and often successful attempts were made at **collectivisation** of economic activity. The advocates of immediate revolution also insisted that the militias were not merely an emergency recourse, but should form the basis of the Republic's defence in the longer war now looming.

It was the militias' ineffectiveness against Franco's experienced regulars (pp85–6) that highlighted the practical problems of these revolutionary policies, and crystallised a very different view of the war among other sectors of the Left. To much of the Socialist Party (PSOE), and even the leadership of the CNT and UGT, the war was not an opportunity, but a mortal threat both to the '*bourgeois*' Republic and to workers. That view, which had also underlain the formation of the Popular Front (p76), now led to its revival in strengthened form when, in September 1936, a new government was formed.

colectivización

collectivisation

Whereas in Soviet Russia collectivisation involved the imposition of large-scale, centrally controlled units of production, in Spain it was associated with **anarchist** (p46) ideas of work on a small scale, involving autonomy and participative management, and consequently opposed by the **Communist Party**. During the early phase of the Civil War it was implemented in some parts of the Republican zone, both on the land, as a sort of spontaneous **land reform** (p70), and in commerce and industry, especially by supporters of the anarcho-syndicalist **CNT** (p47).

The new Prime Minister was the UGT leader Largo Caballero (p75), the figure best placed to unite both sections of the workers' movement. Socialists also filled the majority of cabinet posts. The middle-class parties were reduced to two ministers, although Azaña (p68) remained the Republic's President and figurehead. Two posts also went to the **Communists** and to the Front's regionalist members, the Catalan ERC and the PNV, whose support was sealed by granting Basque devolution. A month later the CNT and, astonishingly, the Iberian Anarchist Federation (p60), abjured their principles and also

---

Partido Comunista de España (PCE)

Spanish Communist Party

Founded in 1921 by dissidents from the Socialist **PSOE** (p45) and anarcho-syndicalist **CNT** (p47), the PCE was banned under the Primo dictatorship and achieved little success during the Second Republic. Strictly obedient to Soviet instructions, in 1936 it reversed its refusal to cooperate with 'bourgeois' parties and backed the **Popular Front** (p76). During the Civil War it acquired significant influence on the Republican side, but the tactics it used to do so alienated many of those who belonged to other parties on the Left. The PCE played a leading part in opposition to the Franco regime (p122), but after 1975 proved unable to capitalise on the prestige that its action had brought (p139). Since 1986 it has been the main component of the United Left alliance, which has also failed to make a significant electoral impact (p156). The PCE is unusual among Communist parties in that its operations have never covered the whole country, Catalonia having its own Communist party known as the Catalan United Socialist Party (PSUC).
See also: **Comisiones Obreras** (p121); **consenso** (p139)

---

accepted cabinet posts, so that the government now included representatives from all sections of the Republic's support.

The most significant aspect of these changes was the inclusion of the Communist PCE. At the start of 1936 it had been little more than a sect, but since then two factors had greatly increased its importance. One was the fact that, as Franco's column bore down on Madrid (p85), the Soviet Union – unlike the Western Powers (p90) – came to the Republic's aid. From the autumn of 1936 it sent large quantities of tanks and planes, and – through the international communist movement – recruited most of the volunteers who formed the International Brigades (*brigadistas*). These reinforcements played an important part, first, in the successful defence of Madrid and then in defeating two further assaults on the capital at the battles of the Jarama and Guadalajara. The crucial intermediary between the Republican authorities' and the source of this precious support was the PCE.

However, the party's ascent also reflected another change; its adoption of pragmatic policies in response to Stalin's decision that the over-riding priority was to defeat the Right. Suddenly, the Communists became fervent opponents of revolutionary activity that might alienate middle-class support. As the only force on the government side solidly behind such moderation, they attracted support from those whose enthusiasm for the Republic did not extend to wanting their own property to be collectivised. Their approach also brought them significant influence among the Republican leadership, not least because it was broadly shared by the PSOE's majority faction, led by Indalecio Prieto (p75).

Together, the PSOE and the PCE were responsible for the new government's efforts to bring revolutionary enthusiasm under control in the interests of the war effort. Law and order were imposed, where necessary by force. The revolutionary committees were disbanded, agricultural collectives suppressed, and industry made increasingly subject to central planning and control. Most controversially, the government moved to integrate the militias – whose weaknesses were again highlighted by the fall of Malaga in early 1937 – into a new People's Army (*Ejército Popular*), organised on the more conventional lines favoured by the Communists.

Resentment at these steps was widespread, above all in Barcelona, where the revolutionaries were especially strong. Conscious that it could not defy them, the regional government had agreed to run the city in tandem with an Anti-Fascist Militia Committee. In May 1937 the third major force in regional politics, the Communist-dominated Catalan United Socialist Party (PSUC) (p88), moved to disband the Committee. Its action was resisted by the POUM, a communist splinter group with anarcho-syndicalist leanings, and by grassroots anarchists. After several days of confused street fighting the revolutionaries were completely defeated, and pragmatic policies were imposed in Catalonia, too.

Their proponents used the disorder in Barcelona as an excuse for Juan Negrín, a Socialist close to Prieto, to replace Largo Caballero as Prime Minister. Under Negrín's leadership, resistance continued for another two years, despite the loss of the vital northern industrial areas over the summer of 1937. On several occasions, most notably in the battles of Teruel (winter 1937/38) and the Ebro (autumn 1938), the People's Army even managed significant local advances. However, it could not reverse the general pattern of defeats, in which the collapse of Republican unity played a key part.

While the Barcelona clashes were not the start of that process, they did accelerate it markedly. First of all, they fatally undermined Catalan enthusiasm for the Republic, not only among workers but also among a middle-class alarmed at the regional government's manifest inability to control events. Crucially, also, Largo's removal prompted the CNT and FAI representatives to withdraw from the government, further weakening its credibility among workers. That same step also added to growing suspicion of the party that, along with Prieto, had engineered it: the PCE.

Doubts had already been aroused by the party's constant efforts to increase its influence, particularly within the People's Army, and by the ruthless nature of its methods. Now the first revelations about Stalin's rule in Russia were mirrored by the Communist secret police's murderous pursuit of the defeated POUM, and other opponents. Another favoured PCE tactic was to mount scurrilous attacks on opponents in their own press, one of which drove Prieto out of government after he attempted to resist PCE influence. As with the resort to terror tactics, the move was ultimately self-defeating. For, even accompanied by the CNT's return to government, Prieto's departure inevitably alienated much of his substantial support within the PSOE.

The chief charge against Prieto was defeatism; like PSOE leader Besteiro (p75), he had questioned the point of continuing with increasingly hopeless resistance. Quite apart from the fact that the Nationalist leadership had no intention of negotiating (p91), though, the two timed their public musings badly, at a time when the Czech crisis seemed, at last, to offer the prospect of Western aid. To encourage it the Republican government disbanded the International Brigades, hoping to quell British fears of Communist influence; the last volunteers left in November 1938. By then, however, the Munich agreement had dashed hopes of an anti-fascist alliance, and also hastened the ending of Soviet support. Now the Republic really was lost.

Its end came tragically with another, pathetic Army uprising. The revolt was led by Colonel Casado, a soldier who had stayed loyal in 1936 and now commanded what remained of the People's Army, Communist interference in which he deeply resented. He was also convinced, quite wrongly, that the sole barrier to a negotiated end to the fighting was the PCE's presence in Negrín's government, which he therefore attempted to overthrow. His futile coup succeeded only in sparking off six days of street fighting in Madrid, at the end of which the capital lay undefended. The war was over, as a triumphant Nationalist communiqué announced on 1 April 1939.

Franco's triumph

Although it was signed by a number of generals, the announcement was issued in one name alone, that of General Franco, a graphic illustration of the importance he had assumed during the war's progress. Of course, there were several reasons for the Nationalists' victory. Franco's leadership was only one of these, but it was crucial in determining the nature of his side's triumph, and in linking it indissolubly to his own person.

To some extent victory was due to factors beyond the Nationalists' control, such as their opponents' divisions, and the stunted economic development of Spain's main industrial region, Catalonia, that rendered its factories ill-suited for conversion to munitions production. Nor could they claim credit for the realities of economic and political geography that left the arms-producing industries of the North an easy prey, and placed Spain's main food-producing areas in their hands from the war's outset. The rather fortunate capture of Seville (p85) was also vital, as it gave the rebels control of the poor southern areas where the Left had solid support, and collectivisation (p87) might have been received as a boon rather than a threat.

Above all, there was the balance of foreign intervention, which was clearly in the Nationalists' favour even before 1938, when France ceased to ignore smuggling across the Pyrenean frontier and Soviet supplies tailed off (p89). Once Hitler and Mussolini had thrown their support behind the insurgency (p85) they were determined to avoid the propaganda setback its defeat would have meant. Indeed, common interest in a Nationalist victory helped prompt their formal alliance of November 1936. Thereafter both sent substantial aid to Franco's troops, virtually unhindered by the **Non-Intervention Pact** they had signed with the Western Powers.

In quantitative terms, the greater contribution came from Italy. The Italians had supplied most of the Spanish Air Force's existing machines, and now they provided

---

Pacto de No Intervención
....
Non-Intervention Pact

Signed in 1936 by Britain, France, Germany and Italy, the Pact was an agreement to refrain from intervening in the Civil War. Its legal basis was questionable – since it effectively accepted the Nationalists' spurious claim to be given equal treatment with the Republican government (p86) – and its practice was downright fraudulent. It was respected by the two Western Powers, thus denying the Republic French aid and impeding supplies to it from third countries. However, since Britain was determined to stay out of conflict, in Spain or elsewhere, the Pact did virtually nothing to prevent Hitler and Mussolini from supplying the Nationalists as they wished.

Guernica (Basque: Gernika)

Guernica

Because of its associations with their **traditional privileges or 'old laws'** (12), Guernica is of enormous symbolic importance to Basques. In 1937, during the Nationalist northern offensive, it was the target of a bombing raid by the German Condor Legion that caused heavy civilian casualties, tactics which were to be perfected in the Second World War. The Basque Statute of Autonomy was signed there in 1979 (p143).

further supplies and back-up to the Nationalists, while denying vital spare parts to the Republicans. Mussolini also committed substantial numbers of ground troops, including armoured units, although they turned out to be of limited value; while they led the capture of Malaga, they failed badly at Guadalajara (p88). Hitler's support was more limited in quantity but of higher quality, consisting of elite air units, including that responsible for the bombing of **Guernica**.

Aid from the Axis powers was crucial in establishing Nationalist military superiority, above all in the air. Ultimately, though, the war was won on the ground, and there the rebels' success in building up an effective Army was vital. The lukewarm response from the armed forces to their initial coup (p85) left them no better off in that respect than the Republicans. Even so, the Nationalists had significant assets in the greater experience of their leaders, especially in Morocco, and the Army of Africa itself; they also had the benefit of German and Italian advice. Above all, the nature of their uprising and the support it had received meant that there was minimal resistance to the imposition of standard military practices in training and action; the Traditionalist and Falange militias (pp84,86) were integrated into a single Nationalist Army without any of the problems experienced on the other side.

As well as its primary role at the front, the rebel Army also served as the chief instrument of organised terror within the Nationalist zone. From an early stage these tactics were associated particularly with Franco. One of the most notorious mass executions occurred at Badajoz during his initial march on Madrid, but once he was established as effective ruler of rebel-held Spain such killings and other forms of brutality were routinely used against known or suspected government supporters. As a result there was little of the uncertainty that wracked Republican Spain, where the better-off were constantly suspected of mere 'geographic loyalty', and rumours abounded of a 'fifth column' of traitors within.

Franco's insistence on stamping out opposition in captured areas before proceeding to a further offensive was one reason why, in strictly military terms, the war lasted longer than necessary. Several times, too, Franco chose tactical options that almost certainly prolonged it. Most glaringly, having defeated the Republicans' Teruel offensive, he ignored the obvious course of a direct attack on Catalonia and instead advanced on Valencia through the difficult terrain of the Maestrazgo district. But such moves were not unintended errors. They were part of a deliberate strategy of attrition (*desgaste*), designed – like the use of terror – quite literally to eliminate his opponents.

Imposition of this approach, which was unmistakably his own, was a mark of Franco's new status as the Nationalists' undisputed leader. The emergence of such a figurehead was assisted by the military ethos of the insurgency, with its emphasis on hierarchy and obedience. Franco's elevation to the role in October 1936 (p86) was partly due to the disappearance of all other contenders in the space of a year; following the deaths of Calvo Sotelo (p77) and Sanjurjo (p85), José Antonio Primo de Rivera (p84) died in a Republican prison in late 1936, and Mola (p85) was killed in another air crash the following summer. But Franco himself also manoeuvred to ensure his pre-eminence, halting his march on Madrid to relieve the rebel garrison besieged in the fortress (*alcázar*) at Toledo, and then exploiting the feat to bolster his own prestige.

Moreover, once installed as effective ruler of Nationalist Spain, Franco worked single-mindedly to consolidate his position, which rested on three pillars. The first was his tremendous standing within the Army. The second was a new political organisation, whose creation reflected his conviction that the main reason for Spain's decline lay in the fractious squabbling of party politics. Determined to avoid any such development in his fief, he decreed the merger of the two largest parties among his support: the Falange and the Traditionalists (p84). All other political organisations were outlawed forthwith.

The clumsy title given to the merged party (p109) betrayed the fundamental incompatibility between Traditionalism and the modernising, socially minded ideas of the Falange. Franco quickly crushed the resultant discontent, imprisoning José Antonio's successor as party leader, Manuel Hedilla. But such methods soon became unnecessary. Membership of the new single party – still known colloquially as the Falange – was a requirement for public office in the Nationalist zone, not to mention an invaluable badge of loyalty. New recruits flocked to it to secure their material interests, and their sheer numbers drowned out dissent from purists, whether Traditionalists or Falangists.

The new Falange was to some extent modeled on the parties created by Mussolini and Hitler, and performed some of the same functions. With its members spread throughout society in the Nationalist zone, it enabled the authorities there to exercise close control over the population. It was also used to promote, through relentless propaganda, a fascist-style leadership cult. Yet the Falange never exercised the control over other institutions, notably the Army, typical of true fascist parties. Nor did Franco assume its leadership, a task he left to his brother-in-law and faithful subordinate, Ramón Serrano Suñer. Instead, his status as *Caudillo*, the nation's hero and predestined leader, rested ultimately on the backing of a very different organisation, the third pillar of his authority.

Outside the Basque Country and Catalonia, the Catholic Church solidly backed the Nationalist cause from the outset. Even the lower clergy, initially more sympathetic to the Republic's cause, had been alienated by its religious legislation (p71) and by anti-clerical violence once war broke out (p87). Franco, for his part, was a firm believer of the traditional school, and regarded the Church as one of the foundations of the 'true Spain' he sought to restore. To that end he quickly set about re-establishing its social role, especially by handing it control over education.

In return, the Church threw its moral authority enthusiastically behind him and the cult of his leadership. Spanish bishops gave their blessing to the elaborate and deliberately old-fashioned ceremonies which became a feature of public life in the

Nationalist zone, and which appeared to give Franco a status close to sainthood. The clergy also sanctioned and promoted his notion of the war as a 'crusade', consciously evoking the country's reconquest from the Moors (pp1–2) – and conveniently over-looking Franco's use of Muslim Moroccan troops, especially in terrorising civilians. The idea was a powerful one in the context of civil war, submerging divided loyalties under the powerful appeal of patriotism.

But while the 'crusade' notion fostered growing unity among Nationalists, it also had deeply divisive implications, both for the present and the future. It implied un-mistakably that the Nationalists' opponents were not truly Spaniards at all, and not merely foreign but inherently hostile to 'true Spain'. Indeed, in Franco's eyes the Republicans embodied an 'anti-Spain' which must be utterly defeated, if not annihilated; at no time would he countenance negotiations with its representatives. His view of them was encapsulated in an extraordinary measure he decreed as the war drew to a close. This 'Political Responsibilities Act' effectively declared all those who had served the Republic – Spain's legitimate government – in any capacity to be guilty of treason. It set the tone for much of what was to follow.

Summary of main points

The 'Nationalist' rebels

- The 1936 rebellion was motivated by distaste for democracy and regionalism, and by ideas of authority and Spanish national unity; hence the designation 'Nationalists' for its supporters.
- Although it enjoyed some influential civilian support – from monarchists, Traditionalists (Carlists) and the Falange – the revolt was overwhelmingly a military affair; even in the armed forces support for it was far from universal.
- As a result, the initial coup attempt failed. However, assistance from the fascist dictators Hitler and Mussolini enabled the rebels to seize half of Spain and declare their own 'state'.

The Republic's defenders

- The initial coup's defeat owed little to the traditional Republican parties, and a great deal to the spontaneous resistance of ordinary people, especially workers. Subsequently, the task of defending the Republic fell mainly to the parties and unions of the Left.
- The Left itself was divided over how to regard the war. Some, especially grassroots anarchists, saw it as the opportunity for a social revolution; others, including the Socialist Prieto and his supporters, as a struggle for survival.
- The main proponents of this second view were the Communists, who were crucial in organising effective resistance to the rebels. But their ruthless and vicious methods were also the main cause of the splits that contributed to the Republican government's defeat.

Franco's triumph

- The Nationalists won the war for various reasons, including their control of economically important regions, the support they received from Germany and Italy, and the possession of a disciplined army with relatively experienced officers.
- Another important factor was the undisputed leadership of Franco, whose personal attitudes were reflected in the savagery and vindictiveness displayed by the Nationalists towards their opponents.
- In turn, Franco used his position as war leader to cement his authority, which rested on the support of three institutions: the Army, the new single party created by amalgamating Falangists with Traditionalists, and the Church.

Exhibit 6.1: The Communist view of the War (1936)

Extract from manifesto issued by the PCE in December

> [...S]i queremos ganar la guerra, no basta ya la improvisación de nuestras Milicias, ni el heroísmo que nuestras fuerzas armadas han demostrado en tantas batallas, sino que es preciso transformar éstas en un gran ejército popular, dotado de la disciplina y de los medios técnicos que exige la guerra, una guerra como ésta que se nos impone contra ejércitos imperialistas bien pertrechados por sus respectivos países. Por esto, la realización de la consigna de crear un ejército popular, férreamente disciplinado, obediente a los mandos y con sólida estructura, consigna lanzada desde los primeros días por nuestro Partido, es hoy de una necesidad imperiosa si queremos ganar rápidamente la guerra. [...] Urge acabar con las fuerzas dispersas, con las Milicias sindicales, de partido, regionales, etc., que si en los momentos iniciales de la lucha fueron la forma obligada para encuadrar rápidamente las fuerzas armadas que hubieron de improvisarse para batir al fascismo, ahora que tenemos enfrente no sólo moros, legionarios, requetés y falangistas, sino un ejército orgánico, formado por tropas alemanas, italianas, portuguesas, ya no bastan, pues, para vencer a este ejército, también nosotros necesitamos un ejército regular, superior al enemigo en armamento, en disciplina, en moral y en combatividad.

> [...I]f we want to win the war, it will take more than our improvised Militias, or the heroism that our troops have displayed in so many battles. What is needed is to transform our forces into one great people's army, possessing the discipline and equipment demanded by a war like the one we are engaged in, against imperialist armies each properly equipped by its own government. Under those circumstances, if we want to win the war quickly there is no option but to create a people's army, strictly disciplined, obedient to its officers, and properly organised – an idea our Party has championed from the outset. [...] We need urgently to do away with small, dispersed units, with Militias organised on the basis of trade unions, parties, regions or whatever. In the early days of the fighting they may have been the necessary means of mobilising rapidly the armed forces which had to be improvised in order to combat the Fascists. But now we are facing not just Moroccans, foreign legionaries, Carlists and Falangists, but a well-organised army of German, Italian and Portuguese troops. And to defeat such an army our Militias are not enough. We too need a regular army, superior to the enemy's in armaments, in discipline, in morale and in the capacity to fight.

Source: Vázquez, M. & Valero, J. (1978) *La Guerra Civil en Madrid.* Madrid: Tebas.

Exhibit 6.2: The Church and the Nationalist uprising (1937)

Extract from a pastoral letter issued jointly by the country's bishops

---

Demos ahora un esbozo del carácter del movimiento llamado "nacional". Creemos justa esta denominación. Primero, por su espíritu; porque la nación española está disociada, en su inmensa mayoría, de una situación estatal que no supo encarnar sus profundas necesidades y aspiraciones; y el movimiento fue aceptado como una esperanza en toda la nación; en las regiones no liberadas sólo espera romper la coraza de las fuerzas comunistas que le oprimen. Es también nacional por su objetivo, por cuanto tiende a salvar y sostener para lo futuro las esencias de un pueblo organizado en un Estado que sepa continuar dignamente su historia. [...]

El movimiento ha fortalecido el sentido de patria, contra el exotismo de las fuerzas que le son contrarias. La patria implica una paternidad; es el ambiente moral, como de una familia dilatada, en que logra el ciudadano su desarrollo total; y el Movimiento Nacional ha determinado una corriente de amor que se ha concentrado alrededor del nombre y de la sustancia histórica de España, con aversión de los elementos forasteros que nos acarrearon su ruina. Y como el amor patrio, cuando se ha sonbrenaturalizado por el amor de Jesucristo, nuestro Díos y Señor, toca las cumbres de la caridad cristiana, hemos visto una explosión de verdadera caridad que ha tenido su expresión máxima en la sangre de millares de españoles que le han dado al grito de "¡Viva España!", "¡Viva Cristo Rey!"

Let us outline the nature of the 'national' movement, as it is known. We believe the epithet to be correct, firstly because of the movement's spirit. For the vast majority of the Spanish nation feels no sympathy with a system of government that was incapable of embodying its fundamental needs and aspirations, and the movement was accepted as bringing hope to the nation as a whole; in those regions which have not yet been liberated it will very soon break the hold of the communist forces that oppress it. The movement is national, too, in its aim, in that it wishes to save, and to preserve for the future, the essence of a people, under a form of state capable of maintaining with dignity its historical traditions. [...]

The movement has strengthened the notion of fatherland, in the face of the alien ideas espoused by the forces that oppose it. Fatherland implies fatherhood; it is a moral climate, like that of an extended family, in which each citizen can develop fully, and the national movement has generated a flow of love focused on the name and the history of Spain, in contrast to the foreign ideas that led us to disaster. And as the love of fatherland, once transformed by the love of Jesus Christ, our Lord God, reaches the very heights of Christian charity, we have witnessed an explosion of true charity whose ultimate expression is the blood of those Spaniards who, in their thousands, have raised the cry of 'Long live Spain', 'Long live Christ the King'.

Source: Aguirre Prado, L. (1964) *La Iglesia y la Guerra Española.* Madrid: Servicio Informativo Español.

Topics

FOR DISCUSSION

- What are the key points of the PCE manifesto (Exhibit 6.1)?
- How does the way they are expressed compare with earlier left-wing documents of this kind, in content and in style (cf Exhibits 2.1, 3.2, 5.2)?
- What themes of Nationalist propaganda are reflected in Exhibit 6.2?

- How would you interpret the notion of 'charity' described in the final lines?
- Could the Republicans have won the Civil War? Would they have been better off without Soviet aid?
- What were the bases of popular support for the Nationalists, initially and as the war progressed?

CHAPTER 7

Back to the future (1939–1959)

From 1939 to 1945 Europe outside the Iberian Peninsula was embroiled in the Second World War. Initially, its course favoured the fascist Axis powers, Germany and Italy. However, in 1942 the balance of forces changed decisively, with the intervention of the United States and Hitler's attack on Russia. Thereafter the Allies slowly but surely turned the tables, and in 1945 achieved complete victory. Almost immediately the Soviets imposed Communist rule in Eastern Europe, and by 1949 the Cold War between the two superpowers had begun, giving rise to new security fears in western Europe. Economically, though, the region had begun a remarkable recovery, greatly helped by US aid under the Marshall Plan. Indeed, it now formed part of an American-dominated western economy, whose foundations were laid at the 1944 Bretton Woods Conference, which established the World Bank and the International Monetary Fund. Along with the Organisation for European Economic Cooperation (later to become the OECD), and the links that culminated in the formation of the European Economic Community in 1957, these bodies provided a framework for steady growth throughout western Europe.

General Franco's victory in 1939 ushered in a period of 36 years during which Spain's history was determined ultimately by his own distinctive attitudes. Yet, even so, the nature of his rule underwent significant changes. Thus, while in the early 1940s his regime flaunted its fascist side, by the 1950s it was attempting to present a democratic face to the outside world. Nevertheless, one thing remained constant throughout both decades: the regime sought its inspiration in the past, be it the Civil War period or an earlier one. For a long time the regime's survival was threatened by the isolation from the contemporary world which, in various senses, that implied. Only when it was relaxed was Franco able to entrench his rule. But, at the same time, he was brought up against the harsh realities of modern international relations, especially the economic ones.

The 'New State'

The form of government imposed by Franco throughout Spain after his triumph in the Civil War was essentially a continuation of arrangements in the Nationalist zone during the conflict. The name he gave it emphasised its affinity with fascism, as did the special status enjoyed by the Falange. Although to a large extent a reflection of Franco's own ideas, its economic policy also had fascist overtones. By the late 1940s it had brought the regime to the verge of collapse.

The wartime character of the new regime was evident from the very top down. The unity of command established in 1936 (p86) was retained, with Franco acting as Head of State, Head of Government, and – last but far from least – Supreme Commander of the Armed Forces. Moreover, his pronouncements made quite plain that the legitimacy of his rule – its ultimate justification – derived not from any constitution or hereditary rights, but quite simply from his victory over the Republic. Hence the constant glorification of the 'uprising' (*alzamiento*), as the 1936 rebellion was now known, and the date (18 July) associated with it (p85).

Nor did the cessation of hostilities mark the end of Franco's 'crusade' against those he regarded not just as his enemies but as Spain's (p93). Rather it provided an opportunity to strike at those of them who previously had been beyond his reach, in the government zone. Initially, his revenge took the form of savage violence; tens of thousands of Republican sympathisers were shot, and many more sentenced to prison sentences, which were often lengthy. Right to the end of his life, the survivors suffered systematic discrimination in access to state benefits and employment.

More generally, the policies pursued by the **Franco regime** favoured those sections of society that had supported the 1936 revolt, in particular large landowners and financiers. Conversely, industrial workers saw their trade unions banned along with other basic freedoms, including those of association and expression, and their wages held down. Regionalists, Franco's other great *bête noire*, also suffered. Devolution was revoked, and stern measures taken to stamp out notions of local or regional distinctiveness. But even there the Civil War was the ultimate yardstick. While the so-called 'rebel' provinces of Guipuzcoa and Vizcaya – who had in fact remained loyal to the country's legitimate government – were stripped of the financial privileges agreed in 1876 (p28), Navarre and Alava, which had largely backed his own anti-constitutional revolt, were allowed to retain theirs.

franquismo

Franco era; Franco regime; Franco's political philosophy

As well as the period during which General Franco ruled, from 1939 to 1975, the Spanish term is used to mean his regime and the ideas that underlay it. Its main features in that sense were: his own supreme authority; an authoritarian, traditionalist concept of Spain based on an idealised image of its past; and an aggressive nationalism, directed less against external enemies than against his opponents, real and imagined, inside Spain.

Another relic of wartime was the continuing high profile of the Armed Forces, especially the Army. In part that was due to the extent and severity of repression. But the forces' role went considerably further; indeed, the new regime flaunted its military character, contrasting its 'virility' with the alleged feebleness of its civilian predecessors. Military men consistently made up a large part of Franco's cabinet (*Consejo de Ministros*), in the early years often filling up to half the portfolios. In the administration, both central and local, their presence was equally marked, and officers even took up key posts in business. Military courts, too, were given wide jurisdiction to deal with civil offences.

Bizarrely, Franco's own preferred designation for the reactionary dictatorship he had imposed was the 'New State'. Yet the name was easily understood in terms of the world situation. For its overtones were clearly fascist, and up to 1941 the fascist Axis leaders who had supported his own campaigns seemed set to win the World War. Anxious to place himself in the victors' camp, Franco made the fascist salute obligatory in Spain, and developed a keen interest in the notion of a Spanish 'race' along Nazi lines.

Franco also played up Spain's indigenous version of fascism, the Falange. Within the larger single party into which Franco had merged it – also called the Falange, for short (p92) – it had been bent to his will during the war, and now the dictator felt confident enough to give it a prominent role in his regime. Thus the Falange emblem, consisting of an arrow and bundle of rods, or fasces, was displayed at the entrance to every town and village; its anthem 'Face the Sun' (*Cara al sol*) was sung at official occasions and school assemblies. The party's founder, José Antonio Primo de Rivera (p84), acquired martyr status and his motto, 'Spain; One, Great, Free', was adopted by Franco. The blue fascist-style shirts worn by Falange members became a common sight, and a 'Blue Division' was sent to fight alongside the Nazis in Russia.

The Falange also took on roles typical of a fascist-style party, most obviously in controlling the government propaganda machine. Directed from 1939 to 1941 by the poet Dionisio Ridruejo, the 'Spanish Goebbels', it ran numerous newspapers and radio stations whose unvarying themes were the regime's triumphs and the evils of its foes at home and abroad, allegedly linked in a conspiracy of communists, freemasons – and Jews. The Falange was also in charge of the strict censorship to which all other media organs were subjected. Meanwhile its network of subsidiary organisations, including the Women's Section (*Sección Femenina*), disseminated the regime's message throughout Spanish society, while also providing the means of snuffing out any sign of dissent.

The Falange also had a government role, being the second main source of ministers in Franco's early cabinets after the military. But its main powerbase lay in the **government-controlled trade unions** and their central 'Syndical Organisation'. Established by the 1938 Labour Charter (*Fuero del Trabajo*), these were the only form of industrial organisation allowed by law, since all independent action by workers in common, including collective bargaining, was banned. As well as their control function, the unions also provided a degree of job security through the system of Labour Tribunals (*Magistraturas de Trabajo*) they ran, which were in some ways reminiscent of arrangements under the Primo regime

> **sindicatos verticales**
> ....
> government-controlled trade unions
>
> ———————————————
>
> Based on the ideas of the **Falange** (p84), which rejected the 'horizontal' notion of class underlying the workers' movement, the 'vertical' unions included all those who worked in a particular industry – managers, workers and even employers. Their importance to the **Franco regime** (p100) was reflected in the term it used to describe its own philosophical basis in the 1940s: National Syndicalism (*Nacional-sindicalismo*). In practice they acted as a means of government control over workers. From the 1960s on they were increasingly infiltrated by opponents of the regime (p121), and were dissolved shortly after Franco's death. See also. **democracia orgánica** (p103)

and the Republic (pp59, 69). They were also behind the introduction of a mild form of social insurance.

All these social measures reflected the influence of fascist ideas, which could be seen also in the economic field. There, the regime' strategy of autarky (*autarquía*) – running the economy in isolation from the outside world – was to some extent dictated by the World War. That it was also in part a deliberate choice was shown by Franco's refusal of US loans when they were first offered. Autarky had the attraction of being associated with Nazi Germany, and of corresponding to Franco's delusion that Spain was well-endowed with resources, and hence naturally rich. But perhaps above all for a simple soldier like Franco, self-sufficiency was a matter of national pride. Hardship – especially when borne chiefly by his enemies – was greatly preferable to dependence.

In its efforts to achieve self-sufficiency, the regime intervened in the economy on a massive scale. Spain's already high tariff barriers were raised still further, as were restrictions on foreign investment. Movement of persons both in and out of the country was strictly controlled. Wages, and some prices, were set by official decree; rationing was introduced. Business activity, in particular the establishment of new firms, was subject to a mass of regulations. The promotion of new industry became chiefly a matter for government, the concern of another Falange stronghold, set up in 1941: the National Industry Agency (*Instituto Nacional de Industria*). Coming on top of all the damage wrought by the Civil War, the effects were disastrous.

Production failed to reach pre-war levels, themselves low by European standards. A thriving black market (*estraperlo*) brought quick riches to a few while millions scraped a bare existence. Deaths from starvation and malnutrition were commonplace, so that the early 1940s became known as the hungry years (*años de hambre*). Conditions in the cities were so hard that Spain experienced a phenomenon unparalleled in modern Europe: a return to the land. Indeed it was actively encouraged by a National Land Settlement Agency (*Instituto Nacional de Colonización*), in a desperate attempt to increase food production by re-cultivating marginal areas.

This was a plan more typical of the Third World, as part of which the UN officially classified Spain towards the decade's end. In any event, it failed to solve the country's grave problems; for several years a genuine famine was kept at bay only by shipments of wheat from Argentina, sent on favourable financial terms. The need for such charity laid bare the abject failure of autarky. But its origin was equally revealing. For, since the defeat of fascism, Peron's Argentina was one of very few countries favourably disposed to Spain. Most of the world seemed happy to see his regime starved into submission (p107). The 'New State', with its strongly fascist overtones, had become a millstone round Franco's neck.

Politics without parties

As soon as it became clear that the western democracies were going to prevail in the World War, Franco began to downplay the fascist side of his regime. At the same time, he began to introduce elements of what he called democracy. It was a cosmetic exercise. Certainly politics existed, in the sense of a struggle for influence, but it continued to be played out, as before, between groups with no democratic basis. Yet below the surface, as it were, significant changes were taking place in the balance of power between them.

Franco distanced himself from fascism in a variety of ways after 1942, and more rapidly after 1945. Thus, the raised-arm salute was dropped, as was the name 'New State' (p101). The Falange representation in government was cut, and its presence in public life generally reduced. Its social measures, too, were watered down. In Labour Tribunals (p101) the dice were loaded increasingly in the employers' favour. Although land settlement measures (p102) included a system of fixed rents, it was large landowners who gained most from the project as a whole. Other aspects of the Falange's social programme were simply abandoned, to the disgust of the party old guard (*camisas viejas*).

The regime's first concession to the forms of democracy also came in 1942, when Franco issued a 'Creation of Parliament Act' re-instituting the Spanish Parliament (*Cortes*). However, as the Act's title implied, the new, single-chamber assembly bore little relation to previous bodies, or the principles on which they had been based. The new Parliament was partly appointed by Franco himself, and partly indirectly elected by institutions under the regime's control, such as the trade unions and local authorities. Up to half of the representatives (*procuradores*) were government-employed civil servants. In any case, they were given only advisory powers; their real function was to play the part of Franco's rubber stamp, and they performed it faithfully.

Then, in 1945, Franco unveiled his Spaniards' Charter (*Fuero de los Españoles*). In it he disavowed his own previous description of his regime as 'totalitarian'; instead he used a new term, **'organic' democracy**. The name was deliberately misleading. The Charter did nothing to prevent continuing discrimination against, and repression of former Republican supporters (p100), and it consolidated censorship and denial of basic rights; Spaniards had the 'right' to express their views, provided they were in agreement with those of the regime! In particular, the ban on political parties was confirmed.

Yet, although overt political activity was banned, jockeying for power and influence continued behind the scenes. Indeed, Franco subtly encouraged it, as it allowed him to play interests off against each other and thereby protect his own authority. Never formally organised, these interests nonetheless formed loose groupings that, at least initially, corresponded to the various elements that had supported the 1936 rising. Their existence, though officially unmentionable, was an open secret, and they were commonly known as the regime's **clans**.

---

democracia orgánica

'organic' democracy

Adopted by the **Franco regime** (p100) in 1945 as a description of its philosophy, 'organic' democracy – as opposed to the 'inorganic', liberal variety – was based on the theory that individuals' interests were best represented, indirectly and collectively, through bodies that were well-established in society. Such natural 'organs' included the **government-controlled trade unions** (p101), professional associations, the Church and, latterly, the family (represented by its male 'head'), but not political parties. The notion bore some resemblance to the ideas of the Austrian Right in the 1930s (p72); as then, it was a cover for dictatorship.

familias
....
clans

Lacking in any official status or formal organisation, the Franco regime's clans were loose groupings among its supporters who shared broadly the same aims or interests, and who competed for influence within and over it. The main ones are usually considered to be: the military; the **Falange** (p84); the Church and its satellite organisations; the **monarchists** (p74); the **Traditionalists** (p84); and, latterly, the civil service (p109).
See also: **tecnócratas** (p118)

In many ways the most crucial clan was the military, including not just the three main forces but also the paramilitary Civil Guard and armed police; as before, Army officers were the key group. Indeed, the end of the Second World War further strengthened the military's already considerable importance (p100), bringing as it did the prospect of international action against a regime that had made no secret of its backing for the Axis. In the event, however, the only attempted invasion was a small affair by Spanish Communist volunteers, which was soon crushed. Thereafter the military's security role reverted to the suppression of occasional strikes and, at a later stage, student demonstrations.

Politically and socially, the military retained a strong influence (p100). Franco's cabinets always contained a military presence, and not merely in the ministries responsible for the forces – when he eventually relinquished the post of prime minister it was to an Admiral (p125). But in some ways the forces fared surprisingly ill; like military spending in general, officers' salaries were kept low, because their loyalty did not need to be bought. Shut off from civilian society in special living quarters and by habitual intermarriage, fed on a constant diet of regime propaganda, the officers corps and their families remained stuck in the 1930s, convinced that only Franco stood between Spain and disaster. In clan politics they only took the initiative in order to block the proposals of others.

Despite its downgrading by Franco, the Falange remained a player in the game. Falangist ministers continued to serve in government, notably José Antonio Girón de Velasco, who as Labour Minister long controlled the powerful unions (p101), and José Luis Arrese, responsible for the introduction of subsidised housing (*viviendas de protección oficial*). Its supporters also kept a strong presence in the media. Yet after 1945 the old-style, fascist-inspired Falange never enjoyed the same influence as before. Instead, it was supplanted by groups connected with traditional Spanish institutions, popular respect for which could help to bolster Franco's authority, as an association with international fascism had before.

Thus Franco's interest in a possible restoration of the monarchy strengthened the position of its many supporters among senior Army officers, large landowners and financiers. Some of these monarchists (p74) were Traditionalists (p84), but most backed the claim of ex-King Alfonso. With his death in 1941, their attention – and Franco's – focused on his exiled son, Don Juan de Borbón. However, Don Juan had his own mildly liberal agenda, and was also aware of his potential symbolic value to the dictator, both domestically and internationally. His advisers had already had talks with exiled Republicans (p107), and in 1945 he offered to assume the throne in agreement with Franco, but only as a constitutional monarch.

For the dictator, and for most influential monarchists, that was too high a price to pay for restoration; Franco's unconstitutional regime had brought them too many benefits. Moreover, as the danger of outside action against the regime receded (p107), so did Don Juan's worth as a proof of its non-fascist nature. In 1947 Franco felt confident enough to pass an Act of Succession ruling out any compromise with Don Juan. While it declared Spain to be a kingdom (*reino*), it also made Franco himself Regent for Life, effectively suspending the monarchy until his death. Moreover, it empowered him to nominate who should then ascend the throne, subordinating the principle of heredity to Franco's own authority. The Act stated that the dictator was responsible only 'to himself and to God'.

Realising that his bluff had been called, Don Juan decided on an accommodation with Franco. In 1948 he agreed that his son, Juan Carlos, should be educated under the dictator's supervision. In return, the monarchists' leading paper, *Abc*, was allowed to reappear, giving them privileged, if limited, access to public opinion. Moreover, just as before 1947, governments contained a good proportion of ministers who sympathised with their ambitions. But they had lost their chance to exert real leverage over Franco, and their influence was increasingly usurped by representatives of an even more venerable and conservative institution.

Franco's alliance with the Church had already been immensely helpful to him during the Civil War (p92), and had remained strong since. For all the fascist-style rhetoric of the New State era, the restored Church influence already apparent in the Nationalist zone had been extended and intensified. All school education was placed under its control, which for the first time reached to the universities. Social mores were governed by strict traditional principles. In 1945 a further aspect became apparent; the political role of Catholic lay organisations.

In a government reshuffle that year, the key post of Foreign Secretary went to Alberto Martín Artajo, a prominent member of the National Catholic Propaganda Association (*Asociación Católica Nacional de Propagandistas [ACNP]*), whose explicit purpose was to extend Church influence into the political sphere. Over the next decade the ACNP achieved considerable success, with several more leading figures becoming ministers. A second important agent of Catholic influence was the pressure group 'Catholic Action', which in 1946 set up a section to work among industrial workers, the Workers' Brotherhood (*Hermandades Obreras de Acción Católica [HOAC]*).

By the 1950s, the Church was clearly the most powerful influence on the regime, and the favoured term to describe its philosophy was now Catholic Nationalism (*Nacionalcatolicismo*). Ultimately however, both the Church and its satellite organisations, like the other clans, were subordinate to the authority Franco had demonstrated in 1942. At that time, after scuffles between their followers, he summarily dismissed the head of the Falange, Ramón Serrano Suñer (p92), and downgraded the Traditionalist leader General Varela. When, 14 years later, he decided on a similar 'judgement of Solomon', the fact that Education Minister Ruiz Giménez was an ACNP member did not save him from the sack along with Suñer's successor.

Nevertheless, the Church's privileged position was underlined in 1953, when a Concordat was signed between Spain and the Vatican to replace that of 1851 (p13). The

Figure 7.1 Franco's ceremonial exit from the requiem for Alfonso XIII in 1941, beneath the canopy previously reserved for royalty, a scene combining the key elements of his regime at the time: the Church, the military and fascism.

agreement gave Franco the right to nominate all Spanish bishops, and implicitly guaranteed that his regime – and its leader – would continue to be bathed in an aura of religiosity (Figure 7.1). Yet on balance the new agreement was extraordinarily favourable to the Church. Spain was declared a confessional state, guided by Catholic precepts; no other religion could be practised in public; and Canon, or Church Law was integrated into the state's Civil Code. These concessions were not just a mark of Franco's piety, or the price of Church backing for his regime within Spain. They also reflected his continuing need for the stamp of the outside approval that 'organic' democracy had so far failed to bring.

International acceptance – and its price

For some time after 1945 the Franco regime's survival was far from assured. While domestic opposition was negligible and the western Allies held back from intervention, the international isolation they imposed threatened the regime with collapse. But slowly the economic situation improved, and in the 1950s isolation was eased by the new circumstances of the Cold War. That assisted the regime to consolidate, but it also meant that Franco's options were greatly constrained, as he soon discovered.

Among Franco's opponents, the defeat of his former Axis backers in the World War raised hopes of support from the victorious allies to overthrow him. The Communist Party was sufficiently encouraged to mount an attempted invasion across the Pyrenees in 1945. It was easily defeated, however. Thereafter internal opposition virtually disappeared, crushed by repression, propaganda, and the parlous living conditions of most Spaniards (p102). Occasional – illegal – strikes occurred, as in 1947, but they were an expression of economic desperation, not political resistance.

Nor did the former Republican leaders who had fled Spain prove any more of a threat, since their chronic divisions had been aggravated by the bitterness of defeat. Because of resentment over Communist behaviour during the Civil War (pp89–90), the government-in-exile set up under José Giral (p86) excluded the group which, despite the setback in 1945, remained best placed to organise underground resistance. It was further divided by the attempts of its leading figure, Indalecio Prieto, to negotiate with the right-wing leader, José María Gil-Robles (pp71–2), now an adviser to monarchist pretender Don Juan. When he then reached an accommodation with Franco in 1948 (p104), the exiles were left in complete disarray.

By then, too, it was clear that the victorious western powers had no intention of overthrowing Franco by force. However, they did seem prepared to impose their will on him by another means: isolation. In 1946 the French closed the Pyrenean frontier, and later the same year Spain was refused admission to the newly formed United Nations on the grounds of its tacit support for Nazi Germany. Almost all countries then followed a UN injunction to withdraw their ambassadors from Madrid, the sole exceptions being Argentina, Portugal, Switzerland and the Vatican. Another sanction that had real material effects was Spain's exclusion from the Marshall Plan, in 1947.

Even these measures failed to shake Franco; indeed, in some ways they actually helped him. For isolation gave real force to his regime's propaganda about an international conspiracy against it, just as the 1945 invasion had been grist to the mill of its anti-communism. Isolation also allowed Franco to justify, even glorify, his strategy of economic self-sufficiency, which had brought Spain to the verge of starvation. That very real threat slowly receded, thanks to continuing Argentinian food aid (p102), until eventually, with the help of a bumper harvest in 1951, it was dispelled altogether. Even so, a wave of strikes that same year was a reminder that the country's appalling economic state continued to threaten the regime's stability.

These various pressures explain the yearning for international acceptance, towards which the 1953 Concordat with the Vatican (pp105–6) was a small but important step. Later the same year came a much more crucial one, the background to which was the outbreak of the Cold War and the development of new weaponry. Long-range strikes against the Soviet bloc were now technically possible, and Spain constituted an excellent potential base for them that the US was determined to secure. Ignoring the continuing reservations of their European allies, the Americans began attempts to woo Franco. When he rejected their offer of cheap loans, they raised the stakes by offering a full-blown treaty.

Formal recognition by the world's most powerful country was too great a prize to sacrifice on the altar of self-sufficiency. In 1953 Franco signed the series of accords known as the **Defence Agreements**. Although their direct material benefits proved disappointing, that was more than compensated by the acquisition of such a powerful friend. In 1955 the advantages of the agreements were illustrated when Spain was admitted to the UN. The regime ascribed this success to the skills of its Foreign

Acuerdos para la Defensa
Defence Agreements (of 1953)

Signed in 1953 between the Spanish and US governments, the Defence Agreements, or 'Pact of Madrid', permitted the Americans to set up and operate four military bases on Spanish soil. They were renewed on a five-yearly basis up to 1978, but thereafter the issue was caught up in the furore surrounding Spain's entry to NATO (pp153–4). After lengthy negotiations a further, partial renewal was agreed in 1988, under which the US retained only the naval base at Rota, near Cadiz.

Minister, Martín Artajo (p105), but in reality the decisive factor in ensuring that the objections of a decade earlier were now overlooked was US pressure. Without the backing of the world's leading economic power, there was no question of an effective trade embargo against the regime.

Having swallowed his national pride, Franco now accepted the financial support he had previously scorned. This provided the Spanish economy with a significant boost, as did the general upswing in the world economy during the early 1950s, especially after the regime relaxed its trade restrictions slightly towards the middle of the decade. Coupled with the policy of state-promoted industrialisation (p102) – and the fact that its starting point was so low – these external factors enabled the country to enjoy a sudden burst of growth. For some years production rose at around six per cent annually, so that pre-war levels were finally surpassed. Living standards rose appreciably, especially for a small but growing middle class.

Insofar as public satisfaction was increased, growth had a stabilising effect. But it also had other, less positive implications for the regime. Reversal of the drift back to the land (p102) revealed the grave lack of adequate urban housing; many poorer Spaniards were condemned to live in shanty-towns (*chabolismo*) which became a breeding-ground for discontent. Prices rose sharply, to the discomfort of workers whose wages continued to be controlled by law. Among the better-off young, prosperity awakened the desire for greater personal freedom. When the Education Minister, Ruiz Giménez, was prompted to partly relax conditions in the universities in 1956, the result was an outbreak of student unrest that cost him his job (p105).

That same year also saw the largest strike wave yet, but this time it did not elicit the usual response. Employers whose businesses were at last getting off the ground were reluctant to have them disrupted, and had the funds to meet wage demands. They found an ally in Labour Minister Girón (p104), who saw a chance to re-assert the Falange's credentials as defender of worker interests (pp101–2). In some industries the government was persuaded to concede wage rises of up to 30 per cent. This policy pacified the strikers, certainly, but for the economy as a whole the effects were disastrous.

Inflation was pushed still higher, increasing the already dangerous disparities between different sectors of the economy, and further reducing the competitiveness of Spanish goods on world markets. This was especially serious given that, as the economy took off, Spanish manufacturers had begun to demand more sophisticated plant and machinery. Yet it was precisely these capital goods that the country could not produce. The result was a soaring import bill and a widening trade gap, which Spain's exports of agricultural produce and low-grade manufactures were quite incapable of closing.

The rapidly worsening situation alarmed the country's new trading partners, of which the US was now the most important. Worried that Spain might be unable to pay its debts, the Americans brought their influence to bear on the International Monetary Fund and the Organisation for European Economic Co-operation. The two agencies agreed to provide further substantial loans, but only in return for changes in economic policy. Spain was required to abolish the system of multiple exchange rates it had used to restrict imports, in contravention of international trade guidelines. Franco had to take another gulp of nationalist pride, and devalue the peseta.

Franco's reaction to these developments came in 1958, in legislation ostensibly concerned with the single party, which had long been a bulwark of his power (p92). Its function had changed considerably since the 1940s, when repression and propaganda were primary tasks of his governments. Now, however, their over-riding concern was to run the apparatus of a modern state. In the absence of democratic politics that gave enormous influence to civil servants, who had emerged as a new, and very influential, clan within the regime (p104). Moreover, the party's title evoked unfortunate memories of fascism. It was accordingly renamed the '**National Movement**', and the use of 'Falange' banned.

However, that was the only concession to change made by the 'Principles of the National Movement Act'. In general, it restated the regime's underlying tenets in fundamentalist terms. Admittedly, it defined Spain not just as a 'traditional, Catholic monarchy', but also as a 'social and representative' one. Yet the basis for doing so was still the 'organic' brand of democracy dreamed up by Franco in the 1940s (p103). All legislation was required to conform to the 'spirit' of the Movement, whose National Council was given the task of checking that it did so. The Movement itself was defined as the 'communion of Spaniards united by belief in the ideals which gave life to the Crusade' – in other words, as one side in the Civil War to which the very name harked back.

In effect, Franco was saying that, as far as he was concerned, nothing had changed. But it had. The partial integration into the world community that had helped the regime to consolidate also meant it was no longer

> ### *Movimiento Nacional*
> ### National Movement
>
> First used as a self-description by the insurgent side in the Civil War (p85), 'National Movement' was adopted in 1958 by the **Franco regime** (p100) as the official designation of the sole political organisation permitted under its rule, replacing the original name *Falange Española Tradicionalista y de las Juntas de Ofensiva Nacional Sindicalista*. All government employees, including military officers, were required to be members. It was assured representation in government – its secretary-general was automatically a minister – and in Parliament, of which its own National Council functioned as an unofficial upper house. The Movement controlled important sectors of Spanish life, in particular the media and the **trade unions** (p101), in both of which old-style **Falangists** (p84) retained some influence. As a whole, however, it was dominated by bureaucrats, many of the **technocrat** type (p118). It was officially dissolved on 1 April 1977.
> See also: **UCD** (p137)

master of its own fate. Indeed, the regime had already tacitly acknowledged this fact: in 1956, by quietly surrendering the Moroccan protectorate that was Spain's last claim to 'greatness', in the imperial sense dear to Franco (p100); and, a year later, in changing its economic tack at America's behest. When the mild changes introduced at that time failed to produce the desired effect, Spain came under renewed US pressure. Eisenhower's Madrid visit of 1959 was lauded by the regime as a signal of acceptance into the US-dominated western economic order. It failed to see that the celebrated embrace with which the American president greeted his fellow general could equally be interpreted as a bear-hug.

Summary of main points

The 'New State'

- The 'New State' established by Franco was essentially a peacetime extension of arrangements during the Civil War. It discriminated harshly against groups and individuals who had supported the Republic, and was to a considerable degree run by the Army.
- It also had markedly fascist features, including the important role of the single party (commonly still known as the Falange), especially in social and labour policy.
- Both fascist ideology and Franco's own ideas led his regime to strive for autarky (self-sufficiency) by intervening extensively in the economy. The results were disastrous; in the 1940s Spain even experienced serious food shortages.

Politics without parties

- After 1942 Franco distanced his regime from fascism, including the social measures associated with it. But moves to introduce aspects of democracy were a sham; basic freedoms continued to be curtailed and political parties remained banned.
- Meanwhile, different groups among the regime's supporters jockeyed for influence. The most important of these so-called clans were the Army, the Falange, Monarchists, Traditionalists, and the Church with its related organisations.
- Although even it remained subordinate to Franco's supreme authority, by the 1950s the Church had emerged as the most influential clan. Its position was further strengthened by the Concordat signed with the Vatican in 1953.

International acceptance – and its price

- For a period in the aftermath of World War II, Spain was almost entirely shut out of the international community. This made it hard to improve the country's appalling economic situation.
- Isolation was effectively ended in 1953 by the US, whose support was decisive in improving the country's situation both diplomatically and economically.

- However, economic growth soon led to various forms of social and economic disruption within Spain, as well as a serious balance of payments deficit. Yet Franco refused to respond to these changed circumstances by altering the regime's nature in any significant way.

Exhibit 7.1: The Principles of the National Movement Act' (1958)

The second last of Franco's 'Basic Laws' (final article omitted)

Yo Franciso Franco Bahamonde, Caudillo de España,
   Consciente de mi responsabilidad ante Díos y ante la Historia, en presencia de las Cortes del Reino, promulgo como Principios del movimiento Nacional, entendido como comunión de los españoles en los ideales que dieron vida a la Cruzada, los siguientes:

I

España es una unidad de destino en lo universal. El servicio a la unidad, grandeza y libertad de la Patria es deber sagrado y tarea colectiva de todos los españoles.

II

La Nación española considera como timbre de honor el acatamiento a la Ley de Díos, según la doctrina de la Santa Iglesia Católica, Apostólica y Romana, única verdadera y fe inseperable de la conciencia nacional, que inspirará su legislación.

III

España, raíz de una gran familia de pueblos, con los que se siente indisolublemente hermanada, aspira a la instauración de la justicia y de la paz entre las naciones.

IV

La unidad entre los hombres y las tierras de España es intangible. La integridad de la Patria y su independencia son exigencias supremas de la comunidad nacional. Los Ejércitos de España, garantía de su seguridad y expresión de las virtudes heroicas de nuestro pueblo, deberán poseer la fortaleza necesaria para el mejor servicio de la Patria.

V

La comunidad nacional se funda en el hombre, como portador de valores eternos, y en la familia, como base de la vida social; pero los intereses individuales y colectivos han de estar subordinados siempre al bien común de la Nación, constituida por las generaciones pasadas, presentes y futuras. La Ley ampara por igual al derecho de todos los españoles.

continued

VI

Las entidades naturales de la vida social: familia, municipio y sindicato, son estructuras básicas de la comunidad nacional. Las instituciones y corporaciones de otro carácter que satisfagan exigencias sociales de interés general deberán ser amparadas para que puedan participar eficazmente en el perfeccionamiento de los fines de la comunidad nacional.

VII

El pueblo español, unido en un orden de Derecho, informado por los postulados de autoridad, libertad y servicio, constituye el Estado Nacional. Su forma política es, dentro de los principios inmutables del Movimiento Nacional y de cuanto determinan la Ley de Sucesión y demás Leyes Fundamentales, la Monarquía tradicional, católica, social y representativa.

VIII

El carácter representativo del orden político es principio básico de nuestras instituciones públicas. La participación del pueblo en las tareas legislativas y en las demás funciones de interés general se llevará a cabo a través de la familia, el municipio, el sindicato y demás entidades con representación orgánica que a este fin reconozcan las leyes. Toda organización política de cualquier índole, al margen de este sistema representativo, será considerada ilegal.

Todos los españoles tendrán acceso a los cargos y funciones públicas según su mérito y capacidad.

IX

Todos los españoles tienen derecho: a una justicia independiente, que será gratuita para aquellos que carezcan de medios económicos; a una educación general y profesional, que nunca podrá dejar de recibirse por falta de medios materiales; a los beneficios de la asistencia y seguridad sociales, y a una equitativa distribución de la renta nacional y de las carga fiscales. El ideal cristiano de la justicia social, reflejado en el Fuero de Trabajo, inspirará la política y las leyes.

X

Se reconoce al trabajo como origen de jerarquía, deber y honor de los españoles, y a la propiedad privada, en todas sus formas, como derecho condicionado a su función social. La iniciativa privada, fundamento de la actividad económica, deberá ser estimulada, encauzada, y, en su caso, suplida por la acción del Estado.

XI

La Empresa, asociación de hombres y medios ordenados a la producción, constituye una comunidad de intereses y una unidad de propósitos. Las relaciones entre los elementos de aquélla deben basarse en la justicia y en la recíproca lealtad, y los valores económicos estarán subordinados a los de orden humano y social. [...]

I, Francisco Franco Bahamonde, Caudillo of Spain:

   Conscious of my responsibility before God and before History, in the presence of the Parliament of the Kingdom, proclaim the following to be the Principles of the National Movement, which being the communion of Spaniards in the ideals that gave birth to the Crusade:

I

Spain's destiny in the world order is one and indivisible. The service of the fatherland's unity, greatness and freedom is a sacred duty and a collective undertaking for all Spaniards.

II

The Spanish nation regards it as a mark of honour to obey the law of God, according to the doctrine of the Holy Catholic Apostolic and Roman Church, the sole true church, whose faith is an integral part of the nation's consciousness and shall inspire its legislation.

III

Spain, the root of a great family of peoples, to whom she feels bound in indissoluble brotherhood, aspires to the establishment of justice and peace between all nations.

IV

The unity which binds the land and men of Spain is inviolable. The country's physical integrity and independence are supreme priorities of the national community. Spain's Armed Forces, as the guarantor of her security and the expression of our people's heroic virtues, shall possess the strength required to serve the fatherland optimally.

V

The national community is founded on man as the bearer of eternal values, and on the family as the basis of social life; but individual and collective interests are always to be subordinated to the common good of the nation, which is made up of past, present and future generations of Spaniards. The law shall protect the rights of all Spaniards equally.

VI

The natural entities of social life – the family, the municipality and the trade union – are the basic structures of the national community. Such other types of institutions and corporations as meet the general needs of society shall be protected, so that they may contribute efficaciously to achieving the national community's aims.

continued

VII

The Spanish people, united under the rule of Law and informed by the notions of authority, freedom and service, make up the National State. In accordance with the immutable principles of the National Movement, and the provisions of the Succession Act and the other Basic Laws, its form shall be that of the traditional, Catholic, social and representative Monarchy.

VIII

The representative nature of the political order is the fundamental principle of our public institutions. Public participation in the legislative process and other tasks of general interest shall take place through the family, the municipality, the trade union, and such other bodies representing the basic organs of society as the law may recognize for that purpose. All political organizations of whatever kind that lie outside this system of representation shall be deemed illegal.

All Spaniards shall have access to public offices and functions according to their merits and abilities.

IX

All Spaniards are entitled to: an independent system of justice, which shall be available free to those lacking financial means; general and vocational education, which none shall fail to receive through want of material means; the benefits of social services and security; and an equitable distribution of the national income and of the burden of taxation. The State's laws and actions shall be inspired by the Christian ideal of social justice, as reflected in the Labour Charter.

X

Work shall be recognized as the basis of Spaniards' rank, duty and honour, and private property in all its forms as a right conditioned by its social function. Private enterprise, the basis of economic activity, shall be encouraged, channelled and, where necessary, supplemented by State intervention.

XI

Business enterprises, which are associations of men and resources for the purpose of production, constitute communities of interests with common aims. The relationships between their various components shall be based on justice and mutual loyalty, with economic values being subordinated to those of a human and social nature.

Topics
FOR DISCUSSION

- To which institutions does Exhibit 7.1 refer, explicitly and implicitly? What roles are they assigned by the Act?
- What attitudes does the Act reflect towards:
  (a) liberal democracy;
  (b) capitalism; and
  (c) regionalism?
- What evidence is there of a desire to improve relations with the outside world?
- What similarities and differences does the Act suggest between Franco's ideas and those of earlier representatives of the Spanish Right (cf. Exhibits 2.2, 3.1, 4.1, 5.2, 6.2)?
- How new was the 'New State', in Spanish terms? Which aspects of it were retained after the designation itself was dropped in the later 1940s?
- What significant changes occurred in Spain, and in the Franco regime itself, between 1939 and 1959?

CHAPTER 8

The bottle half-uncorked (1959–1975)

Throughout the Western world the 1960s were a period of economic growth. It was underpinned by the network of trans-Atlantic institutions set up in the 1940s and extended in 1961, by the creation of the Organisation for Economic Cooperation and Development (OECD). In western Europe a further support was the European Community, as the European Economic Community (EEC) became in 1967; six years later it acquired three new members, including Britain. The decade also saw a trend in favour of social and personal freedom, which, with the liberalising decisions of the Second Vatican Council, even affected the Catholic Church. In 1968 the pressure for change boiled over in widespread protests, especially among the young, who were heavily influenced by new interpretations of Marxist ideas. Change was also reflected in a so-called eurocommunism that rejected the authority of the Soviet Union. The uncertainty caused by these events was heightened by others. In 1971 the western system of fixed exchange rates collapsed; in 1973 came the first 'oil shock', a massive price increase imposed by the producer countries. In 1974 came a different kind of shock, when the Portuguese dictatorship was toppled by Army officers close to the country's Communist Party, the only one in southern Europe not to have gone 'euro-communist'.

At the end of the 1950s the Franco regime was faced with a choice. It could bow to American pressure for radical changes in its economic policies, or it could risk a return to the conditions of the early 1950s. Not even Franco was prepared to contemplate that. Instead, he entrusted his regime's fate to a group of its supporters who felt that the changes were actually in its interest. To a degree, events proved them right; the spectacular economic development brought by the new policies did indeed increase Spaniards' material satisfaction. Yet it also triggered changes that fomented opposition among certain groups, and a more general, if muted dissatisfaction, which some within the regime sought to counter by relaxing its authoritarian nature. As their leader neared his end, however, they once again lost influence in favour of reactionary hardliners determined to resist reform at all costs. Spain was left like a bottle from which the cork had been half removed, on the point of explosion.

Uneven development

For some of its supporters, the grave situation faced by the Franco regime in the late 1950s was not a crisis but an opportunity. They believed that economic change could and should be managed, in order to equip the regime for survival in the

tecnócratas

technocrats

Perhaps better described as 'professional experts', the technocrats were the highly trained specialists, mainly in economics and finance, who acquired decisive influence in the late 1950s. Many were under the influence of the **Opus Dei**, including Mariano Navarro Rubio, appointed Finance Minister in 1957, and Alberto Ullastres, who took over the Trade portfolio at the same time. Other leading technocrats were Gregorio López Bravo, Minister for Industry and subsequently Foreign Minister, and Laureano López Rodó, another Opus member, who co-ordinated the 1959 measures known as the 'Stabilisation Plan' and the various subsequent Development Plans.

contemporary world. Their ideas formed the basis of Spain's astonishing economic development in the 1960s. However, that success also triggered off substantial social changes which were barely compatible with the regime's snail-paced political evolution.

The domestic impetus behind the new course came from elements within the civil service elite, which by now had become very influential (p109). These '**technocrats**' were influenced by – and in some cases members of – the **Opus Dei** organisation, which believed that the survival of a conservative, Catholic regime could only be assured by satisfying the popular desire for better living standards. The necessary economic growth, they believed, was best achieved by allowing market forces free rein through the ending of government intervention in the economy (p102). By contrast, they favoured continued strong control over society, to prevent it going along the liberal, secular road it had taken elsewhere in the West.

The technocrats' influence dated from 1957, when some of the group's leading figures were brought into government to oversee changes in economic policy. Once the inadequacy of those changes gave rise to US pressure for more (p110), they were able to persuade Franco to give them a virtually free hand over economic strategy. The U-turn is now usually associated with 1959, the year in which most of the measures making up the 'Stabilisation Plan' were enacted, while the 'Plan' itself is often seen as being essentially an exercise in cutting intervention and red tape. But, though some deregulation did occur, it was neither new – most price controls were abolished in 1956 – nor by any means complete. As a result, when Franco died, by modern western standards his government was still playing a large economic role.

In the event, two other aspects of the technocrats' strategy proved to be more

Opus Dei

Opus Dei

Founded in 1928 by the Aragonese priest José María Escrivá de Balaguer, Opus Dei (Latin: 'God's Work') is a lay organisation dedicated to preserving conservative Catholic principles in the face of economic modernisation. Under the Franco regime the Opus, as it is frequently known, acquired considerable power, its members and sympathisers filling many top ministerial and administrative posts from 1957 on. Although its political influence was dented by the 1969 Matesa scandal (p126) and, more severely, by Franco's death, the Opus continues to be strongly represented in business, finance and higher education; a number of leading figures in the **People's Party** (p182) are believed to be members. See also: *inmovilistas* (p128) crucial. One was a standard package of deflationary measures (*medidas de ajuste*), introduced in agreement with the OECD and International Monetary Fund, to which Spain was admitted in 1960. Wages were frozen and public spending reduced. The result was a sharp slowdown in the economy, with severe effects on employment and earnings. But the package achieved its aims of bringing down inflation, eliminating many uncompetitive firms and forcing the survivors to become more efficient.

The final plank in the technocrats' strategy was the one most resisted by Franco, since it involved finally abandoning any idea of autarky (p102). The opening up (*apertura*) of Spain's economy that followed had two key aspects. On the one hand, controls on inward investment were relaxed. Foreign capital was now permitted to acquire a controlling stake in companies in all but the most politically sensitive industries, such as defence. On the other hand, restrictions on the movement of persons were eased. Tourism, previously accepted grudgingly at best, was promoted, while Spaniards were allowed, even encouraged, to seek work outside the country.

The effects were dramatic. Investment poured into the country, attracted by low production costs and the helpful industrial relations framework – in plain English, the absence of normal trade union freedoms. Spain launched, at last, a full-blooded process of industrialisation, which now affected not only Catalonia and the Basque Country, but also Madrid and its rapidly growing satellite towns, as well as a number of other regional centres, notably Valladolid. At the same time tourism took off, so that within a few years Spain became the world's leading provider of beach holidays. The result of these twin stimuli was the period of very rapid growth which brought the word 'boom' into the Spanish language, and marked the beginning of what became known as the development years (*años de desarrollo*).

Nor was it just growth that was achieved. Soaring receipts from tourism, combined with the remittance payments (*remesas*) sent by emigrants to their families at home, were more than sufficient to make up for Spain's trade deficit, and so soothe the concerns of its trading partners (p109). Emigration also solved the problem of unemployment inherent in such massive structural change; in effect, it was simply exported. Remittances helped ensure that, although wage-earners paid the vast bulk of taxes, the material benefits of growth were felt almost throughout society, at least in the rapidly expanding cities.

To a degree, rising prosperity had the effect envisaged by the technocrats. Television sets and cars might not necessarily turn workers into enthusiastic supporters of the regime, but they often meant that the resigned resentment of its early years transmuted into apathy. Such indifference was constantly fed by the official media, with its comparisons between 'Franco's peace' and the 'anarchy' that had allegedly preceded it. To those who, for the first time, had significant material possessions to lose, it could seem a powerful argument, especially if they were too young to have their own memories of how 'peace' had been achieved (p100).

But development also had other effects. The decline of agriculture, and the attraction of city jobs, led to depopulation of the countryside on a massive scale (*éxodo rural*). Even in Francoist Spain urban life brought a wider range of experience, especially for the young, many of whom were increasingly resentful of the constraints imposed by strict Catholic morality (p106). Not only that; tourism and emigration meant that more and more Spaniards were coming into contact with outside influences. They became aware that life in other western countries bore no resemblance to the way it was portrayed by the regime's propaganda; instead, it seemed to involve not only higher living standards but also greater personal freedom – and more fun.

These trends contributed to the growth of opposition in the 1960s (p122). It was kept in check by the repression that the technocrats – and Franco – regarded as the natural complement to their economic liberalisation. Harder to deal with, since it could not be combated by the security forces, was the less intense but increasingly wide-spread discontent that represented a potential breeding ground for future protest. It was this longer term threat which led some within the regime to propose a form of liberalisation that went beyond the economic sphere (*aperturismo*).

In most cases such liberalisers were also motivated by dislike of the technocrats. Thus one proposal came from José Solís Ruiz, Secretary-General of the National Movement (p109), an old-style Falangist (p84) deeply distrustful of the new course. For him, liberalisation meant making the government-run unions attractive to workers in the face of competition from illegal alternatives (pp121–2). To do so he proposed the free election of union representatives, and even a limited right to strike. His ideas were blocked, but some leading civil servants opposed to the technocrats were more successful. Their principal representative was the Minister of Information, Manuel Fraga Iribarne, author of the 1966 Press Act.

The Fraga Act, as it became known, brought big changes in the regime's control over the media, including the abolition of 'prior' censorship, i.e. the requirement for editors to get material approved in advance of publication. Instead they now had to judge for themselves what would, and would not, prove acceptable. For those who guessed wrongly, the Act retained harsh punishments, in the form of suspensions and fines. It was also insidious, imposing as it did a form of self-censorship. But its application by Fraga's Ministry was relaxed enough to allow a number of mildly critical journals to appear. For the first time in 30 years a form of public debate was possible, albeit confined to the economic sphere; political criticism was still strictly taboo.

Some political relaxation was, however, apparent in the last of the regime's **basic laws** promulgated in 1967. As well as a degree of religious freedom – for the first time since 1939 faiths other than Catholicism could be practised publicly – this 'Organic Law of the

leyes básicas (del fran-quismo)
....
(Franco regime's) basic laws

In the absence of a constitution, the basic ground rules of government under the **Franco regime** (p100) were set out in legislation passed over a period of almost 30 years. The first of these basic laws were decrees issued in the Nationalist zone during the Civil War, in particular those by which Franco was installed as Head of State and Government (p86), and the 1938 Labour Charter (p101). There followed the 1942 Creation of Parliament Act (p103), the Spaniards' Charter of 1945 (p103), and the 1947 Act of Succession (p105). The most important of the basic laws were the Principles of the National Movement Act, passed in 1958 (p109), and the 1967 'Organic Law of the State'.

State' (LOE) also provided for parliamentary elections. In fact, though, they were as big a sham as earlier aspects of 'organic' democracy (p103). The electorate was restricted to – male – heads of households; the elected representatives remained a small minority in Parliament, most of which continued to be appointed; and the elections were subject to strict control by the authorities, to ensure that only approved candidates were successful.

The LOE was thus proof of how Spain's political evolution continued to lag far behind its economic development. That had not gone unnoticed by her neighbours who, less compliant than their American allies (pp107–8), had rejected her application to join the EEC in 1962 – on the specific grounds that she was not a democracy. The decision was a severe blow to the technocrats, who knew that continuing growth could only be assured by access to wider European markets. More immediately, the gap between political and economic development had the drawback of stimulating opposition of various sorts within Spain itself.

The emergence of opposition

Overt opposition to the regime had never been completely eliminated; indeed, the 1950s had seen several waves of strikes. But it was only in the next decade that unrest among industrial workers became persistent and widespread. The 1960s also saw an upsurge of opposition from regionalists and, ironically, from the institution which had been the regime's chief support: the Church. Indeed, although it rarely turned to anything stronger, by the end of the decade wide sections of Franco's core support were feeling discontent.

It was in reaction to earlier industrial unrest that, in 1958, the regime took what turned out to be a fateful decision. It allowed a degree of collective bargaining over pay, on the condition that the negotiations would take place under the wing of its own trade unions (p101). Yet precisely that stipulation gave an unwitting spur to a process that was already under way: infiltration of the unions by organisations set up by workers themselves in defiance of the regime. At first these **Workers' Commissions** operated locally, but in the 1960s they established a nationwide network, which greatly increased their capacity for effective action.

At the same time, economic growth was changing the status of workers and their own

> ### *Comisiones Obreras (CCOO)*
> #### Workers' Commissions
>
> The Workers' Commissions were illegal associations of workers, created to give employees an alternative form of representation to the Franco regime's own **tightly controlled unions** (p101). The first was set up in 1957. Initially created by separate local initiatives, the Commissions soon came together to form a nationwide underground organisation. Their founders were inspired by widely varying political views, including liberal Catholic ideas (p124), but in the 1960s the Commissions fell under the influence of the **Communist Party** (p88). In the late 1970s they grew dramatically to become Spain's largest labour organisation. Thereafter their appeal to workers was constrained by their militancy and, later, by their Communist ties. Even so, they remain a major player in Spanish industrial relations.

expectations. Skill shortages in key industries greatly increased their bargaining power. Successful businesses, especially those engaged in export, wanted quick solutions to labour problems, and therefore preferred to deal with representatives who could deliver the agreement of employees as a whole – which increasingly meant the Commissions. Moreover, rising wages meant that many workers now had a small financial cushion, and so were readier to undertake strike action if their demands were not met. All these factors strengthened both workers' militancy and the Commissions themselves.

By the mid-1960s the Commissions were effectively under the control of the Communist Party (p88), whose ideas were well-suited to underground operation – and whose objective was to bring down the regime. This contributed to a change in the nature of industrial action, which increasingly focused on political issues. The regime itself also helped the process along, since strikes were routinely suppressed by the security forces, often with considerable brutality, and tended to turn into battles of attrition. This violence bred resentment, and from there it was only a step to political protest. By the time Franco realised the danger and attempted to crack down on the Commissions (pp126–7) they were far too well established, and could no longer be rooted out of his own union apparatus.

Neither of the two main strands of the pre-Civil War workers' movement took any significant part in these developments. The anarcho-syndicalists (p46) had been virtually eliminated by repression in the regime's early years. But the Socialists' abstention from infiltrating the official unions was a deliberate choice, prompted by fears that they would be accused of collaborating as they had done under the earlier Primo dictatorship (p59). Ironically, industrial strife reached its highest levels in the Basque Country, a traditional Socialist stronghold. But that was due to other developments since Franco came to power.

Despite Franco's clampdown on regionalism (p100), the Basque movement did not initially attempt to oppose his regime. It shared some of his conservative ideas (p43), and its supporters often benefited economically from his rule. Moreover, his attempts to stamp out the Basque language meant little in the urban areas, where it had long since effectively disappeared. Regionalism's core, the banned Basque Nationalist Party (p43), showed little appetite for organising resistance.

The situation was changed irrevocably by the economic growth that began in the 1950s, and accelerated in the next decade (p119). It brought a second wave of industrialisation to the region, which penetrated beyond the Bilbao area into the countryside of Guipuzcoa. There it caused enormous social upheaval in the tightly knit rural communities that were the last major stronghold of the Basque language, whose future now looked bleak indeed. They now became the main recruiting ground for a new and very different regionalist organisation; **ETA**.

Part of ETA's efforts were devoted to establishing a network of clandestine Basque-language schools (*ikastolak*) as a means of preserving the language. But its fundamental desire was to strike back at the regime, which led it to get involved in industrial action and – a new departure for Basque regionalists – to establish close links with Spanish workers' organisations of the Left. The conjunction of appeals to national and class solidarity proved a potent mixture, and led to repeated waves of strikes in the region. In response, the regime imposed frequent states of siege and exception, during which indiscriminate brutality by the security forces was the order of the day.

The government's reaction backfired completely, merely serving to bear out ETA's contention that the Basque Country was 'occupied' by a hostile Spanish state. This sense of national conflict was intensified after ETA turned to violence in 1968. From then on its attacks on the security forces, and their persistent over-reaction, fostered the notion of a 'war' in which ETA acted as the Basque 'army'. Moreover, its links with the Left meant that national sentiment was not only deepened but also extended to new sections of Basque society. By the end of the decade it had become the standard-bearer of a radicalised and immeasurably strengthened movement.

The situation in Catalonia was less dramatic, but no less serious for the regime. The business community, the historical core of regionalism (p42), was alienated by Franco's removal of self-government, by his simplistic economic policies (p102) and by the isolation from Europe to which his political ones led (p121). Moreover, much of the middle class deeply resented his attempt to stamp out the Catalan culture, to which they felt strong ties.

Culture certainly formed the initial focus of early underground activities in the region, but, as in other cases, the severity with which the regime cracked down on them broadened

> ### *Euskadi ta Askatasuna (ETA)*
> Basque homeland and liberty
>
> Formed in 1959 by younger members of the **PNV** (p43) to oppose the Franco regime's assault on Basque culture, ETA later adopted a vague form of 'revolutionary' socialism to go with its demand for Basque independence. In 1968 it turned to violence, which was directed initially against the security forces and others closely linked to the dictatorship. In 1974 it split into 'military' and 'politico-military' branches, the second of which disappeared in 1982 (p162). After Franco's death, and despite the granting of Basque autonomy, ETA refused to moderate its demands or abandon violence. It became a significant danger to stability, both in its own right and as the potential excuse for a coup (p143). In the early 1990s it appeared to be on the verge of defeat, but survived, in good part thanks to revelations about a government-sponsored dirty war carried out against it in the 1980s. In 1998 it announced a truce, but resumed killing little more than a year later (p175). In recent years ETA's attacks have been directed increasingly against civilians, especially politicians and others who oppose its activities publicly. See also: **Herri Batasuna** (p162); **caso GAL** (p160); **Pacto de Lizarra** (p174)

the scope of protest. A group led by Jordi Pujol (p164) began the work of nation-building (*fer país*), a long-term strategy of establishing contacts throughout Catalan society and building a consensus on its future once the regime eventually came to an end. By the end of the 1960s virtually all opinion in Catalonia was agreed, not just that democracy had to come, but that it must bring devolution with it.

In both the Basque Country and Catalonia, as in the past, these regionalist protests received backing from the local clergy. Altogether more surprising was the critical stance increasingly adopted by the Spanish Church in general towards the regime. When the Spanish bishops criticised the 1959 Stabilisation Plan (p118) for paying too little attention to the weakest in society, they showed which way the wind was blowing. In the next decade it became a gale.

Part of the cause of the bishops' intervention lay in the Second Vatican Council, which aligned the Church worldwide with demands for human rights and against authoritarian regimes. To Franco this line was as unacceptable as it was inexplicable; he refused to allow one of the Pope's pronouncements to be read in Spain on the grounds that it was heretical. But, despite his powers under the 1953 Concordat (pp105–6), he was unable to prevent the Vatican filling senior positions in the Spanish Church with men whose rejection of his regime was more or less explicit.

Among the lower clergy such attitudes were already common. By the 1960s, references to the Civil War no longer cut much ice with younger Spanish clerics. They were more concerned with issues affecting their parishes in the present, such as the lack of basic freedoms and, in many areas still, abject poverty. Many became involved in more-or-less clandestine political and industrial activity, through the legal Catholic workers organisations, the HOAC (p105) and its offshoot, the Catholic Young Workers (*Juventudes Obreras Católicas*), or even by joining the Workers' Commissions. The Vatican Council and its aftermath meant that these activities often enjoyed the broad support of their superiors.

Meanwhile, lay Catholics led by the former Education Minister, Joaquín Ruiz Giménez (p105), had established an informal Christian Democrat grouping. Taking advantage of the relaxation of censorship in 1966 (p120) it brought out the journal *Cuadernos para el Diálogo*, which became an important arena for debate. It was tolerated by the regime, along with two other mildly critical groups: the monarchists led by José María Gil-Robles (p107), and the so-called 'Social Democrats' set up by a former propaganda chief, Dionisio Ridruejo (p101). They termed themselves jointly a 'democratic' opposition, to emphasise that they would have nothing to do with Communists.

These groups were often accused of being Franco's stooges, and they undoubtedly played into his hands in some ways. By sticking to the unspoken limits of their criticism, they allowed him to claim that his regime accommodated dissent. They sometimes gave the regime's propaganda machine a soft target, as when in 1962 they met in Munich and publicly urged the EEC to reject Spain's application to join (p121). The official media had a field day, condemning the treachery of what they dubbed the Munich conspiracy (*Conturbernio de Munich*). But, at the same time, the 'legal' opposition's existence and criticisms, both widely known, helped to sustain a growing sense of dissatisfaction among what had once been the bedrock of the regime's support, the middle classes.

Middle-class discontent took many forms. The most visible was student protest, which intensified after a number of dissident academics, including the popular Professor Enrique Tierno Galván, were dismissed in 1965 for criticising the regime; it got a further boost from the events of 1968. More generally, the better-off young were increasingly unhappy at being denied the personal freedoms enjoyed by their peers abroad. Not a few joined the Communist Party (PCE), usually because it was the only group organising serious underground opposition rather than for any great belief in its ideas. Finally, exclusion from Europe in another sense – economic – led some business leaders to conclude that there must be political change of some sort. However, like the vast majority of the population, they had tacitly accepted that this was impossible while the dictator lived.

Death throes of dictatorship

In 1970, as his regime entered its fifth decade, Franco was 78. Clearly his death could not be far away, and he had begun making arrangements for it, determined that it should not be a prelude to significant change. In response, his opponents also prepared for outright confrontation. That, in turn encouraged his hard-line supporters to dig in deeper. With the regime, quite literally, in its death throes, those who hoped for some form of gradual relaxation were left with little influence.

By the late 1960s Franco had long since ceased to determine the day-to-day operation of his regime. Indeed, his arms-length approach to government, exemplified by the lengthy shooting holidays he spent with cronies, was common knowledge. But his ultimate authority, which continued to rest essentially on his personal standing, remained uncontested. His forthcoming disappearance thus posed a two-fold threat to his regime, and Franco himself was well aware of the need to make preparations for a world without him (*posfranquismo*).

The planning began in earnest with the 1967 'Organic Law of the State' (pp120–1), which established that the new King would be essentially a figurehead without real power, a Head of State but not of Government. Two years later, Franco at last formally settled the question of who would ascend the throne on his death. In reality, his choice had been clear ever since his 1948 agreement with the legitimate heir Don Juan (p105), whose son had thereafter been carefully groomed by Franco as future King. Prince Juan Carlos, for his part, had given every indication that he knew what was expected of him, to the extent that he had become publicly estranged from his less compliant father. Nevertheless, Franco did not intend to leave him too much option.

Thus, also in 1969, the dictator appointed as deputy Prime Minister his trusted servant Admiral Luis Carrero Blanco, a die-hard conservative who had allied himself with the technocrats and their patron, the Opus Dei (p118). Carrero was clearly earmarked to succeed Franco as Head of Government, a position from which he would be able to exercise tight control over the King. Admittedly, Juan Carlos would have powers of his own in some areas, such as military affairs or designation of the prime minister and other senior figures. But Franco made sure they were subject to ratification by bodies stuffed full of his own appointees: the Parliament (p103), the National Council of the Movement (p109) and, particularly, the Council of the Kingdom (*Consejo del Reino*), a shadowy committee whose powers were greatly extended in 1967. The dictator's confidence in these arrangements was reflected in his assurance that he had left everything 'all tied up' (*atado y bien atado*) (Figure 8.1).

Franco's determination that his regime should continue unchanged (*continuismo*) was also evident in his reaction to an outbreak of bickering in its ranks, caused by various proposals for mild liberalisation. They had been bitterly opposed by the

Figure 8.1 Franco attending a service in memory of Falange leader José Antonio Primo de Rivera, accompanied by three key figures for the survival of his regime, Admiral Carrero Blanco, Torcuato Fernández-Miranda and Prince Juan Carlos, on 20 November 1972 – three years to the day before his death.

aperturistas

liberalisers

Never formally organised, the liberalisers favoured making some concessions to genuine democracy without abandoning the basic authoritarian conservatism of the **Franco regime** (p100). Unlike the so-called democratic opposition (p124) they were members of, or close to the regime, and were to be found in several of its **clans** (p104); their ranks included public servants, **Falangists** (p84) and businessmen.

regime's most conservative supporters. In 1969 a leading **liberaliser**, Manuel Fraga (p120), retaliated by leaking details of a business scandal, the so-called Matesa affair (*caso Matesa*), involving a number of prominent conservatives. As in the past, Franco used the opportunity to exert his authority (p105), sacking both Fraga and National Movement leader, José Solís Ruiz. But this time his judgement was also a clear blow to the liberalisers, among whom, at the time, Solís was counted (p120).

The new government marked a return to the strategy of 1959 (pp118–19). Several leading technocrats (p118) were recalled or promoted, their task being to revive the economic growth whose slowdown had led to business dissatisfaction and an increase in industrial conflict. At the same time, Carrero Blanco – who, in practice now headed the cabinet – was joined by several other hard-liners, with the intention of cracking down on the emerging opposition. Specifically, efforts to stamp out the Workers' Commissions (p121) were intensified. The union's premises were raided and shut down, many activists arrested and a number, including its leader Marcelino Camacho, given long prison terms.

At the same time, a major anti-ETA offensive was launched, and numerous suspected activists arrested. In 1970 sixteen of them were tried by a military court in Burgos; six were sentenced to death. Franco's decision to commute their sentences to life imprisonment did little to still domestic and international outrage, which was prompted as much by the nature of the proceedings as by the verdicts. Both aspects provided further targets for Church criticism of the regime (p124), which had already become more outspoken with the Pope's appointment of Cardinal Enrique y Tarancón as Bishop of Toledo and head of the Spanish clergy.

But it was in the Basque Country itself that the results were most dramatic. Pro-ETA demonstrations multiplied, in which workers increasingly joined as, following a brief recovery in 1971/72, the economy faltered once again. The resultant clashes with the security forces only heightened public support for ETA, giving a major boost to its activities. Bank robberies, kidnappings and attacks on the security forces all increased. Most spectacularly, in December 1973 ETA struck a major blow to Franco's plans when it assassinated Carrero Blanco, who had finally been appointed prime minister just six months before, by setting off a bomb that blew up his official car on a busy Madrid street.

By now Franco's health was deteriorating visibly, and his opponents in general had begun to make preparations for his demise. They were furthest advanced in Catalonia, where the high degree of consensus already achieved (p123) had made it possible to set up a clandestine Assembly, which included representatives of virtually all opinion in the region. Elsewhere, however, such co-operation proved impossible. The problem was the Communist PCE, which had by far the strongest underground organisation of any opposition group, but was distrusted by the others for its ambivalent role during the Civil War (pp89–90).

In an attempt to overcome such reservations, the PCE's leader, Santiago Carrillo, announced his party's conversion to the Eurocommunist ideas pioneered by its Italian counterpart. The move was partly successful. In July 1974 the PCE established a Committee for Democracy (*Junta Democrática*), in which it was joined not only by the Workers' Commissions already under its influence (p122), but also by groups ranging from liberal monarchists to the People's Socialist Party (*Partido Socialista Popular [PSP]*) set up by Professor Tierno Galván (p124).

However, Carrillo's gesture failed to overcome Socialist suspicions, even though control of the PSOE (p45) was wrested from its ageing leadership in 1974, at a party conference held in the French town of Suresnes. Its new leaders were keenly aware that Socialist organisation within Spain had been badly neglected (p122), and had no desire to be swallowed up by the better-prepared PCE. In June 1975 they formed a 'Platform of

---

inmovilistas
....
(Francoist) die-hards

United by their fierce opposition to any relaxation of authoritarian rule after Franco's death, the die-hards formed a loose alliance of convenience in the last years of his regime. They included a number of old-style **Falangists** (p84), such as long-time Labour Minister Girón de Velasco (p104) and the one-time **liberaliser** Solís Ruiz (p120), some **technocrats** close to **Opus Dei** (p118), the openly Fascist Blas Piñar, who set up his own 'New Force' party, and many Army officers.

Democratic Convergence' together with the Basque PNV (p43), the 'legal' Christian Democrats led by Ruiz Giménez (p124) and a number of smaller groups. On one thing, however, Platform and Committee were agreed. Given that the regime showed no willingness to change, there could be no question of compromising with Franco's appointed successors.

These various forms of opposition served to entrench attitudes among the regime's **die-hards**, especially the military officers who were ETA's main target. All the greater was their fury at a speech by Carlos Arias Navarro, Carrero's successor as PM, on 12 February 1974. For Arias appeared to promise a degree of liberalisation, floating the idea of a 'Statute of Associations' that would allow some sort of political debate, albeit within strict limits. But the 'spirit of 12 February' did not last. Its promoter was a colourless figure with none of Carrero's prestige within the regime. Nor was he helped by the April coup in Portugal, which sent a shiver through all its supporters. Soon the die-hards were firmly back in charge.

The first indication came with the dismissal in October of Pío Cabanillas, Fraga's successor as Information Minister (p120), who had largely persevered with the more relaxed censorship policies of his predecessor. The most visible result was the appearance of pornography on Spanish bookstalls, a development that outraged the ultraconservatives – and Franco. Then, in December, the die-hards' renewed ascendancy was confirmed when the eagerly awaited draft of Arias' Statute was finally published. It provided that 'associations' would have to be approved by the National Council of the Movement, a clear sign that no real dissent was to be permitted.

Cabanillas' sacking removed the last liberaliser from government. It provoked several other leading administrators with links to the financial and intellectual communities to resign in despair. Events in 1975 seemed to justify their fears of outright conflict. When Bishop Añoveros of Bilbao spoke out in favour of Basque nationalist aspirations, he was placed under house arrest, leading to a stand-off with the Vatican. Industrial unrest reached new heights as Spain was hit by the effects of the 1973 oil shock and ETA's violence continued unabated. In August, in another triumph for the hard-liners, an Anti-Terrorist Act introduced mandatory death sentences for political killings. A month later, two ETA activists and one from the left-wing FRAP group were executed under its terms. When Franco finally died on 20 November, the chances of a tranquil handover of power looked minimal.

Summary of main points

Uneven development

- Around 1959, so-called technocrats – leading civil servants often associated with the Opus Dei – gained decisive influence over the regime's policies. As a result, Spain's economy was opened up to the outside world in various ways.
- The new strategy led to rapid economic development, which helped to reduce popular resentment. But it also led to new social tensions and to more generalised, lower-level dissatisfaction difficult to combat by outright repression.
- As an alternative response, during the 1960s some moves were made towards mild liberalisation, but they lagged far behind the rate of socio-economic change.

The emergence of opposition

- The economic growth of the 1960s created the conditions for increased labour militancy, channelled mainly through the illegal Workers' Commissions.
- Industrial conflict was most severe in the Basque Country, where it became linked to a nationalist movement greatly strengthened and radicalised by the creation of ETA, and by the regime's brutal response to it.
- In Catalonia regionalism, although less militant, came to enjoy even broader support.
- Large sections of the Church and its followers also turned against the regime, some as part of a tolerated 'democratic opposition', others more clandestinely. Parts of the middle classes and business community, too, became disillusioned with the effects of dictatorship.

Death throes of dictatorship

- Franco made detailed plans for the continuation of his regime. Prince Juan Carlos was designated his successor as Head of State, but real power was to remain with the dictator's most trusted supporters.
- Around 1970 the regime tried to crack down on the resistance of workers and regionalists, but with limited success. Indeed, its opponents both inside and outside Spain became increasingly organised and united.
- As Franco's death approached, the liberalising tendencies within his regime were largely suppressed, and influence returned to the die-hard reactionaries determined to prevent change of any sort.

Exhibit 8.1: Manuel Fraga's early political philosophy (1968)

Extract from one of the leading liberaliser's best-known works

[...] En [las Cortes] se han procurado conjugar las más valiosas enseñanzas de nuestra tradición multisecular con las exigencias debidas al mundo en que vivimos y a la realidad política actual de nuestra nación.

Por eso, cuando esta realidad política lo aconsejaba, se han introducido algunas modificaciones en el sentido de un mayor perfeccionamiento en el mecanismo representativo, uniendo en este alto Cuerpo representativo junto a la representación de los productores la de los consumidores, a través de la Familia, que es la célula básica del consumo en la economía moderna.

Este perfeccionamiento no es, por otra parte, sino un eslabón más en la cadena de mejoras que nos permite un Régimen siempre abierto y previsor de unas instituciones que sirvan fielmente al imperativo de los tiempos. Este realismo político que ha impulsado los pasos del nuevo estado, ha producido ya resultados que a la vista de todos están. Entre ellos son de citar la nueva Ley de Prensa e Imprenta y, sobre todo, la Ley Orgánica del Estado, con toda la serie de perfeccionamientos que prevén los más variados órdenes de nuestra vida política tales como las leyes sobre la Libertad Religiosa, el mundo sindical, el procedimiento electoral, el Régimen Local, así como la reforma de algunas de las Instituciones fundamentales de nuestro Estado [...].

[…] In [the Spanish Parliament] it has proved possible to combine the most valuable lessons of our history that dates back so many centuries with the requirements of the world in which we live and of our country's present political situation.

Thus, when that situation made it advisable, certain changes have been made that enhance still further the system of representation, by bringing together in this top-level representative body the representatives not only of producers but also of consumers, through the agency of the family, which is the basic unit of consumption in today's society.

At the same time, this is merely one in a line of improvements granted to us by a regime always open to new ideas and ever ready to envisage institutions which faithfully fulfil the needs of the time. This political realism, which has inspired the actions of the New State, has already produced results that are evident to all. As examples one should point to the recent Press and Publishing Act and, above all, to the Organic Law of the State, as well as all the enhancements brought by a wide range of measures governing our political life, such as the laws on Religious Liberty, the trade unions, the electoral system and local government, and also the reform of some of our state's basic institutions […].

Source: Fraga Iribarne, M. (1968) *Horizonte español*. Madrid: Héroes.

Exhibit 8.2: The regime promotes itself (1969)

Opening of a typical work issued by the regime's propaganda service

EL MILAGRO DE FRANCO

A lo largo de este año español, tan español que va de 18 de julio a 18 de julio, […], Francisco Franco, que desde aquella inolvidable jornada burgalesa del día primero de octubre de 1936 – con un sol dorado y con toda España metida en las calles de la pequeña ciudad, pequeño rincón de aquella Patria tan dura, tan pequeña también y tan llena de esperanzas – rige con pulso sereno nuestros destinos nacionales, cumplió sus primeros setenta y seis años. La gran aventura de su vida, puesta desde adolescente al servicio de España, siempre en los lugares de mayor riesgo y la mayor responsabilidad, encontró en este aniversario un eco unánime de felicitación popular. Incluso en grandes sectores de la Prensa extranjera, por regla general y constante histórica, tan atrabiliaria a la hora de juzgar a los hombres de España y, por supuesto, a España misma, bajo cualquier signo que la presida, se inició una conversión de frente – entrañable en algunos, admirativa en muchos, fría, pero objetiva, en otros – respecto a este veterano general y estadista que ha dado a los españoles la paz más larga que conoce su Historia y también su tranco político más lleno de realizaciones, prosperidad y posibilidades de futuro. […]

THE MIRACLE THAT IS FRANCO

In the course of this year in the life of Spain, so Spanish in that it ran from one 18th of July to the next, […], Francisco Franco celebrated his 76th birthday. The same Francisco Franco who has been presiding, in all serenity, over the fate of our nation, ever since one unforgettable 1st of October in Burgos[1] – a day of golden sunshine, when it seemed that all of Spain was pressed into the streets of the little city, into one small corner of a Fatherland so harsh, so small too, but so full of hope. This new milestone in the great undertaking that is Franco's life, placed since adolescence at Spain's service, present always where the risks and responsibilities were biggest, was greeted with unanimous popular celebration. Even in large sections of the foreign press, in general and traditionally so mean-spirited in its opinions of Spaniards and, of course, of Spain herself, whoever its ruler might be, began to show a new attitude – of affection in some cases, of admiration in many, of cold objectivity in others – towards the veteran general and statesman who has gifted Spaniards the longest period of peace in their history, and that stage in their political evolution most replete with achievements, prosperity and opportunities for the future. […]

[1] 1 October 1936, when Franco was invested as 'Head of State' of the zone then controlled by his Nationalist forces

Source: Servicio Informativo Español (1969) *Crónica de un año de España.* Madrid.

Topics FOR DISCUSSION

■ How could Fraga's work (Exhibit 8.1) be understood as an argument in favour of change in the Franco regime as it then existed?

■ What role did the family play in most Francoist thinking? What role is it assigned by Fraga in this text?

■ What arguments, explicit and implicit, does Exhibit 8.2 use to glorify Franco? What connotations would the word *milagro* in the title have had?

■ Who would have read such a text in 1969? How credible would it have been to most Spaniards?

■ Who benefited from the 'boom' of the 1960s, and how?

■ To judge by much of what one reads and hears nowadays, opposition to Franco's regime was very widespread towards the end of his rule. How is that impression to be reconciled with the regime's survival until 1975?

CHAPTER 9

A delicate operation (1975–1982)

In the second half of the 1970s the economies of western Europe experienced major problems, aggravated by a further 'oil shock' in 1979. To try and maintain growth the European Community (EC) established an Exchange Rate Mechanism to tie its members' currencies more closely together. Germany, the EC's economic powerhouse, in particular began to eye with interest the prospects offered by the relatively undeveloped markets of southern Europe. There the EC was also keen to ensure that stable democracies emerged from the processes of change that began with the overthrow of right-wing dictatorships in Greece and Portugal during 1974, in the latter case under Communist leadership. Contrary to western – especially American – fears, that turned out to mark the furthest leftward swing of the political pendulum which had begun in the previous decade. Now it moved steadily back towards the Right, accelerated by the election of aggressively free-market, anti-communist governments in Britain (1979) and America (1980). In 1979 the trend was given a further boost by the Soviet invasion of Afghanistan and the renewal of the Cold War. Indeed, the only challenge to the ascendancy of the 'New Right' came in 1981, with the election in France of a Socialist government pledged to resist the advance of free market economic policies.

Like Primo's departure 45 years before, Franco's death in November 1975 left Spain emerging from dictatorship at a time of economic recession. This time, though, the international political environment was much more helpful. Ironically, the delicate process was eased most of all by the fact that Franco's regime was a much sturdier edifice than Primo's, and did not immediately collapse. Consequently change, when it came, was initiated from within the old regime, whose structures could thus be dismantled without provoking the wrath of extreme conservatives. That, in turn, made it possible to begin constructing a new system in co-operation with the left-wing opposition. Only then was the operation threatened by an attempted coup, whose failure provided the renewed impetus required to conclude successfully Spain's transition to democracy.

The Right outmanoeuvred

So long awaited, with apprehension and hope, Franco's death proved rather an anticlimax. Initially, the arrangements he had put in place appeared to work smoothly, and power remained firmly in the hands of the hard-line conservatives who had exercised it in the dictator's last years (p128). Although pressures for change were building up, there seemed to be no way of releasing them while Franco's institutions remained intact. Yet that was precisely what happened from mid-1976 on.

The dictator's plan for the survival of his regime (*continuismo*) was triggered immediately on his death, beginning with the swearing in of King Juan Carlos I (p125). Admittedly, in his investiture speech the new monarch spoke of a desire not just for opening up (*apertura*) but for 'democratisation'. With his encouragement, the first cabinet of the King's reign included several leading liberalisers, notably Manuel Fraga Iribarne (p120). But their room for manoeuvre, and that of Juan Carlos himself, remained tightly circumscribed by the hold exercised by Franco's die-hard supporters (p128) over a range of key institutions, including the Parliament (p103), central and local administration, the National Movement (p109), the judiciary, and the armed forces.

As a result, Juan Carlos had little option but to retain Franco's appointee, Carlos Arias Navarro, as Prime Minister (p128). Arias was seen in some quarters as a liberaliser, but that view said less about him than about the mentality of the die-hard reactionaries who espoused it. His notions of a distinctively Spanish democracy (*democracia a la española*) were firmly based on the 'organic' variety devised by his former master (p103), for whom Arias retained an unswerving admiration. Nonetheless, the fact that he held them at all suggested that, unlike the die-hards, he had some inkling of the pressures on him.

To a large extent these were the delayed result of the 1973 oil shock, the initial impact of which had been muffled by Spain's substantial economic progress in the 1960s. In any case, successive governments had been too preoccupied with the political situation to worry about the country's extreme dependence on foreign oil. Now Spain paid the price for their inaction. Recession in western Europe shut off the safety valve which, for a decade and a half, had released pressure on Spain's labour market (p119); emigration ceased, and those who had left to work abroad began flooding back to their homes in Spain. Unemployment rose steeply, as did prices, fanning the campaign of industrial unrest mounted by the trade unions (p138).

Nor were they alone in demanding change. An alarmed business community lobbied for political concessions to reduce industrial tensions in the short term and, looking further ahead, to allow access to the benefits of EC membership (p121). Externally, the Community itself was anxious for Spain to fulfil the conditions to join, while the Americans were desperate to prevent a repeat of the Communist takeover in Portugal. Both pressed for significant political reform and discreetly supported those who favoured it.

Largely as a result, Arias took some hesitant steps in that direction. Along with a pardon for some political prisoners and a vague commitment to future reforms, he announced the removal of restrictions on the press. Although officially political parties remained banned, in practice they were permitted to begin operation. These moves were bitterly resisted by the most extreme die-hards, who hankered after a return to full-blooded dictatorship (*nostálgicos*), especially the military officers among them (*búnker*). Throughout the first half of 1976 they blocked all moves towards further change as pressure, domestic and external, steadily built up.

Something had to give, and in June it did. When Parliament rejected the central plank in Arias's strategy of minimalist reform – his proposals to legalise political parties under strict conditions – he resigned. Here, clearly, was a chance to break the deadlock. Hopes were high that Juan Carlos would appoint someone with the moral authority and drive to push through real changes. Hence the disappointment and astonishment when, on 1 July, he named Adolfo Suárez, a senior Francoist bureaucrat with no liberalising track-record. That, though, was a prime attraction to the King's adviser, Torcuato Fernández Miranda, an enigmatic figure who had given long and loyal service to Franco, but now played a key role in persuading the institutions left by his old boss to dismantle themselves.

No one was better qualified than the new Prime Minister to implement that strategy – first of all, because he had been secretary-general of the National Movement (p109). On the one hand, that gave him credibility with the reactionaries, on the other a deep knowledge not just of the workings of Franco's institutions but also the personal histories of their members. Secondly, he had served as head of the state-run television service, and understood like no other Spanish politician how the medium could be used to influence opinion. Finally, unlike most of the regime's grey functionaries, he was telegenic, and too young to evoke negative memories of the Civil War and its aftermath (p100).

Suárez's appointment marked the real start of Spain's transition to democracy (*transición democrática*). The key to the operation was that change should be initiated without opposition help, partly because its promoters wanted to prevent change from going too far, and partly because external support would alert the reactionaries. To carry it out Suárez relied on a group of close allies, former Francoist bureaucrats like himself, who wanted limited, controlled change in order to avoid anything more drastic. The most prominent – Rodolfo Martín Villa, Fernando Abril Martorell and Leopoldo Calvo Sotelo – took up key posts in his cabinet; a number of other ministers were drawn from an informal Christian Democrat grouping known as '*Tácito*', whose ranks included both liberalisers and members of the 'legal' opposition tolerated by Franco (p124).

With his team in place, Suárez seized the initiative. Within a month of taking office he announced extensions of various basic liberties, notably freedom of assembly and association. This action reduced the potential for high-profile clashes between opposition demonstrations and the police, as did a further amnesty for political prisoners. Having halted, at least temporarily, the spiral of rising tension, and the consequent hardening of attitudes among both opposition and reactionaries, Suárez made his key move, and announced plans for political liberalisation.

His Political Reform Bill (*Proyecto de Ley de Reforma Política*) was published in September. It proposed a new, two-chamber Parliament, which unlike the existing house (p103), would be fully elected. Parties would be legalised, subject to approval by the government. Beyond that, the proposals were deliberately vague. There was no mention of a new constitution: on the contrary, the old regime's basic laws (p120) would remain in force. Indeed, the fact that Suárez repeatedly had recourse to the extensive decree powers they conferred on him seemed a further sign that major change was not in the offing.

Even so, his plans evoked the reactionaries' fury. The King's role as Supreme Commander of the Armed Forces, and the military connections he had built up during his long apprenticeship, were crucial in keeping them under control. Admittedly the Army Minister, General De Santiago y Díaz de Mendívil, resigned in protest. But that allowed Suárez to replace him with Lieutenant-General Gutiérrez Mellado, a committed democrat, who immediately set about bringing the Army under control by a shrewd combination of discipline and administrative reforms.

With military opposition defused, the next hurdle was the old, Francoist Parliament. Here the key players were Suárez and Fernández Miranda, who occupied the crucial post of Speaker (*presidente*). Their methods were a combination of procedural manipulation and arm-twisting of individual representatives (*procuradores*), backed up by judicious references to the pressures for change from outside Spain. The final vote, held on 18 November, was a testimony to their skills: the Political Reform Act was passed by 425 votes to 59.

Suárez's next obstacle was self-imposed. In order to pre-empt charges that his proposals lacked democratic legitimacy, he had scheduled a national referendum for 15 December 1976. This time it was his media knowledge and skills that were decisive. Shamelessly manipulating coverage by the state television service, and employing his own charisma to the full, he won another overwhelming victory. Over three-quarters of the electorate voted, 94 per cent in favour.

Attention now switched to the general election, which under the terms of his own Act, Suárez had to call no later than 30 June 1977. In preparation for it, he legalised most of the opposition parties in February. However, in the case of the Spanish Communist Party (PCE) the Supreme Court, still dominated by Franco's appointees, overruled him, as the Reform Act allowed it to do. It was a crucial moment. At that time the PCE was seen as the strongest opposition force (p127), and without its participation the election would be meaningless. On the other hand, by legalising the PCE the government risked provoking a coup by military reactionaries. Suárez faced them down, with the King's support (p141), and legalised the PCE by royal decree. Yet, while that solved one problem, from the PM's standpoint it aggravated another, since it ensured even tougher competition in the forthcoming election, and as yet he had no organisation of his own, and no time to create one. His solution was simple: he hijacked an existing party.

The 'Democratic Centre' was one of the innumerable groupings set up in the wake of the Reform Act. Its leader, José María Areilza, was a prominent Francoist who had broken with the dictatorship. Conservative, but unambiguously democratic, it had swallowed up several similar mini-parties and looked well-placed to appeal to middle-class voters. But with virtually no organisation outside Madrid it had little prospect of tapping this potential, which was also limited by Areilza's advanced age and pompous style. When Suárez offered to jump aboard, bringing not just his own growing prestige but also his contacts in the recently wound-up Movement (p109), Areilza's lieutenants summarily ditched their leader and gratefully accepted Suárez as his replacement.

A number of the Prime Minister's own allies also took up senior positions in the hurriedly renamed **Centre Democratic Union** just in time for the election campaign. Once again, Suárez showed himself both skilled and ruthless in exploiting his advantages: civil service back-up, the Movement's countrywide apparatus and, as before, TV exposure. In the poll on 15 June his new party exceeded all outside expectations by winning the largest share of the vote, outpolling not just the barely organised Right, which performed abysmally (pp143–4), but also the historic parties of the Left (p139). Reconfirmed in his position as Prime Minister, this time by parliamentary vote, Suárez was left standing atop the ruins to which, in under a year, he had reduced Franco's seemingly impenetrable defences.

The Left tamed

The 1977 election results endorsed Suárez's strategy. But they also left him no alternative to continuing down the tricky path of reform, while tackling various other pressing problems. Furthermore, they meant that he could no longer, as up to now, govern virtually alone. Instead he was forced to seek support from the leaders of the left-wing opposition who, for their own reasons, were also anxious to work together. Out of their co-operation came the transition's legal foundation – a new constitution.

While the newly-born UCD was the undisputed winner of the 1977 election, and formed a government on its own, it had no overall majority, and won fewer votes than the left-wing opposition as a whole. Having started down the road to change it was clear that Suárez could not stop now, and it was generally agreed that the next step should be a new constitution. But that was by no means the only challenge facing the Prime Minister, since near-crises had emerged on two other fronts.

The first of these related to the law and order situation. Despite splitting into two branches, ETA (p123) had not just continued but stepped up its violence since Franco's death; in the autumn of 1977 the 'military' branch launched a new and more ferocious campaign. Nor were the problems confined to the Basque Country. From December 1976, a shadowy left-wing group, GRAPO, carried out a string of kidnappings, while in January 1977 far-right gunmen shot dead five labour lawyers in the Atocha district of Madrid.

The second crisis was caused by the economy's continuing deterioration (p134). Strikes remained at a very high level, and during 1977 inflation rose to 25 per cent. The

---

Unión de Centro Democrático (UCD)

Centre Democratic Union

Formed to fight the 1977 general election, the UCD was a 'centre' party in the sense that its leadership included both opponents and servants of the Franco regime. As well as a faction drawn from Franco's **National Movement** (p109), whose support for transition was essentially pragmatic, the UCD comprised three main ideological groupings: Christian Democrats, liberals and moderate Social Democrats. Once the **1978 Constitution** (p140) was approved the divisions between them became unbridgeable, and the party crumbled and was dissolved shortly after its cataclysmic defeat at the 1982 election (p156). Its leader, Adolfo Suárez (p135), attempted to construct a successor, the Social and Democratic Centre (CDS), but without success.

See also: **Partido Popular** (p182)

industries that had grown up in the 1960s under the sheltered conditions of dictator-ship were ill-equipped to deal with recession, especially now that their employees enjoyed normal trade union freedoms. Major restructuring was clearly necessary (p153) – and that would inevitably provoke even more unrest among workers.

Some guarantee of industrial peace was thus essential for stability. That, combined with the failure of the Right at the polls, forced Suárez to seek the parliamentary support he needed to his Left – that is, from the Socialists and Communists, who between them had received the vast majority of left-wing votes in June. Luckily for Suárez, both parties were now in a mood for compromise, far removed from the one in which they had entered the transition period.

Back in 1975 the entire opposition had been in favour of making a so-called clean break with the past (*ruptura*). Admittedly, its components disagreed as to what exactly that meant. For some it implied merely political and, perhaps, social reform; others also wanted radical economic changes, such as far-reaching nationalisation and state-directed redistribution of wealth. Nevertheless, there was general agreement that those associated with the Franco regime should play no part in creating its replacement. The unanimity was such that the two umbrella groups which had coalesced around the Communist and Socialist parties (p127) joined forces, under the name of 'Democratic Coordination' (popularly, the *Platajunta*).

The limited extent of change during the first half of 1976 (p134) hardened the opposition's line still more. In the absence of any political forum, its main tactic was industrial action, to which many workers were in any case being pushed by economic circumstances. The resultant strikes repeatedly erupted into violent confrontations with the security forces, especially in the Basque Country, where left-wingers and nationalists continued to make common cause (p123).

One clash in Vitoria during March, which led to five workers being shot and killed, illustrated the dilemma facing the Left's leaders. They were well aware that, contrary to American nightmares, the situation was quite unlike that before the 1974 left-wing revolution in Portugal, where large sections of the Army had gone communist. In Spain the armed forces remained solidly conservative, if not reactionary, and any attempt to force change against their will would involve a bloodbath. Hence the alacrity with which the Left grasped at the chance for negotiated change when Suárez offered it.

Within weeks of his appointment both Felipe González, head of the Socialist Party (PSOE) and Enrique Tierno Galván (p124), leader of the small but influential People's Socialist Party (*Partido Socialista Popular* [PSP]), had agreed to meet the PM for exploratory talks. Even PCE leader Santiago Carrillo had informal contacts with him. When Suárez's proposals for political reform were published (p135), those Christian Democrats who had joined the opposition front (p128) supported them, oblivious of the fact that – like the left-wing leaders' actions – doing so was incompatible with any notion of a clean break.

Yet at the end of October, the opposition leaders publicly reaffirmed that as their goal. When Suárez submitted his proposals to a referendum, they called on voters to abstain. The fact that less than a quarter of the electorate heeded their advice (p136) indicated how far their position had lost credibility. Moreover, the referendum campaign had made painfully clear how effectively Suárez could exploit his privileged access to TV. Even though they would have their own election broadcasts before the upcoming election, his opponents were well aware that the government's control of news coverage would still give it a head start.

Their fears were confirmed by the results (p137), which also abruptly changed the balance of power within the different parties that made up the opposition. Up to then the PCE had been regarded as its strongest component, especially given the party's strong links with the Workers' Commissions (p121), which had been so prominent in organising industrial protest. In contrast, the Socialist union, the UGT (p59), had been relatively cautious in its calls for action; like the PSOE, it had not had sufficient time to rebuild its organisational basis neglected during the dictatorship (p122). Yet in 1977 the Socialists easily outpolled the PCE to become the second largest party in Parliament.

The election results showed that voters preferred younger faces, such as those of Suárez and González, and moderate policies; they were clearly in no mood to relive the conflicts of the Republic and Civil War. The Left's leaders were also aware that talk of radical change increased the already significant danger of a right-wing coup should they ever manage to win power. Consequently, González and Carrillo decided to cut their losses. Abandoning the lost cause of a clean break to various far-left splinter groups, they began to talk in terms of a democratic or agreed break (*ruptura democrática/pactada*) and offered to give Suárez the informal support he needed in return for a say in the next phase of change.

Since 1975 there had already been signs, on both Right and Left, of a spirit of **compromise** that was unusual, to say the least, in Spanish politics: they included the Church's decision not to back an official Christian Democrat party, with its inevitable echoes of the CEDA (p72), and the Communist Party's recognition of the monarchy. By the late summer of 1977 that new spirit had become the transition's *leitmotiv*. Its first concrete result came in October, when the two left-wing parties signed the 'Moncloa Pacts' with the government. The terms, whereby they agreed to persuade their associated unions to tone down industrial action, indicated that they knew the weakness of their position. The left-wing leaders delivered on their promise; inflation was brought down to a more manageable level, and the pressure on Suárez considerably eased. Rather predictably unkept was the promise they received in return, to create more jobs.

---

consenso

(spirit of) compromise

In many ways compromise is the standard stuff of democracy, but the extent to which it was displayed by politicians during the transitional period was remarkably different from the intransigence that had so long characterised Spanish politics. Its protagonists were the **UCD** (p137) government and the leaders of the **Socialist PSOE** (p45) and **Communist PCE** (p88). They were supported to varying degrees by the main trades union federations, the **UGT** (p59) and the **Workers' Commissions** (p121), and the employers. Its main fruits were the Moncloa Pacts, the **1978 Constitution** (p140), and the process known as '**social concertation**' (p158).

The pay-off for the Left's leaders, if not their grassroots supporters, came in the drafting of a constitution. For Suárez abandoned his original intention of having the text drawn up by government lawyers, and instead handed over the task to Parliament, where proposals could only be passed with the Left's approval. As a result, the document finally agreed at the end of 1978 was significantly less conservative than many of the PM's supporters would have wished. Despite – or perhaps because of – that, it was widely hailed as a triumph.

The **1978 Constitution**, which in a formal sense marked the transition's close, settled several conflicts that had bedevilled Spanish politics for a century and more. Thus, the Socialists presented only token objections to the monarchy, happy to accept that Juan Carlos' performance in the role (pp134, 141) had saved them from having to take an awkward decision. Religion caused more controversy, as both the main left-wing parties adamantly opposed granting any special status to the Catholic Church. But eventually they agreed to recognise it as a 'social reality', which was enough to satisfy most conservative opinion. The Constitution also included ingenious provisions to deal with regionalism (p142).

The main error made in drafting the Constitution, which went unnoticed at the time, was to assume that the electoral system made it impossible for a single party to win an overall parliamentary majority (p156). For the moment, though, that assumption proved correct. In fact, the first election held under the new Constitution, in March 1979, produced results very similar to those of 1977. Suárez's party, the UCD, again won most seats, while falling well short of an overall majority. Once again the Left, especially the PCE, had to take on board its electoral weakness. All seemed set for a continuation of the compromise course of the past 18 months. But it was not to be.

Compromise had been a successful strategy for one very particular set of circumstances. However, that moment had passed, and, with the Constitution agreed, politics returned to everyday bread-and-butter issues. Some of these were related to the country's economy, whose serious problems were aggravated by the second oil shock in 1979. Others, symbolised by the possibility of legalising divorce, concerned the type of society that Spain should now become. Many involved fundamental clashes of interest and beliefs that could not be resolved by compromise, but instead needed a strong government able to give a firm lead. That was precisely what Spain lacked.

Constitución del 78

1978 Constitution

The 1978 Constitution was the work of the parliament elected in June 1977, which became in effect a constituent assembly (*Cortes constituyentes*). It was based on a draft produced by a seven-man committee (*ponencia*) known as the 'fathers of the Constitution'. In line with the prevailing **spirit of compromise** (p139) there were three representatives of the governing **UCD** (p137) and one each for the **Socialists**, the **Communists**, the right-wing People's Alliance (p143) and the Catalan regionalist **CiU** (p164). Their text was agreed with only minor amendments, and the final version was overwhelmingly approved in a referendum on 6 December 1978, except in the Basque Country, where the result was ambiguous (p142).
See also: *Estado de las*

The problem was not so much that the government lacked a parliamentary majority; for fear of a coup the Left's leaders still held back from toppling it – despite discontent among their own rank and file, for whom democracy had brought few material benefits. The problem was the UCD's nature. In essence, it was an alliance of convenience between groups that had nothing in common beyond the desire to bring about a smooth transition (p137). With that achieved, at least on paper, there was little to hold its disparate components together.

As a result, the UCD was wracked by a succession of disputes, especially over the legislation of divorce. They were aggravated by Suárez's increasing reliance on a small group of his closest advisers (p135), and by rivalry between the powerful 'barons' who headed its various factions. Although the events have never been fully clarified, it seems to have been these key figures in the party who forced the Prime Minister's surprise resignation in January 1981. Before long it was to become apparent that by ditching its greatest asset the party had merely hastened its own demise (p156). More immediately, however, the uncertainty triggered by Suárez's abrupt departure gave an opportunity to those who found even his brand of reform far too radical, and who had no interest whatsoever in compromise.

Crisis and recovery

It was during the investiture of Suárez's successor that military reactionaries attempted a coup. Although this was a shock, it was hardly a surprise, having been on the cards since the transition's start. The factor most likely to provoke it – regionalist agitation of various sorts – had been growing in importance for some time. Happily, though, the coup was easily put down, and its failure gave a new impetus to the process of reform, hastening the change of government that was so clearly required.

Ever since 1975 the military's propensity for rebellion (*golpismo*) had hovered over Spanish politics. Several times the King's influence was crucial in keeping the Army in check, notably when the PCE was legalised (p136). Subsequently some officers made no attempt to hide their far-right sympathies, and more than once Defence Minister Gutiérrez Mellado (p136) was the target of their abuse. In 1979 and 1980 several plots were uncovered, the biggest known as 'Operation Galaxia'. Although they reflected general Army dissatisfaction at the course of events, these activities were above all a reaction to the revival of the regionalist feeling that their ex-leader had attempted to stamp out.

Ironically, it was the spectacular failure of Franco's efforts to repress such sentiments in Catalonia and the Basque Country (p100) that left Suárez with no option but to concede a measure of self-government. By 1976 feelings in these regions were so strong that its denial would undoubtedly derail plans for a smooth transition (p123). This insight was shared by the leaders of the left-wing opposition, whose activists in the two regions in any case backed devolution. They were thus happy to let Suárez lay the groundwork for it, while at the same time conducting discussions on the Constitution. As a result, by the end of 1977 what amounted to provisional regional governments (*entes preautonómicos*) had been set up in both regions.

Estado de las Autonomías
....
regionalised form of govern-
ment

Neither completely centralised
nor genuinely federal, the
territorial structure of the
government established by the
1978 Constitution (p140) is
based on units known as
Autonomous Communities
(*autonomías/comunidades
autónomas*), the boundaries and
powers of which were left to be
established in individual 'Statutes
of Autonomy'. The three 'historic
nationalities' of the Basque
Country, Catalonia and Galicia
were allowed immediate access
to extensive devolution. Other
regions could only follow this fast
track (*vía rápida*) if they met
demanding requirements to
demonstrate popular support.
Otherwise they had to follow the
slow route (*vía lenta*), which
involved immediate low-level
devolution, with the opportunity
for upgrade after five years. As
a result, devolution has turned
out to be less of a structure and
more of a process (*proceso
autonómico*), which was still
ongoing in 2001 (p184) and in all
probability is not over yet (p188).

The Catalan body was headed by Josep Tarradellas, a popular moderate regionalist who Suárez had brought back from exile for the task. Its views could be fed directly into that process of drafting a constitution thanks to the presence of a Catalan on the committee charged with that task (p140). The final text, with its provisions for a **regionalised form of government**, received massive approval in Catalonia. Thereafter devolution negotiations with the central government were smoothed by the consensus already established within the region on the path to be followed (p123). A Statute of Autonomy was duly approved without major problems. This restored the *Generalitat*, as the regional government was again to be known (p69), and invested it with extensive powers, including education and policing.

In the Basque Country, lack of representation on the constitutional working party was just one, relatively minor problem. This was because regionalists there insisted that self-government was a matter for Basques alone to decide, and that no Spanish constitution could deny them the right to choose independence if they so wished. As far as ETA (p123) was concerned, even talking about devolution was taboo. The non-violent Basque Nationalist Party (PNV) (p43) was willing to do that, especially as its triumph at the recent election allowed it to pose as the Basques' representative *vis-à-vis* Madrid. However, it still refused to back the Constitution, either in Parliament or at the subsequent referendum (p140).

The plebiscite's results in the region complicated the situation still further. For, although there was a majority of 'Yes' votes, widespread abstention meant that they constituted only a minority of the Basque electorate. ETA immediately claimed that the Basques had 'rejected the Constitution', and used that as a justification for its continuing campaign of violence (p137). The message was repeated incessantly by People's Unity (HB) (p162), the political wing set up by ETA's 'military' branch (p123), which in the 1979 election took nearly a sixth of Basque votes on a platform of complete separation from Spain.

At this the PNV took fright. To underpin its nationalist credentials, the region's largest party began emphasising that it, too, believed in independence. It also implied unsubtly that so long as that was denied, violence, if not justified, was at least under-standable. In reality HB's vote, like the frequent and large pro-ETA demonstrations, mainly reflected lingering respect for the armed organisation's resistance to Franco (p123), and the resentment felt against the continuing excesses of the security forces in dealing with anyone suspected of having connections with it. But that was easily over-looked, inside and outside the Basque Country. With the left-wing opposition also demanding wide-ranging devolution, the pressure on Suárez was immense.

As a result, the PNV was able to win major concessions. The Basque Statute of Autonomy, known as the Statute of Guernica (p91), included all the powers granted to Catalonia as well as the tax-collecting powers suppressed by Franco (p100). Like its Catalan equivalent, the Statute was approved by referendum in October 1979. In February 1980 the PNV won a convincing victory in the first regional election, and immediately formed a government. However, it then showed less interest in using its devolved powers than in complaining that they were not greater, and that Navarre had been excluded from the Basque 'Autonomous Community'. In general, the PNV's tendency to portray every issue as a confrontation between the Basques and Madrid both fed on and fed ETA's continuing 'armed struggle', which in 1980 claimed more victims than ever before.

In Catalonia, the first election was unexpectedly won by a new regionalist party, Convergence and Union (p164), whose leader Jordi Pujol (p123) wasted no time in putting his new powers to concrete use. Yet the effects of this different approach were remarkably similar. In the central government's view, some of Pujol's measures exceeded Catalonia's competences as defined jointly by the Constitution and its Statute. Conversely, Pujol claimed that some Madrid laws infringed his region's constitutional rights (a complaint shared by the PNV). Both sides repeatedly appealed to the Constitutional Court (*Tribunal Constitucional*) charged with ruling in such disputes, thereby adding to the impression of conflict between the regions and Madrid.

These developments caused growing concern in the Army and Civil Guard, whose officers were ETA's principal targets and who also tended to have Spanish nationalist views. It was deepened when Andalusian politicians attempted to obtain the same sort of wide-ranging devolution as the Basques and Catalans. The process prescribed in the Constitution for such cases proved to be unsatisfactory, and while it dragged on other regions joined in the clamour for extensive self-government. Wild talk of Spain's imminent disintegration was no longer limited to military circles, and was seized upon by the extreme reactionary officers plotting for a coup; as a sop to military feeling, the Constitution had made the forces responsible for Spain's 'territorial integrity'.

Along with the government's incapacity to maintain law and order, the other justification they offered was that they represented a mood of popular disillusion (*desencanto*). Indeed, many Spaniards were disappointed that reform had not protected them from the effects of economic recession (p138). But the vast majority clearly wanted more change, not less; the only force of any significance saying the opposite was the People's Alliance led by Manuel Fraga (p120) – and in both elections to date it had performed dismally.

(intentona de golpe del) 23-F

1981 coup attempt

The attempted coup of 23 February 1981 only got off the ground in Valencia, where tanks under the command of General Milans del Bosch appeared on the streets, and, most dramatically, in Madrid, where civil guards led by Lieutenant-Colonel Antonio Tejero stormed the Congress of Deputies – the lower house of Parliament – and held at gunpoint MPs attending Leopoldo Calvo Sotelo's investiture as Prime Minister. Prompt action by loyal troops, and the unambiguous opposition of King Juan Carlos, ensured that order was soon restored in both cities.

However, some officers either could not or would not see that the times had changed. In the climate of uncertainty created in early 1981 by the mysterious resignation of Prime Minister Adolfo Suárez (p141), they decided to act. Their **attempted coup** was spectacular, but quickly crushed. Reaction to it underlined just how bogus was their claim to represent public opinion. Spontaneous mass demonstrations in favour of democracy were held all round Spain. The Madrid march was headed by politicians ranging from Fraga to PCE leader Santiago Carrillo. Disillusion, insofar as it had existed, was banished (Figure 9.1).

The coup attempt led the new Prime Minister, Leopoldo Calvo Sotelo, and the main opposition parties to rekindle the spirit of compromise (p139), in order to bring the

Figure 9.1 The head of the pro-democracy march in Madrid on 27 February 1981, made up of leading figures of all persuasions, including Nicolás Redondo (5th from left in front row), Santiago Carrillo (6th), Felipe González (7th) Manuel Fraga (10th) and Marcelimo Camacho (11th).

regional issue under control and so calm Army fears. In the summer they settled on a timetable for resolution of the Andalusian dilemma, but also agreed that no more regions would be granted such extensive devolution. In addition, they pushed through legislation stipulating that, whatever the Autonomy Statutes might say, the Madrid Parliament could always overrule regional laws if it wished. That decision sparked off furious Basque and Catalan protests, and another appeal to the Constitutional Court. But it also countered hysteria about the country falling apart.

Otherwise Calvo's government was completely hamstrung by the progressive disintegration of his UCD party (p141), so that his only other significant initiative was to take Spain into NATO. That, too, was partly designed to ease military tensions, by providing the forces with new tasks to keep them occupied. But NATO entry was decidedly not a product of compromise; it was eventually imposed over Parliament's head, by decree. The Left objected bitterly. Sensing that the danger of another coup was slight, and that the UCD was close to complete collapse, its leaders had decided to go for the kill.

Of the two major left-wing parties the Socialists were now indisputably the UCD's main challenger, having maintained their wide lead over the PCE at the 1979 election. Yet the failure of his party to outpoll the UCD persuaded PSOE leader Felipe González that it must moderate its image. At a party conference in May 1979 he proposed removing all references to Marxism from the PSOE's internal rules. Outvoted, he resigned, a tactical manoeuvre to show that his opponents – left-wingers and party traditionalists – had no alternative strategy or leader. The matter was shelved, pending a special conference. In the meantime, González's henchman Alfonso Guerra took a firm grip on the party apparatus. In September the changes were approved, and González was overwhelmingly re-elected. His authority had been paraded publicly, making him look like the strong leader the country needed.

González's personal standing was an important card in the election that could not be long delayed. Another was the PSOE's anti-NATO campaign, very effective in a country where, thanks to its links with Latin America and the memory of 1898 (p31), anti-US feeling extended across the political spectrum. The Socialists' overall strategy was to ride the wave of enthusiasm for further social and economic change that had been unleashed by the coup attempt, portraying themselves as the only political force capable of delivering such reform. It was a huge success. In the election eventually held on 28 October 1982 the PSOE swept to power (p156). Perhaps more importantly, no voice of any consequence questioned the Socialists' right to assume office. The transition to democracy was complete, not just in constitutional theory but also in political practice.

Summary of main points

The Right outmanoeuvred

- Following Franco's death, change was initially very limited, but pressure for real reform was building up both inside and outside the country.

- The transition to democracy got properly under way in mid-1976, with the appointment of Adolfo Suárez as Prime Minister. Together with a small group of allies, he managed to steer through democratising measures without provoking a reaction from the Right.
- Crucial to Suárez's success were his links to two of the dictatorship's institutions: state-run television and the single party. They enabled him to win both a referendum on his proposals and the first two democratic elections at the head of a newly created party (UCD).

The Left tamed

- After the 1977 election Suárez's lack of an overall parliamentary majority, and the threats posed by terrorist violence and economic recession, forced him to seek support from the Left.
- The Socialist and Communist leaders had originally refused to co-operate with any ex-Francoists, but their disappointing electoral results and the danger of a military coup led them to change their mind.
- The resultant spirit of compromise was reflected above all in the 1978 Constitution. However, it broke down once political debate shifted to bread-and-butter issues, which also led to fatal splits in the governing UCD.

Crisis and recovery

- In the Basque Country and Catalonia demands for self-government were very strong; in 1979 both regions were granted extensive autonomy as part of a wider devolution settlement.
- The arrangements were not fully accepted in the Basque Country, where ETA stepped up its violence, while both new regional governments came into conflict with the central authorities.
- Such tensions, together with fears about Spain's possible break up and popular discontent with economic conditions, prompted military officers to attempt a coup in February 1981.
- The coup's failure, and the massive response by the public and politicians, demonstrated how little support the reactionaries really had, and emboldened the opposition to force an election. Held in October 1982, it was won by the Socialists and marked the end of transition.

Exhibit 9.1: King Juan Carlos addresses Parliament (1977)

Speech at the opening session of the Parliament elected in June 1977

[...] Hace poco más de un año y medio, en mi primer mensaje como Rey de España, afirmé que asumía la Corona con pleno sentido de mi responsabilidad y consciente de la honrosa obligación que supone el cumplimiento de las Leyes y el respeto de la tradición. Se iniciaba una nueva etapa en la Historia de España que había de basarse, ante todo, en una sincera voluntad de concordia nacional y que debía recoger las demandas de evolución que el desarrollo de la cultura, el cambio generacional y el crecimiento material de los tiempos actuales exigían de forma ineludible, como garantía del ejercicio de todas las libertades. Para conseguirlo, propuse como empresa comunitaria la participación de todos en nuestra vida política, pues creo firmemente que la grandeza y fortaleza de la Patria tiene que asentarse en la voluntad manifiesta de cuantos la integramos. [...]

La ley nos obliga a todos por igual. Pero lo decisivo es que nadie pueda sentirse marginado. El éxito del camino que empezamos dependerá en buena medida de que en la participación no haya exclusiones. Con la presencia en estas Cortes de los partidos que a través del voto representan a los españoles, damos un paso importante en esa dirección y debemos disponernos con nobleza a confiar en quienes han sido elegidos para dar testimonio de sus ideas y de sus ilusiones. [...]

Además de estos objetivos, el país tiene pendiente muchos problemas concretos sobre los que el pueblo español espera la acción directa de sus representantes. El primero es crear el marco legal adecuado para las nuevas relaciones sociales, en el orden constitucional, el regional o en el de la comunicación humana.

La Corona desea – y cree interpretar las aspiraciones de las Cortes – una Constitución que dé cabida a todas las peculiaridades de nuestro pueblo y que garantice sus derechos históricos y actuales.

Desea el reconocimiento de la diversa realidad de nuestras comunidades regionales y comparte en este sentido cuantas aspiraciones no debiliten, sino enriquezcan y hagan más robusta la unidad indiscutible de España. [...]

Little more than a year and a half ago, in my first speech as King of Spain, I stated that I was ascending the throne in the full knowledge of my responsibility and aware of the honourable obligations on me to obey the law and respect tradition A new chapter in Spain's history was beginning. It was to be based, above all, on a sincere desire to achieve national harmony. And it would have to take up the demands for our country to evolve that had arisen inevitably from the contemporary trends of cultural development, generational change and material growth, as a guarantee that Spaniards' liberty might be exercised in full. In order to achieve that, I proposed as a common enterprise the participation of all Spaniards in our political life, for I believe firmly that the greatness and strength of our Fatherland must be founded on the clear will of all those who make it up. [...]

The law places the same obligations on us all. But the crux of the matter is that no-one should feel themselves marginalized. The success of the enterprise that we are beginning will depend in large measure on nobody being excluded from participation. With the presence in this parliament of the parties which, through the electoral process, represent Spaniards, we are taking an important step in that direction, and we must be prepared nobly to place our trust in those who have been elected to present their ideas and hopes here. […]

As well as these tasks of a general nature, the country faces other, more specific problems that are still to be resolved, and which the Spanish people expect its representatives to tackle head on. The first of these is to create an appropriate legal framework for new relationships in society, whether in the constitutional or the regional sphere, or in that of human interaction.

I wish – and here I believe myself to be expressing the aspirations of this parliament – to see a Constitution within which all the special features of our people can find a place, and which guarantees their rights, both traditional and contemporary.

I wish also to see the diverse reality of our regions recognised. In that sense I share the aspirations of all those who seek not to weaken but to strengthen and enrich Spain's unquestionable unity. […]

Source: Presidencia del Gobierno (1977) *Mensajes de la Corona.* Madrid: Colección Informe, núm. 15.

Exhibit 9.2: Tejero's manifesto (1981)

Statement issued by the leader of the Civil guards who stormed parliament during the 1981 coup attempt

Españoles: las unidades del Ejército y de la Guardia Civil que desde ayer están ocupando el Congreso de los Diputados a las órdenes del general Milans del Bosch, [...] no tienen otro deseo que el bien de España y de su pueblo.

No admiten más que un Gobierno que instaure una verdadera democracia. No admiten las autonomías separatistas y quieren una España descentralizada, pero no rota. No admiten la impunidad de los asesinos terroristas, contra los que es preciso aplicar todo el rigor de la ley. No pueden aceptar una situación en la que el prestigio de España disminuye día al día; no admiten la inseguridad ciudadana que nos impide vivir en paz.

Aceptan y respetan al Rey, al que quieren ver al frente de los destinos de la Patria, respaldado por sus Fuerzas Armadas. En suma, quieren la unidad de España, la paz, orden y seguridad. ¡Viva España!

Spaniards: the Army and Civil Guard units that, since yesterday, have been occupying the Congress of Deputies on the orders of General Milans del Bosch, […] have only one concern: the good of Spain and her people.

They will not accept any government that fails to introduce a true democracy. They will not accept the existence of separatist regions; they wish to see a Spain that is decentralised, but not broken up. They will not accept the immunity from punishment of terrorist murderers, who must be subject to the full force of the law. They cannot accept a situation in which Spain's prestige is diminishing daily. And they will not accept the absence of law and order that prevents us from living in peace.

They do accept and respect the King, whom they wish to see in charge of the Fatherland's fate, supported by its Armed Forces. In sum, they wish the unity of Spain, peace, order and security. Long live Spain!

Source: *El País* (4 March 1981).

Topics
FOR DISCUSSION

- How does the view of the monarchy's role presented by King Juan Carlos (Exhibit 9.1) compare with that of Cánovas (Exhibit 2.2)?
- Which institutions does he refer to, either directly or indirectly, as having a role to play in the country's future development?
- What aspects of Spain's historical experience appear to have prompted his remarks?

- Judging by Tejero's manifesto (Exhibit 9.2), where does, or should, ultimate authority lie in Spain? What role does it appear to ascribe to the monarchy?
- How did Spain's situation in 1975 resemble that in 1936? Why did events turn out so differently?
- Could the strategy of *ruptura* ever have been practicable? If so, under what circumstances?

CHAPTER 10

Back to the mainstream (1982–1993)

By 1982 the neoliberal ideas of the New Right dominated western thinking, their position reinforced by the rapid abandonment of Socialist economic policies in France. Along with free market economics their main feature was anti-Communism. Renewed stress was laid on the role of NATO, leading to a revival of the arms race. Partly as a result the Soviet bloc crumbled in 1989, with the emergence of new states and the discredit of its underlying ideology. Meanwhile, the western economies experienced a strong recovery, concentrated in the financial sector and other services. It was aided by the European Community's (EC's) removal of remaining barriers to internal competition by the 1989 Single European Act, and enlargement to 12 members. In 1992 these signed the Maastricht Treaty, which, as well as converting the EC into the European Union (EU), established a timetable for Economic and Monetary Union (EMU) by the end of the century. Further steps towards political integration were taken by some members, with the creation of a joint Eurocorps (also in 1992) and the removal of border controls under the Schengen Treaty of 1995. Meanwhile, the strict economic requirements, or convergence criteria, set for EMU candidates served to deepen the recession that, throughout the West, undermined the New Right, and boosted the advocates of a return to the political Centre.

With the smooth transfer of power following the 1982 general election, Spain's long journey to democracy was effectively complete. But there remained two major challenges to face, the first of which was to close the still yawning gap on its neighbours in economic – and social – terms. Both objectively and in the minds of most Spaniards, that was inextricably linked to the second: joining the EC. To a large degree, therefore, the next stage in Spain's story was shaped by the country's belated involvement in the ongoing process of European integration. Its second feature was the extraordinary dominance established over Spanish politics by the Socialist Party, a situation that brought dramatic change to both country and party. Rather from any nationwide force, the main obstacle to complete Socialist hegemony lay in the growth of regional self-government and self-assertiveness that constituted a third major characteristic of the period.

Into Europe

Even before Franco died in 1975 Spanish opinion had swung strongly behind the idea of joining the EC. Yet it was only the arrival in power of the Socialists seven years later that gave decisive impetus to the country's efforts to do so. For the new government was not only willing and able to give top priority to the associated negotiations: it was also prepared to tackle head-on the tricky issue of the country's economic preparedness to join. Membership having been achieved, the Socialists also showed themselves adept in adjusting to the unwritten rules of European politics, the result being to enhance further the considerable benefits it had brought.

By 1982, very few in Spain questioned the desirability, or the importance, of EC membership. Throughout society there was a vague but powerful yearning to see the country accepted by its neighbours as an equal. On the Left, suspicions that the Community was an agent of multinational business were outweighed by the knowledge that workers in the EC were better off, and by the hope that entry would kill off the old reactionary Right. Business, especially the larger, more vocal enterprises, was enthusiastic. This last had been the main factor behind the Franco regime's uncharacteristic, and unsuccessful, decision to apply for admission (p121), and it spurred the centrist governments of the transition era to lodge a new application. Yet, beset as they were by other problems, they lacked the time and energy to pursue it, and little progress was made.

As in many other ways (p157), the Socialists' election marked a turning point. Not only did Spain's new rulers enjoy a large parliamentary majority: the failure of the 1981 coup attempt had effectively dispelled lingering uncertainty about the country's political future. Moreover, they were among the most enthusiastic pro-Europeans (*europeístas*), free from the isolationist complexes that haunted many on the Right. Virtually as soon as they were elected they therefore gave a new priority to the negotiations with Brussels.

At the same time, they were acutely aware that being accepted into the EC club was only half the battle. Spain also had to be made fit to survive once inside. The shaky foundations of development in the 1960s had left the country more vulnerable than her neighbours to the turbulences of the following decade, so that by 1982 her economic situation relative to the rest of western Europe was no better than it had been twenty years before. Indeed, given the increased pace of change it was probably worse. As the third industrial revolution got under way Spain was barely emerging from the first, its economy still dependent on a manufacturing sector within which old-style smokestack industries were heavily over-represented.

The new government, like most Spaniards, took the view that the only way Spain could catch up was through exposure to competition within the EC. But there was the rub. Even the strictly controlled opening of her economy since 1959 had laid bare its lack of international competitiveness (p138). If the cure were not to prove worse than the disease, Spanish industry would have to be prepared for the shock of entry, and on their arrival in power that became the Socialists' top domestic priority. It underlay their reforms in a range of areas, particularly infrastructure and education (p157), but above all their wide-ranging programme of **industrial restructuring**.

Meanwhile a top-ranking delegation was engaged in the tortuous process of actually negotiating entry to the EC. It was headed by Foreign Minister Fernando Morán and one of his senior officials, Manuel Marín, who had long been closely involved in the umbrella organisation of Europe's Socialist parties and had built up an extensive network of contacts as a result. The two faced considerable stumbling blocks, especially French concerns about Spanish agricultural produce and the question of fisheries. Nonetheless, all were overcome, and in 1985 Spain's Treaty of Accession (*Tratado de Adhesión*) was signed.

Under it Spain became a fully fledged Community member on 1 January 1986, although there would be a seven-year transition period (*período transitorio*) before some EC tariffs on Spanish products were removed. Along with significant concessions on fisheries and some aspects of agriculture, that effectively formed the country's entry fee. For the particular sectors and groups affected, such as fishermen and dairy farmers, the price was a high one. But their concerns were drowned in the general euphoria, while handing Brussels control over important areas of economic policy – such a controversial issue

> ### *reconversión industrial*
> ....
> ### industrial restructuring
> ---
> Begun tentatively under the **UCD** governments of the transition period (p137), restructuring aimed to shift the basis of Spanish industry from declining sectors to those with better future prospects, and to encourage the creation of companies large enough to compete in international markets, in particular those within the EC. The comprehensive programme that got under way after 1982 was partially successful in meeting these aims in the medium term. More immediately it had a severe negative impact on sectors such as shipbuilding and steel manufacture, with many plant closures and thousands of workers made redundant.

in the UK – caused barely a ripple in Spain. Indeed the option – virtually standard among prospective new members – of holding a referendum on the terms obtained was scarcely discussed. No-one, euphoric or not, had any doubts as to the outcome.

Another issue, intimately bound up with that of EC entry although the connection was rarely spoken aloud, was not dealt with so easily. It related to Spain's foreign policy in general, and the country's attitude to NATO in particular, which was a cause of concern to her prospective EC colleagues, not to mention the Americans. The worries went back to Adolfo Suárez's time as Prime Minister (p135), when Spain had kept its distance from US policy, notably in Latin America, and presented itself as a bridge between the West and the developing world. Such non-alignment (*tercermundismo*) had been abandoned under Suárez's successor, who took Spain into NATO (p145). But the Socialists had clearly implied they would reverse this decision if elected and, although they made no immediate move to do so, Morán showed signs of reverting to the Suárez line in other respects.

In the climate of the time, that put him out of step with his EC counterparts, who impressed on his boss, Prime Minister Felipe González, that a large, strategically important country like Spain could not be allowed to disrupt the Community's solidly pro-American line. Accepting that withdrawal from NATO was no longer an option, González decided that only endorsement in a referendum would allow him to pull off such a brazen U-turn. Voting was scheduled for 12 March 1986, and the PM set about overturning the large anti-NATO majority shown by opinion polls. First, he persuaded his party to ratify the government's change of tack, arguing that its previous objections had been, not to membership as such, but to the undemocratic way in which the decision to join had been taken (p145). Then, the question actually put to voters made remaining in NATO subject to a number of more or less spurious qualifications, including a commitment to negotiate removal of the US military presence in Spain (p108). Finally González himself, fresh from the triumph of taking Spain into 'Europe', campaigned tirelessly for a 'Yes' vote.

The result was in doubt almost to the last. But in the end, the Prime Minister won a substantial majority, and to all intents and purposes Spain was a full NATO member. The decision marked a turning point. Within months Morán was replaced by Francisco Fernández Ordóñez, who, ironically, had served under Suárez as Finance Minister. However, his mild social democratic views included no trace of anti-Americanism, and under his direction Spain's foreign policy was reoriented along unambiguously pro-western lines. Like the whole NATO affair, that caused bitter resentment among sections of González's own party. But for most Spaniards these issues were soon forgotten amidst the spectacular economic growth that followed EC entry.

In part this resulted from the massive financial support Spain immediately began to receive from the EC's Structural Funds. Even more important was the general upswing in the European economy, which encouraged massive private investment in the newly opened up Spanish market. Heavily concentrated in non-traditional sectors, this contributed to a fundamental change in the country's economy. By the end of the decade dependence on heavy industry was significantly down, and Spain was moving rapidly towards the post-industrial structure typical of the most advanced economies. Indeed, from 1986 to 1990 it grew faster than any other developed country, significantly reducing again the gap between it and its fellow EC members in terms of per capita GDP.

Meantime the government had been at pains to ensure Spain a strong position in the complex world of the EC's internal politics. Its awareness of such issues was apparent in the terms of accession, which gave Spain a weight in the Community's institutions rather greater than would have been merited by its population, never mind its economic strength. Thus it was given the privilege – previously confined to France, Germany, Italy and the UK – of nominating two members of the EC's powerful executive, the European Commission. Indeed, no sooner was Spain admitted than Marín was appointed a Commission Vice-President, a considerable prize for a new member.

Marín himself embodied the Spanish government's strategy of placing well-prepared political heavyweights to serve in Community institutions, an approach that displayed a keen grasp of the demands of EC politics – again in sharp contrast to the UK. It was also apparent in the close relationship struck up by the Socialist González with the Christian Democrat Helmut Kohl, leader of the EC's paymaster and most powerful member, Germany, and in his government's ostentatious readiness to support Community initiatives.

Thus in 1989 Spain not only signed up to the Single European Act – a step about which it had little choice – but also opted voluntarily to join the European Monetary System (EMS). Three years later it enthusiastically adopted the Maastricht Treaty, voicing none of the reservations about further political integration heard in Britain (and Denmark). In 1992, too, it became a founder member of the Eurocorps, and three years later it was to be a founder signatory of the Schengen agreement.

Indeed on occasion the government's desire to be 'at the heart of Europe' seemed to outweigh more material interests. For instance, signing the Single Act made Spain's under-developed services sector vulnerable to foreign domination, and EMS entry, while a guard against inflation, also made the peseta a target for currency speculators. Yet neither of these decisions seemed as daring, perhaps even foolhardy, as the government's determination not to miss out on the biggest project of all; EMU.

Meeting the convergence criteria set at Maastricht for EMU entry would always have been tough for a country that, despite recent advances, remained one of the European Union's poorest. But it became doubly so when, almost as soon as the treaty was signed, Spain was hit, late but severely, by the economic downturn that had struck the entire developed world. On 'Black Thursday' (13 May 1993) the Bank of Spain was forced to devalue the peseta so substantially as to break the EMS rules – a move which, if repeated, would debar the country from EMU. That year the country recorded its worst economic figures for half a century, with unemployment rising to over 20 per cent.

Nonetheless, the government persisted in its determination, which had been graphically demonstrated at the 1992 EU Summit in Edinburgh. There the richer EU members had tried to ditch plans for a Cohesion Fund to assist the poorer members with convergence, of which Spain would be the main beneficiary. González reacted in almost Thatcheresque fashion, threatening to torpedo the whole meeting unless the Fund was retained. He got his way.

At home, his strategy was based on the Convergence Plan (*Programa de Convergencia*), a package of measures adopted in 1992 and composed of budget cuts and strict monetary policy. First signs were not hopeful, as Spain's slow recovery from recession – and the forced devaluation – soon undermined the forecasts on which the Plan was based. But the following year it was relaunched by Finance Minister Pedro Solbes who, ignoring protests that it was further aggravating unemployment, kept it remorselessly on course.

Meanwhile, Spain continued to entrench its position in the EU's internal politics. By the mid-1990s, Spaniards were occupying a disproportionate number of leading positions in the Commission's upper administrative levels and in the European Parliament. Manuel Marín went on to be one of the longest serving Commissioners (albeit his EU career finished under a cloud, when he was at the centre of the mismanagement allegations that led to the entire Commission being voted out of office by the Parliament in 1999). Spain's other Commissioners, always figures of standing, were also given relatively important portfolios. Indeed, among the names most frequently touted as the new Commission President due to be chosen in 1994 was that of González. That was testimony both to Spain's move, in under a decade, from outsider to part of the Union's inner core, and to the stature enjoyed by the PM – and his party – in his own country.

The Socialist hegemony

The victory of the Spanish Socialist Party (PSOE) at the 1982 general election opened a new era in Spanish politics. For the next decade, the PSOE completely dominated the domestic scene and, as a result, was enabled to push through a wide range of reforming measures that brought fundamental changes in many fields. Their nature reflected the priorities of the party's leadership, which in some respects clashed with those of its traditional supporters. The result was a division in the Socialist camp which, together with changes in the PSOE's nature, gradually undermined, and finally broke, the party's exclusive grip on power.

The Socialists' victory in the 1982 general election was, and remains, the most sweeping ever achieved at a genuine election in Spain. With over 10 million votes (47% of the total) they won a more than comfortable overall majority in the Congress of Deputies, something always denied to their predecessors in office, the centrists of UCD (p137). It, by contrast, was almost wiped out, and indeed disbanded the following year, leaving a vacuum on the centre-right of Spanish politics that was to persist for the next decade. Similarly, the Communist PCE also suffered severe losses from which it has never fully recovered, despite its attempted reinvention in 1986 as the United Left (IU).

Faced with so little opposition, the PSOE topped the poll at every major electoral contest for the next eleven years. Despite gradually falling support, it retained its overall majority in the Madrid Parliament, first in 1986 and again, in practice, in 1989 (when it won exactly half of the seats). As a result, it was able repeatedly to circumvent various constitutional checks on executive power (p140). In particular the Socialists were able to cram their own appointees into the swelling apparatus of government agencies, among them the state television monopoly, which they exploited as shamelessly as had UCD (pp136, 139). Moreover, from 1983 on they controlled most of Spain's 17 newly autonomous regions (p160), and most of its larger towns and cities to boot. As a result, politics in the 1980s was to a large extent the internal politics of the PSOE.

It was therefore an important consideration that the party which entered government in 1982 was no longer the mass working-class organisation of the 1930s. That PSOE had been reduced to a small hard core under Franco's rule (p122). Since his death, and above all since the party's near-split in 1979, a new PSOE had been built by a new leadership, dominated by the figure of Felipe González. Although still heavily dependent for votes on the poorer sections of society, especially the expanded industrial labour force, most of its impetus and leadership now came from the middle classes that had also grown under Franco, and from lawyers and educationalists in particular.

Understandably, this new PSOE rejected the old view that socialism was purely a working-class affair (p45), albeit some in it were not averse to exploiting class resentments to win and hold support; González's deputy and close collaborator, Alfonso Guerra, was especially adept at this. Generally, though, the Socialists' leaders were relatively unconcerned with traditional socialist goals of equality or redistribution, and barely needed the warning provided by their unhappy results in France to steer clear of such classic left-wing policies as the nationalisation and regulation of industry. Instead, their focus was on efficiency – 'getting Spain to work properly' as González put it – and in the economic sphere at least their policies were little different from the neoliberal ones popular elsewhere at the time. Together with 'Europe', the Socialists' other watchword was 'modernisation'. In that they resembled the Republicans of the early 1930s, and they had in mind a similarly ambitious programme of reforms (p67).

Indeed, barely an aspect of public life was left untouched in the 1980s. The education system was overhauled and extended, especially at higher level, where numerous new universities were established. A national health service was created on the British model. Crucially, in view of the enormous investment these changes involved, the tax system was revised to make it fairer and, above all, more efficient. Extensive military reforms were implemented that, helped along by Spain's entry into NATO (p154) and its growing involvement in international policing duties, at long last steered the army away from its unhealthy interest in politics.

In the economic field, the considerable advances made were inextricably bound up with what was perhaps the Socialists' greatest achievement: entry into the EC (p153). Industry was restructured in preparation for accession (p153); thereafter the vast improvements in infrastructure that took place under their auspices, in particular those of the grossly inadequate transport network, were heavily funded from Brussels. EU membership was also largely responsible for the renewed rise in Spanish living standards (p154), not just absolutely but also relative to the EU average. As a result, individual Spaniards now enjoyed greatly increased ownership of such goods as cars and electrical appliances, and expanded access to vastly improved social infrastructure, especially schools and hospitals.

The picture was not all rosy, however. As elsewhere in the developed world, Spain's growth in the 1980s was heavily concentrated in light industry and, above all, the services, notably the financial sector. Yet, because of the country's relative economic backwardness, this represented a particularly abrupt change for Spain. The effects were traumatic for some, especially the workforce in the older, heavier industries that were decimated by industrial restructuring (p153). It was that same section of the population – the PSOE's own loyalest supporters – that was also the main loser from the González administration's reforms in two further areas, which involved dismantling the haphazard and unsustainable social policy framework erected by the Franco regime.

The first of these fields was the elaborate system of employment regulation (pp101–2), which made it hard for employers to shed labour, and so react quickly to changes in market conditions. Now that they faced more outside competition, that inbuilt delaying process was a distinct disadvantage; moreover, their complaints were backed up by both the EC and the Organisation for European Economic Cooperation (OECD). In 1984 the government bowed to pressure and, as a first step towards making Spain's labour market less rigid (*flexibilización*), legalised fixed-term contracts.

The second aspect of Franco's legacy was social security provision in general, and state pensions in particular. Flushed with the economic success of the 1960s, the dictatorship had introduced a surprisingly generous system of social support. But it was highly bureaucratic, and assumed that boom conditions would last. Franco's successors were left to pick up the tab caused by rising unemployment, not to mention a rapidly ageing population. The problems were aggravated by the effects of industrial restructuring, which left many workers with no alternative but to take early retirement.

concertación social
....
'social concertation'

A product of the **spirit of
compromise** (p139) that marked
the central period of the transition
in 1977/78, 'social concertation'
was the practice of involving
trade unions and employers'
representatives in economic
policy-making. Foreshadowed
by the Moncloa Pacts (p139),
between 1979 and 1984 it
resulted in a series of agreements
covering industrial relations
issues, specifically wages, and
such matters as employment
creation, social security and
general public spending.
Abandoned by the then ruling
Socialists when the last
agreement lapsed in 1987,
'concertation' was revived by the
conservatives elected in 1996
(p183).

In 1985 the government decided something had to be done, and announced that many state pensions would be reduced.

That was too much for the Socialist trade union federation, the UGT (p59), which had expected a PSOE government to help its members, rather than assign them to the scrapheap and cut their benefits. It was also unhappy at the government's obvious intention to abandon the practice of '**social concertation**'. The UGT's respected leader, Nicolás Redondo, heavily criticised the pension cuts and threatened to resign his MP's seat; two years later he did so in protest at proposals for further cutbacks.

By then, the government's U-turn on NATO (pp153–4) had driven another wedge between it and its sister union, which had not forgiven American support for Franco. Nor were matters helped by the links cultivated by some leading figures in the PSOE – notably Finance Minister Miguel Boyer – with the newly rich celebrities (*los beautiful*) whose doings formed the staple diet of Spain's widely read gossip magazines (*prensa del corazón*). The final straw came in 1988, when the government proposed further deregulating the labour market to allow low-wage contracts for young workers. This move provoked the UGT to throw in its lot with the Workers' Commissions (p121), which had been attacking González's government almost from the time it was first elected in 1982.

On 14 December 1988 the two jointly staged a general strike. For such action, with its almost mythical status for the Spanish workers' movement (p46), to be used against a Socialist government seemed hugely significant, especially as the turnout was impressive. González duly withdrew the offending proposals. But he then took advantage of the favourable economic climate (p154) to call an early election for October 1989 – and won it easily, despite the UGT's unprecedented refusal to endorse the PSOE campaign. Having called the unions' bluff, the PM pressed on with social cutbacks and labour market deregulation as part of his Convergence Plan (p155), ignoring two more general strikes in 1992 and 1994 as well as the continuing high level of unemployment (p155).

The truth was that the PSOE's traditional core support now wielded little clout in the party. Economic change meant that the industrial workforce was shrinking. The party's membership and, above all, its office-bearers, had also come to be dominated by men and women who had been elected or appointed to public positions, and whose over-riding concern was to retain them. Formidably organised by Guerra, this PSOE became a highly cohesive electoral machine, fiercely loyal to González, its electoral trump card. However, just like the old party, which had never been renowned for original thinking (pp44–5), it showed few signs of fresh ideas to replace the traditional ones it had largely ditched. A grandiose project fronted by Guerra intended to do so actually produced little of substance, and the party failed totally to catch the mood of individualism increasingly apparent among the young, especially those in larger cities, from the later 1980s on.

Even more immediately damaging was the impression Socialists often gave of contempt for voters, symbolised by the notorious infrequency of González's appearances in Parliament. Unflattering comparisons were drawn between so-called '**Felipe-ism**' and Francoism. One clear parallel was the prevalence of influence-peddling (*tráfico de influencias*) to swell party coffers. Not that the PSOE was the only culprit; all the main national and regional parties were at fault. But the Socialists held so much more power, and so had many more opportunities. Now, unlike in Franco's day, there was a free press, which

> ### *felipismo*
> ### Felipe-ism
>
> Coined in the 1980s, the term *felipismo* was widely used to refer to various aspects of the **PSOE** (p45) under the leadership of Felipe González. The main ones were: abandonment of the class-based attitudes traditionally associated with Spanish Socialism in favour of an emphasis on economic modernisation (p157); strong, centralised control of the party apparatus; and an approach to electioneering centred on González's charisma. More broadly, the term was applied by opponents to unsavoury aspects of government during his time in power, in particular the practice of steamrollering legislation through Parliament with minimal or no consultation, the widespread incidence of influence-peddling and the major scandals of the 1990s (p181).

gleefully revealed a succession of dubious affairs, mostly involving the PSOE. The biggest was that of a bogus consultancy company, Filesa, which had been set up by prominent party figures to launder illicit income.

Some influence-peddling, on the other hand, was purely a matter of personal gain. One such affair (*caso*), uncovered in 1990, involved Juan Guerra, the brother of González's deputy, who was obliged to resign from office the following year. Given the extent to which the PM had relied on Alfonso Guerra – apart from anything else, he had organised every PSOE election campaign since 1982 – his departure was another grievous blow for the party, whose public image had already suffered immense damage (*desgaste*) from the various financial scandals and the first rumblings of the even more serious **GAL affair**.

As a result of these developments, and because at last they faced a real challenge from the Right (p182), the Socialists were widely expected to lose the 1993 general election. However, they still retained two trump cards. One was González himself, who retained enormous popularity and threw himself into the campaign, making a dramatic personal commitment to act against corruption. The other was the lingering memory of dictatorship, which the PSOE ruthlessly exploited in painting its conservative challengers as a bunch of unreconstructed Francoists bent on reversing the changes of the last decade.

The tactic worked, the party receiving massive support from three sources: the old, the poor rural regions of the South, and public sector workers. Its former base, the

---

caso GAL

GAL affair

Uncovered – partially – in the mid-1990s, the GAL affair centred on the Anti-Terrorist Liberation Groups (*Grupos Antiterroristas de Liberación*), who a decade earlier had claimed responsibility for the killing and kidnapping of a number of Basques, in both Spain and France. Although always suspected to be part of a government-controlled 'dirty war' against **ETA** (p123), the groups were long shrouded in mystery, despite the conviction of two relatively junior police agents in 1988 for involvement in their activities. In 1995, however, the chain of command was traced up to cabinet level, and three years later former Interior Minister José Barrionuevo was jailed for his part in the GAL's activities.

---

industrial workforce, was now far less significant, having been reduced to a shrunken, resentful remnant since 1982. For the group that had swung decisively to the party then, that made up by younger urban voters, 'socialism' had mostly become a dirty word. In consequence, although the Socialists eventually topped the poll, they fell well short of an overall majority. To remain in office they would need support. Given that their increasingly centrist policies had ruled out an alliance with the Communist-led IU, that could come only from what was in any case now established as the third largest block in Parliament: a veritable host of regionalist parties.

Regionalists, new and old

The strength of regionalism was rather ironic, given that the 1978 Constitution was supposed to defuse demands for regional self-government (pp141–2). In fact, though, almost the opposite had occurred, despite – or because of – the devolution process it set in motion. Firstly, devolution itself gave rise to new problems, and to new pressures in areas where regionalism had previously been non-existent or dormant. And, secondly, in attempting to respond to these the government further aggravated the tensions which had never fully disappeared in the Basque Country and Catalonia.

By the time of the 1982 election it was clear that, whatever the framers of the 1978 Constitution may have intended, devolution was to apply to the whole country, not just a few chosen regions (p142). Within another year, all mainland Spain, plus the Balearic and Canary Islands, had been divided up into 17 regions, each with its own parliament and government, and with its Statute of Autonomy defining the extent of its self-government powers. In fact, though, the devolution process (*proceso autonómico*) was only beginning, not least because it was simply impossible for all the devolved powers to be transferred instantly to newly created bodies. Furthermore, the handover of individual areas of responsibility to individual regions (*transferencias*) often became the subject of lengthy wrangling with the central government; indeed, a number of these disputes were still unsettled at the end of the century.

Long before that it had become apparent that the structure which had been established was far from perfect. Certainly, it had brought a long overdue decentralisation of administration, as well as creating alternative powerbases to counterbalance the rather over-mighty central government. However, the structure was also far too complex. Despite the 1981 attempt to stop any more regions taking the 'fast track' to more extensive autonomy (p142), a further three – the Canaries, Navarre and Valencia –

did so. Moreover, as the powers granted to the seven 'fast track' regions were all different, there were no fewer than eight separate models of regional self-government in operation. Understandably, this situation gave rise to considerable administrative problems, prompting the central government to seek ways of streamlining the system.

At the same time, devolution had important effects in the regions themselves. In those that successfully campaigned for 'fast-track' status, feelings of regional identity received a considerable boost. There and elsewhere the new institutions, with the associated symbolism of flags, anthems and so on, served to rekindle the strong feelings of local loyalty virtually omnipresent in Spain but which, since the demise of federal Republicanism (pp23–4), had lacked a political focus.

The process was assisted by the fact that local and regionally based newspapers have always been much more widely read than the Madrid-based press, and later by the blossoming of regional broadcasting. Above all regular regional elections, at which parties inevitably addressed the 'people of Cantabria', or wherever, fostered the notion that those people formed a distinctive group with distinctive, shared interests. By the early 1990s there was barely a region without a party – or parties – whose *raison d'être* was to defend them.

Interestingly, the growth of these new regionalist movements (*nuevos regionalismos*) was not primarily a function of regions' distinctiveness. Thus Galicia, arguably Spain's least typical region in cultural terms, was one of the few in which regionalism made little or no immediate impact. In Andalusia, where it had some tradition, it was soon smothered by the Socialists, who – being in control of central government – could pour public money into a region where they were already well-established (and from where several party bigwigs, Prime Minister González included, originally came).

On the other hand, the persistent weakness of the Spanish right during the 1980s (p156) left an opening for locally based conservative groupings to become important players in several regions where regionalism had little pedigree, notably Navarre, Valencia and Aragon. In the last of these, they could also exploit resentment at the denial of 'fast track' status despite Aragon's strong historical claims to be distinctive (p2). Indeed, once the five-year bar on amending the various regional Statutes of Autonomy expired in 1988 (p142), it was Aragonese regionalists that spearheaded demands from various regions for a devolution review.

Such a move would mean tinkering with the delicate compromises worked out in the first years of democracy, and the Socialists were understandably reluctant to make it without cross-party support. However, the conservative opposition, traditionally suspicious of devolution in any form, was now keen to neutralise what had become a dangerous source of competition. It accordingly agreed to support a package of measures to standardise the system somewhat, finally approved in 1994. As well as extending devolution to Ceuta and Melilla (p58), this gave all regions the right to virtually all the powers previously reserved to the 'fast track' ones. These latter would now be distinguished solely by their control over health services and policing, and by the special tax arrangements applying to Navarre and, most importantly, to the Basque Country (p28).

Herri Batasuna (HB)

People's Unity

Established in 1978 as the political wing of **ETA**'s then 'military' branch (p123), HB's programme was based on the so-called 'KAS alternative'. This demanded independence for an extended Basque Country including Navarre and an area in south-west France (*Euskal Herría*). HB opposed the **1978 Constitution** (p140) and refused to recognise the validity of the Basque autonomy granted under it; its representatives long boycotted both the Spanish and Basque Parliaments. In 1997 HB formed a new front organisation known as Alliance for the Basque People (*Euskal Herritarok* [EH]); four years later it was wound up and re-founded under the name of Unity (*Batasuna*). This new party was banned by the Spanish authorities the following year. Subsequently, ETA's supporters continued operating under a variety of labels, but none of these organisations achieved significant electoral support.
See also: **Pacto de Lizarra** (p174)

There, early and extensive devolution had failed to satisfy regionalists; indeed, it had not even put an end to the 'armed struggle' waged by the most extreme of their factions, ETA (p123). Hopes did rise on that front in September 1982, when ETA's 'politico-military' branch agreed to disband in a deal brokered by Basque Left (*Euskadiko Ezkerra* [EE]), originally the so-called poli-milis' political wing but now an outspoken opponent of violence. However, few activists took up the offer of 'reinsertion' into normal society in return for laying down their arms; most defected to the 'military' branch to form a reunited ETA as committed as ever to violence.

Meanwhile, on the political front, both EE and **People's Unity** were protesting noisily against the 1981 legislation designed to curb regions' real powers (p145), a campaign in which they were joined by the largest regionalist force, the Basque Nationalist Party, or PNV (p43). The effect was to intensify the sense of Basque–Spanish confrontation which the PNV had already been fomenting from its position in regional government (p143) – and which was unfortunately also fed, for their own reasons, by the local Socialists. This strategy brought the PNV large gains at the 1984 regional election, but at the cost of provoking severe tensions within Basque society, and within the party itself. The internal dispute had a number of causes, but at the root of them all was the fact that the PNV's archaic ideas (p43), to which many members clung ferociously, were out-of-tune with contemporary reality.

The outcome was a stand-off between the party's traditionalist boss Xabier Arzalluz and the head of the new regional executive (*lehendakari*), Carlos Garaikoetxea, who resigned in 1985. The following year he set up a breakaway party, Basque Solidarity (*Eusko Alkartasuna* [EA]), and forced an early regional election. Held in November 1986, it complicated matters still further. The PNV suffered heavy losses, mainly to EA, and, while the combined nationalist vote rose to a new high of over 60%, it was now so fragmented that no single party was anywhere near to winning a parliamentary majority. On top of the region's already massive problems – ETA's relentless terror; the social and economic effects of restructuring (p153) on its heavy industry – this political crisis threatened to render it ungovernable.

In the event, it had the opposite effect. Against all expectations a coalition government was formed in early 1987 by the PNV and the PSOE's Basque section, whose relations had previously been deteriorating into bitter animosity. Now, united by a common desire for stability and a hold on power, they were forced to patch up their differences, at least in public, thus removing one cause of tension in the region. Over the next year the main one was also mitigated, though for very different reasons.

Initially the 1986 crisis had prompted ETA to step up its attacks, particularly those on the new regional police force, the *Ertzaintza*, whose ranks were filled mainly with nationalist sympathisers. Other victims now included ETA's own former activists who had opted for 'reinsertion', and also members of the public; in June 1987, a bomb in a Barcelona hypermarket killed 15 people. These tactics led even most nationalist voters, many of whom had retained a certain sympathy with ETA because of its anti-Francoist origins (p123), to turn sharply against it and its political backers.

In January 1988 all parties in the regional parliament, with the exception of HB, signed an agreement that condemned all violence, irrespective of its alleged motives. This 'Ajuria Enea Pact' – in the negotiation of which EE played a key role – effectively isolated ETA and its supporters, and greatly normalised relations among the other parties. Above all, by forcing the PNV to take a clear stand against violence (p143), it obliged the region's key political force to stop flirting with HB, which continued to command the support of a sixth of Basque voters. Toning down its demands for increased self-government, the PNV began to concentrate on using those powers already devolved to address the region's economic problems, with no little success. Partly as a result, the Basque Country was able to share in the economic upturn after 1986 (p150), a development that helped to ease tension further.

The PNV's new line also brought benefits for the party itself; buoyed by the growing popularity of Garaikoetxea's successor as regional First Minister, the calm and moderate José Antonio Ardanza, it regained much of its lost support at the next regional election in 1990. By then developments in eastern Europe, in particular the Baltic states' successful bid for independence, were rekindling demands for Basques to be given the same status. Succumbing to temptation, the PNV formed an all-nationalist government with EA and EE. However, mindful that its supporters in the Basque business community wanted stability above all else, it soon backtracked and renewed its Socialist alliance. With 1992 seeing major police successes against ETA on both sides of the Pyrenees, including the capture of the group's leadership at Bidart in the French Basque Country, it seemed that the 'Basque problem' might truly be on the way to solution.

In Catalonia, meanwhile, events were taking a less dramatic, but in some ways equally problematic course. That was something of a surprise. Catalan devolution had been a relatively painless process, backed by the local Socialists and Communists as well as by regionalists. These were by tradition moderate in their demands and approach; violent extremism was limited to a tiny grouplet called Free Homeland (*Terra Lliure*). Certainly the Catalan Republican Left (p70) criticised devolution as inadequate, but it was completely overshadowed by the newly emerged **Convergence and Union**, which initially took a more conciliatory line.

Yet, even during its first term in regional government, the CiU began to show signs of a more confrontational style (p143). After it won an overall majority at the second

---

Convergència i Unió (CiU)

Convergence and Union

Formed in 1977 by the merger of Catalan Democratic Convergence (CDC) with the older Catalan Democratic Union (UDC), the CiU quickly came to dominate internal Catalan politics, running the regional government alone from its creation in 1980. The CiU's success was closely associated with its leader, the regional first minister Jordi Pujol (p123), and its distinctively assertive brand of centre-right regionalism is known as 'Pujolism'. Between 1993 and 2000 the CiU propped up minority central governments of both Left and Right (pp172–3), exercising considerable influence as a result. However, particularly its alliance with the conservative **People's Party** (p182) cost the CiU support and in 2003, when Pujol stepped down after an astonishing 23 years in office, it was ousted from the regional government (p176).

---

regional election in 1984 this became so marked that a new term was coined to describe it: Pujolism, after party leader and regional First Minister Jordi Pujol (p123). This new brand of regionalism had three main features, the first being an aggressively pro-Catalan language policy, which aroused some anxieties among monoglot Castilian speakers in the region. The second was a harder line on the self-government issue; on several occasions, notably following Baltic independence, Pujol speculated publicly about Catalonia taking the same option, albeit he always followed up with assurances of loyalty to Spain. Finally, Pujolism involved identifying the CiU and its leader as the region's sole representatives, and implying – or even stating – that its opponents were not true Catalans.

The main object of these attacks was the CiU's main rival, the Catalan Socialist Party (PSC), which at general elections regularly topped the Catalan poll. And that even though the PSC, which enjoys a uniquely autonomous status within the Spanish Socialist Party, not only supported devolution but even defied its own Madrid leadership by proposing that Spain should be turned into a federation – the traditional stance of moderate Catalan regionalism (p42)! Yet routinely the CiU, and Pujol in particular, portrayed the PSC as the agent of a central government whose policies it claimed – equally routinely – were damaging Catalonia. Interestingly, though, he was more measured in his criticism of the Socialists' Madrid leadership. One thing that Pujolism undoubtedly shared with traditional Catalan regionalism was awareness that the region's interests could be furthered by exercising influence in Madrid, the opportunities for which were greatly expanded by the results of the 1993 general election (pp159–60).

Summary of main points

Into Europe

- Although there had for some time been overwhelming support in Spain for joining the EC, the Socialist government elected in 1982 was decisive in preparing the country for membership and in negotiating its terms. One unspoken condition of joining was that Spain would remain a member of NATO.

- The Socialists also showed themselves adept at playing internal EC politics in generally supporting Community initiatives, even where the material benefits appeared dubious (as with EMU). As a result, they ensured an important role in Community institutions for Spain and its representatives.
- Initially, EC membership gave a massive boost to the Spanish economy. In the early 1990s, the effects of world recession were aggravated by efforts to meet the criteria for EMU, but these problems were soon overcome.

Socialist hegemony

- Following its crushing victory in the 1982 general election, the PSOE dominated Spanish politics at all levels for a decade.
- During that time it carried through a sweeping program of reforms that, together with entry into the EC, brought huge advances in Spain's economic situation and public services. However, the party's traditional supporters benefited relatively little, and were actually harmed by a number of measures.
- By 1982 the PSOE was less concerned with improving conditions for workers than with efficiency of the economy as a whole. In office, the party's top priority effectively became to retain power.
- From 1989 on, the Socialists were involved in a growing number of financial scandals and other affairs. Even so, they won the 1993 election, but without an overall majority.

Regionalists, new and old

- By late 1983, devolution had been extended to the whole of Spain. The new arrangements were administratively complex, and also encouraged the development of new regionalist movements in several regions. As a result, a further round of devolution was initiated.
- In the Basque Country, tension and violence continued, and even increased. In 1986 the region's largest party, the PNV, suffered a crisis, the effects of which forced it to adopt a less confrontational approach. Additionally, ETA came under increasing pressure, and in 1992 seemed on the verge of defeat.
- In Catalonia, a new party, the CiU, emerged as the main representative of regionalism, and took control of the regional government. It developed a new, more assertive style of regionalism that caused considerable friction, especially within the region.

Exhibit 10.1: Felipe González assesses Spain's situation (1987)

Extracts from a press interview

Estamos a una década de las primeras elecciones democráticas; del comienzo de los debates sobre la Constitución; de los Pactos de la Moncloa. Buena ocasión para describir el cuadro general de la situación de España.

Desde hacía más de un siglo, vivíamos en un claro aislamiento político y cultural, con miedo o rechazo a todo lo que venía de fuera, sin asimilar la pérdida del imperio colonial. España estaba enquistada en sus propias fronteras y se cocía en su propia salsa. Este aislamiento produjo períodos autoritarios, le dio una fuerza relativa mayor a las posiciones políticas de los extremos y se la quitó a las más templadas, la mayoría más amplia de nuestra sociedad. Con el aislamiento político se correspondía, también, un sistema económico cerrado, hiperproteccionista, y perdimos el tren de la primera y la segunda revolución industrial.

La década democrática ha producido una apertura al mundo sin precedentes, y un cambio sustancial en las reglas de juego del funcionamiento socioeconómico. Se ha roto el aislamiento político y nos integramos en espacios más amplios – Europa y Occidente, – y se pasa de un sistema hiperproteccionista a una eliminación de barreras arancelarias y de controles burocráticos al desarrollo de las actividades económicas, tratando de ganar competitividad interna y externa. [...]

El cambio en las reglas de juego del funcionamiento de la economía se deriva, primero, de un esfuerzo interior y, segundo, de nuestra incorporación a Europa. Empieza a notarse en España la entrada de aire fresco, de competencia, de libertad de movimiento en la economía. [...] Tenemos algunas amenazas, naturalmente; no podemos descuidar la vigilancia sobre la inflación, ni perder de vista que una balanza comercial negativa no puede sostenerse indefinidamente. Pero podemos tener la razonable esperanza de que al final de la década, España, además de un salto considerable en la competitividad y modernización del aparato productivo, siga por esa senda de crecimiento. [...]

It is now ten years since the first democratic elections; since the start of discussion about the Constitution; since the Moncloa Pacts. A good time, therefore, to review Spain's situation in general terms.

At that time we had been living for more than a century in a state of patent political and cultural isolation, fearing and rejecting anything that came from outside, having failed to come to terms with the loss of our colonies. Spain was imprisoned within its own borders; it was stewing in its own juice. Isolation resulted in periods of autocratic government; it exaggerated the importance of the political extremes while reducing that of the moderates who make up the great majority of Spanish society. Moreover, political isolation went hand in hand with a closed economy, protectionist in the extreme, which meant that we missed out on both the first and the second industrial revolutions.

These ten years of democracy have brought an unprecedented opening up to the outside world, and a substantial change in the way our country functions, both socially and economically. Now we are no longer isolated politically, and we are integrating ourselves into larger units – Europe, the western world as a whole – and we have gone from extreme protectionism to the removal of tariff barriers and of bureaucratic controls over the development of economic activity, in an attempt to become more competitive, both at home and abroad. […]

The change in the way our economy works is the result, first, of our own efforts and, second, of our entry into Europe. The Spanish economy is starting to feel the effects of some fresh air, of competition, of freedom of movement. […] Of course, we face some dangers: we must keep a close eye on inflation; we must never lose sight of the fact that a negative trade balance cannot be maintained indefinitely. But we can reasonably expect that, by the end of the decade, Spain will not only have greatly modernised its industry and improved its competitiveness but also be continuing to experience growth.

Source: El País (8 November 1987).

Exhibit 10.2: ETA's violence (1993)

Extracts from a book written by a former ETA activist who later became leader of Basque Left (EE), and who was one of the architects of the anti-ETA 'Ajuria Enea Pact' of 1988

ETA […] ha desempeñado, desempeña y posiblemente siga desempeñando el papel de símbolo. Su entorno social proyesta hacia él sus propias impotencias, sus miedos o incluso la mala conciencia por su falta de compromiso o de acción. Su existencia y su veneración redimen a quienes la apoyan. Se ha ido constituyendo en una referencia mesiánica de identificación colectiva. […]

Poco a poco ETA se convierte en el principio y el fin de toda una serie de referencias simbólicas en las que la violencia se interna y termina cosificando. Se representa – simboliza – la voluntad de un colectivo – Euskal Herría en su doble acepción social y territorial –; se totaliza su representación – MLNV – simbolizándola; se simboliza el objetivo – independencia y socialismo – en la Alternativa KAS, que es lo genuino aunque no habla ni de independencia ni de socialismo. ETA es el soporte y el garante de todo ese universo simbólico, y todo lo que de una manera u otra puede servir a la violencia termina formando parte de su imaginario [sic]. […]

Incluso el propio sentido de la «estrategia del contrapoder» que se practica, su gran logro, no se encuentra en el hecho de haber abierto perspectiva alguna de alternativa a la democracia realmente existente y al proceso estatutario. Su gran logro ha consistido en la construcción de toda una trama que ha permitido a una parte nada insignificante de ciudadanos vascos, vivir su relación con la realidad política y social, con la cultura, participar de una visión histórica desarrollada al margen de los restantes vascos, es decir, al margen de la mayoría. Ésa ha sido la gran victoria, la gran construcción de la violencia, en la que su fuerza simbólica ha constituido el elemento de mayor cohesión.

ETA's role [...] has been, is and may continue to be, that of a symbol. Those who form part of its milieu project onto ETA their own feelings of impotence, of fear and even of guilt at their own failure to make a commitment or take action. Its supporters are redeemed by its existence and their own veneration for it. Gradually it has become the focus of a messianic form of collective identification. [...]

Little by little, ETA has come to incorporate a whole range of symbolic references through which its violence is accepted and, eventually, reproduced. It stands for, or symbolises, the collective will of the 'Basque people', or the 'Basque Country', a will it claims to represent exclusively, and so to symbolise, through the Basque National Liberation Movement,[1] and whose aims – independence and socialism – it symbolises in the 'KAS alternative', which is presented as the only legitimate goal even though it mentions neither of these two concepts. ETA is the basis and the guarantor of this entire symbolic universe, and everything that in one way or another can be of service to its strategy of violence ends up forming part of its imagery. [...]

ETA's great success has been its strategy of creating a so-called 'anti-authority', but not because that has opened up the least prospect of an alternative to Spain's existing democratic system or to devolution as it has developed under the Statute of Autonomy. What it has succeeded in doing is to construct an entire framework within which a not inconsiderable number of Basques can live out their social, political and cultural relations on the basis of an interpretation of history that has been developed in isolation from their fellows, that is, from the majority of Basques. That has been the great triumph of ETA's violence, its major construct, which is held together above all by ETA's power as a symbol.

[1] The name used by ETA to describe the network of its related organisations and supporters.

Source: Aulestia, K. (1993) *Días de viento sur: La violencia en Euskadi.* Barcelona: Antártida/Empúries.

Topics
FOR DISCUSSION

■ Judging by Exhibit 10.1, what does González appear to regard as the main achievements of his time in power up to 1987? To what extent do they correspond to the hopes of the Spaniards who voted for his party in 1982?

■ He implicitly criticises aspects of Spanish political behaviour in the past (*posiciones políticas de los extremos*). Who could reasonably be seen as the object of such criticism?

■ Exhibit 10.2 talks about the symbolism of violence. Can you think of any such symbols exploited by ETA (or other terrorist groups)? Why do you think their effect was so powerful in the Basque Country?

■ How would you rate Felipe González's contribution to Spain?

■ Did Spain go the right way about tackling the issues posed by regionalism between 1982 and 1993? Could it have taken any other approach?

CHAPTER 11

Between regionalism and globalisation (1993–2004)

The election victories of Bill Clinton (1992) and Tony Blair (1997) ended the supremacy of the 'New Right'. Yet both leaders retained an over-riding belief in free markets strongly at variance with most mainstream thinking in the EU, especially France and Germany. Their approach appeared to be vindicated, the US in particular growing considerably faster than continental Europe. The European Commission therefore tried to promote liberalisation as best it could, in parallel with its efforts to keep the process of Monetary Union on track through the Stability and Growth Pact setting limits to budget deficits within 'Euroland'. Politically, the EU's most pressing need was for an institutional structure capable of accommodating enlargement to eastern Europe; one was agreed at Nice in 2000, but it was an uneasy compromise. The following year Al-Qaida's terrorist onslaught further accentuated Europe's problems, turning the world economic downturn into a recession from which the continent was much slower to recover than the US. Inside the EU opinions were sharply divided on how to react; in the end, France and Germany effectively opted out of the Stability Pact. Further divisions were introduced by the British-backed US invasion of Iraq in 2003 and by proposals for a Union 'Constitution' which would change some of the arrangements made at Nice.

The period from 1993 to 2004 saw Spain's assimilation into the family of developed western countries virtually completed. Economically, strong growth continued to narrow the wealth gap with its neighbours. Politically, a second transfer of power, this time from Left to Right, was accomplished in the best democratic manner. Internationally, too, the country began to play a role more consonant with her size and importance. Yet, at the same time, the very notion of Spain as a single and autonomous entity was called into question. On the one hand, Basque and Catalan regionalists became the single most important factor in Spanish politics as a whole, and their appetite for self-government showed no signs of slackening. On the other, events within Spain were increasingly inter-linked with those abroad, in Europe and beyond. The connection became indisputable with the dramatic events of March 2004, which brought to an abrupt end the ascendancy established in the previous eight years by the conservative People's Party.

The regionalist spiral

The 1993 general election ushered in a period during which Spanish politics was influenced to an unprecedented degree by regionalists and their concerns. Indeed, for the next seven years successive central governments were significantly constrained by their reliance on the Catalan CiU. The impact of Basque regionalism was less direct, but even greater. For, far from stabilising as had seemed possible in the early 1990s, the situation in the Basque Country became steadily tenser, as the continuing scourge of ETA violence was aggravated by an escalating confrontation between the central authorities and the increasingly radicalised Basque Nationalist Party (PNV).

Following its narrow win in the 1993 general election (pp159–60), the Socialist Party (PSOE) turned for the support it needed to form a stable government to the CiU (p164). Its leader Jordi Pujol drove a hard bargain, declining to enter a formal coalition, as Catalans had on occasion done in the past (pp49–50). Instead he offered Prime Minister Felipe González only parliamentary support – and even that only on certain specific issues. In effect, he held the government's fate in his hands at minimal risk to himself. Not for nothing did he soon come to be widely regarded as Spain's most powerful politician.

In return for propping the government up, Pujol demanded – and obtained – a considerable price. Thus, he stiffened the government's resolve to meet the criteria for the European Monetary Union (EMU), a high priority for his backers among the Catalan business community, in the face of growing unrest among PSOE supporters at the consequences of this course (p181). Conversely, in fields where his Catalan government wished to follow different policies from those favoured in Madrid, notably in allowing wide scope for private suppliers of health and education services, he simply went his own way. Most importantly, he insisted on changes to the system of regional funding to allow regional governments to retain 15 per cent of income tax collected within their territories, a move the CiU believed would benefit Catalonia as one of Spain's richest regions.

Most outside observers agreed, and the measure, passed in 1994, was bitterly contested by the poorer regions. Since these were mostly run by the PSOE, the change did nothing to help relations between the two parties, although those between Pujol himself and Spanish Prime Minister Felipe González developed surprisingly well. Nonetheless, when the 1995 regional election brought a small but salutary setback for the CiU, he had no compunction in breaking his ties to a government and party whose reputation was in free fall (p181). He withdrew his backing for González, effectively forcing the PM to call an early election for March 1996, the outcome of which again made Pujol's backing essential for a stable government to be formed (p183).

This time it was the conservative People's Party (PP), now the largest party, who solicited his favours. On paper an agreement with it seemed unlikely. On the one hand, the PP (p182) was by tradition unsympathetic to regionalism in general, and Catalan demands in particular. On the other, the conservatives were a direct competitor for the CiU's core middle-class support, into which they had already begun to make inroads. Yet that was precisely because their philosophy was close to Pujol's in a number of respects. Crucially, the PP was so desperate to govern that it was prepared to pay an even higher price for his backing than the PSOE had in 1993. Thus, regions' share of income tax was now doubled, to 30 per cent – even though the conservatives had previously opposed any such 'fiscal co-responsibility'! Moreover, the PP's leaders in Catalonia were obliged by party bosses in Madrid to cease their attacks on Pujol's controversial language policies (p164).

In 1999, however, the tables were turned. At that year's regional election the CiU was outpolled by an alliance of the Catalan Socialists (p164) with other left-wing forces. Only the vagaries of the region's electoral system allowed it to remain the largest parliamentary party. To remain first minister, Pujol in turn was obliged to rely on the local PP for support, and so lost much of his leverage over the conservative government in Madrid. The following year that was finally neutralised by the PP's convincing general election victory (p183). Pujol's seven-year reign as arbiter of Spain's fate was over.

That same period had witnessed a slowdown in the rise of new regionalist movements (p161), and to some extent its reversal. Some of the parties which had emerged in the 1980s transpired to be merely vehicles for particular individuals; others were snuffed out by the PP's success in filling the vacuum on the political Right. On the other hand, the PSOE's decline was accompanied in some regions by the growth of local left-wing parties, notably the Galician National Alliance (BNG), which in 1997 became the region's second electoral force. Otherwise, before and after 2000, regionalists remained strong where there were genuinely regional issues to exploit: for instance, in the Canaries, by virtual geographical imperative, and in Aragon, which along with Catalonia would be the main loser from government plans to divert water from the Ebro to the market gardens of Valencia and Murcia. In none of these cases, though, were they so strong or so radical as to present a challenge to the constitutional order.

In the Basque Country they did exactly that. There, where regionalism shaded into nationalism, the optimism of the early 1990s (p163) soon dissolved, for various reasons. One, the impact of which is hard to judge but certainly significant, was the GAL affair (p160), which poisoned relations between the two parties whose alliance had been crucial to the stabilisation of Basque politics: the PSOE and the nationalist PNV (pp162–3). Another was a renewed upsurge in ETA terrorism, much of it directed now, not at the military, but at representatives of the Spanish parties.

Particularly targeted was the PP, whose leader was nearly assassinated by a car bomb attack in 1994. Three years later a young conservative councillor in the town of Ermua, Miguel Angel Blanco, was the victim of a particularly callous killing. It sparked off an unprecedented wave of popular anger against ETA that momentarily transcended the divisions among all other political forces. But such unity did not last.

Instead, events were shaped by a burgeoning confrontation between the PP and the PNV, which as recently as 1996 had appeared close to an alliance. Then the main nationalist force – notoriously pragmatic, and itself conservative in many of its views – had voted for the new government's investiture in return for various concessions, notably a favourable deal on the Basque Country's contribution to central revenues for the next four years (p28). Thereafter, though, relations rapidly deteriorated, partly because of the government's intransigence (p184) and partly because the PNV felt itself under increasing pressure. Thus it believed – not without justification – that the Basque Country's special constitutional status as a 'historic nationality' (p142) was under threat from the PP's plans to extend devolution equally to the country as a whole (p184). It was concerned, too, at the progressive erosion of total nationalist support, and of its own vote by the PP. Less forgivably, it may have feared that the security forces' latest offensive against ETA would effectively eliminate one of its best bargaining counters.

The PNV was united in believing that these dangers could only be averted by securing greater self-government than that set out in the existing Statute of Autonomy, but divided on how that was best achieved. The party's moderate wing wanted to build a broad consensus for change, including the Spanish parties as well as non-violent nationalists. In 1998 the regional First Minister, José Antonio Ardanza (p163), floated proposals intended to do that. The 'Ardanza Plan' accepted that the 'Basque problem' was essentially a dispute among Basques themselves – rather than between the Basque Country and Spain – that could only be solved once violence ended. But it also asserted that the solution was a matter for Basques alone; whatever they agreed on, up to and including independence, must be accepted by Madrid. That the central government would not – arguably could not – accept. The Plan's rejection ended Ardanza's career, as well as the cross-party Ajuria Enea Pact (p163).

It also handed the initiative inside the PNV to the radicals headed by party boss Xabier Arzalluz, who saw salvation not in consensus but in increased pressure. In their view that could be exerted only by reunifying the nationalist movement as a whole, which in the 1980s had fragmented into four different parties (p162). Since then, however, the only one of the four opposed to reunification in principle, EE, had effectively disappeared, having merged in 1993 with the PSOE's Basque section (now known as PSE-EE). A second, EA, had been losing votes steadily for a decade, and was already little more than a junior partner to the PNV. That left only ETA's political wing HB, which in 1997 was thrown into disarray by the arrest of its entire leadership for allowing ETA activists to appear in one of its election broadcasts (a decision revoked two years later by the Supreme Court).

Seeing their chance, the PNV's radicals opened secret negotiations with HB. The following year these resulted in the **Lizarra Pact**, which effectively asserted the notion

---

Pacto de Lizarra

Lizarra Pact

Signed on 12 September 1998 in the Navarrese town of Estella (Basque: *Lizarra*), the Pact was effectively a joint declaration by the main Basque nationalist parties – the **PNV** (p43), Herri Batasuna (**HB**) (p162) and EA (p162) – and a number of other organisations. Inspired by the Good Friday agreement in Northern Ireland, it ostensibly set out a framework for peace negotiations in the Basque region, involving basically: an unconditional ETA ceasefire, openness of the talks (i.e. no participants or subjects to be excluded), and recognition of Basques', right to 'self-determination'. However, its critics argued that the Pact implicitly reiterated positions long held by **ETA** (p123): for instance, it viewed the conflict as one between Basques and Spain rather than amongst Basques; it referred to an enlarged Basque Country as conceived by HB; and it ignored the existing, democratically legitimated Statute of Autonomy (p143). This interpretation was given added weight when ETA subsequently revealed the existence of a parallel, secret agreement between it and the PNV to work for the Statute's overthrow.

See also: **Plan Ibarretxe** (p175)

that sovereignty, the right to decide their region's future, lay exclusively with Basques (*soberantismo*). Almost immediately ETA announced a ceasefire. Although the Pact was bitterly criticised by the Spanish government and parties, in the Basque Country it unleashed a mood of near euphoria, which the PNV attempted to exploit by calling an early regional election. Its main effect was to strengthen ETA's supporters, now known as EH (p162), whose support was essential to the minority government formed by the PNV and EA under a new first minister, Juan José Ibarretxe.

Its fate hung on progress towards a permanent end to violence. But, whether because of the PP's intransigence (p184), as many nationalists alleged, or because the truce was a fraud all along, as the government claimed, that never came. In late 1999 ETA declared the ceasefire over. Early the following year it resumed killing, critical journalists now joining political opponents among its victims, and the familiar atmosphere of fear and distrust returned to the small towns and rural areas where the extremists were strongest.

Even then the PNV refused to back down; although it repudiated its alliance with EH, it stuck to the position set out in their joint Pact. Equally, the central government refused to contemplate any change to the existing constitutional framework, and routinely bracketed the PNV and ETA together as a threat to it. The PP's line was slavishly taken up by the Basque Socialists – and by much of the Madrid-based media – so that the regional election Ibarretxe was forced to call in 2001 became a duel between nationalists and self-styled 'constitutionalists'.

Even though the PP made further gains, overall the results were a setback for it. For the PNV and EA, now standing together, did even better and were able to form a more stable – but still minority – government with the small, but symbolically important addition of United Left. EH's vote having halved, hopes of a compromise again rose, only to be dashed again.

Possibly over-confident after its win, possibly provoked by the PP's latest attempt to round off the devolution process once and for all (p184), the First Minister now launched his own proposals. The '**Ibarretxe Plan**' was considerably more radical than Ardanza's, being effectively a timetable for independence in stages. Detailed proposals for the first of these, a 'Free Association' agreement between Spain and the region, were worked out over the next two years and passed by the Basque Parliament with the votes of the governing coalition alone. Ibarretxe then announced his intention to submit the agree-

Plan Ibarretxe
Ibarretxe Plan

First announced by the Basque First Minister Juan José Ibarretxe in 2001, the 'Plan' set out a blueprint by which an extended Basque Country as conceived by **HB** (p162) could achieve independence once a definitive ETA ceasefire was in place. The first step would be to replace the existing region's Statute of Autonomy (p143) by a much looser 'Free Association' agreement with Spain (a model taken from Quebec nationalists), including provision for a binding referendum to be held in the region on its implementation. As that indicates, the Plan's focus was almost exclusively on the supposed conflict between the Basque Country and Spain; the internal dimension of conflict – i.e. the divisions among Basques themselves was virtually ignored.

ment to a referendum in the region, a move that could only heighten tension and divisions. In a situation where ETA continued to kill in the name of Basque independence, even some nationalists, while sympathising with Ibarretxe's aims, disagreed with his initiative.

Nor was the reaction of the Madrid government designed to cool the situation. It broke off all relations with its Basque counterpart and with the PNV as a party, took Ibarretxe's proposals to the Constitutional Court, and passed a law that threatened him with imprisonment should he proceed with his referendum. Meanwhile, it focused its efforts on destroying ETA's social and political base. In 2002 a new Political Parties Act (*Ley de Partidos Políticos*) was passed, with Socialist backing, which empowered the Spanish Parliament to ban formations linked to terrorism. The measure was clearly directed against Unity (*Batasuna*), the latest manifestation of HB, which was duly outlawed later the same year.

This move enjoyed some success; attendance at demonstrations linked to ETA, and the level of street violence incited by it (*kale borroka*), both fell. Yet the ban's democratic validity, was opposed by most Basques, nationalist or not, a point the PNV exploited to block its extension to the Basque Parliament. Meanwhile, though the detention of successive ETA leaderships kept the level of violence low, there were worrying signs that, increasingly desperate, the organisation was planning mass attacks on civilians outside the Basque Country. Indeed, as the general election due in 2004 approached, the Basque conflict in its various dimensions dominated the political scene, not just in the region but throughout Spain.

Meanwhile, some of the same tensions had surfaced in Catalonia, albeit there without any hint of violence. Some were caused by the CiU (p164) which, like the PNV, feared for its region's privileged status. Allied with the PP, it also perceived a need to distance itself from the conservatives' persistently negative attitude and tone towards Catalan – and other – regionalist aspirations (p184). In 1998 it therefore joined the PNV (and the Galician BNG) in the Barcelona Declaration, which asserted the 'sovereignty' of the three 'historic nationalities'. Subsequently Pujol back-pedalled on that; instead he started to make more concrete demands for a new, extended Statute of Autonomy, in particular to give Catalonia greater control over its own finances.

In that he was echoing a demand long voiced by the left-wing regionalists of Catalan Republican Left (ERC) (p70), who made substantial gains at the regional election held in November 2003. Indeed, their support was now essential to building a viable regional government. After lengthy negotiations ERC rejected an alliance with the CiU. Instead it joined a left-wing coalition headed by Pasqual Maragall, a popular ex-mayor of Barcelona and leader of the local Socialists, the PSC (p164), themselves advocates of 'asymmetric federalism'. As well as certain changes to Spanish central institutions, in particular the Upper House of Parliament, this notion too was based on the principle that Catalonia (and the other 'historic nationalities') should enjoy markedly more autonomy than other regions. Thus, while the new government promised significant changes to the CiU's social and economic policies, its commitment to extending Catalan self-government was as strong as, perhaps even stronger than, that of its predecessor.

In the time of globalisation

If the constraints placed on Spain's central government by regionalism between 1993 and 2004 were unprecedented, its involvement in foreign affairs was greater than at any time since the seventeenth century (p2). The most immediate sphere of action was the European Union where, for various reasons, relations with the country's partners became increasingly problematic. At the same time, though, those with the US grew closer, while globalisation – the process of rapidly developing inter-connection between events around the whole world – affected Spain in a number of ways.

During Felipe González's last term in office the restrictive policies required to qualify for EMU caused considerable hardship to some Spaniards, many of them traditional Socialist voters (p181). Yet, despite the adversarial political climate of the time (pp182–3), this was one issue the then opposition People's Party (PP) refrained from making political capital out of. Its restraint was testimony to the almost complete consensus among Spain's political elite on EMU's importance for Spain. Not surprisingly, then, the PP (p182) maintained exactly the same course once it came to power in 1996.

The efforts of both governments were so successful that, when the decision on countries' eligibility for EMU was taken in 1997, Spain satisfied the conditions with some ease. Admittedly, its public debt was still too high, but agreement had already been reached to relax that test when it became clear that several leading EU members, notably Germany, would also fail it. In fact, and quite contrary to early forecasts, Spain was one of the best qualified countries in terms of the five criteria as a whole. Subsequently, the continuing success of its economy meant that it had no difficulty in satisfying the budget conditions on EMU members established by the Stability Pact – again in sharp contrast to other, richer countries.

In another area, too, there was continuity of policy after 1996. Like his predecessor, the new PM José María Aznar made a habit of sending political heavyweights to Brussels (p154). Thus, when the Commission was almost entirely renewed in 1999, he nominated his Agriculture Minister, Loyola de Palacio, who was promptly given Vice-President's rank and one of the more important portfolios (Transport and Infrastructure). An even greater prize went to Spain's other new Commissioner, Pedro Solbes (p155), who was given responsibility for Economics and Finance and so became effective overlord of the EMU process as a whole. More generally, too, the country continued to enjoy a disproportionately high share of top posts in the EU machinery.

Spain's biggest coup in this regard came in 1999, when the Union appointed its first High Representative for foreign and security policy, a high-prestige and potentially key post. It went to Javier Solana, an ever-present in the Socialist governments of the 1980s and 1990s who had ended his domestic career as Foreign Minister and González's heir apparent in the PSOE. On the other hand, no more was heard of the former PM himself as a future Commission President. Of course, that reflected the damage done to his reputation during his final years in office (p181). But it was also part of a broader trend, a mild but growing anti-Spanish feeling that became increasingly apparent over the PP's time in power.

That, in turn, mirrored the party's attitude towards the EU, significantly different from that of the Socialists. It was not that the PP was eurosceptic, in the British sense of distrusting European integration in general, and its political dimension in particular. Yet, not least for generational reasons, its leaders did not share their predecessors' unbridled enthusiasm for the EU and all its works (p152). For them, Europe was not the realisation of a dream but a mere political reality, less a community of partners than an arena in which to compete for influence and resources. Added to that was the fact that the PP did not fit readily into the EU's ideological grid (p182); it was no coincidence that in internal Union disputes Aznar regularly found himself allied with Britain's Tony Blair, whose 'New' Labour Party was also an outsider in those terms, and whose enthusiasm for deregulation the Spanish PM shared (p185).

Conversely, the years around the turn of the century witnessed a sharp deterioration of Spain's relations with Germany. With Germany's Chancellor now being a Social Democrat, Gerhard Schröder, the differences were to some extent ideological. Understandably, he and Aznar took opposing positions on such issues as the pace of liberalisation and privatisation or, later, the need to maintain the strict terms of the Stability Pact.

Another factor was changing circumstances. As Germany's own economy stuttered and its attention shifted to prospective new partners in the East, its willingness to continue transferring very large sums of money to Spain under the Structural Funds (p154) understandably diminished. At the 1999 Berlin Summit, where a decision on allocation of such funding up to 2006 had to be taken, Aznar simply refused to agree to any settlement which failed to preserve Spain's share. In the end he won, but his success came at a price. From then on he was known in Union circles as '*Señor No*'.

The following year, at Nice, the battleground changed to the EU's post-enlargement institutional arrangements. Again Aznar successfully held out for an extremely advantageous deal; in particular, Spain was allocated 27 votes in the European Council, only two less than the largest countries, including Germany. This time Schröder was not prepared to accept defeat. He reopened the dispute as part of the discussions on an EU constitution, and eventually persuaded almost all his colleagues to revise the Nice Treaty in this respect.

Yet Aznar, backed only by Poland, refused to compromise, thus effectively blocking adoption of the constitution – which, if nothing else, had great symbolic significance for much of Europe's political elite. Nor was it merely that Aznar's positions tended to be extreme: it was the fact that he defended them in the same assertive and uncompromising style also apparent in domestic affairs (p184). In that sense he contributed to what by 2004 was a significant rift between Spain and several of its EU partners, above all France and Germany.

On the other hand, the Aznar years saw a remarkable strengthening of Spain's relations with the US, which had been problematic on occasions during the transition period and threatened to be so under the Socialists (p153). However, they had begun to improve with the confirmation of NATO membership in 1986 (p154), while a new defence agreement signed two years later effectively settled the thorny issue of US bases on Spanish soil (p108). In 1990 these played an important support role during the

Gulf War against Iraq, in which Spanish naval vessels also played a minor, non-combative part. Five years later Javier Solana landed his first big international post, as NATO Secretary-General. Nevertheless, it was left to the PP to complete Spain's integration into the alliance's military structure soon after it came to power in 1996, a move that met with little opposition, either popular or political. Three years later Spanish warplanes participated in the alliance's bombing of Kosovo, albeit in very small numbers.

Up to now Spain had acted in conjunction with its main EU partners, but that changed once US President Bush announced his so-called war on terrorism. For whatever reason – perhaps the ETA threat in general, or his own narrow escape from a bomb attack (p173) – that struck a particular chord with Aznar, who seems to have been the first European leader to offer troops for peace-keeping duties in Afghanistan. Then, in the run-up to the Iraq War of 2003, he was the prime mover behind a letter sent by the leaders of eight EU member states, existing and prospective, to their colleagues, supporting the Americans and British in their plans to invade. The action was a direct challenge to the main opponents of invasion, France and Germany, with whom it was another cause of division.

Undeterred, Aznar attended a well-publicised pre-invasion meeting with Bush and Blair, and generally cultivated the impression that he formed part of a triumvirate. In fact, that was far from being the case; the 'coalition' of American allies involved a number of other countries, and the 1,300-strong contingent Spain eventually dispatched to Iraq was one of the more modest contributions, especially relative to its population. But the contrast with France and Germany, and Aznar's propensity to make hawkish statements, made him a virtual hero in the US. At home the position was very different, with polls showing over 80 per cent opposition to the war and Spain's involvement in it, both before and after it took place, despite which the PM blocked all attempts to debate the matter in Parliament.

Events in Iraq may have provided the most dramatic illustration of globalisation's impact on Spain, but it was by no means the only one. Since 1986 the country's trade within the EU had expanded rapidly and it had also become a major recipient of investment from its new partners. In the later 1990s, however, Spanish companies themselves began to invest heavily abroad, above all in Latin America. Indeed, within only a few years Spain had become by far the biggest investor in the region apart from the US. This brought problems, notably due to the successive crises experienced by Argentina, but also enabled Spanish companies to expand in ways that were previously unthinkable. It made Spain into a net exporter of capital.

The end of the century also saw the reversal of another type of cross-border flow. For centuries the country had been exporting population; now, suddenly, it started to attract immigrants in substantial numbers. EC accession in 1986 had already made the short crossing from North Africa one of the principal clandestine entry points to 'Europe' as a whole. Initially, though, most of those who made it across the Straits of Gibraltar – notoriously, many died in the attempt, and still do – saw Spain merely as a staging post on the way to its richer neighbours. By the late 1990s, however, rising affluence had made it an attractive destination in its own right.

Previously, the relatively modest rise in immigration had been accounted for mainly by well-off retirees from northern Europe, who presented few problems of social integration. On the other hand, if anything their presence aggravated those posed by Spain's perilously low birth rate and rapidly ageing population structure. In that sense the latest arrivals, notably more fertile than indigenous Spaniards and mostly anxious to work, were to be welcomed. But these same characteristics could also be perceived as threatening by those native Spaniards, often the least well-educated and worst-off, who came into closest contact with the newcomers, most of whom came from very different cultural backgrounds in Latin America, sub-Saharan Africa and the Islamic world.

The bulk of these new immigrants were illegal, lacking as they did the necessary documentation (*indocumentados*). Officially barred from working they had little choice but to accept the poor pay and conditions prevailing in the 'underground economy'. As a result they found it hard to obtain the record of their stay in Spain needed to justify regularisation of their situation under the amnesties provided by successive amendments to the Aliens Act (*Ley de Extranjería*). These changes also tightened up the conditions affecting those who were not regularised, for instance by restricting their access to health care and social services. Such steps were justified as a necessary response to public anxieties. But they also served to nourish them, as did the irresponsible comments of some politicians, mainly but not exclusively of the Right, who effectively accused immigrants of responsibility for rising crime rates.

These, in turn, may have been one reason why the over-stretched police did little to stop employment of illegal immigrants. But it is also undeniable that, for powerful interests close to the governing conservatives, these were a welcome source of cheap and docile labour, at a time when falling unemployment was drying up the native supply. This was especially true of the labour-intensive, often seasonal, activities involved in the booming production of fruit and vegetables along the southern and eastern coasts. The labourers there tended to live in makeshift shanty towns or similarly sub-standard conditions, and their relations with the indigenous population were often poor, resulting in clashes of varying degrees of seriousness.

Such incidents most frequently affected the Moroccans who formed the largest group among new immigrants in general and were especially predominant among agricultural labourers. In particular, they were the victims of the near race-riot that occurred in the town of El Ejido, near Almería, in February 2000. Immigration-related issues also contributed to a sharp deterioration in Spain's diplomatic relations with Morocco itself, which culminated in July 2002 with the comic-opera invasion of Parsley Island (*Isla del Perejil*), one of various islets off the African coast belonging to Spain.

These circumstances may or may not be connected to the fact that Moroccans accounted for most of those detained or pursued by the Spanish authorities following the **terrorist attack in Madrid** on 11 March 2004. Undoubtedly, though, the outrage provided grim evidence of Spain's irrevocable integration into the wider world order; almost a quarter of the victims were non-Spaniards working in the country. And it soon became clear that the attack was the work, not of home-grown terrorists, but of Islamic fundamentalists linked in some way to Al-Qaida (*Al-Qaeda*) (pp187–8).

The PP ascendant

As it transpired, the Madrid attack was to prove the nemesis of the conservative People's Party (PP), which had been governing Spain since 1996. Its rise was closely linked to the errors of its main rival, the Socialist PSOE, first in office and then in opposition. Once in power itself, the PP displayed undoubted qualities of its own, above all in the economic field, and was resoundingly re-elected in 2000 as a result. On the other hand, in a number of areas it also displayed a lack of sensitivity, which became increasingly marked during its second term of office.

The PSOE's unexpected election victory in 1993 (p159) was probably bad for Spain; for the party itself it was an undoubted disaster. Bound by its commitment to EMU and its alliance with the Catalan CiU (p172), the Socialists had no option but to pursue a deflationary economic policy the burden of which fell most heavily on social groups or regions on which they depended for support (p155). Even more damagingly, a succession of public figures linked to the PSOE were found to be involved in financial irregularities far more serious than earlier affairs (p159). Among those implicated were such senior figures as the Governor of Spain's central bank, Mariano Rubio, and the paramilitary Civil Guard's first civilian head, Luis Roldán. Worst of all, investigations into the GAL affair (p160) revealed that government ministers had directed the 'dirty war' waged against ETA in the 1980s.

Given these various factors, the government was universally expected to suffer a heavy defeat at the general election it was forced to call for March 1996 (p172). However, as had happened three years before (p160), fear of such an outcome impelled both employees and beneficiaries of the greatly expanded public service sector to turn out in force. As a result, although the conservative PP won a clear victory, it fell well short of an overall majority in Parliament. Felipe González, who remained PSOE leader, spoke of a 'sweet defeat'. Yet actually the result was another calamity for his party, allowing it to continue in a state of denial about its long-standing problems (p159).

In consequence, the much-needed renewal of leadership and ideas was again postponed. When González finally resigned in 1997 he was replaced by Joaquín Almunia, an ex-minister admittedly untouched by scandal, but equally bereft of voter appeal. There followed a disastrous primary election (*elecciones primarias*), designed to confirm him as the party's prime ministerial candidate, but which Almunia lost to another ex-minister, José Borrell – who was then forced to resign by his remote association with one more murky affair. Finally, in the run-up to the 2000 general

---

(matanza del) 11-M

terrorist attack in Madrid on 11 March 2004

At around 7.40 on the morning of 11 March, a total of 10 bombs exploded in four busy commuter trains heading for Madrid's Atocha station, killing 191 people and injuring some 1,500. The devices had been hidden in rucksacks, along with the mobile telephones used to detonate them remotely, one of which failed to operate and was crucial in identifying the perpetrators, members of the Al-Qaida (*Al-Qaeda*) network. A number of these were subsequently detained; seven, including the group's leader, blew themselves up along with a police officer after being cornered in a flat in Leganés, close to Madrid.

Partido Popular (PP)

People's Party

Founded under its present name in 1989, the PP was the direct successor of the right-wing People's Alliance (*Alianza Popular* [AP]) created by Manuel Fraga Iribarne (pp143–4) following Franco's death, although its ranks also included some veterans of the centrist **UCD** (p137). More recently, the main features of the party's ideas have been Spanish nationalism and a neoliberal approach to economic issues. Previously the official opposition, the PP was elected to government in 1996 and for the next eight years held a dominant position in Spanish politics. However, it was surprisingly defeated at the 2004 general election, largely because of its apparent attempt to manipulate reaction to the **terrorist attack in Madrid on 11 March** of that year (p181).

---

election, Almunia concluded an alliance with the Communist-led United Left (IU), with which the PSOE had been in bitter dispute for over a decade. The results were catastrophic. The Socialist vote fell by over a sixth, to its lowest level since 1979 (the IU fared even worse). The PSOE was left stunned, unable for the next few years to oppose seriously the party that had replaced it as Spain's undisputed master.

The rise to power of the **PP** had been a lengthy process. It began in 1989, when Manuel Fraga (p120) stepped down as leader of the People's Alliance to become First Minister of his native Galicia. His replacement was José María Aznar, who had previously held the same post in Castile-Leon, but who was sufficiently young to be free of the Francoist associations that clung to his predecessor. As part of its makeover the party also received a new label, designed to give it a more modern, European image; 'People's Party' is the designation used by the largest right-of-centre group in the European Parliament, the Christian Democrats (*democristianos*), which the PP now joined.

Like many labels, this one was deceptive. In fact, Aznar and his allies in the party rejected more or less explicitly the economic and social interventionism characteristic of European Christian Democracy – and Francoism (p100) – in favour of the neoliberal attitudes of the New Right. And, though their policies did sometimes display a religious tinge, it was not of the progressive, ecumenical shade espoused by most of their new allies in Strasbourg. Rather it was the traditional Catholic variety associated with their other main trait: a strongly centralist Spanish nationalism which did indeed prove reminiscent of the former dictatorship on occasions.

The desire to escape such electorally damaging associations (p159) was a prime motive behind Aznar's attempts in the mid-nineties to rebrand his party as 'centrist'. At the same time, though, those made it hard for the PP to distinguish itself from the ruling Socialists, who had long since been occupying that part of the spectrum (pp156–7). Aznar accordingly adopted a two-pronged approach. On the one hand, he built up a highly organised and strictly disciplined party machine to match the PSOE's. On the other, he focused relentlessly on the Socialists' all-too-obvious ethical problems.

In this he was assisted by several leading Madrid dailies, notably *Abc* and *El Mundo*, and by two of the three private TV stations which the government had licensed in 1989 after long prevarication. Their role was questionable, to say the least, given that their financial backers were mainly close to the PP and themselves not always free from the taint of scandal. Moreover, several of their exposés later turned out to have no basis.

With state-controlled television and pro-government papers hitting back, sometimes with similarly low blows, Spanish politics acquired an ugly air of rising tension (*crispación*) unprecedented in the democratic era.

Be that as it may, Aznar's strategy bore fruit. At the 1994 European elections the PP inflicted the PSOE's first nationwide defeat for twelve years. The following year it won a more significant victory, taking control of most regions and the great bulk of local government, before 1996 finally brought it success at Spanish level. Yet the narrow margin of its win forced the PP to rely on regionalist support to form a government. As a result, the party was obliged to restrain its centralist instincts and make several concessions on the devolution front. Indeed, whether or not for the same reason, over the next four years the PP proved generally more flexible than its origins and nature might have suggested.

Flexibility was most apparent in the new government's dealings with the trade unions, relations with which had been a running sore for the previous decade (p158). The PP not only adhered scrupulously to the Toledo Pact, a 1995 cross-party agreement to maintain pensions largely unchanged, which was a major consideration for the unions; it also encouraged a return to the practice of 'social concertation' (p158), promoting and underwriting union–employer agreements on social security funding and a further reduction in labour market rigidity (p157). The effects were highly positive. For the first time since 1982–86 Spain went through a legislature period without a general strike, and industrial strife generally was markedly reduced.

That, in turn, contributed to the great success story of Aznar's first term in office. Between 1996 and 2000, Spain outperformed a world economy that was itself expanding rapidly. In the European context, the country's growth rate stood out even more, being by some distance the fastest of the larger economies. Spain also led the EU in job creation, and so was finally able to tackle its grave unemployment problem (p155); although the jobless rate remained above the EU average, the difference was now much reduced. These achievements were all the more impressive in that they entailed no extremes of either monetary or fiscal policy; interest rates actually came down and the budget remained in a healthy state, helping Spain to qualify easily for EMU (p177).

Economic success was the main reason for the landslide by which the PP was re-elected in 2000 – again to the discomfiture of opinion pollsters, who greatly underestimated the scale of its victory. That was large indeed. The party's 10.3 million votes, a total even greater than that won by the Socialists in 1982, put it no less than ten per cent ahead of the PSOE. In fact, that lead was due essentially to low turnout among a considerably expanded electorate and, above all, among left-leaning voters; barely three Spanish electors out of ten had actually voted for the conservatives. For the moment, though, what mattered was the situation in Parliament, where their 183 seats represented the first overall majority for any party since 1986, and the first ever for a party of the Right in a truly democratic election.

The victory was a personal triumph for Aznar, to whose own growing authority it gave a further boost. Almost immediately the PM announced that he would not seek re-election for a third term. The motives for his unusual step cannot be known. Arguably it was a laudable attempt to counteract the tendency, apparent both inside and outside Spain, for leaders to remain in power too long. In effect, though, it also exempted him from the need to face the electorate again. At the same time the election result freed his party, which the previous year had reasserted its control over most of local and regional government, from the need to build alliances with awkward allies. These two factors were reflected in the move away from the 'centre' that typified the PP's second term. Indeed, the government increasingly displayed an assertiveness and even arrogance, already presaged in some aspects before 2000 and clearly apparent in its conduct of foreign policy (pp178–9).

Domestically, this tendency was most obvious in dealings with the regions. These began on a positive note; in 1996 more competences were transferred to the 'slow route' regions as a means to improve the workings of devolution (p160–1). But, as it transpired, the PP also had another aim in mind. It wanted to standardise – and so cap – the level of autonomy across Spain. So much became clear in 2001, when devolution of health powers was made general. A number of smaller regions, several PP-run, did not actually want the new responsibilities, and had to be bullied into accepting them by threats of reduced funding.

Where regions did want a greater say, as in relations with the EU, their wishes were over-ridden, often in the most dismissive of terms. As for Basque and Catalan concerns about the erosion of their special constitutional status (p142), these were derided as irrational and backward-looking – and equated, sometimes explicitly, with ETA's violence. To halt that, the government ruled out negotiation, even during the ceasefire of 1998/99 (p175), and relied exclusively on police methods – admittedly with considerable success, and with a marked decline in the abuses of former years (p160). Meantime, the PP itself promoted a 'constitutional patriotism', for instance by the prominent display of symbols such as the Spanish flag, which often seemed to ignore not just the complexity of Spaniards' feelings and identities but also the Constitution's actual provisions on devolution.

After the 2000 election, similar insensitivity poisoned the government's previously good relations with the unions. Despite some efforts to maintain dialogue these deteriorated rapidly, to the extent that two years later Spain was facing its first general strike since 1994. Yet the PM in particular virtually incited the unions to act by refusing to discuss their proposals for new labour market changes and by using the most extravagant of rhetoric – about what were essentially technical matters, not grand principles. Then, after the event, the government withdrew most of the proposals, tacitly admitting that negotiation should have been the way ahead all along.

The same bulldozer approach was evident in a second highly sensitive field: education. Here, the reforms introduced in the 1980s at secondary and tertiary level had certainly widened access as well as modernising course structures and content. But equally they had failed to solve all existing problems, notably failure to develop high-quality skills and promote research, and had arguably contributed to some new ones, such as pupil disinterest and resource shortages. As a result, and just as with the job market, there was broad agreement that further change was needed. Yet the government did little during its first term of office, other than to provoke a dispute with several regions over a proposed new, uniform history syllabus with a strong (Spanish) nationalist bias.

No sooner had it won an overall majority, however, than it drew up plans virtually without consulting either professionals or the public. The extensive changes they proposed were highly controversial, involving a return to earlier, discredited practice in several respects. Somewhat surprisingly given the manifest decline in its social importance, they also made the Catholic Church two significant concessions: the upgrading of religion as a secondary-school subject, and exemption from some of the requirements for establishing private universities. These latter, like the health trusts (*fundaciones sanitarias*) set up during its first term, were in themselves another controversial feature of PP policy.

Privatisation in another sense, that of selling off state-owned firms, was a cornerstone of the PP's economic policy, both before and after 2000. This was a course on which the Socialists had already embarked while in office. The PP went much further, however, disposing of virtually all the state's main holdings. In doing so it effectively eliminated the gap between Spain and other (continental) European economies in this regard; by 2003 Spain's public sector was not significantly larger than those of its main EU partners.

On the related issue of liberalising its utility markets the country actually proceeded faster than required by the Union's directives, or in theory it did. In practice, deregulation brought few of the hoped-for benefits in terms of greater choice and lower prices. That was because the sectors supposedly 'liberalised', in particular the energy industry, continued to be dominated by a few large enterprises linked together by mutual share holdings or co-operation agreements. Typically these involved one or other of the two big players left by progressive consolidation of the banking sector. Aznar's governments, moreover, took an active part in shaping these oligopolies, promoting certain links and discouraging others.

Meanwhile, the regulatory bodies established to oversee the new 'liberalised' markets were starved of the resources needed to carry out their job properly – and subjected to extensive government influence. The same was true of those companies that were privatised, key holdings in which tended to land in the hands of firms or even individuals with close political or personal connections to the government. The most notorious case was that of Juan Villalonga, who prided himself on having gone to school with Aznar, and who became head of the largest of all the privatised prizes, the telecommunications giant *Telefónica*. That in itself was controversial. What made it downright alarming, though, was that Villalonga wasted little time in using his newly acquired financial clout to buy into the media business.

That had long been an obsession of the PP's leaders, who felt – not without justification – that the Right had been disadvantaged by news coverage while the PSOE was in power. At that time it had had to contend both with the undoubted bias of state television and with the fact that the country's most powerful media group, *PRISA*, whose organs included the highly respected top-selling daily *El País*, was broadly sympathetic to the Socialists. After 1996, though, the tables turned. Not only did the state channels – and parts of the private media – continue their attacks on the Socialists as if they were still in power, virtually ignoring any bad news affecting the government; legislation was also passed specifically to damage *PRISA*'s interests in the area of digital broadcasting, and its head was prosecuted on charges that subsequently transpired to have been trumped up.

In that context, the acquisition by *Telefónica* of various media interests, including a highly popular private TV channel, came as a bombshell. The effects were soon felt; observers rated overall media coverage of the 2000 election as the most unbalanced of the democratic era – no small claim, given the extent of previous abuse in this area. Its extent now provoked a substantial outcry that, along with the considerable costs involved in the media business, led to Villalonga's fall and his successor's decision that *Telefónica* should gradually withdraw from the field. That was not the end of the story, however, since the stakes sold off stayed within the circle of the PP's associates and supporters.

On the economic front, too, Aznar's second term saw the emergence of some problems. Inflation rose, slightly by historical Spanish standards but significantly given the country's new, more open situation. A very high proportion of new employment was short term and low in quality, reflecting a failure to increase skills and education levels sufficiently. Furthermore, the rise in housing prices that had been underway for some years gathered pace alarmingly, leading to a steep increase in private debts and significant hardship for some. Overall, though, the country's performance continued to be impressive. Spain's growth rate was again among the very highest in the EU, and for the bulk of the population living standards continued to rise steadily. As a result, there was a general expectation that, for all its blemishes, the government would be re-elected for a third term.

Postscript: The 2004 general election

It was therefore an enormous shock when the general election on 14 March 2004 actually resulted in a victory for the Socialist Party (PSOE). The poll took place in the shadow of the terrorist attack in Madrid three days before (p181), and some observers were tempted to see the result as a vote against Spain's involvement in Iraq. The reality was rather more complex, however.

It is true that, even before 11 March, the PSOE's fervent opposition to the Iraq War had contributed to a marked recovery from the disaster of the 2000 election (p183). Its fortunes started to turn later that same year at the party conference held to find a new leader, Joaquín Almunia (p181) having characteristically accepted the blame for defeat and resigned. The party establishment's candidate, and hot favourite, was José Bono, the long-serving first minister of Castile-La Mancha. Nevertheless, in the poll of party members he was narrowly beaten by the young and virtually unknown José Luis Rodríguez Zapatero.

In itself, the result sent a much-needed signal of renewal, which Zapatero sensibly followed up by replacing virtually all of the old leadership. He also brought a new, and electorally appealing, approach to the task of opposition, actively seeking cross-party agreements with the government and concluding two (on the response to ETA, and on reforms to Spain's hopelessly overloaded court system). Zapatero was also helped by various other factors. Several government ministers were implicated in financial scandals, the most notable being the *Gescartera* affair involving Economics Minister Rodrigo Rato. When the oil tanker *Prestige* ruptured off the Galician coast in late 2002, the government mishandled the immediate crisis and then reacted clumsily to the resultant massive oil spill. Some voters were alienated by the PP's increasingly high-handed style of government, typified by the way it committed Spanish forces in Iraq against overwhelming public opposition (p179). Yet, even so, at the local and regional elections held in May 2003 the Socialists could make only minor gains.

Towards the year's end, the PP finally revealed who was to replace Aznar as its leader. Mariano Rajoy was an experienced and successful minister, but far from charismatic. Nonetheless, the surrounding publicity sufficed to restore the government's poll lead. It then focused relentlessly on Spain's economic success, and on the threat posed by ETA – and, by extension, regionalism in general. Once the campaign proper got underway, the PP leaked classified information about contacts between ETA and the leader of the Catalan grouping ERC, now second-in-command of the regional government (p176), to the embarrassment of ERC's Socialist partners (and the dismay of the security forces, who stood to lose valuable informants). Thereafter, the government lost no opportunity to present the election as a choice between itself and a rag-bag of Socialists, far leftists, regionalists and terrorists.

This strategy proved effective. By the time of the Al-Qaida attack on Madrid (p181), three days before the election, the only doubt in virtually all minds was whether the government would secure another overall majority. Yet, in the event, the PSOE beat the PP so decisively in both votes (42.6 per cent to 37.6 per cent) and seats (164 to 148) that its return to government was assured. So different was the outcome from the results of polls taken shortly before 11 March that it must surely have been influenced by the attack on that day. Indeed some commentators, especially in the US, interpreted it as a capitulation to terrorism, pointing to Zapatero's promise to withdraw Spanish troops from Iraq should he be elected.

However, that interpretation hardly squares with the PP's conviction, based on opinion poll evidence, that its hard line against ETA terrorism was a vote winner. Nor does the idea of a last-minute swing caused by fear fit well with the fact that the 9.6 million votes the PP actually received was little, if any, lower than predicted. Indeed, overall turnout was considerably higher than forecast; at 78 per cent, it was the third highest of the democratic era. In very crude terms, many of the Socialist non-voters from 2000 (p183), plus a disproportionate number of new voters, opted for the PSOE in 2004; a significant proportion of those who did so made their decision after 11 March. Rather than fear, the most likely motive for their behaviour was the emotion on display at the demonstrations that took place in front of PP offices all round the country in the wake of the Madrid attack: anger.

Its target was the government's blatant attempt to pin the blame for the Madrid attack on ETA. In the light of other recent incidents (p176), that initially seemed a reasonable conclusion. It was also a conclusion that not just the government but also much of the Madrid establishment, journalists included, was disposed to accept, since it fitted so well with their demonisation of Basque nationalism (p175). But it was not a conclusion supported by the evidence gathered over the crucial three days, which pointed unequivocally to Islamic fundamentalists. Yet the government continued to insist publicly on ETA's involvement, and instructed official Spanish spokespersons worldwide – and the government-controlled media – to take the same line.

This unsubtle news management, of which the public soon got wind, seemed all too obviously designed to influence voters' intentions. It also fell into something of a pattern. Thus, the year before, the death of 70 Spanish troops in an air crash while returning from service in Afghanistan had been followed by a clumsy attempt to prevent some of the circumstances from emerging. And both the manner and the timing of the leak about ERC–ETA contacts gave substance to an accusation long levelled by Basque nationalists: that Aznar routinely exploited terrorism-related issues for party advantage. All in all, while it is certainly an exaggeration to say that Al-Qaida won the election, there is good evidence to suggest that the PP lost it, through its partisan and clumsy response to the 11 March attack. In that sense, the 2004 election was indeed decided by international terrorism.

Conversely, never has a Spanish election result attracted such attention from international media because of its potential impact abroad. Given the prominence of his predecessor in supporting the original invasion (p179), a withdrawal of Spanish troops from Iraq as promised by Zapatero would inevitably have serious repercussions for the situation there. Not surprisingly, within days, he had been sought out by both US Secretary-of-State Colin Powell and Tony Blair. The UK Premier would have had a second cause for concern, because Socialist leaders had already made clear that they would return to Spain's traditional alliance with Germany and France inside the EU; indeed, Zapatero indicated that he would make concessions on Spain's weight in the Union institutions, thus ending Aznar's blockade of the proposed constitution (p178).

Finally, as regards regionalist issues, the election results suggested a strong reaction against the PP's policies in both Catalonia and the Basque Country, where the swing to the PSOE was particularly strong. In Catalonia, they also provided a vote of confidence in the new regional coalition (p176), since the ERC advanced strongly at the expense of the CiU. Given that his party has already espoused the concept of 'asymmetric federalism' (p000), Zapatero would seem to be well placed to reach a compromise, especially as the region's case is now being argued by his fellow Socialist Maragall.

In the Basque case, too, Zapatero has indicated that he will attempt to reopen dialogue with non-violent nationalists, although that may not be easy so long as the Ibarretxe Plan is on the table (p175). One hopeful sign is that the PNV, for whom the election also brought gains, had already chosen to replace its retiring party leader Xabier Arzalluz (p174) by the more moderate Jon Josu Imaz. There must also be a chance that the 11 March attack will have a salutary effect on both ETA and, just as important, the attitudes of its supporters. Should that indeed prove true, the victims of 11 March would not have died entirely in vain.

Summary of main points

The regionalist spiral

- Between 1993 and 2000 the CiU's Jordi Pujol exerted a strong influence over successive central governments. He used it, in particular, to extend Catalonia's financial autonomy.
- In the mid-1990s renewed ETA violence, and a breakdown in relations between the PNV and the main Spanish parties, greatly increased tensions in the Basque Country.
- After the failure of the ETA truce in 1998/99 the situation deteriorated further, the PNV hardening its demands for outright independence and the central government refusing to negotiate at all, concentrating instead on crushing ETA and its political base.
- In 2003 the CiU lost power in Catalonia to a coalition made up of Socialists and left-wing regionalists, and set on significantly extending the region's self-government.

In the time of globalisation

- The conservative government elected in 1996 completed the process of qualifying Spain for EMU. However, owing to its different ideas and changing circumstances it came increasingly into conflict with its EU partners, notably Germany, over a number of issues.
- Under the conservatives, Spain became more closely involved in NATO, and was at the forefront of support for the American invasion of Iraq, even though this was highly unpopular at home.
- Globalisation affected Spain in various ways, notably a large rise in immigration, much of it illegal, from the developing world. Many immigrants suffered poor conditions in the underground economy and also experienced friction with indigenous Spaniards.
- Moroccans were the group most affected by these circumstances.

The PP ascendant

- After 1993 the Socialist government was involved in a succession of scandals, and lost power as a result in 1996. In opposition, the Socialists' decline continued.
- Their successor in power, the People's Party (PP) under José María Aznar, initially showed surprising flexibility in dealing with trade unions and regionalists. It also presided over a further period of strong economic growth and was re-elected by a landslide in 2000.
- Thereafter the government showed a growing tendency, both in foreign affairs and domestically, to ignore opinions other than its own. Another cause for concern was its apparent desire to extend its influence into business and the media sector, through dubious privatisation policies.

- Despite some blemishes, on balance the economy continued to perform well up to 2004.

The 2004 general election

- Although the Socialists (PSOE) had recovered somewhat under a new leader, José Luis Rodríguez Zapatero, they were generally expected to lose the election until the 11 March terrorist attack.
- The election produced a clear PSOE victory, seemingly due to a swing of opinion after the attack.
- The most likely reason for the turnround was reaction against the government's apparent attempt to mislead public opinion by blaming the attack on ETA.

Exhibit 11.1: The People's Party's inheritance (1995)

Extracts from a book written by the party's leader

El resultado de[l poder socialista] no es otro que una democracia más débil, una sociedad más débil, una economía más débil, una nación más débil. La suma de estas debilidades es *nuestro problema*.

Y nosotros queremos contribuir a su solución con una propuesta política general, que se ha ido elaborando a partir del análisis de nuestras necesidades y con la renovación de nuestras ideas.

Y digo *renovación*, porque no es cierto que vengamos de ninguna parte.

Nuestro partido es joven, pero nos consideramos, con legítimo orgullo, herederos de una corriente que, con aportaciones de diverso signo, ha estado presente en la vida nacional durante más de doscientos años. La construcción del Estado liberal, a partir de la Constitución de 1812, la creación de un mercado nacional, la modernización jurídica, con obras de tanta fecundidad como nuestros venerables Códigos del XIX, han sido pilares fundamentales en la configuración de la España de hoy. El respeto a las libertades, el imperio de la Ley, la sujeción del Estado al Derecho, el protagonismo de la sociedad fueron los motores de una vasta obra, hecha con la impronta del espíritu liberal. Con demasiada frecuencia se ha querido desfigurar nuestra más reciente historia. La corriente reaccionaria ha pretendido siempre descalificar e incluso ahogar los logros modernizadores del pensamiento moderado y liberal español. Una cierta izquierda ha elaborado, por su parte, una visión maniquea de nuestra historia contemporánea, metiendo en el mismo saco todo lo que no se identificaba con sus planteamientos. Nosotros, por el contrario, reivindicamos el vigor de una opción con perfiles propios que a través de las sucesivas generaciones defendió la primacía del valor de la libertad y de la ley de un Estado sometido a èl, de una democracia en la que cupiera holgadamente la España plural y en cuyo marco se pudieran llevar adelante las reformas que demandaba una sociedad más justa. [...]

What [the Socialist government] has done is to weaken democracy, to weaken society, to weaken the economy, to weaken the nation. Taken together, these weaknesses are the problem we face.

We want to help to solve that problem with a broad political programme, drawn up gradually and based on an analysis of our needs, and with the renewal of our ideas.

I say 'renewal' because it is not true that we have arrived out of nowhere.

Our party is a young one, but we consider ourselves – with legitimate pride – as the heirs to a strand of opinion which, with contributions from various quarters, has been present in Spain for more than 200 years. The building of a liberal state based on the 1812 Constitution; the creation of a national market; the modernisation of our legal system, the valuable products of which included the venerable codes of law drawn up in the nineteenth century: all these were fundamental in shaping today's Spain. Respect for freedoms, the rule of law – extended to cover the actions of government – and the participation of society as a whole were the driving forces of a vast project that bears the imprint of liberal ideas. All too often attempts have been made to distort Spain's modern history. Reactionaries have always sought to disparage or even reverse the modernising achievements of Spanish moderates and liberals. At the same time, part of the left sees our recent history in strictly black and white terms, lumping together all those who do not share its views. By contrast, we lay claim to the dynamism of a third, distinct tradition that, down the generations, has championed the causes of liberty; of the rule of law and a state subject to it; of a democracy with ample room for a pluralistic vision of Spain, within which it would be possible to implement the reforms needed to create a more just society.

Source: Aznar, J.M. (1995) *España: La Segunda Transición.* Madrid: Espasa.

Exhibit 11.2: The Ibarretxe Plan (2003)

Extracts from the 'Political Statute for the Community of Euskadi', approved by the Basque Parliament with the support of PNV, EA and the Basque section of United Left.

PREÁMBULO
El Pueblo Vasco o Euskal Herría es un Pueblo con identidad propia en el conjunto de los pueblos de Europa, depositario de un patrimonio histórico, social y cultural singular, que se asienta geográficamente en siete Territorios actualmente articulados en tres ámbitos jurídico-políticos diferentes ubicados en dos estados.
[...]
   [...]

Artículo 1. – De la Comunidad de Euskadi
[...L]os Territorios vascos de Araba, Bizkaia y Gipuzkoa, así como los ciudadanos y ciudadanas que la integran, en el ejercicio del derecho a decidir libre y democráticamente su propio marco de organización y de relaciones políticas, y como expresión de su nacionalidad y garantía de autogobierno, se constituyen en una Comunidad vasca libremente asociada al estado español bajo la denominación de Comunidad de Euskadi.
   [...]

Artículo 13. – Ejercicio democrático del Derecho a Decidir
A los efectos del ejercicio democrático del derecho de libre decisión de los ciudadanos y ciudadanas vascas [sic], del que emana la legitimidad democrática del presente Estatuto, las Instituciones de la Comunidad de Euskadi ostentan la potestad para regular y gestionar la realizacion de consultas democráticas a la ciudadanía vasca por vía de referéndum, tanto en lo que corresponde a asuntos de su ámbito competencial como a las relaciones que desean tener con otros Territorios y Comunidades del Pueblo Vasco, así como en lo relativo a las relaciones con el Estado español y sus Comunidades Autónomas, y a las relaciones en el ámbito europeo e internacional.
   [...]
   Cuando en el ejercicio democrático de su libre decisión, los ciudadanos y ciudadanas vascas [sic] manifestaran [...] su voluntad clara e inequívoca de alterar integra o sustancialmente el modelo y régimen de relación política con el Estado español, así como las relaciones en el ámbito europeo e internacional [...], las Instituciones vascas y las del estado se entenderán comprometidas a garantizar un proceso de negociación parar establecer las nuevas condiciones poíticas que permitan materializar, de común acuerdo, la voluntad democrática de la sociedad vasca.
   [...]

Artículo 65. – Unión Europea
[...]
2. De conformidad con la normativa comunitaria europea, la Comunidad de Euskadi dispondrá de representación directa en los órganos de la Unión Europea. A tal efecto, el Gobierno español habilitará los cauces precisos para posibilitar la participación activa del Gobierno Vasco en los diferentes procedimientos de toma de decisiones de las Instituciones Comunitarias en aquellos asuntos que afectan al contenido de las políticas públicas que les son exclusivas.
   [...]

PREAMBLE
The People of the Basque Country (*Euskal Herria*) have a distinct collective identity within the community of Europe's peoples. They are the bearers of a unique historic, social and cultural heritage, and their homeland is made up of seven territories which are currently divided between three legal and political jurisdictions located in two states. [...]
  [...]

Article 1. – The Community of Euskadi
[...I]n the exercise of their right to decide freely and democratically their own administrative and political structure, and as an expression of their nationhood and a guarantee of their self-government, the Basque territories of Alava, Vizcaya and Guipúzcoa, together with their citizens, hereby constitute themselves as a Basque community freely associated with the Spanish state, under the name 'Community of Euskadi'.
  [...]

Article 13.– Democratic Exercise of the Right to Decide
In order to permit Basques the democratic exercise of their right of free decision making, from which this Statute derives its democratic legitimacy, the institutions of the said Community shall have the power to regulate, and to organise the carrying out of, democratic consultations of all Basques by means of referendums, relating to:

● matters lying within the scope of their competence;
● the relations which they wish to maintain with other territories or communities forming part of the Basque People; and
● their relations with the Spanish state and its constituent regions, and to their external relations in the European and international spheres.

  [...]
  As and when Basques, in the democratic exercise of their right of free decision making, manifest [...] their clear and unequivocal will to amend, wholly or substantially, the principle and mechanism governing their political relationship with the Spanish state, or their external relations in the European and international spheres [...], the institutions of the Community of Euskadi and of the Spanish state shall be deemed to have committed themselves to ensuring a process of negotiation designed to establish such new political circumstances as would permit the expression, by mutual agreement, of the democratic will of Basque society.
  [...]

Article 65.– European Union
[...]
2. The Community of Euskadi shall enjoy direct representation in the institutions of the European Union, in accordance with the norms and regulations of the said Union. To that end, the Spanish government shall establish the arrangements necessary to enable the active participation of the Basque government in the various decision-making procedures of the Union's institutions in all matters affecting those areas of public policy which are the exclusive responsibility of those institutions.
  [...]

Topics

- In Exhibit 11.1, Aznar portrays his party as the heirs of the Spanish liberal movement. How realistic a picture does he present of that? How credible is his claim?
- How far did Aznar's performance in office reflect the picture presented in Exhibit 11.1?
- How extreme are the demands implicitly set out in Exhibit 11.2, for example relative to those made by Scottish and Welsh nationalists? Why do you think they are so controversial in Spain?
- How would you rate Jordi Pujol's contributions to Spain and to Catalonia?
- Was the foreign policy followed by the PP governments a sound one for Spain?

Afterword

Over the last few years Spain has become increasingly and patently integrated into European and global developments, not just politically and economically, but also – in an important sense not touched on here – culturally. Does that mean that an appreciation of its history has become irrelevant? The answer, surely, is 'No'. Even in the era of globalisation, each country's involvement in the wider world comes to some extent on its own terms – as the very differing reactions to the Iraq War within Europe have demonstrated. Nowhere in the Western world does that apply more than in Spain, whose experience was so distinctive until so recently.

Thinking first of relations with the outside world, it is easy to forget that the world's eighth largest economy was so cut off for so long. At the start of the nineteenth century, Spain was already a backwater. After the brief and traumatic experience of the War of Independence it became ever more detached from the outside, virtually uninvolved in trade, colonial disputes or even incipient recreational travel, being seen as an occasional destination for the more intrepid. Even the soul-searching inspired by the events of 1898 did little to increase contacts; economically, the inward turn of later 'regenerationist' thinking was paralleled by Primo's raising of the protectionist barriers first erected during the Restoration period.

During the tensest and most unhappy decade of the last century Spain was briefly drawn back into European affairs, but once the Second World War was over it was again largely cut off from the developments that shaped the late-twentieth-century western community of states. Yet by the later stages of the Franco regime, for all the propaganda disseminated by the State, most Spaniards had enough contact with the outside world to know that their country was regarded as economically backward and politically unsavoury – and that both views had some foundation.

Against that background it is easier to understand Spanish attitudes since Franco's death to the outside world in general, and the rest of western Europe in particular. To an astonishing degree, the desire to be recognised as an equal partner has often seemed to over-ride all other considerations. There was virtually general acclaim when Javier Solana was appointed NATO Secretary-General, even though he had opposed Spain's participation in the alliance less than 15 years before. Support for European integration, too, has been extraordinarily resilient even when, as in the early 1990s, it brought considerable material costs for many. The post-Communist Left's insistence on pointing out such unfortunate realities was one of the main reasons why it found life so much harder in Spain than in Italy after 1989.

Spanish 'Europhilia' is all the more striking when compared with attitudes in the other peripheral country which has traditionally seen 'Europe' as being somewhere else: the UK. But unlike Britain – or at least England – Spain did not have an unthinkingly accepted notion of nationhood to which European integration posed a threat. Within living memory, a country whose sense of common identity was never highly developed had experienced a civil war, followed by four decades of propaganda to the effect that a large proportion of its own inhabitants were its bitter enemies. On the other hand, many, perhaps the majority, were deeply unhappy with the notion of Spanishness imposed by the Franco regime. Under those circumstances, being European offered, and continues to offer a way to sidestep awkward debates about Spain's essential nature.

The question of national identity bridges the external and internal aspects of Spain's contemporary situation. For the relative weakness of feelings of common Spanishness is inseparable from the strength of loyalties to particular parts and regions of the country. Given new life by the conditions of the War of Independence, they underlay Republicanism's federalist period and its extreme expression in the cantonalist movement of the 1870s. Now, in the post-Franco era, they have re-emerged with even greater vigour, which this time is being channelled in the particular form of regionalism.

Such feelings, like 'Europhilia', are both powerful and widespread, as Manuel Fraga's career illustrates. Having been a minister under the ferociously centralist Franco regime, and a fervent critic of what he regarded as excessive devolution in the 1980s, becoming First Minister of his native Galicia seemed to be no more than a step on the way to his retirement from nationwide politics in 1989. Yet subsequently Fraga – who remains in office 15 years on – was to display a strong regionalist streak, advocating a standardised administrative system that would put more responsibilities in the hands of regions in general, and doughtily defending Galicia's particular interests. More than once he found himself in agreement with his long-time Catalan equivalent, Jordi Pujol – whose own regionalist sympathies meant that he spent part of the Franco era, not in a ministerial office, but in a prison cell.

Pujol was a phenomenon in his own right who, in a sense, single-handedly wrenched Catalan regionalism away from its historical roots. But, at the same time, his brand of regionalism was essentially a new attempt to address the problem that plagued the Regionalist League at the turn of the century: how to mobilise mass political support for the economic interests of a small, privileged group – and how to control it once mobilised. Pujol's resolution of that dilemma depended heavily on his own personal standing; now that he has gone it is likely to re-emerge in its full force. Certainly, the resurgence of ERC and the cementing of a Socialist–regionalist alliance is uncannily reminiscent of events in the 1930s.

If history still weighs heavily in Catalonia, in the Basque Country its presence is almost overpowering. For one thing, the very weakness of historical claims to Basque nationhood means that, for many nationalists, it is all the more important that they be asserted as loudly and as often as possible. The irony is that by the 1990s most non-nationalists had accepted the proposition of Basques' distinctiveness, albeit not necessarily on historical grounds – a situation that, to judge by opinion polls, has not been changed significantly by the People's Party's subsequent reversion to more centralist attitudes.

The traditionalist aspect of Basque nationalism has been enormously important, even for ETA. In its communiqués down the years, 'revolutionary socialist' demands have sat oddly alongside those for the restoration of Basques' traditional rights. Many observers have commented on the clearly traceable links between its intransigent, irrational, violent approach to politics and the Carlist movement of the last century, from which a number of early nationalists emerged. But even more important for ETA's development, and attitudes to it, has been the Basque Country's more recent history.

For nearly four decades now, the region has experienced one sort of trauma after another: the virtually endemic industrial conflict which formed the background to the early stages of ETA's 'armed struggle'; the often bitter debates over devolution of the decade after 1975, against a background of increased violence; the political crisis of the mid-1980s; and ETA's later evolution into a marginalised but still highly effective terrorist group. Add to that a savage industrial restructuring that threw thousands out of work and destroyed whole communities, a massive drug problem among young people and the persistent security force abuses which have killed and maimed scores, and caused less extreme harm to hundreds more – not to mention the GAL revelations of the 1990s. The contradictory impact of these various factors has been much in evidence since 1996, and will doubtless continue to be so.

There is a sense in which the GAL affair, while especially alarming because of its nature, is merely one example of a more general phenomenon that, once again, derives from Spain's particular historical experience. The apparatus of the Spanish state was constructed late in comparison to most of its neighbours – in many fields only in the 1950s, and in some not until the 1970s. It also came into being under the special circumstances of dictatorship. In 1975, the Spanish public service had little or no ethos of public accountability. Indeed, in the military and security forces the concept made no sense; there the key virtue was obedience, ultimately to a leader whose only responsibility was before God. More than two decades of democratic rule have brought some changes, but the sense that rulers and administrators occupy their positions by right and are answerable to no one has been hard to dislodge.

Another feature of contemporary Spanish government also reflects the experience of the Franco era. Dictatorships anywhere fill the administration with their own supporters. In Spain, though, the practice was already common under the façade of democratic conditions of the last century, when the successive pairs of embryonic parties – first Moderates and Progressives, later Conservatives and Liberals – used the gift of public jobs as a way of buying support. During the Socialist hegemony of the 1980s patronage recovered that function, but more often served as a means of securing party control over government, at central, regional and local level. Once the pendulum swung, and the People's Party acquired a similarly strong hold on government, the same process was visible, with the PP in turn 'colonising' large tracts of the public service and its related agencies. In that sense, one of the most encouraging aspects of the investiture speech given by José Luis Rodríguez Zapatero was his explicit reference to such problems, and proposal of concrete measures to address them, for instance by reducing government control over public broadcasting.

The parties and the system they compose also show a strong historical imprint, their development heavily conditioned by the very limited scope for their normal activities prior to 1975. Only the PNV and, in certain areas, the PSOE ever became the sort of mass party common in most of western Europe. Not only that: for various reasons, parties as institutions were poorly regarded by very wide sections of opinion – a rare point of agreement between Franco and the anarchist movement! In both these respects, Spain can be said to have anticipated developments elsewhere, towards a media-centred, personalised style of politics in which mass parties play little part, and are held in low esteem by voters. Similarly, the PP's relative lack of ideological baggage and long-standing commitments to particular interests may have helped it to survive the mid-nineties swing to the Left so much better than most of its European counterparts.

Another reason, though, is a question of timing, or rather the way in which recent history has left the political cycle in Spain completely out of step with that in western Europe as a whole. In 1982 the after-effects of the Franco regime, which included the Right's complete disarray, meant that the Left swept into power just as everywhere else the pendulum was swinging hard in the opposite direction. Then, in power, the Socialists were faced with carrying out the sort of free market reforms being undertaken throughout the West, which in Spain involved attacking welfare provisions put in place by Franco but now defended by their own traditional supporters. Just as, elsewhere, the Right was eventually undermined by a reaction against neo-liberalism and a general mood of staleness, so was the PSOE, and at much the same time. Whether, given the circumstances, the party's return to power in 2004 can be seen in the same terms is more doubtful. But the strength of opposition, both popular and among the political elite, to involvement in Iraq would certainly suggest that Spain is still, as the old advertising slogan had it, 'different'.

Further reading

The following comments cannot pretend to be comprehensive. They are intended merely to offer a range of sources suitable for readers who are not specialist historians but feel ready to take the next step beyond the material provided here. A number of authors (Carr, Payne, Preston) have written so widely on the period that for reasons of space only a selection of their output can be mentioned here. There is emphatically no intention to deter readers from sampling their other works – quite the reverse, in fact.

General works

The standard academic work in English, covering most of the period in considerable detail, is Carr's massive tome (8). Much more accessible is the 'pocket version' (7) which starts with the Restoration period rather than at the outset of the liberal era, whereas the latter and its antecedents are covered in their entirety by Esdaile (15). Shubert (46) provides an account that goes below the political surface, and covers more than the social history indicated by the title; he is particularly useful on the Franco era. For a very different approach from all these, concerned almost entirely with overview rather than chronological detail, try Vilar (51), in particular the later chapters, and for a Spanish view of the whole period see Fusi and Palafox (16). Finally, although it was written over half a century ago, to my mind Brenan's classic (6) still provides the best introduction to pre-Civil War Spain; its topic-based arrangement and down-to-earth style allow the non-specialist reader to see the wood for the trees.

Chapter 1

Here there is very little written in English other than for specialists, although the early parts of Payne's work (35) on the military are accessible as well as enlightening. To get a feel for nineteenth-century Spain there is no better source than the novels of Galdós; one of the most famous is now available in translation (17).

Chapter 2

The articles by Harper (23) and Chandler (10), unfortunately difficult to locate, are excellent introductions to the First Republic and Restoration respectively, while Kern (30) includes a useful chapter on the operation of clientilism.

Chapter 3

For a discussion of 'regenerationist' ideas and their impact, see the articles by Harrison (24) and Ortega (33). The standard work on early Basque regionalism is by Payne (36), although Heiberg (25) offers an equally interesting view; for the Catalan variety, see Balcells (1). The comparative treatments by Conversi (12) and Díez Medrano (14) offer contrasting interpretations of the differences between the two movements; both are rewarding if not particularly light reading. Bookchin (5) provides a useful introduction to Spanish anarchism, while Geary (18) sets the Spanish labour movement in international perspective. Specifically on the PSOE, see Heywood (26), or Gillespie's detailed party history (19).

Chapter 4

The article by Ben-Ami (2) gives the best overview of the Primo dictatorship; for a more detailed account see the relevant chapters in the book by the same author (3). The relevant chapters of the works by Payne (35) and Preston (43) on the military are also useful.

Chapter 5

A considerable amount has been written on the Second Republic; given the nature of the period, treatments tend to vary significantly in their assessments. Jackson (29) and Preston (42), alone or in the international treatment written jointly with Graham (21), tend broadly to sympathise with the Left, Payne (38) with the Right, whose nature is in turn revealingly analysed by Preston (43). The article by Graham (20) explores the crucial differences within the Socialist movement.

Chapter 6

Here both the quantity of material and the degree of partisanship is even more marked. Again, Jackson (29) and Preston and Mackenzie (44) offer eminently readable accounts from a basically Republican perspective, while the differences between the early and late editions of Thomas' work (48, 49) reflect changes in the author's own political standpoint. For an understanding of the Nationalist side, Preston's biography of Franco (41) is particularly recommended. The article by Casanova (9) offers an interesting insight into the revolutionary view of the war on the Left. Moving towards literature, Orwell's account of the 1937 Barcelona clashes (34) retains its power, while Ken Loach's film *Land and Freedom* gives an unashamedly partisan, but incredibly immediate picture of the left-wing militias. Finally, for an intriguing analysis of Britain's role in the conflict, see Moradiellos (31).

Chapters 7 and 8

Payne (37), Blaye (4), and Grugel and Rees (22) all provide analyses of the Franco regime's nature, on which Preston's massive but highly readable biography of its master (41) is also most enlightening. The opening chapter of the same author's study of the transition (40) gives a very useful overview of the opposition forces.

Chapters 9–11

Here history and political science begin to overlap: the different viewpoints are apparent in the many studies of the transition to democracy; see, for example, Higley and Gunther (28) and Preston (40). Powell (39) provides a useful overview of most of the period, although his coverage naturally becomes progressively less detailed, while Tusell (50) covers the very recent past with remarkable perspective. Heywood (27) analyses the Socialist era from the standpoint of a political scientist. In Spanish, the same period is covered very thoroughly – from the same standpoint – in the volume edited by Cotarelo (13), although readers should bear in mind the close connections of most of its authors with the Socialist party. ETA has been the subject of several studies; those by Clark (11) and Sullivan (47) both require committed reading but are highly informative, while Onaindía (32) offers a fascinating and highly personal insight into the 'Basque problem' as a whole. Finally, for an overview of recent developments I can tentatively recommend my own contribution (45).

List of further reading

1. Balcells, A. (1996) *Catalan Nationalism: Past and Present*. London: Macmillan.
2. Ben-Ami, S. 'The dictatorship of Primo de Rivera' in *The Journal of Contemporary History*, January 1977.
3. Ben-Ami, S. (1978) *The Origins of the Second Republic in Spain*. Oxford: Oxford University Press.
4. Blaye, E. de (1974) *Franco and the Politics of Spain*. Harmondsworth: Penguin.
5. Bookchin, M. (1977) *The Spanish Anarchists*. New York: Freelife.
6. Brenan, G. (1990) *The Spanish Labyrinth*. Cambridge: Cambridge University Press.
7. Carr, R. (1980) *Modern Spain 1875–1980*. Oxford: Oxford University Press.
8. Carr, R. (1982) *Spain 1808–1975*. Oxford: The Clarendon Press.
9. Casanova, J. 'The egalitarian dream' in *Journal of the Association of Iberian Studies*, Autumn 1989.
10. Chandler, J. 'The self-destructive nature of the Spanish Restoration' in *Iberian Studies*, Autumn 1973.

11. Clark, R. (1984) *The Basque Insurgents: 1952–1980.* Reno: University of Nevada Press.

12. Conversi, D. (1997) *The Basques, the Catalans and Spain.* London: Hurst.

13. Cotarelo, R. (ed.) (1992) *Transición política y consolidación democrática.* Madrid: Centro de Investigaciones Sociológicas.

14. Díez Medrano, J. (1995) *Divided Nations.* Ithaca: Cornell University Press.

15. Esdaile, C. J. (2000) *Spain in the Liberal Age.* Oxford: Blackwell.

16. Fusi, J. P. and Palafox J. (1998) *España 1808–1996: El desafío de la modernidad.* Madrid: Espasa.

17. Galdós, B. Pérez (1988) *Fortunata and Jacinta.* London: Penguin.

18. Geary, D. (1989) Labour and Socialist Movements in Europe before 1914. Oxford: Berg.

19. Gillespie, R. (1989) The Spanish Socialist Party. A History of Factionalism. Oxford: The Clarendon Press.

20. Graham, H. 'Spanish Socialism in crisis' in *Journal of the Association of Iberian Studies*, Spring 1990.

21. Graham, H. and Preston P. (1987) *The Popular Front in Europe.* Basingstoke: Macmillan.

22. Grugel, J. and Rees T. (1997) *Franco's Spain.* London: Arnold.

23. Harper, G. 'The birth of the first Spanish Republic' in *Iberian Studies*, 16(1&2), 1987.

24. Harrison, J. 'The regenerationist movement in Spain' in *European Studies Review*, January 1979.

25. Heiberg, M. (1989) *The Making of the Basque Nation.* Cambridge: Cambridge University Press.

26. Heywood, P. (1990) *Marxism and the Failure of Organised Socialism in Spain.* Cambridge: Cambridge University Press.

27. Heywood, P. (1995) *The Government and Politics of Spain.* London: Macmillan.

28. Higley, J. and Gunther R. (1992) *Elites and Democratic Consolidation in Latin America and Southern Europe.* Cambridge: Cambridge University Press.

29. Jackson, G. (1965) *The Spanish Republic and the Civil War.* Princeton: Princeton University Press.

30. Kern, R. (1973) *The Caciques.* Albuquerque: University of New Mexico Press.

31. Moradiellos, E. 'The British government and the Spanish Civil War' in *International Journal of Iberian Studies*, 12/1, 1999.

32. Onaindía, M. (2000) *Guía para orientarse en el laberinto vasco*. Madrid: Temas de hoy.

33. Ortega, J. 'Aftermath of splendid disaster' in *Journal of Contemporary History*, April 1980.

34. Orwell, G. (1986) *Homage to Catalonia*. London: Secker and Warburg.

35. Payne, S. (1967) *Politics and the Military in Modern Spain*. Stanford: Stanford University Press.

36. Payne, S. (1975) *Basque Nationalism*. Reno: University of Nevada Press.

37. Payne, S. (1987) *The Franco Regime*. Madison: University of Wisconsin Press.

38. Payne, S. (1993) *Spain's First Democracy*. Madison: University of Wisconsin Press.

39. Powell, C. *España en democracia, 1975–2000*. Madrid: Debolsillo.

40. Preston, P. (1986) *The Triumph of Democracy in Spain*. London: Methuen.

41. Preston, P. (1993) *Franco*. London: HarperCollins.

42. Preston, P. (1994) *The Coming of the Spanish Civil War*. London: Routledge.

43. Preston, P. (1995) *The Politics of Revenge*. London: Routledge.

44. Preston, P. and Mackenzie A. (1996) *The Republic Besieged*. Edinburgh: Edinburgh University Press.

45. Ross, C. J. (2002) *Contemporary Spain. A Handbook*. London: Arnold.

46. Shubert, A. (1990) *A Social History of Modern Spain*. London: Unwin Hyman.

47. Sullivan, J. (1988) *ETA and Basque Nationalism*. London: Routledge.

48. Thomas, H. (1961) *The Spanish Civil War*. London: Penguin.

49. Thomas, H. (1990) The Spanish Civil War. Harmondsworth: Penguin.

50. Tusell, J. (2004) El Aznarato. El gobierno del Partido Popular, 1996–2003. Madrid: Aguilar.

51. Vilar, P. (1977) *Spain, a Brief History*. Oxford: Pergamon.

For reference purposes

Jordan, B. (2002) *Spanish Culture and Society: A Glossary*. London: Arnold.

Smith, A. (1996) *Historical Dictionary of Spain*. Lanham, Michigan: Scarecrow.

Index/Glossary

A page number in **bold** indicates an insert dedicated to the entry
A page number followed by 'i' indicates a reference to the entry in an insert

this image may accurately reflect the experience of some fathers who do face an uphill struggle and who have been unfairly excluded. But it is also a narrative that embraces the compulsive and manipulative father who refuses to give up his attempts to control the life of his former wife and children. The heroic narrative is therefore not spoken only by heroes.

> Philip: I kept asking through my solicitors for more time and tried to get her to see that I could not, that it was too upsetting for me and for the boy, but she would not move at all and in the end I kept going back to court and in the end I was deemed to be a vexatious litigant and they hit me with a section 91.14 which is a really draconian order; basically it means that you cannot make any more orders without the leave of a judge. And that has stayed in place until 2004. Every year I go to court asking to progress my case and he does not, and he knows what I think of him and he knows that I know his days are numbered. The man is a dinosaur.

Philip had taken his case to the Court of Appeal, had challenged the Court Welfare Officer and spent much of his time agitating against CAFCASS and family court judges. His experiences are validated by groups like Families Need Fathers, which publish such accounts in their newsletters and document similar examples of (apparent) injustice, providing a supportive context for this kind of anger. What is more, we also know that these accounts are given increasing credence in the media, which in turn provide a validation of experiences of injustice. It is clear that these 'heroic' fathers identify with a new political script and that this is empowering for them.

Conclusion

In this chapter, I have drawn together ideas about how moral claims to fatherhood are being framed into a new recognisable narrative. Claims to justice and rights are utilised to reposition (disadvantaged) fathers in relation to (over-privileged) mothers. Claims based on the welfare of the child are now routine, while claims based on care are a newer element. These draw both on assertions about fathers' love for their children and on the wider policy context in which it is held that fathers are necessary to their children's well-being and that all responsible parents should parent jointly. As Wallbank has argued, mothers who appear to resist these arguments are now castigated.[34]

At this point, however, it becomes necessary to recognise the limits of this analysis. It is possible to carry out an analysis of emergent narratives and the ways in which different 'elements' such as care or rights are put together to create a new vision of fatherhood. It is also possible to see how debates around specific issues like residence and contact are shifting in line with these evolving narratives. We can also see how some of these narratives become discursive – by this I mean they may become part of how fathers re-envision and reconceive themselves. Hence, we should not really be surprised that more and more fathers may position themselves and understand themselves in these new terms. But the problem arises when, in

---

34 Wallbank (1998).

tracing these developments, one's analysis fails to do justice to the experiences that fathers may be trying to articulate because some of the claims made by the fathers' movement and some individual fathers are so problematic (for children and for mothers). It is also a problem if it is assumed that the new claims that are emerging (especially claims to care) are treated as if they are cynical or politically motivated strategies designed solely to defeat motherhood.[35]

Above, I raised the issue of there being a range of registers through which the new narratives of fatherhood can be presented. I suggested that it is important to be attentive to the tone and emphasis of what is said, but it is also important to hear the quieter statements and not only those that are delivered at high decibels and in an intimidating fashion. Take for example this statement:

> Paul: Contact was stopped sometimes, it has never been as bad as some, as what some non-custodial parents have had, who I have known, some have not seen their children for nine months, over a year, some have not seen them again. It's never been that bad but contact at the moment is one weekend out of every two from the Friday night to the Sunday night, but we don't have any contact during school hours, which I find very difficult to feel involved with the children's growing process if you know what I mean. I know very few of their friends at school or their parents, so I feel slightly isolated from the children, but we do have an exceptionally good time when they do come, but you are not part of their general life.

This father is subscribing to some extent to the widely held view of vindictive residential mothers, although it is interesting that he does not gender his account; he sees it in terms of residential and contact parents, rather than in terms of mothers and fathers. In this way, he shifts the debate away from a simple gender war towards a recognition of the relative powerlessness of the contact parent (of either gender) compared with the residential parent. But he then goes on to capture, in very straightforward terms, what it means to be a parent who cannot share in the everyday life of their child or children. He depicts the sense of exclusion and the hurt that goes with this, but he is not constructing his story as a blame narrative; rather it is one of regret and sadness.

There is therefore a range of registers when it comes to fathers' voices, and it may be that, in listening, we need to become more attuned to these differences. The rise of the more aggressive fathers' rights movement may cloak some very problematic patriarchal and hostile attitudes towards women and children, and may even express a yearning for a golden age when women and children were dependent and powerless. But equally some voices may be seeking to express an emergent change in how fathers wish to relate to their children, and this may signal a shift in fatherhood which is not dependent upon a denigration of motherhood. It would, of course, be unwise to predict how the current struggles over motherhood and fatherhood will unfold. But it is interesting that fathers may be signalling a shift in fatherhood by using ethical claims which were developed in the context of trying to give a place to values associated with care. Returning to the theme originated by Gilligan, one might have predicted that fathers would

---

35 Fineman (1995).

seek to advance their case in relation to an ethic of justice, yet, although this is an important element in their narratives, I have argued that it is claims formulated within an ethic of care that seem to be particularly significant. Of course, whether one sees this as the cynical co-option of feminist ideas for the benefit of men,[36] or as a more complex interplay between shifting values, a recognition of the importance of care relationships and a discursive reconstruction of fatherhood will determine how these changes are viewed.

Acknowledgments

I would like to acknowledge the importance of my collaboration with Dr Vanessa May at the University of Leeds in the work we carried out on the project funded by the Department for Constitutional Affairs. The interviews with fathers from which extracts have been used in this chapter were collected as part of that project.

References

Advisory Board on Family Law: Children Act Sub-Committee (2002) *Making Contact Work: A Report to the Lord Chancellor on the Facilitation of Arrangements for Contact between Children and Their Non-Residential Parents and the Enforcement of Court Orders for Contact*, London: Lord Chancellor's Department

Amato, P and Booth, A (1997) *A Generation at Risk: Growing Up in an Era of Family Upheaval*, Cambridge, MA: Harvard University Press

Bailey-Harris, R (2001) 'Contact – challenging conventional wisdom?', 13 *Child and Family Law Quarterly* 361

Bainham, A (2003a) 'Contact as a right and obligation', in Bainham, A, Lindley, B, Richards, M and Trinder, L (eds) *Children and their Families: Contact, Rights and Welfare*, Oxford: Hart Publishing

Bainham, A (2003b) 'Men and women behaving badly: Is fault dead in English family law?', in Bainham, A, Lindley, B, Richards, M and Trinder, L (eds) *Children and their Families: Contact, Rights and Welfare*, Oxford: Hart Publishing

Brophy, J (1982) 'Parental rights and children's welfare: Some problems of feminists' strategy in the 1920s', 10 *International J of the Sociology of Law* 149

Cantwell, B, Roberts, J and Young, V (1999) 'Presumption of contact in private law – an interdisciplinary issue', 29 *Family Law* 226

Collier, R (1995) *Masculinity, Law and the Family*, London: Routledge

Day Sclater, S (1999) *Divorce: A Psychosocial Study*, Aldershot: Ashgate

---

36 *Ibid.*

Department for Education and Skills (2005) *Draft Children (Contact) and Adoption Bill*, London: HMSO (Cm 6462)

Diduck, A (2003) *Law's Families*, London: LexisNexis UK

Geldof, B (2003) 'The real love that dare not speak its name', in Bainham, A, Londley, B, Richards, M and Trinder, L (eds) *Children and their Families: Contact, Rights and Welfare*, Oxford: Hart Publishing

Gillies, V (2005) 'Meeting parents' needs? Discourses of "support" and "inclusion" in family policy', 25(1) *Critical Social Policy* 70

Gilligan, C (1982) *In a Different Voice*, London: Harvard University Press

Fineman, M (1995) *The Neutered Mother, The Sexual Family and Other Twentieth Century Tragedies*, London: Routledge

James, A and Hay, W (1993) *Court Welfare in Action: Practice and Theory*, London: Harvester Wheatsheaf

Marsden, D (1969) *Mothers Alone*, London: Allen Lane

Morgan, P (1998) 'An endangered species?', in David, M (ed) *The Fragmenting Family: Does It Matter?* London: Institute of Economic Affairs, Choice in Welfare Series No 44

Murch, M (1980) *Justice and Welfare in Divorce*, London: Sweet and Maxwell

Sevenhuijsen, S (1998) *Citizenship and the Ethics of Care*, London: Routledge

Sheldon, S (2001) ' "Sperm bandits", birth control fraud and the battle of the sexes', 21(3) *Legal Studies* 460

Smart, C, May, V, Wade, A and Furniss, C (2003) *Residence and Contact Disputes in Court – Volume 1* (Research Series 6/03), London: Department for Constitutional Affairs

Smart, C and May, V (2005) *Residence and Contact Disputes in Court – Volume II* (Research Series), London: Department for Constitutional Affairs

Smart, C and Sevenhuijsen, S (eds) (1989) *Child Custody and the Politics of Gender*, London: Routledge

Tronto, J (1993) *Moral Boundaries*, London: Routledge

Wallbank, J (1998) 'Castigating mothers: The judicial response to "wilful" women in disputes over paternal contact in English law', 20 *J of Social Welfare and Family Law* 357

Chapter 8

Domestic Violence, Men's Groups and the Equivalence Argument
Felicity Kaganas

Introduction

Feminism and feminist activists have made their mark when it comes to domestic violence. It is largely through feminist efforts that men's violence to women has become visible and that domestic violence is now seen as a serious social problem.[1] Since the days of the 1970s, when the Chiswick women's refuge was established, the issue has moved steadily up the legislative and political agendas; in the United Kingdom, women's organisations have played an important role in achieving this.[2] Changes have been introduced into the law with a view to increasing protection for victims and strengthening the criminal justice response to perpetrators. And, while it is true that changes to the law[3] do not necessarily lead to changes in material circumstances, it appears that, in this area, change has been more than merely cosmetic and that it extends beyond the law. Government policies have been formulated, which are directed at meeting the needs of victims, and services appear to be making some attempt to implement these policies.

The influence that feminist activism and research have had on the law, on policies and on debate concerning domestic violence has extended to definitions of domestic violence, explanations of it and recommendations on how to respond to it.[4] Perhaps most significantly, domestic violence is now seen predominantly as a problem of men's violence and as being linked to men's power and control over women.[5]

A number of men's groups, however, reject this view and are seeking to argue that it is women's violence against men that should be preoccupying the authorities. They maintain that men are subjected to domestic violence and that their suffering is being ignored. Men, they say, are the silent and silenced victims of violent women, of an indifferent state, of callous welfare agencies and of an unheeding criminal justice system. They complain about lack of resources, they call for better services and they insist that it is the punishment of women that should be the priority.

This chapter will provide a brief overview of the impact of feminist thought on policy, practice and the law. It will then turn to consider the claims of the men's groups in the light of the research evidence regarding the prevalence of male victims of domestic violence. And it will conclude that, while these groups are, to

---

1   This recognition has occurred on an international scale. See Declaration on the Elimination of Violence Against Women 1993, Article 2; Council of Europe Committee of Ministers (2002), Appendix, para 1.
2   See Hearn (1998), pp 7–8. See also Mawby and Walklate (1994); Itzin (2000).
3   On feminist engagement with law, see Lewis *et al* (2001).
4   See Itzin (2000).
5   See Mullender and Morley (1994), p 7; Hearn (1998), p 11; Itzin (2000), p 360.

some extent, concerned about men who are abused,[6] they neither produce evidence to prove that abuse of men is a major social problem nor place protection and help high on their agendas. Their main interest lies elsewhere. Their primary aims, rather, are to reverse what they see as the gains that women have made and, most importantly, to store up ammunition in a gender war over shared parenting and paternal contact with children.

Feminism and domestic violence: Impact on law and policy

Since the late 1990s, a number of government initiatives have been devised to tackle domestic violence,[7] all of them focusing on women as victims; civil remedies in cases of domestic violence have been strengthened;[8] and there has been law reform[9] to address feminist criticisms of the way in which crimes involving violence against women[10] have been dealt with by the police and in the courts.

Moreover, it is not only the substantive law that has changed; official discourse and practice has also been affected by feminist research and activism. For instance, guidance issued to the police[11] and also Crown Prosecution Service policy[12] acknowledge that the majority of violent and repeated assaults between intimates are perpetrated by men on their female partners. In addition, both the guidance and the policy document refer to domination, abuse of power and control,[13] as well as to post-separation violence and to women's persisting fear. Even the judiciary, who have been criticised for not treating domestic violence sufficiently seriously,[14] may not be impervious. At least one judge[15] has recently said that there is a 'wider appreciation[16] of the profound and often long-term effects on women and children of serious and chronic domestic violence'.[17] And he himself accepts that domestic violence is a gendered problem and that it is linked to control and domination.[18]

Admittedly, it is still the case that women who are abused face enormous

---

6 It is not the intention here to draw definitive conclusions about the prevalence or otherwise of male victims of domestic violence. The intention is to point out that those groups contending that women's violence against men is a major problem do not produce evidence that it is.

7 See Cabinet Office and Home Office (1999); Home Office (2000a); Home Office (2003). See further Diduck and Kaganas (2006) ch 10.

8 See, for example, Family Law Act 1996, as amended, ss 1, 4 and 46(3A).

9 Domestic Violence, Crime and Victims Act 2004; Protection from Harassment Act 1997, ss 5A and 12; Youth Justice and Criminal Evidence Act 1999, s 17. See further Diduck and Kaganas (2006), ch 10.

10 Including rape: see Sentencing Advisory Panel (2002); *R v Millberry* [2003] 1 WLR 546. See also, on domestic violence in the context of domestic homicide, Law Commission (2003).

11 Home Office (2000b). See also Metropolitan Police (2001).

12 Crown Prosecution Service (2001).

13 See also Sentencing Advisory Panel (2004), para 9.

14 See, for a summary of criticisms, Diduck and Kaganas (2006), ch 10.

15 See also Mitchell (2004).

16 The judge's observations were, however, made in the context of contact disputes.

17 Hamilton (2003), p 5.

18 *Ibid*, p 7.

difficulties in getting help and protection from the law and agencies of the state.[19] But the momentum for change has been maintained and still more reforms are being contemplated. Complaints about lenient sentencing in domestic violence cases are being addressed.[20] Specialist domestic violence courts are being piloted.[21] Priority is being given to training for prosecutors and the judiciary.[22] Better information for victims is now regarded as necessary to reduce risks where a perpetrator is released.[23] Measures are being taken to ensure that child contact is safe.[24] More refuges are planned, as well as outreach and resettlement services.[25]

There can be no doubt that feminist research and the efforts of domestic violence activists have greatly contributed to these initiatives, and that feminism has had an important influence on the way that domestic violence has come to be understood. Newburn and Stanko have observed that 'certain forms of victimisation only become visible when they do, because of the campaigning work of representative groups'.[26] The role of modern moral entrepreneurs[27] in this context is one that has been fulfilled by domestic violence activists along with feminist and pro-feminist researchers. As a result of these people's efforts, domestic violence is now, to a large extent, perceived as a serious social problem and, in particular, as a problem of men and masculinity.

In order to achieve what they have, it was necessary for these 'entrepreneurs' to show that domestic violence affected large numbers of women in profound ways. This the campaigners were certainly able to do. For one thing, abused women themselves made the problem visible. They both articulated it and provided evidence of the needs it created.[28] As more and more women began to seek shelter in overcrowded refuges,[29] activists not only tried to deal with the practical challenges they faced, but also sought to raise public awareness.[30] And as the extent of the problem began to become apparent, public pressure mounted.[31]

Alongside the work of domestic violence activists, the work of researchers and scholars provided further evidence of the plight of abused women. Using in-depth interviews with women as well as analysis of official documents, they managed to 'fill out the statistics with human dimensions and make the social facts comprehensible'.[32]

---

19 See Diduck and Kaganas (2006), ch 10. See also HM Crown Prosecution Service Inspectorate and HM Inspectorate of Constabulary, 2004.
20 Sentencing Advisory Panel (2004).
21 Home Office (2003), p 28. See, on specialist courts, Cook *et al* (2004).
22 Home Office (2003), pp 26–7.
23 *Ibid*, p 28.
24 *Ibid*, pp 38–40.
25 *Ibid*, pp 42–4.
26 Newburn and Stanko (1994), p 155.
27 See Diduck and Kaganas (2006), ch 10.
28 See, for example, Dobash and Dobash (1992), pp 26 and 63.
29 *Ibid* (1992), pp 63–6.
30 See *ibid*, pp 27 and 118.
31 See, for example, *ibid*, pp 112–13.
32 Dobash and Dobash (2000), p 190.

Men as victims

The scale of the problem

Every now and then, and certainly in recent years, these feminist, and now official, accounts of domestic violence have been challenged. The challenge has come from family violence researchers and it has been enthusiastically taken up by groups campaigning for men. These groups seek to draw attention to men's victimisation and to construct domestic violence against men as a major social problem, comparable with the problem of woman abuse. At first blush, then, it might be thought that they are the new moral entrepreneurs engaged in revealing a hidden problem of violent women and victimised men, which is not being adequately addressed by the state.

However, these men's groups tend not to produce, or to produce very little, evidence of the extent of the problem. Some of them rely on American sources; there are websites that provide links to the publications of one American writer, Fontes, in particular.[33] But all of the United Kingdom groups rely primarily on the 1996 British Crime Survey in their literature and on their websites. That survey notoriously concluded that one in four women and one in six men suffer abuse, and it has had the effect that 'the message that "women do domestic violence too" now has official confirmation'.[34] Other findings reported in the survey,[35] indicating that women are more likely than men to suffer serious injury, to suffer post-separation violence, to be afraid and to lack the resources to escape, have not been permitted to mute this message.

The message, moreover, gains additional support from other research studies that show relatively high levels of abuse of men,[36] such as the Scottish Crime Survey[37] and the 2001 British Crime Survey.[38] There is also some support in the most recent British Crime Survey,[39] which reported that 67 per cent of victims of domestic violence were women and 33 per cent were men.[40]

Findings like these are difficult to reconcile with those reported by feminist

---

33 Fontes conducted research in the USA for his PhD and has published a number of pieces on the web on the topic of male victimisation. He claims to have dealt with abused men in his professional capacity, but restricts his evidence to an anecdote about one man and to the bald statement that he 'was surprised by the number of men who shared with [him] their stories of being physically assaulted by their female partners' (Fontes (1998), accessed 19 July 2004). However, he does rely on surveys by family violence researchers using the Conflict Tactics Scale (see Fontes (1998: 2003), 20ff, accessed 27 May 2004). See below for criticisms of this methodology. Fontes also relies on the rising arrest statistics for women, but does not explore the extent to which this might be the effect of arrest policies; in some areas in America the police have been known to arrest both parties routinely (Chesney-Lind, 2002).

34 Worrall (2002), p 55.

35 See Mirrlees-Black (1999), pp 37, 39, 61–2.

36 The research usually includes abuse by women and by other men, without providing separate figures for these categories.

37 See, for discussion, Gadd *et al* (2002).

38 Simmons *et al* (2002).

39 As was the case for the earlier British Crime Survey, these figures do not include sexual offences.

40 Dodd *et al* (2004), Table 5.01.

researchers, which show an overwhelming predominance of male-on-female violence. One explanation for the discrepancy, which is suggested by Dobash and Dobash, lies in the different research methods used.[41] They draw a distinction between 'family violence' research and 'violence against women' research.

Family violence researchers claim that intimate violence is 'symmetrical', with men and women equally likely to be perpetrators.[42] They have relied mainly on measuring discrete 'acts', such as a slap or a punch. In contrast, 'violence against women' researchers claim that intimate violence is 'asymmetrical', with men as the main perpetrators.[43] They argue that violence cannot be understood unless context is taken into account, and that purely act-based research fails to do this. When violence is considered in the context of a relationship, the evidence suggests that men's violence is often associated with a ' "constellation of abuse" that includes a variety of additional intimidating, aggressive and controlling acts'.[44] This same phenomenon is not apparent in reports about women's violence against male partners.[45] Women's violence is normally associated with self-defence or retaliation against men's violence.[46]

The research methods

It appears that when context is taken into account, and when searching interviews are part of the methodology, useful information about the prevalence and the meaning of violence can be garnered. Dobash and Dobash note that women's accounts 'reveal the nature of men's violence, the sources of conflict leading to attacks, their own emotions and reactions'.[47] Men's accounts in turn show them minimising their own violence and denying responsibility for their actions.[48] Hearn, for instance, quotes one man as saying: 'I wasn't violent . . . I picked her up twice and threw her against the wall . . . I've never struck a woman . . .'[49] Another said he had only been 'really' violent twice, although he admitted to slapping his victim frequently: 'I don't see slapping as being really violent.'[50]

Family violence research is not designed to reveal attitudes like these, and Dobash and Dobash[51] argue that family violence methodology gives rise to a skewed picture. The act-based approach relies on lists of items designed to measure conflict and abuse. The main instrument used is the Conflict Tactics Scale.[52]

---

41 Dobash and Dobash (2004), p 324. See also Barnish (2004), para 2.1.
42 Dobash and Dobash (2004), p 326.
43 *Ibid*, p 327.
44 *Ibid*, p 328.
45 *Ibid*, p 328. But see *Dispatches*, shown on Channel 4 on 7 January 1998. See Dewar Research (1998).
46 Dobash and Dobash (2004), p 328.
47 Dobash and Dobash (2000), p 190.
48 *Ibid*, p 190.
49 *Ibid*, p 117. See also pp 111–12. See also Barnish (2004), para 4.3.
50 *Ibid*, p 115. See also Barnish (2004), para 4.3.
51 Dobash and Dobash (2004).
52 See further Dobash and Dobash (1992), ch 8.

This research tool does not distinguish between serious and trivial consequences. Nor can the meaning of acts and their outcome be discerned.[53] The Conflict Tactics Scale ignores motivation such as self-defence.[54] In addition, act-based measures often do not reveal frequency or seriousness.[55] The studies also conflate physical and sexual violence with behaviour such as shouting. And although Dobash and Dobash agree that non-violent acts of abuse are significant, they argue that it can be misleading not to separate them from physical violence.[56] Indeed, Dobash suggests that the 'conflation of physical attack with conflict, intimidation and threats . . . may be a primary source of the notion that men and women are equally likely to be "violent" to an intimate partner'.[57]

Examining the research

The Dobashes' contention that domestic violence is asymmetrical appears to be borne out by research examining more closely the studies showing high levels of male victimisation.

First, Gadd et al[58] designed a research project to assess the nature and extent of domestic violence against men in Scotland, in the light of the Scottish Crime Survey 2000. The study revealed that some male respondents included in the statistics as victims were not victims at all. In follow-up interviews, one in four denied having experienced domestic abuse.[59] Some indicated that they were referring to vandalism or theft around the home and/or acts of stranger or acquaintance violence when they reported victimisation.[60]

Of course, there were men who did say they had been abused, and there were some who reported life-threatening events. But many of the men described the abuse as 'rare and relatively inconsequential'.[61] About half of the men interviewed said they were also abusive, although some said this was retaliatory. Only a minority of the men perceived themselves as victims.[62]

Second, Walby and Allen[63] conducted a study examining responses from a questionnaire which was included in the 2001 British Crime Survey. They used a questionnaire based on the Conflict Tactics Scale,[64] but even so, their report[65] does not support the view that domestic violence is symmetrical.[66]

---

53 See, for example, Dobash and Dobash (2004), p 329.
54 *Ibid*, p 329.
55 *Ibid*, p 330.
56 *Ibid*, p 331.
57 Dobash (2003), p 314.
58 Gadd *et al* (2002).
59 *Ibid*, p 1.
60 *Ibid*, p 3.
61 *Ibid*, p 3.
62 *Ibid*, p 3.
63 Walby and Allen (2004).
64 *Ibid*, p 15: albeit adapted to take account of criticism.
65 *Ibid*.
66 See, for example, *ibid*, p 37.

They[67] found that 'women are the overwhelming majority of the most heavily abused group'.[68] They report that it is largely women who 'suffer multiple attacks and are subject to more than one form of inter-personal violence'.[69] Of those respondents who had been subjected by their abuser to four or more incidents of domestic violence, 89 per cent were women.[70] Women also outnumbered men when it came to severe injury[71] and mental or emotional harm.[72] Ten times more women than men reported potentially life-threatening violence in the form of being choked or strangled.[73] The number of sexual assaults against women greatly exceeded those against men.[74] Women were more likely to be subjected to aggravated stalking,[75] by an 'intimate or former intimate'.[76] They were also more likely to suffer post-separation violence, notably in the context of child contact.[77]

Walby and Allen state that far more women then men reported being frightened of threats.[78] And fear, they say, is important 'in the understanding of domestic violence as a pattern of coercive control'.[79] Fontes, on the other hand, who contends that violence is symmetrical, argues that men are 'trained' to 'ignore or suppress fear',[80] or do not tell anyone about their plight since they feel ashamed.[81]

Walby and Allen's research findings do suggest that under-reporting is more common for men than for women,[82] although the picture changes when sexual assaults are included.[83] However, the reasons for under-reporting that Walby and Allen found to be prevalent do not bear out Fontes's theory. A more plausible explanation is that violence against women tended to be more serious.

First, there is a correlation between disclosure and the frequency and severity of the violence.[84] Because women suffer considerably more repeat violence and the violence against them is more frequently severe, it is not surprising that they disclose more. Second, contrary to the view that men are deterred by embarrassment at higher rates than women, a slightly larger proportion of women (7 per cent)

---

67 See also Barnish (2004), para 2.3.
68 Walby and Allen (2004), p vii.
69 *Ibid*, p 11. See further pp 18, 29–31.
70 *Ibid*, p vii. See further pp 23 and 25.
71 *Ibid* p viii.
72 *Ibid*, p viii. See further pp 33–7. Domestic violence also appears to affect women's health but not men's (p 87).
73 *Ibid*, p 19.
74 *Ibid*, p vii. Of the women who were raped, 45 per cent were raped by a husband or partner and 9 per cent by a former husband or partner (p ix).
75 Cases where there was violence in addition to stalking.
76 Walby and Allen (2004), pp ix and 61.
77 *Ibid*, p ix.
78 *Ibid*, p 19.
79 *Ibid*, p 19.
80 See also Stanko and Hobdell (1993), pp 401 and 413; Goody (1997).
81 Fontes (1998: 2003), p 39.
82 Walby and Allen (2004), p 91. See also Barnish (2004), para 2.5.
83 See Walby and Allen (2004), p x and p 94. See also p 53.
84 *Ibid*, p 98.

than men (5 per cent) said they did not report because they did not want any further humiliation.[85] Indeed, it seems that the most common reason for not reporting among men is that the incident was not seen as serious: 68 per cent of men compared with 41 per cent of women said they did not disclose because they thought the incident was too trivial. 'No discernible percentage of men' and 13 per cent of women said that they feared more violence or that the situation would worsen if they reported to the police.[86]

It seems, then, that on closer scrutiny neither the British Crime Survey nor the Scottish Crime Survey proves gender symmetry. And the most recent research conducted by Dobash and Dobash[87] also demonstrates differences between the prevalence and consequences of violence committed by men and women.[88] Their definition of violence was framed so as to distinguish between physical abuse and what they see as less damaging emotional and financial abuse. Unlike the Conflict Tactics Scale, they distinguish serious and frequent violence from behaviour associated with conflict, such as shouting and acts such as a one-off push.

All the men in the study had been convicted of an offence involving violence against their partners. Just under half agreed that there had been no violence on the part of the woman. Men and women alike reported more male than female violence, and it appears that men perpetrate more of every kind of violent act and that they inflict more injuries.[89] However, men appeared to minimise their violence; a larger percentage of women than men reported their own violence[90] and women reported being subject to more severe and more frequent violence than their partners admitted to inflicting.[91] Nevertheless, men's violence was perceived by both men and women as 'serious' or 'very serious', while women's violence was seen as 'not serious' or 'slightly serious'.[92] Women often said they acted in self-defence or for 'self-protection'.[93] Only a few used serious or injurious violence, even though they had all been subjected to repeated physical violence from their partners. Also, women did not use the kind of controlling behaviour that characterises the 'constellation of abuse'.

The study also reveals significant differences in the effects of violence on men and women. Most women said they were usually 'frightened', and that they felt helpless, trapped and angry. In contrast, the men mostly said they were 'not bothered', or ridiculed the woman. The men found the violence inconsequential and rarely sought protection from the authorities.[94] Only a few felt 'victimized';[95] '[u]nlike the women, few of the men reacted to the violence in ways that suggested

---

85 *Ibid*, p x.
86 *Ibid*, p x. See further pp 101–2.
87 Dobash and Dobash (2004).
88 See *ibid*, pp 343–4.
89 *Ibid*, pp 336–7.
90 *Ibid*, p 336.
91 *Ibid*, p 338.
92 *Ibid*, p 338.
93 *Ibid*, p 314.
94 *Ibid*, p 343.
95 *Ibid*, p 340.

it had seriously affected their sense of well-being or the routines of their daily life'.[96]

The 'search for equivalence'

The available evidence does suggest that there are men who are subjected to violence at the hands of their partners or former partners. Nevertheless, it seems clear that it is primarily women who suffer as a result of domestic violence.

The question, then, is what lies behind the campaigns by men's groups seeking to establish women's violence against men as a serious social problem. These campaigns would be perfectly understandable if they were designed to draw attention to any unmet needs of male victims. Certainly, that is what groups such as Women's Aid have done and are continuing to do for women. But women's organisations have been faced with overwhelming evidence that large numbers of women are abused, that many suffer serious injuries and that women often have no means of escape.

Yet there is nothing to suggest that men's groups have been confronted with such palpable exigency. Their 'search for equivalence'[97] in relation to domestic violence appears to be driven primarily by other considerations. This seems to be a campaign based on anecdote, contested research evidence and 'rhetorical resort to notions of equality'.[98] One of the main grievances appears to be that things have changed and the pendulum has swung too far in favour of women.

A number of writers have suggested that what lies behind the search for equivalence is an attempt to obscure or divert attention from gender inequality. Feminist researchers have argued that domestic violence is a manifestation of power and control, and the demonstration of a sense of possessiveness and entitlement. To say that women are equally violent is a way of denying that inequality exists in society or that women are oppressed.

> Now what is striking is that when each discovery [of abuse] is made, and somehow made real in the world, the response has been: it happens to men too. If women are hurt, men are hurt. If women are raped, men are raped. If women are sexually harassed, men are sexually harassed. If women are battered, men are battered. Symmetry must be reasserted. Neutrality must be reclaimed. Equality must be re-established.[99]

The equivalence argument means that violence and abuse can again be legitimately analysed in terms other than those of gender inequality.[100] As Worrall, quoting MacKinnon,[101] says: ' "All of this 'men too' stuff means that people don't really believe" that women are victims of anything anymore.'[102]

---

96 *Ibid*, p 341.
97 This term is borrowed from Forbes (1992).
98 Graycar (2000), para E.
99 MacKinnon (1987), p 170.
100 Worrall (2002), p 48.
101 MacKinnon (1987), p 171.
102 Worrall (2002), p 48.

Similarly Forbes[103] argues that the 'search for equivalence' legitimates a return to a gender-neutral analysis of abuse. It entails a return to explanations focusing on individual or family pathology and social pressures, rather than those focusing on inequality and the exercise of male power.[104] And the assertion of equivalence sends a message to professionals that they 'can get back to the business of understanding and treating (ungendered) deviant behaviour'.[105]

The equivalence argument may also serve another function: that of rendering men, and fathers in particular, safe. Collier observes that men's groups complain that men have become the new victims of divorce[106] and that the law has moved too far in favour of women.[107] Their vilification of women and mothers is in part an effort to defuse what has been seen as a 'crisis of paternal masculinity'.[108] Men's groups maintain that fathers are crucial to the healthy functioning of families[109] but that feminism has ousted the father.[110] In order to reinstate fathers at the centre of the family, it has been necessary to render fatherhood 'safe'.[111] For fathers to be equal partners in the family, it is important that they do not embody the 'threat of the undomesticated male'.[112] Familial masculinity, he says, has been constructed as something remote from drunkenness, violence and sexuality.[113]

Feminist research, in contrast, has of course focused on men's dangerousness and has sought to expose men's violence in the home. Research into violent men in the 1980s, say Mullender et al,[114] painted a picture of men who appeared to reflect little on their role as fathers. More recently, research has drawn links between violence against women and child abuse and has explored the effects on children of domestic violence.[115] This research, therefore, calls into question the fitness as parents of violent fathers.

The equivalence argument can be used to deflect such questions. To assert that women are as violent as men and as likely to abuse their children means that men cannot be singled out as a source of danger to their partners and children. The equivalence argument also enables violence to be seen in terms of mutual combat or simple conflict; something far less dangerous than sustained and overwhelming attacks on a terrified and demoralised victim. Men, therefore, are no worse than, and are as safe as, women. Accordingly, they should maintain a central role in the nuclear or bi-nuclear family.

Finally, the equivalence argument may have the effect of downgrading the

---

103 (1992). She discusses the 'discovery' of the female sexual abuser.
104 *Ibid*, pp 107–8.
105 *Ibid*, p 109.
106 Collier (1999), p 126.
107 Collier (1995).
108 Collier (1999), p 127.
109 Collier (1995), p 202.
110 *Ibid*, p 177.
111 *Ibid*, p 202.
112 *Ibid*, p 202.
113 *Ibid*, p 212.
114 Mullender *et al* (2002), p 180.
115 See, for example, Mullender *et al* (2002).

importance attached to men's violence and, to some extent, substituting under-standing for condemnation of it. As Rock says, becoming a victim carries rewards: '... sympathy, attention, being treated as blameless ... exoneration, absolution ... exemption from prosecution, mitigation of punishment.'[116]

An examination of the material produced by various men's groups and pub-lished on their websites suggests that they are using the equivalence argument in all of these ways. And this argument, along with others,[117] is being deployed in a bid to counter what they see as the ascendancy of feminism and the denigration and marginalisation of men.

The websites

The scale of the problem

This chapter will focus primarily on the four groups that seem to be most active in lobbying for, and offering support to, abused men.[118] The most recently estab-lished of these is the 'it does happen network', set up in September 2004. Its website states that it was first created to provide a 'safe haven for *men* to seek information, help, advice, support and a place to talk and share their experi-ences'.[119] It claims that within the first two weeks of its existence over 3,000 men had made contact. It is not clear, however, what counts as contact. Nor is it clear how many of these contacts were made by victims of domestic violence.

Another group, the Mankind Initiative, is an organisation concerned with fight-ing what it sees as discrimination against men and boys in fields such as education, employment, and 'family abuse'.[120] It has produced a document, 'The Mankind Family Abuse Campaign',[121] which sets out to draw attention to the abuse of men by women. Only seven case studies are provided, but the organisation is at pains to stress that these are 'just the tip of the iceberg'. However, even the studies that are documented are difficult to evaluate. Some are phrased in the form of simple assertions such as 'Mr B and his two children suffered years of abuse'; no indication is given of the form that the abuse took. In only three studies is any relevant detail given. One woman broke a window with a cricket bat. Another is described as abusive for denigrating her husband and throwing a table. Yet this woman is also said to have 'engineer[ed] arguments' so as to provoke 'a verbal

---

116 Rock (2002), p 14.
117 Some websites include material that is simply misogynous. See, for example, Manorama, Door 3: http://homepage.ntlworld.com.verismo/index.html (accessed 19 July 2004).
118 It is not claimed that any of these groups is representative of a significant segment of the British male population. However, these groups are significant in that they seek to influence law and policy and it is these groups that lobby politicians and policy makers, ostensibly on behalf of men as a constituency.
119 The 'it does happen network' at www.itdoeshappen.org/mambo/index.php?option= content&task=view&id=8&it (accessed 5 November 2004; emphasis in original).
120 See The Mankind Initiative at www.mankind.org.uk/charter.html (accessed 1 June 2004). It is also a strong proponent of the 'traditional family'.
121 See at www.mankind.org.uk/dv.html (accessed 26 November 2004).

reaction or better still a physical reaction'. She made 'false allegations' and was able to 'play the DV card' in order to get the man out of the house. A further case also involved 'provocation into an argument followed by a false accusation' resulting in cautions and, after a subsequent allegation, the man's arrest.

These descriptions, with their references to provocation, give some grounds for suspecting that at least some of the men may themselves have been violent. No information is given to substantiate the claim that the women's allegations were false and, in one case, violence by the man is conceded. In any event, the studies are insufficiently informative or numerous to make a convincing case that abuse of men is an unrecognised and serious social problem.

The Men's Aid website is no more enlightening. This organisation was originally established specifically to help male[122] victims of domestic violence as well as men engaged in contact disputes. Yet despite its central role in lobbying for, and offering support to, abused men, the organisation is somewhat vague on the question of the prevalence of male victims and the nature of their unmet needs. As regards the scale of the problem, there is no information on their newly reorganised website.[123] Until recently, however, their website included a report that, in 2002, they were receiving around 700 requests for help each month. But since changing their statistical recording methods, they were receiving fewer.[124] They say they 'support' fifty families 'with a comparable sized waiting list'.[125] It is somewhat surprising, therefore, to read in their response to the government consultation on domestic violence a reference to the 'many hundreds of thousands of men, women and children that we support'.[126]

This discrepancy in the figures is difficult to explain and the figures themselves are difficult to interpret. This is because Men's Aid, like other men's organisations, has been seeking to expand the definition of domestic violence to encompass what they see as a major problem: mothers who deny fathers contact with their children. There is no way of knowing whether the families they are 'supporting' are victims of women's violence, 'falsely' accused men or protagonists in contact disputes. On the basis of its own figures, it seems that most of Men's Aid's referrals concern contact disputes and that the number of men coming forward because of violence is relatively small. Gordon, writing the group's response to the government's consultation paper, says that '[m]ore than 60% of the men

---

122 Although the organisation states that it is gender neutral, Men's Aid has undergone organisational change and has completely rewritten its website since the bulk of the research for this paper was done. Parts of the website appeared to be still under construction at the time of writing, and by proof stage it contained almost no information about domestic violence on men. Gordon's paper (2003) had disappeared (see below).

123 www.crisisline.co.uk/mensaid/ (accessed 5 November 2004).

124 See at www.mensaid.org/history.htm (accessed 25 May 2004). Women constitute about 45 per cent of their contacts (Gordon (2003), p 5) and most of these are mothers, sisters and daughters of male victims of domestic violence. See www. mensaid.org/domestic-violence.htm (accessed 6 May 2004).

125 Gordon (2003), p 5.

126 Ibid, p 21. They also refer to 'the hundred thousand or so female perpetrators' (p 24).

that approach Men's Aid for assistance are being consistently abused by their ex-partners by deliberately refusing reasonable child contact'.[127]

There does appear to be some demand for refuge space. The 'it does happen network'[128] and Men's Aid report plans to provide 'refuge space for men and their children'.[129] The Mankind Initiative is also establishing a refuge and has set up helplines for men.[130] Yet, although men's groups complain of discrimination[131] and deplore the lack of refuges, it is not clear whether the kind of refuges that some are setting up are needed. Men's Aid, for example, says that 'most male victims would find communal refuge solutions inappropriate'.[132] In any event, none of the organisations shows the existence of a large number of men subjected to abuse that is comparable with that suffered by women.[133] Neither the numbers cited nor the broad definitions used[134] support the equivalence argument.

Nor is it apparent from the websites that all the groups prioritise domestic violence. With the possible exceptions of 'the it does happen network' and the Mankind Initiative, which are focusing on refuge provision and seeking to secure resources, they seem to be primarily concerned with agendas other than protection of victims of violence: they want to prevent men from being removed from the home; they want to place men at the centre of the family; and they want to gain control over women and their sexuality. A statement from Men's Aid neatly encapsulates all these themes:

> The state's willingness to accept a women's (*sic*) allegation as an evidential truth sufficient enough to have a man removed from his home, and have him separated from his children is unpardonable, a power arbitrarily afforded to women alone, which is often employed by female abusers to further abuse their partners. There is also evidence that many women 'let their hair down' after separation.[135]

For Families Need Fathers, as for some of the other groups, the greatest significance of the incidence of domestic violence evidently lies in its implications for contact disputes.[136] Families Need Fathers is clear about its concerns: '[T]here are attempts to create a stereotype of fathers being a danger to their children . . . If false stereotypes are believed, this will cause social policy and decisions about families to be based on prejudice.'[137] It goes on to say that: 'Secondly, our work is affected when accusations of domestic violence are raised in individual cases where residence and contact are being decided . . . Because of discriminatory and

---

127 *Ibid*, p 27.
128 www.itdoeshappen.org/mambo/ (accessed 5 November 2004).
129 www.crisisline.co.uk/mensaid/dv.htm (accessed 26 November 2004).
130 www.mankind.org.uk/dv.html (accessed 1 June 2004).
131 See, for example, Gordon (2003), p 12.
132 *Ibid*, p 55.
133 But see Dewar Research (1998). See also Richards (2004), para 5.1.7.
134 See, for example, The Mankind Initiative (2004), para 3.2, which refers to 'verbal' abuse, a term that could extend to 'nagging'.
135 Gordon (2003), p 14.
136 See Smart, Chapter 7 in this volume.
137 Families Need Fathers (undated), p 3.

prejudicial stereotypes many individual cases are not judged fairly and on their merits.'[138] It appears, therefore, that the main task that groups like Families Need Fathers have set themselves is to render the family man safe.

The strategies

Central to the strategy of rendering men safe and essential to the proper functioning of the family is the equivalence argument. It is also crucial to the re-assertion of equality and the move to introduce gender-neutral terminology into the debate. In addition, it is used to excuse and explain men's violence.

Equivalence, equality and gender neutrality

The 1996 British Crime Survey statistics[139] feature prominently on some of the websites, and all put forward the equivalence argument. Families Need Fathers is the only organisation to concede that there are differences in the severity of violence; the British Crime Survey, it says, 'suggests that men and women report broadly similar levels of domestic violence overall, though the majority of serious injuries are sustained by women'.[140] Nevertheless, it still invokes the notion of equivalence: 'There are perpetrators of violence of both sexes, but the propaganda is only about men.'[141] The statistics, it is alleged, are misleading, as men find it difficult to report because they are not taken seriously or they are treated as perpetrators. There are few services to which they can turn: 'These feelings of course affect the statistics, making female on male accusations a self-filling prophecy (sic).'[142] In reality, it is suggested, domestic violence is frequently characterised by mutual combat: confrontations are 'instigated by [the] mother or father or, as we suspect is commonly the case, by both'.[143]

Men's groups accordingly promote gender-neutral understandings of domestic violence. The 'it does happen network' proclaims that: 'It's not a Gender issue, it's a *human issue*!'[144] Families Need Fathers asserts that 'the gender assumptions in the proposals [relating to contact between children and violent parents] are both ill-founded and offensive'.[145] Similarly, The Mankind Initiative argues that the definition of abuse needs to be free of references to gender and 'free of gender politics'.[146] The language of equality is pressed into service to prove that women

---

138 *Ibid*, p 3.
139 The Justice for Fathers UK website links to a page entitled 'The Truth About Domestic Violence. Exposing Stanko's Big Lie of 1 in 4' (www.justiceinfamilylaw.co.uk/ The%20big%20lie.htm). This webpage refers to the 1996 British Crime Survey to show equivalence (accessed 9 February 2004). See also The Mankind Initiative, at www.mankind.org.uk/charter.html.
140 Families Need Fathers (2001) (accessed 26 November 2004).
141 Families Need Fathers (undated), p 3.
142 *Ibid*, p 4.
143 *Ibid*, p 4.
144 The 'it does not happen network' at www.itdoeshappen.org/mambo/ (accessed 5 November 2004, emphasis in original).
145 Families Need Fathers (1999), p 3. See also Families Need Fathers (1999), p 9.
146 The Mankind Initiative at www.mankind.org.uk/dv.html (accessed 1 June 2004).

and men hold power in equal measure and that women must surely abuse it in the same way:[147]

> Domestic abuse is no longer about the subjugation of women by men; . . . it is time the government recognised that women are not inferior and have the same capacity for creation and destruction as men.[148]

This insistence on equality and gender neutrality is designed to shift the focus away from men's dangerousness.

Rendering men safe

One strategy aimed at downplaying the threat that some men present is to suggest that the problem of violence, and male violence in particular, is being exaggerated. Fathers4Justice, for example, suggest that domestic violence may be being used as a 'bogus argument and smokescreen to remove fathers from their children'.[149] Families Need Fathers, in turn, warns that children's relationships with their fathers 'should not be imperilled by excessive reactions to other problems'.[150] The numbers involved are not as great as they seem: 'The behaviour of a minority in each sex is generalised to other members of that sex.'[151] And in any event, violence, as long as it is not severe, is normal and is something that women engage in as well as men: 'Domestic violence is, if some definitions are used, common but gender neutral, or, if other definitions are used, male on female but affecting a small minority.'[152] The incidence of domestic murders, perpetrated predominantly by men, does not 'indicate any need for concerns about violence to be the drive contact arrangements (sic) in the hundreds of thousands of families who divide each year without violence'.[153] So, extreme violence is sufficiently rare to be discounted in formulating policy, and less extreme violence is common and gender neutral, and, therefore, presumably of little import. On the contrary, the state is 'over-protective':[154] 'In the past the shortfall in the concern about domestic violence put people at risk. There is now a risk of damage to adults and children because of an overshoot.'[155]

Another approach is to maintain that much of men's violence is apparent rather than real; women make false allegations. Mothers engaged in residence or contact disputes are particularly prone to lie. According to Men's Aid:

> In assisting victims of domestic violence and their families we have become aware that false allegations of domestic violence and child abuse are common practices by the abusers in order to gain a better standing, greater support and sympathy and

---

147 *Ibid* and Fontes (1998).
148 Gordon (2003), p 8.
149 Fathers4Justice (2003), p 11.
150 Families Need Fathers (undated), p 2.
151 *Ibid*, p 3. See also p 5.
152 *Ibid*, p 6.
153 *Ibid*, p 6.
154 *Ibid*, p 8.
155 *Ibid*, p 5.

inevitably residence of any children – a position from which they can continue to abuse and control the victim.[156]

Families Need Fathers, in a similar vein,[157] observes:

> Allegations of domestic violence towards the mother are frequently made in response to a father's application for a Contact Order. Many children lose contact with their father as a result, irrespective of the truth, for such criminal allegations are rarely examined properly in family cases[158] . . . An unsubstantiated allegation of domestic violence is therefore a key weapon for those wishing to obstruct contact.[159]

It is suggested by Families Need Fathers that women are fuelled by bitterness and motivated to lie by the benefits to be gained by denying contact to a 'hated ex', by gaining control of housing and by the prospect of 'improved incomes'.[160] What is more, it is these women who are portrayed as dangerous, not the accused men. Along with the denial of violence comes an attempt to shift the focus of blame and to establish a new form of victimisation: 'There are also victims, adults and children, of false allegations.'[161]

Yet another strategy is to deny any risk to children, even when there is evidence of violence against women. Men's groups seek to draw a clear distinction between woman abuse and child abuse, indicating that the former is irrelevant to the latter. It is irrelevant because it is in the past[162] or because it does not affect the children. Men's Aid, for example, recommends that 'perpetrators found guilty of domestic violence [be] permitted child contact',[163] although they might have to be kept from direct contact with the victim.[164] They also suggest that children should not necessarily be placed with the victim of domestic violence rather than the perpetrator: 'Being a victim of domestic violence does not assume that person to be a better parent, as being a perpetrator does not automatically assume that individual would do anything to harm the children.'[165] Families Need Fathers is adamant in its defence of contact between fathers and children: '[W]e believe that the removal or restriction of a parent's contact with his/her child is a draconian measure which should only be taken when there is a *demonstrable* risk of *direct* harm to the child.'[166]

---

156 The Men's Aid Philosophy, at www.crisisline.co.uk/mensaid/philosophy.htm (accessed 5 November 2004). Although this does not refer to the gender of the parties, it is clear that it is the resident parent, normally the mother, who is alleged to have lied.
157 See also Gordon (2003), p 27.
158 It is suggested that allegations of violence be removed altogether from the family courts and be confined to criminal courts with the criminal standard of proof (Families Need Fathers (1999), p 2).
159 Families Need Fathers (2001). See also Families Need Fathers (1999), p 2.
160 Families Need Fathers (undated), p 8.
161 *Ibid*, p 11. See also Mankind Initiative, 'Family Policy Document' at www.mankind.org.uk/fampol.htm (accessed 1 June 2004); Men's Aid 'Domestic Violence' at www.crisisline.co.uk/mensaid/dv.htm (accessed 5 November 2004).
162 Families Need Fathers (undated), p 9.
163 Gordon (2003), p 27.
164 *Ibid*, p 50.
165 See at www.crisisline.co.uk/mensaid/philosophy.htm (accessed 5 November 2004).
166 Families Need Fathers (2001) (emphasis added). See also Families Need Fathers (1999), p 3; Gordon (2003), p 30.

It seems that, with assertions like this, Families Need Fathers is attempting to counter the thinking that has since led to the amendment of the definition of 'harm' in the Children Act 1989 to include the harm caused by witnessing domestic violence. It is also seeking to break the links forged by feminist research between woman abuse and child abuse. Indeed, Families Need Fathers manages both to break this link and to impugn women's credibility at the same time:

> The claim is often made that there is 'an association' between violence inflicted on partners and violence and other ill-treatment inflicted on children . . . But how strong is the association is highly problematic. It is based primarily on reports of residents of women's refuges, highly likely to hate their ex's.[167]

And even if children are harmed by witnessing violence, women's bad behaviour also exposes children to risk. While Families Need Fathers concedes that equivalence in terms of severity of violence cannot be asserted, there is equivalence in relation to harm to children, irrespective of whether there is actual violence or there is family conflict:

> [T]here is no reason to think the all harm (*sic*) to children is when there is violence and none occurs when there is hostile and aggressive behaviour of other sorts. The pattern asserted below – that extreme behaviour is often more male on female than the other way around, but affects a small minority of families, but that other undesirable behaviours are more common but more equally balanced by gender, applies here too.[168]

Having downplayed the risks posed to children by violent men, Families Need Fathers goes on to stress the importance of fathers to their children's well-being. The harm that we should be concerned about is the harm to children and to society should children's links with fathers become attenuated:

> There would be nothing less than tragedies in individual cases if a child were effectively orphaned from a loved and loving father on false on insufficient (*sic*) grounds. It would cause general social damage if this happens on any significant scale, granted the impact on children and society.[169]

Rendering women abusive and dangerous

Men's groups have deployed the equivalence argument to render men, and fathers in particular, safe or no more dangerous than women. But they also seek to show the converse: that women are as dangerous, or can be more dangerous, than men. Men's Aid stresses the need 'to appreciate that being female does not lessen the seriousness of their domestic abuse perpetration, and being male does not reduce the seriousness of the abuse that is suffered'.[170] And it is not only men who are victimised, it is children too. Men's Aid, for example, states that it is seeking to

---

167 Families Need Fathers (undated), p 5. Walby and Allen (2004, p ix) report that in 2 per cent of cases of post-separation contact involving violent men there had been threats to the children and in 1 per cent of cases, the perpetrator hurt the children.
168 Families Need Fathers (undated), p 5.
169 *Ibid*, p 5.
170 Gordon (2003), p 8.

alleviate the plight of 'men, who have so far been left, with their children . . .
to suffer often chronic domestic violence at the hands of their partners and
ex-partners'.[171]

The aim of Men's Aid and similar organisations appears to be to show that
mothers cannot always be trusted to protect their children or to safeguard their
best interests. More specifically, their aim is to discredit mothers who oppose
contact. In order to achieve this, men's groups have sought to construct new
categories of harm. Denial of contact is in itself classified as harmful; mothers
who resist contact are defined as perpetrators of 'child abuse' and of 'domestic
violence', terms which condemn them out of hand. Fathers and children are portrayed as victims, their suffering at the hands of the same oppressor uniting them
on the same side in the contact battle.

Families Need Fathers, for example, maintain that the 'most common form of
domestic violence amongst separating couples may be the deliberate thwarting of
contact by the controlling parent'[172] and say that mothers who engage in such
behaviour are emotionally abusive.[173] Men's Aid too refers to abuse and domestic
violence: 'One in six men are victims of domestic violence and many more men are
abused through being unreasonably refused child contact, itself an act of domestic
violence.'[174]

This use of language seeks to expand the definition of domestic violence beyond
its currently accepted usage.[175] However, Men's Aid has attempted to bring it
within the parameters of established usage. The somewhat disingenuous explanation entails subverting the notion of the 'constellation of abuse', which includes
social isolation as an element of abusive behaviour, in order to support the contact
argument:

> We . . . accept the national definition of domestic violence which states that being
> prevented access to 'your family and friends' is an act of domestic violence and,
> therefore, being refused reasonable contact with your child after separation and
> divorce is an act of domestic violence.[176]

Denial of contact is also designated as child abuse. According to Justice for
Fathers UK, for instance, women emotionally abuse their children 'by using them
as pawns'.[177] In addition, mothers are dangerous because they physically abuse
their children or expose them to abuse from their new sexual partners.

Women in general are considered to be irresponsible and out of control.

---

171 *Ibid*, p 5.
172 Families Need Fathers (1999), p 11.
173 *Ibid*, p 2. See also p 10.
174 Men's Aid at www.mensaid.org/general-info.htm (accessed 25 May 2004).
175 Of course, women's groups have also used and expanded the definition of domestic violence
     in strategic ways.
176 www.mensaid.org/about-us.htm (accessed 6 May 2004).
177 www.justiceinfamilylaw.co.uk (accessed 9 February 2004). See also the Mankind Charter at
     www.mankind.org.uk/charter.html (accessed 1 June 2004). The courts too, in a limited range
     of cases, have held children to have been emotionally abused by mothers who have made
     unfounded allegations of sexual abuse. See *Re M (Intractable Contact Dispute: Interim Care
     Order)* [2003] EWHC 1024 (Fam), [2003] 2 FLR 636; *V v V (Contact: Implacable Hostility)*
     [2004] EWHC 1215 (Fam), [2004] 2 FLR 851.

The Mankind Initiative, for example, complains that: 'Women are searching for the perfect man who does not exist – a man who will permit them to indulge in excessive behaviour or enable them to change the rules as and when it suits.'[178] This irresponsibility, combined with uncontrolled sexuality, presents a major risk to children, a risk that can only be countered by the presence of the father:

> The children's likelihood of being abused by their 'single' mothers, already the most likely person to abuse the children, is increased, and the woman's probability of meeting strangers is increased which in turn further increases the woman's and child's likelihood of being abused, particularly true as the main protector of the family is absent.[179]

Indeed, many allegations of domestic violence are falsely made, it is said, in order to eject the 'true victim' from the home and to allow the 'true perpetrator' to move in with a new partner, so perpetuating the cycle of abuse.[180] And the greatest danger to children is presented by the mothers' new partners.[181] Some men, it seems, are violent but these are sexual men, not family men and 'natural' fathers.

Even in the absence of a new partner, women cannot be trusted. Families Need Fathers points out that 'NSPCC[182] research . . . showed that the people most likely to be violent to children are their mothers'.[183] This can be explained, they say, by the fact that mothers 'have most involvement with children and therefore more stress'.[184] Lone mothers may be unable to cope and so abuse their children:

> A lot of . . . abuse is when the children and the abusing parent are on their own and without support. There is no-one to stop them hurting their children and help them control themselves . . . Shared parenting can reduce this stress by sharing the work and the tensions.[185]

The involvement of 'natural parents', namely fathers, prevents ill treatment of children.[186]

Fathers, then, are cast as the protectors of children against the violence of mothers. In this way, men are rendered safe. They are also the victims, along with their children, of dangerous women. Men, and fathers in particular, are distanced from violence in the vast majority of cases. Moreover, where they are violent, this is often understandable and the fault of the women concerned and of an unfair legal system.

---

178 The Mankind Initiative 'Denigration' at www.mankind.org.uk/denigrat.html (accessed 9 February 2004).
179 Gordon (2003), p 16.
180 *Ibid*, p 55.
181 See Families Need Fathers (undated), p 3. See also Families Need Fathers (1999).
182 National Society for the Prevention of Cruelty to Children.
183 Families Need Fathers (undated), p 3. See also Sacks (undated); Fathers4Justice (2003), p 8.
184 Families Need Fathers (undated), p 3. See also Families Need Fathers (1999).
185 Families Need Fathers (undated), p 7.
186 *Ibid*, p 7.

Excusing and explaining men's violence

If men are violent, this is because they are hard done by; they are provoked:[187]

> The immediate aftermath of parental separation seems to be a flash point for violence. A possible factor in this is that the mother so often seizes the children and the father risks, or feels he risks, loss not only of the central adult relationship of his life but the children and much else.[188]

The solution, therefore, is to ensure that there is a 'clear understanding' that the relationships between both parents and their children will be preserved.[189] Even when domestic violence occurs during contact, this is the result of provocation. Men who were not previously abusive 'suddenly find that their children's mothers can continue to control them through dictating child contact'. There should therefore be 'equal contact, except in cases where criminal evidence shows that a parent is violent and a clear and present danger of causing harm to the children'.[190] Otherwise women will continue to 'control and abuse' men.

The notion of provocation and the shifting of blame are discernible also in the assertion that perpetrator programmes should be 'less focused on blame and undermining the position of the perpetrators ... but focus more on appreciated, appropriate behaviour and how to respond appropriately to inappropriate behaviour'.[191] 'Therefore it should be emphasised that using violence as a reaction to domestic violence is not appropriate and constitutes a criminal offence ... This would require that the police actually do their job properly and arrest perpetrators of domestic violence, even if they are women.'[192]

The law is unfair and biased against men

The call to punish men less and to punish women more recurs frequently throughout these websites and is tied up with allegations of discrimination against men. Men are unfairly stereotyped and unjustly accused of violence, while women can behave badly with impunity. To remedy this injustice, women's transgressions should be dealt with severely. False allegations of domestic violence 'should be properly punished to the full extent of the law'.[193] Women should also be punished if they do not allow child contact.[194] More generally, the law should 'recognise the cruelty of persistent or unrelenting verbal and emotional abuse which women can use ... against men, and which may provoke a violent reaction.'[195]

Families Need Fathers reports that female-on-male violence is not taken

---

187 According to Fontes, 'emotional abuse', in the form of 'yelling', constitutes provocation that can lead to physical violence by the man (Fontes (1998: 2003), p 31).
188 Families Need Fathers (undated), p 10.
189 *Ibid*, p 10.
190 Gordon (2003), p 16.
191 *Ibid*, p 24.
192 *Ibid*, p 25.
193 *Ibid*, p 26. See also *ibid* p 27.
194 *Ibid*, p 38.
195 The Mankind Initiative (2004), para 3.1.

seriously and that male victims are treated as perpetrators:[196] '[W]hatever the exchanges and events that might have preceded allegations of violence, it is the male of the couple that takes the rap.'[197] Gordon[198] takes a similar view:

> Men feel that the criminal justice system is heavily stacked against them. If they hit their partner they are punished, if their partner hits them, then little or nothing is done. All too often this means that the man has to defend himself, if that defence involves any level of violence, then he is the perpetrator.[199]

The Domestic Violence, Crime and Victims Bill (now Act) was seen as further evidence of unfair discrimination: '[T]hey [the government] are now forcing the criminal courts to become as corrupt as the family courts.'[200] Certainly, there is a perception that men are being disadvantaged. A 'Comment' from the *Daily Mail* linked to the Fathers4Justice website and reproduced on the Justice in Family Law site says of the Bill:

> From a government that has shown its contempt for marriage comes another assault on men, whose rights under the law are being systematically dismantled . . . [T]he British political establishment, including the judiciary, are declaring war on half the human race, creating a new official received wisdom that men are programmed to be violent towards women and children while women are blameless. In fact all the evidence suggests that women are as violent towards men as men are towards women.[201]

The impact of feminism

Not only are men discriminated against, according to these groups; they are demonised as a consequence of feminist influence: 'Violent women are treated more leniently than violent men . . . This is a result of the demonisation of men by radical feminists.'[202] Men and their interests are also marginalised: 'Giving women

---

196 See also Families Need Fathers (1999), p 1.
197 Families Need Fathers (undated), p 4.
198 See also Gordon (2003), p 10.
199 *Ibid*, p 26.
200 www.justiceinfamilylaw.co.uk (accessed 26 November 2004). The family law system has come under sustained attack from men's groups. Bob Geldof, for example, in the context of contact with children, has posted a message on the Families Need Fathers website alleging that 'family law remains flagrantly biased, prejudicial and discriminatory', and that 'men and our children are forced through this disgusting and baleful construct, cruelly and surely ironically called "Family" law' (Geldof, undated). Fathers4Justice say in their manifesto: '*We challenge the bias inherent in the family law system*' and '*advocate the dismantling of every element of the existing grotesque, cruel, unjust and unaccountable Family Law Industry and the removal of all existing family court judges*' and seek to '*expose miscarriages of justice*' (emphasis in original), at http://homepage.ntlworld.com/f4jswansea/manifesto.htm (accessed 9 February 2004). The UK Men's Movement (UKMM) alleges that 'feminists have almost entirely succeeded in destroying men's rights in marriage and the family'. And the law, it says, gives rise to 'persecution of honest and decent men, and massive privileges for women' (UKMM, undated a). Fathers4Justice claims there is a 'war on Fatherhood' with 'mass fatherlessness' leading to social decay (Fathers4Justice (2003), p 12). For an exceptionally intemperate attack, see at www.justiceinfamilylaw.co.uk (accessed 26 November 2004).
201 *Daily Mail* (2003) at www.justiceinfamilyaw.co.uk (accessed 26 November 2004).
202 The Mankind Initiative (2004), para 3.8. See also UKMM (undated b); www.mankind.org.uk/denigrat.html (accessed 9 February 2004).

ing.

equal value to their voice is one thing, making their voice *more* valuable than the wisdom and voice of men is quite another. Today a growing number of feminists have devalued the voice of men.'[203] Moreover, '[g]ender feminists have become a formable (*sic*) obstacle in raising the real needs of the male victim'.[204]

Feminists are said to have a disproportionate and dangerous level of influence over academics, policy makers and law makers. The Mankind Initiative deplores what it regards as the 'corruption' of research by radical feminists and by feminist ideology.[205] It argues that the Law Commission is unduly influenced by 'feminist ideology that has no regard for the rights of men'[206] and it rails against discrimination:

> After decades of feminist ascendancy in society, men in generally (*sic*) experience sex discrimination in many ways . . . In the recent past, the Law Commission itself has been highly responsive to the radical feminist activists, who have begun to secure privileges for women (in respect of sexual and domestic violence, and family law) at the expense of men's basic human rights.[207]

'The problem with the "domestic violence movement" ', says Fontes,[208] 'is that it has become a feminist political movement'. 'Gender politics' ensures that all the available funding goes to women victims[209] at the expense of men. UKMM,[210] in turn, proclaims that:

> There can be no greater folly or degeneracy than to provide further support, via Ministers for Women etc. to the most privileged group in our society – women – while denying the disadvantaged, suppressed and persecuted group – men – any representation at all . . . The question of whether 'feminism has gone too far' is perhaps less important than 'why feminism was established at all'. Feminism is an aberration, like Nazism and communism – a blight on our society.[211]

The zero sum game in which many of these campaigners and groups see themselves as involved extends to embrace money, power and the fate of the traditional family.[212] As one piece appearing on the website of the Equal Justice Foundation, an American website, states:

> [T]he feminist matriarchy has had considerable negative influence on domestic tranquillity in the form of Draconian Big Sister laws that . . . are destroying families . . . Are we the only ones who regard the present unsubstantiated, radical social engineering based on the destruction of the patriarchy as extremely dangerous?[213]

203 Fontes (1998: 2003), p 42 (emphasis in original).
204 *Ibid*, p 46.
205 The Mankind Initiative (2004), paras 5.1–2.
206 *Ibid*, para 6.10.
207 *Ibid*, p 1.
208 Fontes (1998: 2003), p 49.
209 *Ibid*, p 47. See also Gordon (2003), p 9.
210 UK Men's Movement.
211 UKMM (2001), Conclusions (accessed 1 June 2004).
212 See also Collier (1999), p 127.
213 Corry (2002).

Conclusion

In the context of domestic violence, the search for equivalence is intended to divert attention from male power and to seek acceptance for a construction of women as aggressive, controlling and out of control. It casts doubt on the veracity of women's allegations and seeks to shift concern from men's violence to women's mendacity; it is the latter, rather than the former, that warrants the attention of the law. It minimises the extent and severity of men's abuse of women, suggesting that it is something that has been exaggerated or that men are unfairly blamed for violence they do not commit. In addition, and most importantly, it is an attempt to make men appear safe; they are no more dangerous than women and perhaps less so. To deny men contact with their children is therefore an irrational over-reaction and unjustified.

The main concern of most men's groups is not to gain victim status for abused men in an effort to secure help and resources for them. What seems central to their campaign is the drive to establish perpetrator status for women, so that they cannot be believed or trusted to make decisions regarding their children or to keep them safe. Within this account, fathers are central to their children's well-being; it is only they who can provide some protection from mothers' cruelty or at least fecklessness and the consequences of their undiscriminating sexual appetites. With this strategy, men's groups seek to re-assert the place of the father in the nuclear or bi-nuclear family, as well as to counter the 'rampant' feminism that is undermining men's rights and that must be brought under control.

References

Barnish, M (2004) *Domestic Violence: A Literature Review*, London: HM Inspectorate of Probation

Cabinet Office and Home Office (1999) *Living Without Fear: An Integrated Approach to Tackling Violence Against Women*, London: Cabinet Office

Chesney-Lind, M (2002) 'Criminalizing victimization: the unintended consequences of pro-arrest policies for girls and women', 2 *Criminology and Public Policy* 81

Collier, R (1995) *Masculinity, Law and the Family*, London: Routledge

Collier, R (1999) 'From women's emancipation to sex war? Men, heterosexuality and the politics of divorce', in Day Sclater, S and Piper, C (eds) *Undercurrents of Divorce*, Aldershot: Ashgate

Cook, D, Burton, M, Robinson, A and Vallely, C (2004) *Evaluation of Specialist Domestic Violence Courts/Fast Track Systems*, London: Crown Prosecution Service and Department of Constitutional Affairs

Corry, C (2002) 'The role of patriarchy in domestic violence', Equal Justice Foundation: www.dvmen.org/dv–38.htm (accessed 20 July 2004)

Council of Europe Committee of Ministers (2002) *Recommendation (2002)5 of the Committee of Ministers to Member States on the protection of women against violence*

Crown Prosecution Service (2001) *Crown Prosecution Service Policy on Prosecuting Cases of Domestic Violence*, London: Crown Prosecution Service

Daily Mail (2003) 'Comment: Putting prejudice before justice' (3 December)

Diduck, A and Kaganas, F (2006) *Family Law, Gender and the State*, Oxford: Hart Publishing

Dewar Research (1998) 'Dispatches: "Battered men survey" ': www.dewar4research.org

Dobash, RE (2003) 'Domestic violence: Arrest, prosecution and reducing violence', 2 *Criminology and Public Policy* 313

Dobash, RE and Dobash, RP (1992) *Women, Violence and Social Change*, London: Routledge

Dobash, RE and Dobash, RP (2000) 'The politics and policies of responding to violence against women', in Hanmer, J and Itzin, C with Quaid, S and Wigglesworth, D (eds) *Home Truths About Domestic Violence: Feminist Influences on Policy and Practice – A Reader*, London: Routledge

Dobash, RP and Dobash, RE (2004) 'Women's violence to men in intimate relationships: Working on a puzzle', 44 *British J of Criminology* 324

Dodd, T, Nicholas, S, Povey, D and Walker, A (2004) *Crime in England and Wales 2003/4*, Home Office Statistical Bulletin, London: Home Office

Families Need Fathers (undated) *Safety and Justice. The Government's Proposals on Domestic Violence. Reply to Consultation from Families Need Fathers*, www.fnf.org.uk

Families Need Fathers (1999) *Response to the Consultation Paper Contact Between Children and Violent Parents*, www.fnf.org.uk/subs/dvresp.htm

Families Need Fathers (2001) 'Domestic violence', www.fnf.org.uk/domviol.htm (accessed 26 November 2004)

Fathers4Justice (2003) *A Damning Indictment of the Policies of the Lord Chancellor's Department, The Government and the Growing Crisis in UK Family Law. Fathers 4 Justice Report for MP's (sic)*, www.fathers-4-justice.org

Fontes, D (1998) 'The politics of the domestic violence movement', www.dvmen.org/dv–43.htm (accessed 19 July 2004)

Fontes, D (1998: revised 2003) 'Violent touch: Breaking through the stereotype', www.safe4all.org (accessed 27 May 2004)

Forbes, J (1992) 'Female sexual abusers: The contemporary search for equivalence', 6(2) *Practice* 102

Gadd, D, Farrall, S, Dallimore, D and Lombard, N (2002) *Domestic Abuse Against Men in Scotland*, Edinburgh: Scottish Executive

Geldof, B (undated) 'A message to Families Need Fathers from Bob Geldof', www.fnf.org/bobg.htm (accessed 9 February 2004)

Goody, J (1997) 'Boys don't cry: Masculinities, fear of crime and fearlessness', 37(3) *British J of Criminology* 401

Gordon, D (2003) *Men's Aid, Response to the Government Consultation Paper on Domestic Violence. Safety and Justice*, Fife: Men's Aid

Graycar, R (2000) 'Law reform by frozen chook: Family law reform for the new millennium?', 24 *Melbourne University Law Review* 737

Hamilton, I (2003) 'Domestic violence and the family lawyer – the way forward', 27 *Association of Lawyers for Children Newsletter* 5

Hearn, J (1998) *The Violences of Men: How Men Talk about and How Agencies Respond to Men's Violence to Women*, London: Sage

HM Crown Prosecution Service Inspectorate and HM Inspectorate of Constabulary (2004) *A Joint Inspection of the Investigation and Prosecution of Cases Involving Domestic Violence*

Home Office (2000a) *Domestic Violence: Break the Chain Multi-Agency Guidance for Addressing Domestic Violence*, London: HMSO

Home Office (2000b) *Domestic Violence: Revised Circular to the Police*, London: Home Office (Home Office Circular No 19/2000)

Home Office (2003) *Safety and Justice: The Government's Proposals on Domestic Violence*, London: HMSO (Cm 5847)

Itzin, C (2000) 'Gendering domestic violence: The influence of feminism on policy and practice', in Hanmer, J and Itzin, C, with Quaid, S and Wigglesworth, D (eds) *Home Truths About Domestic Violence: Feminist Influences on Policy and Practice – A Reader*, London: Routledge

Law Commission (2003) *Partial Defences to Murder*, Consultation Paper No 173, London: The Law Commission

Lewis, R, Dobash, RE, Dobash, RP and Cavanagh, K (2001) 'Law's progressive potential: The value of engagement with the law for domestic violence', 10(1) *Social and Legal Studies* 105

MacKinnon, C (1987) *Feminism Unmodified*, Cambridge, MA: Harvard University Press

Mankind Initiative, The (2004) *The Law Commission Consultation Paper 173. Partial Defences to Murder. Submission by the Mankind Initiative*, www.mankind.org.uk

Mawby, R and Walklate, S (1994) *Critical Victimology*, London: Sage Publications

Metropolitan Police (2001) *Enough is Enough: Domestic Violence Strategy*, London: Metropolitan Police

Mirrlees-Black, C (1999) *Domestic Violence: Findings from a New British Crime*

Survey Self-Completion Questionnaire, Home Office Research Study 191, London: Home Office

Mitchell, District Judge J (2004) 'Contact in Practice', [2004] *Family Law* 662

Mullender, A and Morley, R (eds) (1994) *Children Living with Domestic Violence*, London: Whiting & Birch

Mullender, A, Hague, G, Imam, I, Kelly, L, Malos, E and Regan, L (2002) *Children's Perspectives on Domestic Violence*, London: Sage Publications

Newburn, T and Stanko, E (1994) 'When men are victims', in Newburn, T and Stanko, E (eds) *Just Boys Doing Business*, London: Routlege

Richards, L (2004) *'Getting Away With It': A Strategic Overview of Domestic Violence, Sexual Assault and 'Serious' Incident Analysis*, London: Metropolitan Police Service

Rock, P (2002) 'On becoming a victim', in Hoyle, C and Young, R (eds) *New Visions of Crime Victims*, Oxford: Hart Publishing

Sacks, G (undated) 'Four feminist myths about domestic violence', Manorama website, http://homepage.ntlworld.com/verismo (accessed 19 July 2004)

Sentencing Advisory Panel (2002) *Advice to the Court of Appeal – 9: Rape*, London: Sentencing Advisory Panel

Sentencing Advisory Panel (2004) *Sentencing Guidelines on Domestic Violence Cases*, Consultation Paper, London: Sentencing Advisory Panel

Simmons, J *et al* (2002) *Crime in England and Wales 2001/2*, Home Office Statistical Bulletin 07/02, London: Home Office

Stanko, E and Hobdell, K (1993) 'Assault on men: Masculinity and male victimization', 33(3) *British J of Criminology* 400

UKMM (undated a) *Women are Oppressed by Marriage – Part of The Big Lie for our Time*, www.ukmm.org.uk/issues/biglie-m&fl.htm (accessed 26 November 2004)

UKMM (undated b) *Domestic Violence – Part of the Big Lie for our Time*, www.ukmm.org.uk/issues/biglie-dv.htm (accessed 26 November 2004)

UKMM (2001) *Discrimination Against Men in the UK*, http://www.ukmm.org.uk/issues/dam.htm (accessed 1 June 2004)

Walby, S and Allen, J (2004) *Domestic Violence, Sexual Assault and Stalking: Findings from the British Crime Survey*, Home Office Research Study 276, London: Home Office

Worrall, A (2002) 'Rendering women punishable: The making of a penal crisis', in Carlen, P (ed) *Women and Punishment: The Struggle for Justice*, Cullompton: Willan Publishing

Chapter 9

Feminist Perspectives on Youth Justice
Christine Piper

Introduction

Gender issues are not high on the youth justice policy agenda in the UK. 'Boys' and 'girls' or 'young men' and 'young women' rarely appear in practice and policy documents, and yet the Home Office is concerned about gender differences in the causes of offending.[1] This paradox runs throughout responses to children who offend. On the one hand, the increasing use of 'youth' as a descriptor and policy focus renders girls and young women invisible in a criminal justice system in which, it is true, the vast majority of those processed and punished are male. On the other hand, there is an increased visibility of what has been referred to in a Canadian article as 'female youth',[2] notably in media and policy concern at the perceived proliferation of 'girl gangs' and the rise in convictions of girls.

The existence of such apparent inconsistencies has often been the spur to feminist analyses and this chapter is no exception. It will, consequently, examine the ways in which minors who offend are described in policy documents, the media and practice guidance, and will also assess what we know about the offending of girls and young women in comparison with their male counterparts. In addition, it will seek to establish whether feminist analyses of gender issues in the sentencing and punishment of adult women apply also to girls and young women.

However, this book is bringing together feminist perspectives on family law and its effects, not just on family life but also on social and legal meanings ascribed to 'good' families and 'good' mothers. Law's construction or endorsement of values has given it a crucial role in the 'remoralisation' agenda which underpinned social, criminal justice and family policy in the 1990s and continues as a theme of New Labour policy.[3] The desire to support and also discipline the family as a means of strengthening the moral basis for an ordered society has encouraged an approach to offending children and their families which draws on older ideas about the child's need for discipline.[4] So, current policy holds families responsible for preventing their children offending or re-offending, at the same time as it deems children to be responsible from an early age for their own wrongdoing.

One implication of this development is that there is a potential gender issue in the extent to which mothers and fathers are held 'culpable' for their child's behaviour or pressured to be involved in informal justice, treatment or punishment. Policy and practice in relation to parenting orders, parental fines and parental involvement in restorative conferences (when their child receives a warning from

---

1   See Farrington and Painter (2004).
2   Boyle *et al* (2002).
3   See Day Sclater and Piper (2000).
4   See Fortin (2003), p 556.

the police),[5] and referral order meetings with the youth justice panel,[6] are of particular concern.

Gender implications for parents?

Research on the effects of policies directed at parents in the educational and child protection systems suggests mothers are disproportionately burdened and blamed by the encouragement of 'parental' involvement and responsibility in these systems.[7] The policy focus on parental responsibility and the involvement of parents in the youth justice system has the same potential to discriminate against female carers.

Parenting orders, introduced by ss 8–11 of the Crime and Disorder Act 1998, are triggered if the child or young person is subject to a child safety order, an anti-social behaviour order or a sex offender order, is convicted of a criminal offence or fails to comply with a school attendance order.[8] Parenting orders can last up to 12 months and can specify particular requirements, if that would be desirable to prevent further anti-social behaviour or offending. Parents must also attend parenting classes or counselling for a concurrent period not exceeding three months and not more than once a week. The Anti-Social Behaviour Act 2003 widened the scope and use of parenting orders, giving the court the power to impose a residential requirement in the order. Section 25 of the Act also puts parenting contracts on a statutory footing so that failure to enter into or comply with the terms of a voluntary 'contract' made between a parent and a youth offending team can be taken into account when the court decides whether or not to make a parenting order.

These are potentially very controlling orders, notwithstanding their aim of helping parents to acquire more effective parenting skills. The government's guidance on reparation orders gives a similarly ambivalent message to parents:

> The Government believes that parents have an important role to play in supporting their children when they are involved in any court proceedings. Magistrates' courts, including youth courts, have powers to enforce parental attendance at court where appropriate. Section 34A of the Children and Young Persons Act 1933 provides that where a child or young person is charged with an offence or is for any other reason brought before a court, the court may in any case – and *shall* in the case of a child or young person who is under the age of 16 – require a person who is a parent or guardian to attend at the court during all stages of the proceedings, unless the court is satisfied that it would be unreasonable to do so.[9]

A survey by Campbell (see below) would suggest that, in these new processes, mothers are again bearing the brunt of involvement and, in this case, potentially

---

5 For reprimands and warnings, see the Crime and Disorder Act 1998, ss 65–6.
6 For referral orders see Powers of Criminal Courts (Sentencing) Act 2000, ss 16–27.
7 See Piper (1994), and the references therein.
8 Under the Education Act 1996, ss 443–4; Crime and Disorder Act 1998, s 8(1)(d). For guidance on parenting contracts and orders see Home Office *et al* (2004).
9 Home Office (2000), para 3.17

being stigmatised. For example, the pilots for parenting orders revealed that 80 per cent of the children and young people involved were males, but over 80 per cent of the parents involved were females.[10] Despite the relative invisibility in the youth justice system of the problematic situation of young offenders' mothers, the government's proposal in *Youth Justice – The Next Steps* to encourage youth justice agencies to make more use of parenting orders and contracts 'more actively *engaging fathers*, making sure *both parents* generally come to court and ensuring courts consider a Parenting Order when they fail to attend court [emphasis in the original]'[11] is of concern. Arguably, 'the Government, the Home Office and the Youth Justice Board are reluctant to confront the stark correlation between gender, violence and anti-social behaviour'.[12]

Further, given the currently significant 'cross-overs' of law and resources between youth justice and child protection/children's services, the impact on families of the above policy developments is greater than might be anticipated. Children who are not offenders – and their parents – are being dealt with by youth justice teams, whilst relevant civil law measures are increasingly being backed up with criminal sanctions. The disciplinary net, justified by a focus on actual or potential juvenile offending or misbehaviour, is being cast over a much larger number of boys and girls and mothers and fathers.

The widening remit of youth offending teams

The youth justice system is part of the criminal justice system, operating with the offences, procedures and evidential rules established by the criminal law, but, in recent developments, the remit of the system covers young males and females who are not eligible to be in the youth justice system. There are two developments, focusing on the control of 'sub-criminal' behaviour, especially 'anti-social' behaviour and truanting,[13] or on pre-criminal behaviour, notably preventative schemes. The Crime and Disorder Act 1998 introduced civil orders to deal with sub-criminal behaviour, the relevant order for those aged ten and over being the anti-social behaviour order. The criterion for making an anti-social behaviour order (in s 1 of the Act) is one of the criteria in s 11(3) for imposing a child safety order on a child aged under ten: '. . . that the person (child) has acted . . . in a manner that caused or was likely to cause harassment, alarm or distress to one or more persons not of the same household as himself.'[14]

That these provisions fudge the line between criminal and civil can be seen, for example, in the 'Executive Summary' in *Every Child Matters*. Under the bullet point 'reforms to the youth justice system', a brief paragraph begins: 'The Government intends to revise the Child Safety Order to make it more effective and

---

10 Campbell (2003).
11 Home Office (2003b), para 9, p 5.
12 Campbell (2003), p 3.
13 See, for example, DfES (2004b), a recent research report on risk of becoming involved in criminal or anti-social behaviour.
14 See Piper (1999).

build on the success of the Intensive Supervision and Surveillance Programme by using it more widely as an alternative to custody.'[15] This statement evidences child safety orders as part of a discourse of 'youth justice', despite the fact that only Family Proceedings Courts can make such an order, and elides in one sentence provisions for under-ten year olds being mentioned in the same sentence as a community programme for offenders over ten years old. This elision reflects the trend of government policy. After the consultation exercise following the publication of *Youth Justice – The Next Steps*,[16] the government proposed to include preventing anti-social behaviour in the duties of the Youth Justice Board and youth offending teams. Before the general election in May 2005, the government stated that this duty would be included in a subsequent Youth Justice Bill.[17]

Another example of this policy trend is the development of Youth Inclusion Support Panels through the Children's Fund. This fund is used for projects which target 5- to 13-year-old disadvantaged children and is administered by the Children, Young People and Families Directorate at the DfES. Of this budget, 25 per cent is allocated to preventative projects for children aged 8 to 13 who are seen as most heavily at risk of offending. The government's aim is that there should be a youth support panel in each youth offending team area.[18] Funding for preventative projects managed by youth offending teams is increasingly provided by crime and disorder reduction partnerships and the government intends to expand by 50 per cent youth inclusion and early intervention projects across England and Wales.[19]

This conflation of risk of offending by boys and girls and risk of harm to them, particularly in the context of the social inclusion–exclusion policy agenda, raises the possibility of early 'stigmatisation' of children and their parents and allows for potentially 'unnecessary' intervention in families.[20] This may seem far removed from this chapter's focus on offending girls and their mothers, but what these developments signify is that more girls, as well as boys, are being drawn into an increasingly important system in which the risk of offending normally takes priority over the risk of harm, or the latter risk is subsumed in the former. Further, there is evidence that the risks of engaging in offending are different for boys and girls in a way that might mean that those parents, particularly lone-mother parents, living in poverty may be more at risk of having their children's behaviour scrutinised.

The current focus in policy and research is on isolating factors correlated with risk of offending and desistance from offending. Farrington and Painter have recently conducted research on gender differences in this respect, using brothers and sisters.[21] This research found that the most important factors for offending

---

15 DfES (2003); see also DfES (2004a).

16 Home Office (2003b).

17 See: www.commonsleader.gov.uk/output/page798.asp. However, whilst a Youth Justice Bill was announced in the Queen's Speech in 2004 and drafted in the 2004–5 session, such Bill is not in the list of Bills for 2005–6; see the Queen's Speech, May 2005, at www.number–10.gov.uk/output/Page7489.asp.

18 Youth Justice Board (2004), para 6.3.

19 *Ibid*, para 6.6.

20 See Piper (2005); for the use of 'criminalisation' as a state response to poverty and educational disadvantage, see Drakeford and Vanstone (2000).

21 Farrington and Painter (2004).

and frequent offending were similar for brothers and sisters, but that 'risk factors predicted offending by sisters more strongly than offending by brothers'.[22] The example they give is of the influence of the factor of low family income on early-onset offending, where the proportion of sisters who were convicted increased from 1 per cent to 11 per cent according to the absence or presence of this factor, whereas for their brothers the increase was from 14 per cent to 33 per cent. After controlling for other risk factors, 'the partial odds ratios were 15.5 for sisters and 2.1 for brothers'.[23] They also found that socio-economic and child-rearing factors were more important in predicting offending of sisters, whilst parenting-related factors were more important for brothers. Farrington and Painter use their conclusions to note the cost-effectiveness implications of focusing preventative interventions on those risk factors which are most – and also differentially – influential on girls and boys respectively.[24]

This focus on risk assessment may, therefore, impact differentially on girls and boys and also on mothers and fathers, whilst the colonisation by crime prevention agencies of work and funding for children's services aimed at prevention of offending might mean that other aspects of the child's life and welfare are obscured, including those where gender issues are potentially significant.[25] Further, it means girls – whether or not they have offended – are being drawn into a system in which the 'child as youth' is the dominant concept.

'Youth'

Until legislation in the 1990s, in England and Wales, children and young people under 17 were the 'juveniles' who were processed in a juvenile justice system and prosecuted in the juvenile court set up by the Children Act 1908. Since the implementation of the Criminal Justice Act 1991, the criminal court for minors has been the youth court, with the upper age raised from 17 to 18[26] and, since implementation of the Crime and Disorder Act 1998, minors who have offended are now dealt with in a youth justice system. There are youth offending teams and youth offending panels providing youth justice services and operating with a published youth justice plan, within a system overseen by a national Youth Justice Board.[27]

In England and Wales, the word 'youth' has also gradually emerged through successive versions of the Code for Crown Prosecutors to refer to the child or young person; before that, the reference was to the juvenile, or a young person, or, in its penultimate version, a youth offender.[28] Similarly, in Northern Ireland, where

---

22 *Ibid*, p 56.
23 *Ibid*. In this sample, 12 per cent of sisters and 44 per cent of brothers were convicted.
24 *Ibid*, pp 57–8.
25 See the discussion below concerning the ASSET assessment tool.
26 At the same time, non-criminal cases were moved to the newly created Family Proceedings Court: Criminal Justice Act 1991, s 68 and Schedule 8; Children (Allocation of Proceedings) Order 1991, SI 1991/1677.
27 See Crime and Disorder Act 1998, ss 37–41.
28 See Piper (2001).

different legislation and terminology apply to many aspects of the treatment of minors, the same trend is to be found. In 1999, Northern Ireland re-named its juvenile court as the youth court (Criminal Justice (Children) Order 1998, article 27) and s 63 of the Justice (Northern Ireland) Act 2002 raised the upper limit from 17 to 18 years.

'Juveniles' have not disappeared from policy and administration: the Juvenile Offenders Unit at the Home Office sponsors the Youth Justice Board and 'is responsible for youth justice policy, law, processes and organisation covering 10 to 17 year olds in England and Wales'.[29] There is also still a Juvenile Operations Management Group in the Prison Service and juvenile secure accommodation. Further, in *Youth Justice – The Next Steps*,[30] the companion document to the Green Paper *Every Child Matters*,[31] the juvenile reappears in references to juvenile sentences, juvenile court orders and juvenile custody.[32]

Neither juvenile nor youth are morally or culturally neutral terms. 'Juvenile' has pejorative connotations: it suggests, perhaps, the offender as 'young and silly'. Arguably, however, 'youth' not only has more negative associations but is inherently gendered. If our associations with the word youth are pleasant ones of youth clubs, youth and community projects, or youth orchestras and choirs, where the two genders mixed on equal terms and the age range was not confined to older teenagers, there is no problem with the word 'youth'. However, Burney suggests that 'youths hanging about' have become 'the universal symbol of disorder and, increasingly, menace',[33] so that the meanings constructed around 'youth' are negative.

The significance of this change in terminology is increased by the abolition, in the Crime and Disorder Act 1988, of the presumption that children aged 10–13 years old are *doli incapax*: that is, incapable of being held criminally responsible.[34] From the tenth birthday, a child can legally be prosecuted and punished, so that a 'youth' in the criminal justice system now refers in law and practice to a girl or boy aged 10–17 inclusive. This has been widely criticised, not least by those concerned with the rights of children.[35] *Children in Trouble*, a report by the children's charity Barnardo's, criticised this 'tendency to criminalise children unnecessarily and at younger ages, and a corresponding tendency to treat them as adults too soon'.[36] Such a trend is encouraged by the use of the word 'youth', with its connotations of the older male person. Further, if policy and practice is – consciously or otherwise – geared to older male youths, then there is a risk that female youths – as well as younger youths of both sexes – will receive inappropriate responses to their offending.

---

29 www.homeoffice.gov.uk/inside/org/dob/direct/jou.html.
30 Home Office (2003b).
31 DfES (2003).
32 Home Office (2003b). See, for example pp 4–6 and 8.
33 Burney (2002), p 473.
34 Crime and Disorder Act 1998, s 34.
35 Fortin (2004), especially pp 256–7.
36 Hibbert *et al* (2003), p 6.

Offending by girls

Whilst girls who offend or behave anti-socially are increasingly and routinely subsumed into 'youths', there is, at the same time, a selective but increasing visibility of some children and young people as offenders because they are girls and young women. Girl gangs have been a recurrent focus of media attention. They are the new lads or 'ladettes' at the level of minor offending and, most recently, in relation to drunkenness. In media reports, the implicit message is that girls are doubly culpable – of offending and also of not conforming to popular notions of femininity, of how girls and women should behave. For example, one of the on-line responses to a BBC *Inside Out* feature on 'binge drinking' and the new licensing laws ended, without explanation as to why one gender is being singled out, with the question: 'Lastly, why do girls behave so badly?'[37] Two national daily newspapers have run similar stories. An article in the *Telegraph* on the latest complex report of the 'European School Survey Project on Alcohol and Other Drugs' was simply entitled 'Girls overtake boys in binge-drinking study'.[38] The *Daily Mirror* began an article entitled 'Bottle of the Sexes' with: 'In bingeing Britain the boys still outdrink the girls . . . but the gap is getting dangerously smaller.'[39] The 'problem' is not presented as the long-term trend of boys' alcohol abuse, but the fact that girls are catching up with them.

More significantly perhaps, fears have been expressed that there has been a rapid increase in the number of violent girls. In the 1990s, these fears gave rise to headlines of the 'Sugar 'n' spice . . . not at all nice' variety.[40] More recently, a former US police chief is reported as saying of violence among American girls: 'This is vicious, I-want-to-hurt-you fighting. It is a nationwide phenomenon and is catching us all off guard.'[41] This statement, and its reporting in the British press, indicates a significant level of social anxiety about the behaviour of girls.

That there has been a rise in reported offending by girls is not in question. In England and Wales, the number of girls convicted of indictable offences rose, with a corresponding increase from 11.1 per cent to 13.2 per cent in the proportion of girls in the sentenced population between 1992 and 1999.[42] Increases can also be found elsewhere. In Scotland, the number of 17–19-year-old females who had a charge proved increased between 1987 and 1997, as did the number of referrals to a Reporter (children's hearings) on an offence ground.[43] However, statistics would suggest that this does not represent a significant surge in offending by young females. The National Association for the Care and Resettlement of Offenders (NACRO) points out that, in the 1990s, the *total* number of girls who were

---

37 www.bbc.co.uk/insideout/southwest/series5/drinking_binge_pubs.shtml
38 See article by C Hall on 15 December 2004.
39 *Daily Mirror*, 4 February 2005. See, for a balanced analysis, the article on motivations and outcomes of a study on underage drinking in *Childright*, April 2005.
40 *Sunday Times*, 27 November 1994.
41 Jansen Robinson, quoted in *The Times*, 28 April 2002, p 2.
42 National Association for the Care and Resettlement of Offenders (NACRO) (2001), p 2.
43 Glasgow: Girls and Violence Project. See www.gla.ac.uk/girlsandviolence/facts.htm

cautioned or convicted for indictable offences fell by almost a third, from 33,600 to 24,800, and that the number of girls sentenced for *violent* offences *fell* in the period 1992–9.[44] Further, the Edinburgh University Study of Youth Transitions and Crime found that, at age 15, boys are three times more likely than girls to carry a weapon and twice as likely to be involved in fighting, and that specific forms of the more serious offending – carrying a weapon, housebreaking, robbery, theft from cars, and cruelty to animals – are still much more common among boys than girls.[45]

The overwhelming majority of offenders in this age group are, however, still males: the Youth Justice Board estimated in 2001 that girls made up about 18 per cent of the offending youth population.[46] Further, the latest Criminal Statistics would suggest that the number of the more serious young offenders – of both genders – has now peaked in England and Wales. In 2002, a total of 3,713 ten to under-18 year olds, including 453 girls, were found guilty at the Crown Court for indictable offences.[47] In 2003, the total was 2,790, including 340 females.[48] For both years, the proportion of girls in these totals was 12 per cent. NACRO concludes that the rise in convictions of girls is, then, a function of reduced measures to divert them from court.[49] In Canada, too, an analysis of official statistics would suggest that female young offenders accounted for only 7.3 per cent of all cases brought before the youth court at the end of the 1990s.[50]

However, a major problem is that – until recently – there has been relatively little research in the UK since the 1980s on the experience and treatment of young female offenders, except in relation to ethnic minority girls and to gangs. Whilst the *Research on Girls and Violence* project based at Glasgow University has been important in the process of addressing that deficit, particularly as it is using research methods developed by feminists,[51] research on the treatment of women in the criminal justice system is still a necessary source of insights into the treatment of girls.

Invisible?

A standard feminist analysis of adult offenders is that women become 'invisible' in policy and practice because of the preponderance of men, and that this invisibility works to their disadvantage. So, whilst policy documents talk in apparently gender-neutral terms about offenders, the generic term used may actually be applicable only to men. The resulting issue is whether the different structural and personal factors relevant to women should lead to differential – rather than equal – treatment if substantive justice is to be achieved.

---

44 NACRO (2001).
45 See www.regard.ac.uk/research_findings/R000239150/report.pdf. See also www.ed.ac.uk/news/truancy.html.
46 NACRO (2001), p 2.
47 Home Office (2003c), Table S2.1E.
48 Home Office (2004b), Table S2.1E.
49 NACRO (2001).
50 Boyle *et al* (2002), p 393.
51 Burman *et al* (2001); see also Batchelor and Burman (2004).

What is not yet so clear is whether girls and young women are also invisible, treated inappropriately equally or discriminated against in the youth justice system. It is certainly possible in youth justice texts to find instances where it appears unlikely that the commentator is thinking about girls when he or she is referring to youths. For example, when referring to Operation Spotlight, Muncie explains that 'after-hours revellers, groups of youths on the streets and truants' were targeted in Glasgow in 1996.[52] No gender is specified. Muncie goes on: 'As a result, charges for drinking alcohol in public places increased by 2,240 per cent, dropping litter by 320 per cent and urinating on the street by 140 per cent.'[53] Whilst it is not unknown for the last activity to be engaged in by girls and women, our dominant image is of males. Further, the latest Audit Commission report on youth justice mentions differences in terms of race but not in terms of gender.[54] 'Males' are only referred to, therefore, in the context of 'black',[55] and gender is not an issue anywhere in the report. Likewise, the recent *Youth Matters* consultation paper on wider youth policy has only one brief reference to gender.[56] This may be significant, given the conclusions of criminologists in relation to the treatment of adult women offenders.

Feminist criminologists have focused on differential gender treatment in the contexts of both sentencing and punishment. In relation to the latter, research has documented forms of disadvantage to female offenders in custodial regimes[57] and in the provision of community punishments. As regards sentencing, research suggests that constructions of femininity and the 'normal' woman could lead to either more lenient or less lenient sentencing treatment. Two types of response can 'save' a woman from imprisonment: the medicalisation of women – the 'not bad but mad' approach; or the paternalistic approach – the chivalrous protection of the 'weaker' sex or the 'social casualty'.[58] Feminist researchers in the 1980s drew attention to the fact that women were two or three times more likely than men to receive an absolute or conditional discharge on conviction for an indictable offence, and three times less likely to receive a custodial sentence.[59] More recent research has found similar discrepancies in relation to specific offences. For example, women are less likely than a comparable man to receive a custodial sentence for shoplifting and drug offences.[60]

---

52 Muncie (2003), p 54.
53 *Ibid*.
54 Since the implementation of s 95 of the Criminal Justice Act 1991, the agencies of the criminal justice system must provide statistics broken down into different race and sex categories and so sentencing statistics are available by age, sex and race.
55 Audit Commission, *Youth Justice* (Home Office (2004a), p 81).
56 DfES (2005), para 169 in reference to the need for careers advisers to challenge gender stereotypes. The words 'girl', 'boy', 'young women' and 'young men' do not feature in the report.
57 See Carlen (1983), for an early detailed study of women in Corton Vale Prison in Scotland; see Easton and Piper (2005), ch 12, for a recent review of research about women and custody.
58 See, for example, Edwards (1984); Gelsthorpe (1986); Morris (1988); and Pearson (1976) for early, seminal work on these issues.
59 See, for example, Morris (1988), p 163.
60 Hedderman and Gelsthorpe (1997), pp vii–viii, and also Part 1.

On the other hand, the 'double deviancy' of offending and acting in an unwomanly fashion could lead to more intensive punishment than a man would receive for a similar instance of offending, particularly if the generally less serious criminal histories of women offenders are taken into account. Carlen, for example, found in her sample of judges in Scotland that the women they sentenced to custody were those who, in their eyes, had failed as mothers: 'Thus Sheriffs not only wanted to know whether a woman was a mother, but whether she was a *good* mother.'[61]

Hedderman and Gelsthorpe more recently found that some magistrates still treated female, but not male, defendants as 'troubled' offenders to whom they ascribed different motives, even if, for example, men were stealing bacon and coffee rather than alcohol or items to sell.[62] Consequently, they chose sentences to 'help' rather than punish them. However, their comparatively low use of fines for women (because they had no independent means) could mean that women were given a community sentence, a higher tariff sentence reserved for offences 'serious enough' to justify it.[63] There was also some suggestion that the conclusions of earlier research are still valid: that magistrates do take into account the demeanour of women in court when making sentencing decisions.[64]

Sentencing girls

First, a caveat: strictly speaking, we should not refer to 'sentencing' girls. Juveniles are not 'sentenced' after 'conviction'; instead, since the implementation of the Children and Young Persons Act 1933, the youth court 'makes an order upon a finding of guilt' (s 59) in relation to those minors who have been successfully prosecuted.

Second, we simply do not know enough about this decision-making process with minors. In 1986, Heidensohn reviewed research about girls and young women as well as adult women. That research – stemming mainly from the 1970s and early 1980s when a more welfare-focused juvenile justice system operated – concluded that 'delinquent girls', like adult women, were 'subject to a particular regulatory censure' stemming from ideas about what was normally expected of adolescent girls.[65] In particular, the response to male offending signified by 'boys will be boys' contrasts with the response to the 'waywardness' of delinquent girls.[66] So, for Heidensohn, research evidence that females of all ages risk the penalties of double jeopardy emphasises the fact that, 'while this is a man's world it will be his conception of justice which will prevail',[67] in relation to minors as well as adults.

---

61 Carlen (1983), discussed in Morris (1988), pp 166–7.
62 Hedderman and Gelsthorpe (1997), p viii.
63 *Ibid.* The sentencing criterion is now to be found in the Criminal Justice Act 2003 at s 148(1).
64 Hedderman and Gelsthorpe (1997), p viii and ch 2.
65 See Harris and Webb (1987), p 134; see also Webb's 1978 research on the supervision order (Webb, 1984).
66 Harris and Webb (1987), p 134.
67 Heidensohn (1986), p 297.

It is tempting to use twenty-year-old research to prove discrimination in the present. For example, Annie Hudson, in her chapter on 'Troublesome girls' in a compendium on youth justice issues published in 2002, perhaps does rely too much on conclusions drawn in the 1980s.[68] A NACRO briefing in 2001 noted that data was not available 'at a sufficient level of detail' to know whether the factors identified in the 1980s currently influence sentencing outcomes for offending girls. Further, even in 1987, Harris and Webb had concluded: 'With the sole (and major) exception of the control of girls' sexual behaviour, the differences between the treatment of boys and girls are of degree and not kind.'[69]

The reliance on possibly out-of-date research on the experiences of girl offenders is also problematic because of changes in penal policy and theory since the 1980s, which may be influencing the treatment of women offenders and reducing the likelihood that girls are still facing the discriminatory treatment that research in the 1980s suggested.[70] First, the 'just deserts' sentencing framework set up by the Criminal Justice Act 1991 mandated an approach primarily in terms of pro-portionality to offence seriousness and, whilst the Criminal Justice Act 2003 has amended this framework in relation to persistence of offending, this retributivist starting point is still important.[71] The current focus on the young person's responsibility and accountability also increases the focus on the offence. In theory at least, these developments should have reduced the sentencing discretion that permitted different outcomes for girls and women.

However, in 1994, Hudson argued that the focus on proportionate punishment could work against the interests of female offenders: 'Young women's needs are marginalised as the criminal justice system becomes ever more offence-focused, and the sort of justice they are offered is of equal access to male provision, rather than gender-appropriate provision.'[72] A potentially gender-levelling focus on proportionality may also have been outweighed by the focus on risk. At the sen-tencing stage, minors and adults who have committed sexual and violent offences and are deemed to be dangerous must be dealt with 'disproportionately'.[73] New provisions in the Criminal Justice Act 2003 relating to persistence (previous convictions) may also undermine proportionality. The punishment stage is also infused with risk management and the use of ever more intensive community programmes – for adults and minors.

According to Hudson,[74] 'the factors which had been seen as bringing about harsher and more interventive sentencing of socially disadvantaged offenders . . . have reappeared as "risk of offending" factors'. The focus on risk factors can mean

---

68 Hudson, A (2002).
69 Harris and Webb (1987), p 135.
70 See Hudson, B (2002), p 21.
71 See Easton and Piper (2005), ch 3.
72 Hudson, B (1994), p 10.
73 Criminal Justice Act 2003, chapter 12; see Easton and Piper (2005), ch 5, particularly pp 145–6. There is also a focus on persistence in relation to drug offences and burglary through the 'three strikes' legislation; see Powers of Criminal Courts (Sentencing) Act 2000, ss 110–11.
74 Hudson, B (2002), p 25.

that life history factors increase an offender's risk score whilst the choice of preventative programmes or sentencing outcome ignores that context. For girls and women, then, the assessment of risk may itself be discriminatory.

Let us focus on a girl or boy from an abusive home who has committed a criminal offence. ASSET is the young offender assessment profiling tool used by youth offending teams to assess children and young people in relation to various interventions. There is some evidence from a national evaluation of Final Warning Projects that ASSET is not always properly used and needs are consequently not addressed.[75] One component of the form (section 2) on 'family and personal relationships' includes not only factors about the criminality or the health problems of the young offender's family but also has tick boxes for 'experience of abuse' and 'witnessing other violence' in the family context. At the bottom of the page, the professional conducting the assessment has to rate on a scale of one to four the extent to which the family relationships 'are associated with the likelihood of further offending'. This is one of 12 ratings which have to be totalled at the end with a maximum high-risk score of 48. A high score may lead to intensive supervision, which ignores the factors which led to the risk score. For a girl, this might mean a mixed-sex community project or pressure to stay with her family, when in neither context does she feel safe and may not be safe.

As noted above, Home Office research on siblings also points to gender implications of the prediction of risk of offending.[76] The finding that 'socio-economic factors such as low social class, low family income, poor housing and large family size predicted offending more strongly for sisters than brothers' might also confirm that girls and young women in custody are more likely to have experienced 'structural' disadvantage in their lives, which needs more targeted programmes as part of punishment. There is also an increasing awareness that not only are the young disproportionately at risk of violence, but that females experience different forms of violence, notably violence within the home.[77]

A telephone survey of criminal justice practitioners by Beatrix Campbell suggested that professionals in the front line are aware of gender issues.[78] The cases summarised by practitioner respondents reveal boys 'watching their mothers beaten to hell by their fathers' and mothers who felt disempowered and defeated. Campbell noted that government guidelines on the use of parenting orders 'refer only to "inadequate" or "harsh and erratic" parenting as risk factors, and cite no references to the significant volume of research on domestic violence and its impact on children'.[79]

Campbell's comments were based on draft guidance, the final version being issued in March 2004. This states that both parents should be seen if they both participate in the child's upbringing, 'unless a parent is estranged, for instance

---

75 See Holdaway and Desborough (2004).
76 Farrington and Painter (2004).
77 Burman *et al* (2001), p 446.
78 Campbell (2003).
79 *Ibid*, pp 4–5.

because of domestic violence'.[80] It further states that 'information that emerges during the intervention and assessment process about domestic violence or abuse will need to be passed on to police and social services for action' and practitioners should establish with other agencies whether they have such information.[81] However, as research on practitioners in the family justice system has shown[82] and as one of Campbell's respondents phrased it, domestic violence 'won't come out unless you create a climate'.[83]

The violence and harm that may be done to girls and young women – as offenders, as the mothers of offenders or as young offenders who are themselves mothers – does not get highlighted. Instead, as the Howard League pointed out, the focus is on the violence done *by* girls, and that results in an increasing tendency to give more severe sentences to girls than boys where violence is involved.[84]

Punishing girls

Ofsted has recently completed a report, *Girls in Prison*, which is a survey of female juveniles completing detention and training orders, conducted between October 2002 and April 2003 at three secure establishments.[85] Because the second half of a detention and training order is spent on supervision in the community, the findings cover the experiences of girls in detention and on licence. The main findings of this report are:

- the majority of young women interviewed had poor educational histories with low levels of attainment;
- all but a small minority of the surveyed group had exceptionally low levels of self-esteem (around half had experienced severe depression during sentence, of whom a significant number had a history of self-harm);
- attendance at education during custody was highly valued by the majority of those interviewed;
- the community aspect of the detention and training order did not provide sufficient structure or support to cope with personal problems or help them to progress to further education, training or employment;
- the quality of careers information, advice and guidance was extremely variable and too often inadequate; and
- the availability of suitable programmes and support structures for young women on licence was inconsistent from one youth offending team area to another.

---

80 Home Office (2004a), para 2.17.
81 *Ibid*, paras 2.20 and 2.21 respectively. A note by Judy Renshaw to the Youth Justice Board, *Advice on Accommodation* (YJB(00)72), noted at paras 44 and 51 that 16–17 year olds who are 'fleeing domestic violence' are now treated as 'vulnerable' under housing legislation and the Safer Communities Housing Fund; see www.youth-justice-board.gov.uk/Publications/Downloads/AccomVulnerYP.pdf.
82 Piper and Kaganas (1997).
83 Campbell (2003), p 5.
84 Howard League (1997).
85 Office for Standards in Education (2004).

This summary is taken from the website of HM Prison Service and reveals an acknowledgment that girls may not be well served by the Prison Service, the Probation Services or youth offending teams.

In the community

The latest Criminal Statistics would suggest that there may still be differential sentencing in relation to community penalties whereby girls receive more regulatory, and fewer practical, penalties. The overall figures for under-18 year olds in 2003 reveal that 12 per cent of total convictions at the Crown Court are in relation to girls and young women, but the proportion given supervisory sentences is higher than this, whilst the proportion is lower for other community sentences. For example, only 18 community punishment (previously community service) orders (10 per cent of the total imposed on girls and boys) and no reparation orders were imposed on girls or young women in 2003, but they received 78 supervision orders (18 per cent of the total) and 17 community rehabilitation (previously probation) orders (17 per cent of the total).

The Ofsted report noted above included a variety of negative comments on the community part of a sentence of detention and training made by the girls surveyed. For example, they said that some community projects were too 'risky' for them and they criticised the standard of resettlement support.[86] As Carlen has pointed out, it is difficult to establish and maintain community projects designed for girls and women, ostensibly because of funding problems that mask other shortcomings such as non-use by the courts.[87] This results in pressure to extend the projects to men to avoid closure, so that survival requires ring-fenced funding and excellent public relations.

There is also potential gender discrimination arising from the increasing importance given to restorative justice in community programmes in the youth justice system. Below is an extract from government guidance on examples of suitable content for reparation orders.

- A 15 year old boy is found guilty of daubing graffiti on the walls of a newsagent's shop. He is sentenced to a reparation order which, with the agreement of the newsagent, requires the offender to clean the graffiti from the walls, and to spend one hour under supervision every Saturday morning for two months helping the newsagent to sort out his stock.
- A 12 year old girl is found guilty of vandalising an elderly lady's garden and shouting abusive language at her. She is sentenced to a reparation order which requires her, with the victim's agreement, to meet the victim in order to hear her describe the effect that this behaviour has had on her, and to allow the offender to explain why she has behaved in this way, and to apologise. This meeting might be arranged and supervised by a local voluntary organisation working with victims and offenders, in support of the youth offending team.
- A 16 year old boy has caused damage to a local children's playground. The court

---

86 Ofsted (2004).
87 Carlen (2001–2), p 44. For a discussion of one particular community-based project see Roberts (2002).

sentences him to a reparation order. As there is no obvious, specific victim in this case, the reparation is designed to benefit the community at large, many of whom use the playground; the offender is required to spend one hour every weekend under supervision helping to repair the damage that he has caused.

- A 14 year old boy is found guilty of damaging the greenhouse of an elderly man. The victim wants no further contact with the offender, but the court feels that some form of reparation activity would be appropriate. The offender is therefore required to spend two hours per week under supervision assisting the gardener at the local old people's home.[88]

In these examples, the three boys were given practical reparation, the girl met her victim to apologise and, it was hoped, to feel remorse at the effects of her offending. The crucial variable here could have been age, with 14 being seen as a minimum age for gardening. Nevertheless, the choice of examples is intriguing, as are the summaries below of two of the case studies included in the government's *Restorative Justice* Consultation Paper.[89]

> **Case study 02** 'A 28 year old man was assaulted by a group of 11 youths, four of whom were girls aged 14–16 . . . The four girls were all given referral orders.' A video was made of the first Panel meeting with the victim and this was shown to the others: 'both the victim and the attacker were visibly moved'. One of the girls went on to do a peer mentoring course and became a peer mentor for the youth offending team.

> **Case study 05** The 'offender' was serving a four and a half-year custodial sentence. 'During the restorative conference one of the offender's supporters was her grandmother', who was 'appalled' at what she heard. The offender was 'overwhelmed with remorse' at this. 'By the end the victim said her view of the offender had changed from a monster to a broken little girl.'

This is not to make the point that boys in the case studies were never remorseful; simply to draw attention to the choice of examples and the tone of the narratives. They serve to emphasise how little is known about the gender implications of these new processes, and how gender could be operating differentially without proper monitoring. Alder has pointed out that what we know about the greater intolerance by the public of offending and anti-social behaviour by girls, and different social expectations of girls, must be taken into account when developing programmes for girls.[90] Girls may be more likely to feel shame and guilt, and restorative programmes should not endorse the continuance of shame as a tool to control women. They should also be aware of the 'delicate balance between exhibiting contrition and remorse, and feelings of guilt and self-blame and self-harm.'[91]

In prison

Again, this title is technically incorrect: minors are not imprisoned or given custodial sentences, but are 'detained'. They currently receive orders for detention

---

88 Home Office (2000), para 6.3.
89 Home Office (2003a).
90 Alder (2003), p 119.
91 *Ibid*, p 120.

and training, detention for a specified period, or detention at Her Majesty's plea-sure.[92] Section 226 of the Criminal Justice Act 2003 adds detention for life or detention for public protection to this custodial repertoire for the under-18s. The period of detention for all these orders may take place in a prison service estab-lishment (generally a young offender institution), a secure training centre[93] or a local authority (social services) secure children's home. In practice, many girls and boys are in prison. The DfES website in mid-2005 gave a figure of 2,700 juveniles (15–17 year olds) in custody, either sentenced or on remand, of whom approxi-mately 80 were females. Male juveniles are normally held in young offender institutions, but provisions for female juveniles have been unsatisfactory.

A recent report of the Howard League for Penal Reform gives a figure of 90 girls aged under 18 in prison on any one day and points out that, unlike for boys, there are no prisons which are solely for girls. Sentenced girls are therefore held in four designated prisons, where they may be placed on a separate wing for juveniles or on wings which also hold women aged over 18. The report provides evidence of what amounts to discriminatory treatment of girls in custodial establishments, stemming from the much smaller numbers of young female detainees and from their different needs.[94] Her Majesty's Chief Inspector of Prisons, Anne Owers, has implicitly accepted that justice for girls requires that they have facilities specifically geared towards their needs. She has argued that no girl aged under 17 should be held in prison, given the lack of separate facilities for girls, and has drawn attention to examples of girls inappropriately placed in custody, such as a pregnant 16-year-old girl and a 17-year-old girl with serious mental health problems.[95] She points out that this is sometimes because the appropriate facilities are not available. Five new 16-bed units for juveniles in female prisons were opened by Autumn 2006 to provide specialist provision for this age group; this will improve matters.

It is also encouraging that Owers is aware that 'many of the children coming into prisons have been abused, and that the issue of strip-searching is, consequently, a very sensitive one'.[96] For girls in particular, such intimate searches are problem-atic because there is evidence to suggest that girls are more likely than boys to be victims of sexual abuse. For example, the NSPCC's[97] international survey of studies of the prevalence and incidence of child sexual abuse reveals higher figures for women and girls in all the jurisdictions included in the survey.[98] Likewise, a study of children on child protection registers in England and Wales on 31 March 2003 found there were more girls than boys on the registers for sexual abuse, although the situation was reversed in relation to physical abuse.[99] A review of North

---

92 Under the Powers of Criminal Courts (Sentencing) Act 2000, ss 100, 91 and 90 respectively.
93 Four privately run institutions with health and educational services, inspected by the CSCI (Commission for Social Care Inspection).
94 Howard League for Penal Reform (2004).
95 Owers in conversation with Wadsworth (2005), pp 10–11.
96 Ibid, pp 9–10.
97 National Society for the Prevention of Cruelty to Children.
98 Creighton (2004), Table 1.
99 DfES (2004c), paras 6.8 and 6.9.

American research reaches similar conclusions.[100] This should also be noted in relation to the fact that prison staff may not have been properly vetted. Owers's recent inspection of Holloway Prison revealed that no adult working with children and young people had been subject to the required checks from the Criminal Records Bureau.[101]

Juveniles in Custody,[102] a report by the Prison Inspectorate, also found gender differences in regard to feelings of insecurity: over one-third of the cohort of 15–18 year olds surveyed had felt unsafe at some time whilst in custody, but this included *all* the 15-year-old girls. These and other findings emphasise what is already known: that girls and young women in prison are very vulnerable and often psychologically damaged and that they frequently self-harm. In 2003, for example, women constituted 6 per cent of the prison population but were responsible for 46 per cent of recorded incidents of self-harm.[103]

A research study undertaken in 2002–3 aimed to shed light on this, using a sample of 15 women aged 19–50 years. Whilst this research did not include minors, its results reveal in its sample of women histories of self-harm and suicide attempts going back to early adolescence, and also a disproportionate incidence of chronic mental illness, sexual abuse, assault and rape.[104] All but one of the women interviewed said they had wanted to die, and all were in custodial situations where their trauma and medical problems were intensified. There is no evidence to suggest that the situation is considerably better for girls aged under 19 who are in detention.

As has happened in adult prisons, one problem is that there may not be sufficient staff trained to deal with the specific problems of vulnerable (young) females: the title of the Howard League 2004 Report, *Advice, Understanding and Underwear*, gives an indication of what these might be. Another problem is that – with only four institutions – there is a greater likelihood of being placed far from home. The Response from the Gender and Justice Policy Network to the Halliday Report made the point that, with the serious shortage of places for girls and young women in young offender institutions in the south of England, many girls are transferred to places of detention in the north of the country, 'increasing the distance from home and community and making the maintenance of family ties more difficult'.[105]

The search for equivalence

A development which has, perhaps, hidden the particular safety as well as physical and emotional needs of girls is what has been called the search for equivalence. This refers to the aim of some campaigning groups to gain equivalent public interest in the problems or misdeeds of the other gender where, historically, the

---

100 Chesney-Lind and Pasko (2004), pp 25–7.
101 HM Inspectorate of Prisons (2005).
102 HM Inspectorate of Prisons (2004).
103 See Borrill *et al* (2005), p 57.
104 *Ibid*, pp 6–61.
105 Gender and Justice Policy Network (2001), para 2.3.2.

focus has been on only one gender. The clearest examples are to be found in family law practice. There we find, for example, the construction of women (rather than just men) as perpetrators of domestic violence and child abuse,[106] and also pressure, from men's groups, for men (rather than just women) to be constructed as victims of parental separation.[107] What such 'evening up' may do is to hide the different extents and natures of those phenomena that are united by a common name. This can lead to the assumption that there is no need for gender-specific approaches to dealing with the problems. Specifically, it hides any need to treat girls and boys who offend differently if their needs and family backgrounds are different.[108] It also legitimates the use of gender-neutral risk assessment tools such as those already mentioned.

Arguably, the assessment, supervision and detention of young male and female offenders are not given adequate analysis in theory or in policy. This may well stem from the fact that youth victimology, as Muncie points out, is non-existent and it is still not fully appreciated that young people are often both victims and offenders.[109] The findings of the *Girls in Prison* report, summarised above, support the finding of many research studies, which reveal that the proportion of offenders with abusive backgrounds is far higher than that of the general population.[110] A recent survey found that, prior to custody, 83 per cent of the boys and 65 per cent of the girls had been excluded from school, whilst 37 per cent of boys and 43 per cent of girls had been accommodated by the local authority.[111] Further, in 2000, of 15–20 year olds in prison service establishments, 90 per cent had a diagnosable mental health problem.[112] Offending not only re-categorises the child from victim to offender, but also removes him or her – temporarily or permanently – from the family justice system or the mainstream health service. Almost half of all girls in custody have been the subject of that move.[113]

Conclusions

Developments in policy relating to children who offend have significant implications for family life. What we know about the background and treatment of girls who engage in anti-social or offending behaviour suggests the potential for parental behaviour to have differential impacts in relation to their male and female children, and that parents face different outcomes for their male and female children who end up in the youth justice system. Further, the ability of the family justice system and family law to protect such girls must be assessed in the light of the increasing

---

106 See, for example, Kaganas, Chapter 8 in this volume.
107 See, for example, Smart, Chapter 7, and Collier, Chapter 12, both in this volume.
108 Worrall (2002).
109 Muncie (2003).
110 See, for example, Crowley (1998), for research evidence of the abusive backgrounds of 12–14 year olds eligible for what are now detention and training orders.
111 HM Inspectorate of Prisons (2004).
112 Lyon *et al* (2000).
113 Walklate has also argued that there is a gendered victimology with an unhelpful 'deeply embedded male view of the problem of victimisation' (2003, pp 32–3).

scope, powers and resources of the youth justice agencies. Indeed, Danner[114] has pointed out that the mothers of such girls may be disadvantaged by the movement of resources from social welfare to criminal justice policies, not simply in reduced benefits but also in reduced opportunities for traditional 'female' work in social services. Women generally are also being disadvantaged by the extra caring responsibilities resulting from the rising imprisonment rate: they may be left caring single-handedly for (the father's) children, or they may find themselves looking after the children of imprisoned daughters. Consequently: 'It is often the women and children who are left out, sometimes unintentionally . . . by the cumulative impact of crime control policies which adversely harm women.'[115]

Yet, despite the media and research focus on the offending of girls, girls and their mothers are virtually invisible in the processes of responding to their offending or their anti-social behaviour, particularly in analyses of 'youth' sentencing and punishment. There is now a growing focus on girls in prison but still very little attention to girls punished in the community or diverted to preventative projects in the community. Whilst there is, as now, inequality of opportunity, of societal expectations and of life experiences for girls and young women who offend, differential treatment is potentially necessary and should be considered in all individual assessments and in devising general programmes and institutional regimes. As a first step, there should be proper monitoring of gender in the ever-widening youth justice system. The difficulty is currently in finding out what is happening to young female offenders – and those girls being brought within the system because of their risk of offending – and this chapter has, consequently, prompted far more questions than it has answered.

There are, however, signs of change. Anne Owers, as HM Chief Inspector of Prisons, has given valuable publicity to the shortcomings of prisons for women and girls. Campaigning groups such as the Howard League and NACRO are again focusing on the experiences of girls in the youth justice system and in detention, as references to important research reports have evidenced. Further, the concern about the perceived increasing 'danger' from girl criminals is itself forcing policy development of responses. The urgent need, then, is for more empirical research – on boys and girls – and for that research to be brought to the attention of policy makers. Currently, the standard of the conditions in which children are held in penal detention is far below that envisaged by rights conventions. When addressing these shortcomings, there needs to be explicit attention to girls and boys. What is also required is an assessment of the role of, and burdens on, mothers, at least to counterbalance the assumptions about the importance of fathers.

References

Alder, C (2003) 'Young women offenders and the challenge of restorative justice', in McLaughlin, E, Fergusson, R, Hughes, G and Westmarland, L (eds) *Restorative*

---

114 Danner (1998).
115 Miller (1998), p xviii.

Justice, Critical Issues, London/Milton Keynes: Sage Publications/Open University Press

Batchelor, S and Burman, M (2004) 'Working with girls and young women', in McIvor, G (ed) *Research Highlights in Social Work: Female Offenders and Female Offending*, London: Jessica Kingsley

Borrill, J, Snow, L, Medlicott, D, Teers, R and Paton, J (2005) 'Learning from "near misses": Interviews with women who survived an incident of self-harm in prison', 44(1) *Howard J* 57

Boyle, C, Fairbridge, S, Kinch, K, Cochran, P, Smyth, R and Chunn, D (2002) 'The criminalization of young women: An editor's forum', 14 *Canadian J of Women and the Law* 389

Burman, M, Batchelor, S and Brown, J (2001) 'Researching girls and violence', 41 *British J of Criminology* 443

Burney, E (2002) 'Talking tough, acting coy: What happened to the anti-social behaviour order?', 41(5) *Howard J* 469

Campbell, B (2003) ' "Infant warriors": Boys, mothers, men and domestic violence', 54 *Criminal Justice Matters* 4

Carlen, P (1983) *Women's Imprisonment*, London: Routledge and Kegan Paul

Carlen, P (2001–2) 'Gender-specific projects for female lawbreakers: Questions of survival', 46 *Criminal Justice Matters* 44

Chesney-Lind, M and Pasko, L (2004) *The Female Offender: Girls, Women and Crime*, 2nd edn, Thousand Oaks and London: Sage

Creighton, S (2004) *Prevalence and Incidence of Child Abuse: International Comparisons*, London: NSPCC

Crowley, A (1998) *A Criminal Waste: A Study of Child Offenders Eligible for Secure Training Centres*, London: The Children's Society

Danner, M (1998) 'Three strikes and it's women who are out', in Miller, S (ed) *Crime Control and Women*, Thousand Oaks and London: Sage

Day Sclater, S and Piper, C (2000) 'Re-moralising the family? Family policy, family law and youth justice', 12(2) *Child and Family Law Quarterly* 135

Department for Education and Skills (DfES) (2003) *Every Child Matters*, www.dfes.gov.uk/everychildmatters/

DfES (2004a) *Every Child Matters: Next Steps*, www.dfes.gov.uk/everychildmatters/pdfs/EveryChild MattersNextSteps.pdf

DfES (2004b) *Offenders of the Future? Assessing the Risk of Children and Young People becoming Involved in Criminal or Antisocial Behaviour*, Research Report, London: DfES

DfES (2004c) *Referrals, Assessments and Children and Young People on Child Protection Registers: Year ending 31st March 2004*, London: HMSO

DfES (2005) *Youth Matters*, CM 6299, London: DfES

Drakeford, M and Vanstone, M (2000) 'Social exclusion and the politics of criminal justice: A tale of two administrations', 39(4) *Howard Journal* 369

Easton, S and Piper, C (2005) *Sentencing and Punishment: The Quest for Justice*, Oxford: Oxford University Press

Edwards, S (1984) *Women on Trial*, Manchester: Manchester University Press

Farrington, D and Painter, K (2004) *Gender Differences in Offending: Implications for Risk-Focused Offending*, Home Office Online Report 09/04, London: Home Office

Fortin, J (2003) *Children's Rights and the Developing Law*, 2nd edn, London: Lexis Nexis

Fortin, J (2004) 'Children's rights: Are the courts now taking them seriously?' 15 *King's College LJ* 253

Gelsthorpe, L (1986) 'Towards a sceptical look at sexism', 14 *International J of Sociology of Law* 25

Gender and Justice Policy Network (2001) *Response to the Halliday Report*

Harris, R and Webb, D (1987) *Welfare, Power and Juvenile Justice*, London: Tavistock Publications

Hedderman, C and Gelsthorpe, L (1997) *Understanding the Sentencing of Women*, Home Office Research Study 170, London: Home Office

Heidensohn, F (1986) 'Models of justice: Portia or Persephone? Some thoughts on equality, fairness and gender in the field of criminal justice', 14 *International J of Sociology of Law* 287

Hibbert, P, Moore, S and Monaghan, G (2003) *Children in Trouble – Time for Change*, Ilford: Barnardo's

HM Inspectorate of Prisons (in conjunction with the Youth Justice Board) (2004) *Juveniles in Custody: A Unique Insight into the Perceptions of Young People Held in Prison Service Custody in English and Wales*, London: HM Inspectorate of Prisons

HM Inspectorate of Prisons (2005) *Inspection of HMP Holloway*, London: HM Inspectorate of Prisons

Holdaway, S and Desborough, S (2004) *Final warning Projects: The National Evaluation of the Youth Justice Board's Final Warning Projects*, London: Youth Justice Board

Home Office (2000) *The Crime and Disorder Act, Guidance Document: Reparation Order*, London: Home Office

Home Office (2003a) *Restorative Justice: The Government's Strategy*, Consultation Paper, London: Home Office

Home Office (2003b) *Youth Justice – The Next Steps*, London: Home Office

Home Office (2003c) *Criminal Statistics, England and Wales 2002* (Cm 6054)

Home Office (2004a) *Youth Justice – The Next Steps: Summary of Responses and the Government's Proposals*, London: Home Office

Home Office (2004b) *Criminal Statistics, England and Wales 2003*, (Cm 6361)

Home Office, Dept for Constitutional Affairs, Youth Justice Board (2004) *Parenting Contracts & Orders Guidance*, London: Home Office

Howard League (1997) *Lost Inside – The Imprisonment of Teenage Girls*, London: Howard League

Howard League for Penal Reform (2004) *Advice, Understanding and Underwear: Working with Girls in Prison*, London: Howard League

Hudson, A (2002) ' "Troublesome girls": Towards alternative definitions and policies', in Muncie, J, Hughes, G and McLaughlin, E (eds) *Youth Justice: Critical Readings*, London: Sage/Open University Press

Hudson, B (1994) 'Discrimination and the young adult offender', NACRO Conference, 20–22 April, Sheffield

Hudson, B (2002) 'Gender issues in penal policy and penal theory', in Carlen, P (ed) *Women and Punishment: The Struggle for Justice*, Cullompton: Willan Publishing

Lyon, J, Dennison, C and Wilson, A (2000) *Tell Them So They Listen: Messages from Young People in Custody*, Home Office Research Study 201, London: HMSO

Miller, S (1998) 'Introduction', in Miller, S (ed) *Crime Control and Women*, Thousand Oaks and London: Sage

Morris, A (1988) 'Sex and sentencing', [1988] *Criminal Law Review* 163

Muncie, J (2003) 'Youth, risk and victimisation', in Davies, P, Francis, P and Jupp, V (eds) *Victimisation: Theory, Research and Policy*, Basingstoke: Palgrave Macmillan

NACRO Youth Crime (2001) 'Girls in the youth justice system', Youth Crime Briefing, London: NACRO

Office for Standards in Education (2004) *Girls in Prison: The Education and Training of Under-18s Serving Detention and Training Orders*, London: HM Inspectorate of Prisons

Owers, A in conversation with Wadsworth, N (2005) 'Interview', 213 *Childright* 8

Pearson, R (1976) 'Women defendants in Magistrates' Courts', 3 *British J of Law and Society* 265

Piper, C (1994) 'Parental responsibility and the Education Acts', 24 *Family Law* 146

Piper, C (1999) 'The Crime and Disorder Act – child or community safety?', 62 *Modern Law Review* 397

Piper, C (2001) 'Who are these youths? Language in the service of policy', 1(2) *Youth Justice* 30

Piper, C (2005) 'Welfare, social exclusion and the importance of being at risk', Seminar on Children and the Concept of Best Interests, 5 May, Keele University

Piper, C and Kaganas, F (1997) 'The Family Law Act 1996 s1(d): How will "they" know there is a risk of violence?', 9(3) *Child and Family Law Quarterly* 269

Roberts, J (2002) 'Women-centred: The West Mercia community-based programme for women offenders', in Carlen, P (ed) *Women and Punishment: The Struggle for Justice*, Cullompton: Willan Publishing

Walklate, S (2003) 'Can there be a feminist victimology?' in Davies, P, Francis, P and Jupp, V (eds) *Victimisation: Theory, Research and Policy*, London: Palgrave Macmillan

Webb, D (1984) 'More on gender and justice: Girl offenders on supervision', 18(3) *Sociology* 367

Worrall, A (2002) 'Rendering women punishable: The making of a penal crisis', in Carlen, P (ed) *Women and Punishment: The Struggle for Justice*, Cullompton: Willan Publishing

Youth Justice Board (2004) *Government Response to the Audit Commission Report – Youth Justice 2004: A Review of the Reformed Youth Justice System*, London: Youth Justice Board

Chapter 10
Working towards Credit for Parenting: A Consideration of Tax Credits as a Feminist Enterprise

Ann Mumford[1]

Introduction

As Sainsbury has compellingly argued, 'the tax system is a crucial nexus of the state, the family, and the market'.[2] The intent of this chapter is to consider the current tax credit system for families, at the intersection of all of these factors. The impact of such initiatives on family decision making, in particular, will be addressed. Through incentives provided via the tax system, different types of families may be 'privileged', some members encouraged to enter the labour market or to leave it,[3] and this chapter will investigate the extent to which gendered tax incentives influence those choices and thus have an impact upon the division of family labour and gender relations within the home.[4] This chapter will confront the fact that tax incentives historically have encouraged fathers to work outside of the home and mothers to work inside of it, and, now, may be seeking to redress this balance. Put simply, this chapter will seek to demonstrate that tax plays a significant role in fashioning the subject of family law.

It is almost a truism that '[t]he tension between official legal forms and functional families has created issues for centuries'.[5] Through the study of tax credits, this chapter will reveal the government's latest vision for the ideal family. Tax, in particular, plays a crucial role in the government's vision.

On the question of this issue's importance, the Women's Budget Group have suggested that

> [t]he government is already encouraging the development of family friendly employment practices. Employer contributions to their employees' childcare costs should be on both trade union and employers' bargaining agendas. A more supportive tax regime would encourage both parties to take the issue more seriously.[6]

Perhaps the association of child care and family budget issues with tax, as opposed to benefits, takes the issue into the mainstream of cultural debate. This question will be considered, as will the thorny question of whether tax credits are

---

1 The author would like to express warmest thanks to Prof Lisa Philipps of Osgoode Hall Law School for her invaluable assistance in the writing of this chapter; and, also, to acknowledge the contribution of the Issues in Taxation class (2005–6) at the LSE, whose feedback on earlier drafts is very much appreciated.
2 Sainsbury (1999), p 185.
3 *Ibid.*
4 *Ibid.*
5 Minow (1991), p 270, cited at Kornhauser (1993), p 64.
6 Women's Budget Group (2003).

truly 'credits' at all. Further, in addition to family decision making, tax credits have an impact upon the range of choice that is available to women. They are presented as feminist initiatives. The extent to which tax credits live up to their promise will be considered. This 'promise' will be considered along the lines as suggested by Bennett, in that

> [a] key question to be asked of any policy proposal from a gender perspective . . . is not only whether it will make men's and women's 'choices' in the present easier, but also whether it will help to transform the existing gender roles and relationships that currently structure, and constrain, those choices, to allow both sexes to fulfil their capabilities to the full.[7]

Towards this end, whether tax credits assist mothers to 'fulfil their capabilities to the full' will be a recurrent, investigatory theme of this chapter. Most of all, this chapter will investigate the place of tax credits within a feminist vision of family law.

Child tax credits: Introduction to the legislation

The family tax credits upon which this chapter will focus are relatively recent initiatives: Child Tax Credit and Working Tax Credit have been payable from April 2003.[8] Couples are required to apply for tax credits jointly, and members of couples are precluded from applying for tax credits separately.[9] The Child Tax Credit, which is the primary focus of this chapter, is payable to people caring for at least one child, and is paid directly to the carer. According to Her Majesty's Revenue & Customs, nine out of ten families with young children qualify for tax credits, so the reach is very wide.[10] Families with income of up to the income threshold[11] per year are able to claim, and the claim lasts until 1 September following the child's 16th birthday.[12]

Child Tax Credit came into effect with the Tax Credits Act,[13] which abolished the Working Families' Tax Credit and Disabled Person's Tax Credit. The credits include a 'child care element', which 'is an element in respect of a prescribed proportion of so much of any relevant child care charges as does not exceed a prescribed amount'.[14] Child Tax Credit is, in design, an earned income tax credit, which may be defined as a benefit linked to paid employment. Confusion, which will be discussed below, exists as to whether the modern Child Tax Credit is a benefit, and thus a form of welfare payment; or a credit which may be deducted

---

7 Bennett (2002), p 579.
8 *Per* Tax Credits Act 2002, Ch 21.
9 *Ibid*, at s 3(a). Section 5A, as amended by the Civil Partnership Act 2004, defines 'couple' as those who are either married or civilly registered and not living separate, or those who are living as husband and wife or as civil partners.
10 www.taxcredits.inlandrevenue.gov.uk/HomeIR.aspx.
11 Tax Credits Act 2002, s 7(1)(a). For 2005–6, see http://www.hmrc.gov.uk/pbr2004/pn02.htm.
12 Tax Credits Act 2002, s 8(4)(a).
13 Tax Credits Act, *ibid*.
14 *Ibid*, s 12.

against ultimate tax owed. The fact of the matter is that the Child Tax Credit carries features of both. Its ultimate purpose is to guarantee families who work in the marketplace a minimum amount of income through the allocation of a benefit. As this payment is linked to money earned, it shares features, in spirit at least, with a tax credit, for the benefit increases and decreases proportionately (much like a tax credit).[15]

Tax credits were particularly 1990s, New Labour – and in the US, Clintonian – initiatives. The development of the UK's tax credits (earlier known as the Working Families' Tax Credit, or WFTC) and the US's earned income tax credits (or EITC) followed strikingly parallel lines, although, as Gerfin and Leu explain,

> [t]he main difference between the Earned Income Tax Credits and the Working Families Tax Credit is that the Earned Income Tax Credit has a wage subsidy component at low incomes (in the so called phase-in region), whereas the Working Families Tax Credit replaces the phase-in region by a minimum working hours requirement of 16 hours per week.[16]

The Working Families Tax Credit, now Child Tax Credit, chose to focus on working hours, as opposed to income, perhaps as part of an effort to render the initiative potentially relevant to the middle classes. This relevance is strikingly absent in the US, where Staudt has described the Earned Income Tax Credit as part of a 'push' to force 'poor' mothers into work.[17]

In the UK, the tax credits were part of a package of initiatives targeted at families living in poverty. The Working Families Tax Credit and New Deal (the latter aimed at 18–24 year olds with a history of at least six months of unemployment) were directed specifically at families with low income and low levels of 'skill', and low-income workers more generally.[18] The focus of the Working Families Tax Credit, however, was the provision of an encouragement to enter the marketplace, viewed in the context of what the government perceived as the very powerful deterrent of a generous benefits provision for families.[19]

Studies conducted by Blundell et al have concluded that the effects of these initiatives have been 'significant but relatively small'; that whilst some families have received 'unambiguous' enticement to enter the marketplace, the number of families who have received this is relatively small.[20] Additionally, the Women's Budget Group has warned that 'the tax credit scheme is only reaching a minority of families who would like to make use of formal childcare to take employment'.[21] Given such studies, it is likely that the tax credits will be extended to reach a wider range of families.

---

15 See Mumford (2001).
16 Gerfin and Leu (2003), p 13.
17 Staudt (1997), p 542.
18 Blundell (2004), p 234.
19 *Ibid.*
20 *Ibid*, p 235.
21 Women's Budget Group (2003).

Historical background

It is important to view tax credits within the context of tax legislation in its entirety, and not as a separate, independent, perhaps feminist initiative. As Blumberg famously argued in 1972, the forces which conspire to prevent women from having the access to work that men enjoy are to be found in a variety of tax provisions.[22] Additionally, the progress towards tax credits over the second half of the last century reveals much about the position of women in this nexus between 'state, family and the market'.[23]

The 1950s, with its norm of 'male-breadwinner families', produced a tax system in which joint taxation of husbands and wives was the rule, supported by deductions for men for their wives, and forms of relief for men and their children.[24] Amongst the changes the tax system has seen since the 1950s are the introduction of individual taxation and child allowances paid to the mother.[25]

The history of earned income tax credits reveals that they are very much conservative initiatives. Tax credits were first proposed by Edward Heath's government in 1972, although the proposal was dropped when Harold Wilson came into power in 1974.[26] Tax credits were part of a movement towards tax reform under Heath's government, which also included, in 1971, the introduction of the Family Income Supplement.[27] In the US, earned income tax credits were introduced during Gerald Ford's administration in 1975.[28] Adler stresses that what distinguishes the early-style tax credits from their modern counterparts is the design of a system which seeks to ensure that a recipient receives more money by working within the marketplace than if s/he were to stay at home.[29] He explains that, '[c]onsidered alongside the continued decline of national (social) insurance, it represents an alternative social security approach to those that have hitherto been associated with any of the familiar welfare state regimes'.[30]

The modern tax credit saw its genesis perhaps in 1988, when Harold Wilson's Family Income Supplement was replaced by the Family Credit – which, in 1999, was replaced by the Working Families' Tax Credit.[31] It is, in fact, the Family Credit which is the true ancestor of the current Child and Working Tax Credits, as the Family Credit targeted low-wage families, specifically.[32] The year 1999 also saw a

---

22 Blumberg (1972), cited at Staudt (1997), p 535.
23 Sainsbury (1999), p 185.
24 *Ibid*, pp 186–7.
25 *Ibid*, p 187.
26 Adler (2004), p 87, citing HM Treasury (1972) *Proposals for a Tax Credit System*, Green Paper, London: HMSO (Cmnd 5116).
27 Ochel (2001), p 6.
28 Adler (2004), p 88, citing Brewer, M (2000) *Comparing In-Work Benefits and Financial Incentives for Low-Income Families in the US and the UK*, Working Paper WP 00/16, London: Institute of Fiscal Studies.
29 *Ibid*.
30 *Ibid*.
31 Ochel (2001), p 6.
32 Blundell and Meghir (2002), p 10.

significant increase in the amount of the credit, and, importantly, the introduction of a minimum wage.[33]

Tax credits within a system defining women's financial independence

Part of the philosophy behind the Child Tax Credit is an assumption or hope that the tax system may provide a means by which women can choose to define a degree of financial independence. The idea of financial independence for women achieved much prominence in the 1990s, which, in addition to giving rise to the growth of the tax credit initiatives, also witnessed the end of the joint taxation of a married couple's income. Joint taxation ended on 6 April 1990, after which date husbands and wives have had the option to be taxed separately.[34] This was a striking moment in feminist history, and in many ways all tax measures which follow in its still-early wake must be considered in this context. It was also a moment to challenge assumptions at the basis of tax policy more widely.

Traditionally, questions of attribution of income in tax systems are answered by determining who has ultimate control or authority.[35] This has particular resonance in the context of the wife whose income, until so recently, was compelled to be merged with that of her husband. Contributing to the delay in the adoption of individual filing is thought to be a 1980 study by Feenberg and Rosen arguing that, in a family, not only is a great deal of property jointly owned, but, even if not, then a system which remained focused on individual ownership would entice spouses to transfer ownership of property from one spouse to another in order to achieve the lowest possible tax burden.[36] These were dangers which were assumed as written in 1990, when the decision to allow independent taxation of couples nonetheless went ahead.

Independent taxation did not end the gendered biases in income taxation. Indeed, a criticism of independent taxation is that it reinforces marriage as a societal ideal. The reason for this is found in the basis of the tax system itself. The tax system in the UK is based upon income; a choice which may be justified, among other policy grounds, on the argument that taxing income is based in fairness. Put simply, if one is fortunate enough to have both ability and motivation, the extent of both may be taxed in a system based on income (which may be described as taxing the 'sweat off one's brow').[37] Income taxation also incorporates progressivity more easily than consumption taxes, which have the potential to fall more harshly on lower earners.[38] So an income tax system is based on initiative, ability, and the individual. Joint income taxation moves away from

---

33 Leigh (2004), p 16.
34 See generally Andrews (1991).
35 As Kornhauser explains, '[t]raditionally, the power to manage and control determines whether income should be attributed to a taxpayer': (1993), p 74.
36 Feenberg and Rosen (1980).
37 Oberst (1988), p 671–2.
38 Kornhauser (1997).

that paradigm and into something else. This is potentially difficult, because it means that the taxation of families may not fit easily into the rest of the tax system, which remains based on the individual.

So where do tax credits fit within this redesign? Blundell has asked whether it is 'possible to design an effective training incentive within an individually based tax credit system'.[39] More broadly, the construction of that individual, in taxation and in the marketplace, will not escape the patriarchy underlying society (and the tax system that supports it), especially within the context of liberal feminism.

Perhaps an answer lies in (traditionally defined) 'liberal feminism', submitting that people are both individuals and self-governing, and that the choices they make are self-directed.[40] In this design, the more options from which individuals may choose, the happier they will be.[41] 'Sexism', Becker argues, 'operates by pressuring or requiring, sometimes by law, individuals to fulfil male and female roles regardless of their individual preferences'.[42] The female role is not subsumed within a system of joint taxation of income; rather, it is reinforced. Choices are denied in a system of jointly taxed income because the system itself is based on the model of the family, which itself is drawn along gendered lines. Jointly taxed income is derived from a family model which has been reinforced, even designed, by the tax system along lines of gender. What is being taxed are the gendered roles of male and female, joined together in the legal forms that define the family.[43]

Bennett proposes that the ideal of independent taxation should be taken a step further, such that 'a fundamental step towards achieving [financial autonomy for women] could be to base benefit entitlements and obligations on the individual rather than the family or household'.[44] He explains this point cogently, suggesting that 'the government often has a tendency to see couples as "one flesh", rather than as individual men and women'.[45] This has the consequence of increasing the importance placed on the stresses faced by, for example, one-earner as opposed to two-earner families, and 'working families' as opposed to 'out of work' families.[46] This point also has been seized upon by fathers' rights activists, who have enjoyed some success in litigation arguing that equal entitlement to tax credit is not superseded by any legitimate policy aim.[47]

---

39 Blundell (2004), p 245.
40 Becker (1999), p 32.
41 *Ibid.*
42 *Ibid.*
43 The Civil Partnership Act 2004, Pt 14, s 3(c), ensures that 'two people of the same sex who are civil partners of each other' will be entitled to claim tax credits. This need not impact, however, on the gendered roles that continue to define the family, as explained in Eskridge (1995), pp 62–3.
44 Bennett (2002), p 564.
45 *Ibid*, p 579.
46 *Ibid.*
47 See *Hockenjos v Secretary of State for Social Security* [2004] EWCA Civ 1749, [2005] Fam Law 464.

Mothers, citizens and the economy

This section will consider, to some extent, why both men and women are taxed in the first place. Discussion will largely relate to concepts of societal obligation and citizenship. The very concept of citizenship, however, may 'negat[e] consideration of gender-based inequalities'.[48] When 'the paid worker in the public sphere is the model, and the appropriate citizenship rights are those associated with paid employment', women, inevitably, are marginalised.[49] Women often have a greater role in the private sphere (for example, as carers and homemakers) than men, and thus are excluded from models of citizenship which depend upon public roles.[50] Further, these responsibilities in the private sphere can act to preclude women's entrance into the public sphere, for example, of the marketplace.[51]

Fredman describes this move away from welfare and into paid employment as part of a 'push/pull' strategy by Labour: 'On the "push" side have been the welfare to work programmes centred on the New Deal; while on the "pull side" have been the minimum wage, working families tax credit (now child tax credit and working tax credit) and the national childcare strategy.'[52] Into what, exactly, are mothers being pushed?

Tax credits are designed to increase employment and net income in 'low-wage areas' without burdening the government's budget.[53] A contradiction of such initiatives is that whilst the problem of 'low wages' is their target, in some ways, tax credits may act to ensure that areas which suffer low wages continue to do so. As Adler has explained, a key aspect of the new earned income tax credits proposals is that they, by design, in effect force people to accept poorly paid employment.[54] Tax credits ameliorate the effects of low wages, but do not act to raise the wages themselves. Further, employers are given an opportunity by these initiatives to lower wages.[55]

Additionally, studies have suggested that '[e]mployment-conditional tax credits and benefits do not only affect the decision whether or not to participate in the labour market; they also affect the volume of labour services which those who are already in employment are prepared to supply'.[56] The reason for this, Ochel suggests, is a reaction against a structure through which, as a worker's income increases, so the level of credit decreases; and simultaneously, as a worker progresses up the rate brackets, so the rate of income taxation increases.[57] Put simply, although earned income tax credits are designed to ensure that working parents who may be classified as low wage can afford to work (ie, they are no longer

---

48 Kilkey and Bradshaw (1999), p 148.
49 *Ibid*.
50 *Ibid*, p 149.
51 *Ibid*.
52 Fredman (2004), p 299.
53 Ochel (2001), p 3.
54 Adler (2004).
55 Ochel (2001), p 18.
56 *Ibid*, p 5.
57 *Ibid*.

effectively prohibited from working because of taxation and the costs of child care), nonetheless, the fact that the more one works, the less one retains, may act as a disincentive to increase volume of work.[58]

It is worth stressing the argument that much of the work concerning the increase in the volume of labour supply emanates from studies of the US's earned income tax credits.[59] Leigh's study of the UK revealed similar results, focused on the specifics of the UK system, yet with some surprising caveats. His study considered specifically the increases that both welfare and the tax credits received in 1999, and '[w]hile theory suggests that the difference between welfare and in-work benefits will be a key factor determining the employment effect, the stigma associated with welfare may be such that a comparable increase in both welfare and the tax credit will nonetheless induce a rise in labour supply'.[60]

On the other hand, stark analysis of tax credits reveals that the economy may be injured by tax credit programmes.[61] Their attractiveness lies not in the amount of beneficial economic activity that is increased, it is suggested, but in the extent to which they increase the attractiveness of marriage for men (if not for women).

> First, poor families will get extra income that should allow them to invest more time and resources in their children. Second, it should make marriage a more attractive option for males, since single males are taxed without receiving any subsidy. On the downside, the attractiveness of marriage for females, however, might decline. Second, the beneficial aspects of this policy for children may be dissipated by larger family size. The long-run health of the economy is not helped by this policy.[62]

This research needs to be considered against a background of high rates of unemployment, which provided the background for the redevelopment of earned income tax credits in 2001 not only in the UK, but in Australia, Canada, Ireland, New Zealand, Finland, France and the United States as well.[63] Initiatives like tax credits are particularly effective techniques in such economic climates because, as explained above, of the opportunity they provide for employers to lower wages.[64] This can reduce the cost of labour, and hence stimulate the demand for more workers.[65]

High levels of unemployment, generally, may have provided a backdrop to the refashioning of the tax credits in 2001, but it was the under-employment of single mothers, specifically, as Blundell and Meghir explain, which truly commanded the government's attention in the structuring of these initiatives.[66] This was a particular concern, because single mothers remained a persistently 'under-employed'

---

58 Ibid.
59 Leigh (2004), p 2.
60 Ibid, p 18.
61 Or, in their analysis, 'subsidies' for children.
62 Greenwood et al (2000), p 35.
63 Ochel (2001), generally.
64 Ibid, p 18.
65 Ibid.
66 Blundell and Meghir (2002), p 6.

group throughout growths in employment for other types of women.[67] The Women's Budget Group has defined the issue plainly: 'The government has accepted that we should collectively share with parents the maintenance costs of children by introducing the new child tax credit alongside universal child benefit (formerly family allowance). . .'[68]

On this question of sharing maintenance costs, Alstott has constructed a more radical platform. She suggests that society should contribute money, directly, to parents.[69] She points out that 'in the not-so-distant past' raising children made economic sense in terms of their expected contribution to the family business (even during childhood), and support during old age.[70] Now, parents are expected to provide emotional and financial support for almost twenty years, without immediate financial reward.[71] Given this shift, Alstott submits, it is not only unsurprising that parents need help from society, but proper that they should receive it.[72]

Alstott explicitly rejects the 'libertarian' response, which would suggest that, even if parenting makes less financial sense than it did not so long ago, nonetheless this is an activity which participants choose.[73] The skills valued under the tax credits legislation would include recognition of the fact that one should choose only to have children which one can afford, *without* state assistance. The end-game of the Child Tax Credit is a 'working parent', working in the marketplace.

In this context, it is worth remembering that fourteen years ago, Fineman suggested that the symbolism evoked by such initiatives may be that the state will move to the side, and then the father will step in to assume his rightful place.[74] This symbolism is particularly redolent when class enters the analysis, and the discussion of the extent of society's obligation to parents may disintegrate to: 'I don't mind paying to help people in need, but I don't want my tax (dollars) to pay for the sexual pleasure of adolescents who won't use birth control.'[75] The legislation enacting the Child Tax Credit is not, however, necessarily focused on the father. Its goal is a working parent, whether the mother or the father, to some extent liberated from the otherwise financially prohibitive demands of child care.

The libertarian objection, however, is not dependent on stereotypes of gender and class in the formulation of its argument that society owes no obligation to those who chose an activity of which the benefits, pleasures, struggles and demands are publicised and celebrated in equal measure. The flaw in this argument, Alstott suggests, is child care. She argues that 'continuity of care' is crucial to a child's development, and, if a child grows into a troubled teenager, or student, and eventually troubled adult, then society will suffer in a number of ways.[76]

---

67 *Ibid.*
68 Women's Budget Group (2003).
69 Alstott (2004). This might be described as a radical version of the UK's Child Benefit.
70 *Ibid.*
71 *Ibid.*
72 *Ibid.*
73 *Ibid.*
74 Fineman (1991).
75 *Ibid*, p 282.
76 Alstott (2004).

Given the incentive society has in minimising the products of poor parenting, Alstott argues, it makes sense to make the job of parenting easier through financial assistance, even if parents probably would try their hardest to care for their children with whatever resources they had.[77] Alstott's proposal is to keep mothers out of the marketplace.

The lynchpin for Alstott's analyses are studies in child psychology. She writes that, '[s]tudies document the serious and lasting emotional harm suffered by children denied continuity of care for long periods or during formative stages'.[78] Social science also is relied upon to establish the impact suffered by parents by their choice to have children, and, in particular, the effect wrought on women's position in the marketplace. Alstott writes that '[s]ocial science research is often equivocal, but on the cost of parenthood to mothers in particular a truckload of research exists to establish how it limits economic options in every class'.[79] Her characterisation of the demands made of the twenty-first-century parent is stark: 'No exit.'[80] At the core of Alstott's philosophy is the argument that one affirmative choice (ie, to become a parent) should not provide the excuse for 'unlimited regulation' of the remainder (or, at the least, a very significant portion) of a parent's life ... without more.[81] Direct financial assistance to parents is that 'something more', and, at the least, it provides the possibility of remedying the enormous limitations that parenthood places on women in particular.[82]

In some ways, the value of Alstott's suggestions is what Livingston has described as 'the narrative or consciousness-raising side of feminist scholarship, the ability of an author to make us think about gender in a different way than we did before, even if her proposals are politically unrealistic or inconsistent with some versions of feminist theory'.[83] Alstott's direct subsidy proposals offer an alternative for those uncomfortable with the proposal of the marketplace, with all of its gendered assumptions, as the locus for women's liberation. Typical ripostes to feminist suggestions about tax include, as Livingston explains, 'political unrealism', 'flawed technical analysis' and 'failure to take adequate notice of the differences among various strains of feminist theory'.[84] Taking what could be posed as Livingston's challenge to view Alstott's proposal in terms of consciousness raising, then what do we learn about motherhood, tax and the marketplace from these suggestions?

First, we learn that the perceived impact upon children of care which is not provided by parents is increasing the attention placed upon (primarily) women's work within the home. We learn also, as Minow describes it, that '[t]he dominant discourse of economic necessity and market choice risks squeezing out the equally

---

77 *Ibid.*
78 *Ibid.*
79 *Ibid.*
80 *Ibid.*
81 *Ibid.*
82 *Ibid.*
83 Livingston (1998), p 1801.
84 *Ibid*, p 1802.

important language of responsibility, care, equality, fairness, and compassion'.[85] This is a contribution, as well, to a model – the family – which imposes limitations on women. It may be that 'family is one of the most important contexts for the structuring of women's lives . . . [and] feminists identify the family as a key site of male power over women'.[86] The family is *also* the basis for welfare distribution.[87] Kilkey and Bradshaw explain that '[l]argely as a result of gendered-power relations, familial welfare in all countries remains overwhelmingly the responsibility of women'.[88]

All of this suggests that society has a stake in parenting, and that we all take some benefit from a child that is well 'supported'. From a strictly economist's (ie, not feminist) perspective, it is all actually a rather more complicated series of sacrifices:

> Women in the lower strata of the economy are better off with a child tax credit. The rest are slightly worse off. The poorest women have the largest number of children so a tax credit helps them the most. Since women value children more than men (single men don't value them at all), the overall effect of the tax credit on women's expected utility is less detrimental than it is for men.[89]

Indeed, studies have explored whether child tax credits may be detrimental to society, in that they either encourage families to have greater numbers of children, or at least make it more possible for them to do so.[90] The (albeit limited) value of such research to a feminist analysis might focus on the inevitably broad question of whether or not 'women' actually 'want' tax credits. There is some empirical evidence indicating that they do.

A study by Alvarez and McCaffery revealed that, in the US, women were more likely to prefer initiatives such as earned income tax credits to, for example, reducing the national debt (which was favoured by men).[91] When informed that tax laws were biased against families with two workers, the study found that men adjusted their preferences to support initiatives such as earned income tax credits, although men objected to tax relief for child care.[92] Women were more predisposed towards child-care tax relief, but less inclined towards tax relief for the 'working poor' than men.[93]

The authors of this study explained that

> [t]he decline in support for general rate reduction and the increase in support for working poor tax credits, but not child-care relief, suggests that the prime had the effect of making respondents think more of general redistribution to the poor: that

---

85 Minow (1998), p 342.
86 Kilkey and Bradshaw (1999), p 149.
87 *Ibid.*
88 *Ibid.*
89 *Ibid*, p 36.
90 Greenwood *et al* (2000), p 7.
91 Alvarez and McCaffery (2000).
92 *Ibid.*
93 *Ibid*, p 19. Interestingly, however, women also were significantly more likely to express 'no opinion' than men, and to emphasise their 'ignorance' about tax law and policy (*Ibid*).

the 'problem' of working mothers triggers an economic, not a familial demographic, response.[94]

What this reveals is that, with the focus taken away from the parent, or at least from the parent's gender, and redirected towards the economy, it is actually the child that is at centre stage. Or, perhaps, the transferring of income from families without children, to families with them, is at centre stage.[95] It is perhaps for this reason that the child-care element of the tax credit system can have important feminist consequences. For, as Orloff explains, 'the impact upon women of inadequate resources and support for childcare is well documented'.[96] Where lack of support impedes women's abilities to participate in the economy, there is an impression that they are prevented from participating in a fuller sense of citizenship as well. On the question of citizenship, Lardy has investigated whether the participatory benefits (civic and personal, even emotional) of voting ought to be made compulsory.[97] Then, in effect, everyone would be able to feel good for 'doing the right thing', even if forced to do so. This has intriguing resonance for tax credits, which seek to encourage (perhaps, financially, push?) women into the marketplace. Work traditionally has been viewed as a key aspect of citizenship theory, to the point that feminists have suggested that the denial of access to work directly impedes women's equality.[98] Focusing solely on work, of any kind, as the desired goal ignores the restrictions imposed by lack of education and other restrictions of opportunity.[99] The assumptions underlying such discourse reveal much about the value placed on the act of parenting.

Tax or benefit? The changing face of tax administration

As far back as 1972, the government realised that the amalgamation of taxes and benefits presented daunting administrative challenges.[100] A key facet of the (later) Working Families Tax Credit was that it was to be paid to the earning family member through his or her employer. Thus, the credit would usually be paid to men, not women. The government hoped through this approach that the 'stigma' associated with receiving what might be viewed as a 'handout' would be lessened, because the credit would be associated with the income tax system (as opposed to benefits).[101] This policy was never popular with child advocacy groups, however, who, along with influential research conducted by Goode *et al*[102] managed to convince the government of the old adage that money would be more

---

94 *Ibid*, p 12.
95 Greenwood *et al* (2000), p 34.
96 Orloff (2002), p 113.
97 Lardy (2004), p 303.
98 Staudt (1997), pp 542–3.
99 *Ibid*, p 543.
100 Adler (2004), p 91.
101 Bennett (2002), p 566.
102 Goode, J, Callender, C and Lister, R (1998) *Purse or Wallet? Gender Inequalities and Income Distribution within Families on Benefits*, London: Policy Studies Institute, cited at Bennett (2002), p 566.

likely to reach children 'going into the women's "purse" rather than the man's "wallet" '.[103]

The perception of whether or not 'assistance' through the tax system is a credit or a benefit may be linked to the class and gender of the recipient. What may be perceived as 'welfare' when received by taxpayers struggling with poverty may be viewed as 'a way of helping hard-working "independent" taxpayers' when directed towards the middle class.[104] The Child Tax Credit legislation is part of a process which began when the Inland Revenue[105] commenced administration of some benefits. Undertaken for reasons of efficiency, this was a startling development in the modern history of this agency. In 1999, the Benefits Agency units charged with administering the old-style Family Credit and Disability Working Allowance were moved from the Department of Social Security to the Inland Revenue.[106] The transfer was attributed to plans for establishing the infrastructure that would be needed for the then-upcoming Working Families Tax Credit and Disabled Person's Tax Credit, and to a hope that this merger would save employers some of the costs associated with administering the new legislation.[107]

Tax credits are distinguishable from benefits in that benefits typically are dependent upon a specified period of unemployment, and are limited in duration.[108] Tax credits need not be limited in duration.[109] Tax credits are meant to provide long-term assistance to families, to encourage them to alter their behaviour and to attain new skills, so the lack of time limits is logical from that perspective. That a tax collection authority should hand some of the money collected *back* was, simply, startling, but it seemed to make sense. Given the administrative infrastructure of the Inland Revenue, it was perhaps logical to attempt to employ these resources more efficiently.

Is the Child Tax Credit, in truth, anything to do with tax? Is it not simply a benefit? If so, may the title simply be dismissed as a cynical attempt at re-branding? Perhaps, but the importance of language in these initiatives, and its relevance to a feminist analysis of them are not to be underestimated. Brewer explains that although the tax credits originally were introduced as part of a government package to reduce child poverty, their administrative structure indicated a growing dissatisfaction with PAYE[110] as a means of identifying household need and targeting benefits.[111] Passing the burden to both the taxpayer and the employer, he suggests, may contain significant portent for the future.[112] If it worked

---

103 *Ibid.*
104 Orloff (2002), p 112.
105 As then was.
106 Inland Revenue Annual Report (1998). The Inland Revenue has now been merged with HM Customs and Excise to form one, combined 'new' organisation. See the O'Donnell Report (2004).
107 *Ibid.*
108 Blundell (2004), p 234.
109 *Ibid.*
110 Pay As You Earn.
111 Brewer (2002), p 245.
112 *Ibid.*

well, perhaps the introduction of self-assessment for self-employed taxpayers might be extended to non-self-assessing taxpayers, in a 'self-assessed benefit' of a sort. As of the end of 2004, however, it could not easily be suggested that it *had* worked well. Andrews, for example, warned in 2001 that the complexity of the credits' structure actually was not worth it when compared to the amount of money that families would be receiving.[113] Their early structure also led to initial misunderstandings about 'credit' and 'relief'. Andrews explained that the early Child Tax Credit was, in fact, a true credit of £520, which could be deducted from a taxpayer's ultimate liability to tax.[114] The Working Family Tax Credit, however, was 'welfare payment redesignated as a tax credit', or, simply, a benefit with the name 'credit' tagged on.[115] This, however, in these still early days, has proved to be the least of the problems faced by these initiatives.

Perhaps most unfortunate has been the problem of overpayment. Approximately 80,000 families were placed in the position of having to ask the Revenue if they could keep excess payments with which they mistakenly had been issued.[116] Worse, Ann Redston, chair of the personal taxation committee at the Chartered Institution of Taxation, warned that 80,000 was 'the tip of the iceberg' in terms of the poor administration of the credits.[117] Given that the Revenue has announced that it in fact intends to recover much of this overpayment,[118] these fears would appear to be well placed. The attempt to recover these funds has been criticised as 'over-zealous', especially when viewed in light of the aims of the legislation. In perhaps the worst case scenario, one mother announced that she now would need to work additional hours to be in a position to refund the overpayment – hardly the balance indicated as an objective by the legislation. Families have the right to challenge requests to refund overpayment if the blame may be ascribed to the Revenue, but fears were expressed that this right is not widely known (nor publicised).[119]

There are other levels of confusion. Wikeley has suggested that: 'While Child Tax Credit might just as well have been named Child Benefit Plus, there are features of Working Tax Credit that are genuinely new and would not fit comfortably in a social security scheme.'[120] This lack of clarity also has implications for the place that the credits should assume within the structure of the taxation of the family, generally – in other words, should the tax credits be 'taken at their word' and considered as part of a system of joint taxation (ie, taxation of the family), or are the credits really about the 'mother', and hence part of individual taxation? As the Women's Budget Group has explained, '... either tax credits are in effect means-tested benefits, and should be treated as public expenditure rather than

---

113 Andrews (2001), p 306.
114 *Ibid*, p 307.
115 *Ibid*.
116 BBC, 10 November 2004.
117 *Ibid*.
118 *Ibid*.
119 *Ibid*.
120 Wikeley (2004), p 22.

revenue foregone as other benefits are, or that they are part of the income tax system and the principle of independent taxation has been breached'.[121] Intriguingly, the Women's Budget Group believes that

> the government has now agreed to implement the OECD[122] conventions on accounting procedures for purposes of international comparison – ie that the refundable part of tax credits should count as public expenditure and the remainder as revenue foregone; but we are not aware of any commitment to change HM Treasury documents to reflect this agreement.[123]

Generally, the credits are part of a system which is supported by a fundamental adherence to joint taxation. As the credits address basic concerns founded along lines of gender, the gender implications of joint assessment might have been considered by the government prior to their introduction, and the Women's Budget Group consider it 'unfortunate' that this did not occur.[124]

It is particularly unfortunate, perhaps, when considered in the context of what Bennett believes to be Labour's track record on gender awareness. Included among Labour's accomplishments in this area are 'some progress on producing better statistics using a gender perspective'; the development (soon after assuming office) of a 'policy appraisal for equal treatment'; and research into social security initiatives.[125] Research and policies aside, Bennett suggests that the gendered perspective has been neglected as Labour's tenure has progressed, to the point that intentions seldom have produced results for women. Bennett explains that '[t]his lack of gender awareness is clearly not a product of ignorance amongst Treasury civil servants. Instead, it must reflect a particular conceptualisation of the major issues facing the UK and the government's resulting policy priorities'.

What is the problem, though, with programmes that may be described as, perhaps, mildly successful? Other than the fact that the problems which the tax credits are addressing are urgent, and more needs to be done, is there not an argument for applauding steps in the right direction? If such programmes are indeed steps in the right direction, then perhaps, but Staudt described the danger of tax laws which seriously impede women's efforts towards financial independence whilst giving the illusion of equality.[126] This is a debate which can also become subsumed in concerns over the societal 'devaluing' of work performed within the home.[127]

The tax credits are tools with intriguing feminist potential because they are designed to encourage women to work outside of the home. A traditional feminist critique of tax legislation is that it encourages women to stay at home, and thereby increases women's financial dependence on men.[128] Yet, as has been suggested at

---

121 Women's Budget Group (2001).
122 Organization for Economic Cooperation and Development.
123 Women's Budget Group (2001).
124 *Ibid.*
125 Bennett (2002), pp 561–2.
126 Staudt (1997), p 533.
127 See Graglia (1995).
128 *Ibid.*

earlier points in this chapter, the economic literature addressing whether or not tax credits actually 'work', from the perspective of the government's objectives, is not at all clear. In fact, Gerfin and Leu suggest that

> . . . changing the wife's labour supply would affect disposable income which can be increased above the poverty line. This is the reason why in the public discussion it is argued that this kind of tax credit makes work pay. Theoretically, however, it is well known that the labour supply effects of the tax credit are unambiguously negative.[129]

This has particular relevance when placed in the context of Alstott's response to proposals, first, to reduce the marginal rate of tax for working mothers; and second, to repeal legislation which ensures equal pay for men and women (in favour of women) with what she describes as 'feminist' objections.[130] For example, 'feminists who see the devaluation of women's family labour as the central obstacle to women's autonomy, power, or happiness could oppose market work tax incentives'.[131]

The undoubted political attractiveness of these initiatives aside, 'if', as Orloff has argued, 'strategies based on employment are the only politically viable option, one must still confront the fact that the workplace and the labor market remain deeply structured by gender, race and residence, and care giving responsibilities create a number of problems for many mothers and other caregivers who are or would like to be employed, particularly when they are poor and unpartnered'.[132] The marketplace is a curious destination for mothers, for women, if this is a feminist journey. Of course, marketplace work leads to increased financial independence, but the marketplace is largely drawn along lines of 'neoclassical economic assumptions [which] do not adequately serve the interests of the vast majority of people, especially those who are less powerful'.[133]

The target of the Child Tax Credit is constructed by the media and by government along hazy lines of deliberate confusion. The former Leader of the Conservative Party, Michael Howard, seized on this confusion, and gave it the 'spin' of 'Labour tends to believe it's all or nothing. You're either a stay at home mum or a career woman. You're either Kate Reddy or Gwyneth Paltrow'.[134] Howard proposed to reform child-care tax credits by expanding them, such that they may be spent on child-care options beyond the 'formal', 'registered' carer.[135] He also promised that the Conservatives are 'looking at ways' to reduce

---

129   Gerfin and Leu (2003), p 15.
130   Alstott (1996), p 2033, citing McCaffery, E (1993) 'Taxation and the family: A fresh look at behavioral gender biases in the code' 40 UCLA L Rev 983, and McCaffery, E (1993) 'Slouching towards equality: Gender discrimination, market efficiency, and social change' 103 *Yale LJ* 595.
131   *Ibid*, p 2035.
132   Orloff (2002), p 114.
133   Dennis (1993), p 34. As Bennett observed, '[w]hen the government *has* applied a gender lens to its tax and benefit policies, it has typically tended to focus on mothers'. Bennett (2002), p 563.
134   Howard, speech, 11 November 2004.
135   *Ibid*.

administrative burdens which are 'unfair' on the employer, such that, for example, credits might be paid directly to parents.[136] Additionally, he proposed reforms which would protect parents from the needlessly 'bureaucratic' requirement of having to inform the Revenue every time their circumstances change.[137] The latter proposal was potentially, particularly significant, as it indicates that the Tories considered removing the 'tax credit' element (confused though it may be) of the Child Tax Credit and rendering it a pure benefit (which, presumably, would be less dependent on information concerning a parent's changing circumstances, particularly if constructed along the lines of Child Benefit). Howard proposed also to consider including a deduction for child care as part of his platform.[138]

As a final question for this chapter, then, what is, potentially, the relationship of the tax–benefit conundrum to the debate surrounding the possible impact of the market on motherhood, or the debate surrounding the commodification of gendered labour?[139] Because the social constructs of class, gender and race are interconnected, the way in which one of these factors affects an individual is related to one's experience of the other two.[140] A woman's experience of the gendered construct of motherhood is inevitably affected by her relationship to class. It should be stressed, however, that de-commodification, with its focus on 'social rights free individuals from reliance on the market',[141] is equally problematic. Kilkey and Bradshaw argue that this concept is related to the male-breadwinner model of dependence on the market, and is thus of 'only limited relevance to women'.[142] What, then, constitutes 'independence' for women? Freedom, not from the marketplace, but from male dominance over their lives.[143] This may be achieved through a variety of means, including access to independent income, giving 'women "voice" to negotiate power relations within families, and "exit" to opt out of an unsatisfactory relationship'.[144] The ability of tax credits to provide this exit, however, is less than certain.

Conclusion

The family tax credits upon which this chapter has focused are relatively recent initiatives, born of the political sphere surrounding definitions of the family. Child Tax Credit, in design, is an earned income tax credit, which may be defined as a benefit linked to paid employment. The end-game of earned income tax credits is a 'working parent', working in the marketplace. This chapter has drawn attention to research demonstrating that some women in the lower strata of the economy

---

136 *Ibid.*
137 *Ibid.*
138 *Ibid.*
139 Cahn (2001).
140 Matthaei and Brandt (2001).
141 Kilkey and Bradshaw (1999), p 149.
142 *Ibid.*
143 *Ibid.*
144 *Ibid.*

are better off with a child tax credit. But tax credits are presented as being about children: all of society's children. Child tax credits are designed to elevate the welfare of all children in the economy. This focus on how a mother raises her children can have important feminist consequences.

These consequences include the place of tax credits within a structure which, over the past decade and a half, has acknowledged women's financial independence as an underlying value of the tax system. Although the place of women's financial independence on the value hierarchy (potentially) presently may be at risk, tax credits have been presented as a further (not necessarily connected) initiative towards this end. Interestingly, though, this independence is being achieved through her status, not independently, but *within* a family. It is the marketplace, with all of its gendered constructs, which is the locus for women's liberation. Davis explained that '[t]o the extent that the tax system is a source or a subsidizer of patriarchy, the tax system is in fact responsible for the continued oppression of women in this society'.[145] By encouraging women's participation, tax credits support, even reinforce, the patriarchy of the marketplace.

What will the feminist consequences of these initiatives be? The answer may lie in the fact that this chapter has considered tax credits as part of the changing face of tax administration. Tax credits may simply be refashioned benefits, part of a new administrative order, but this chapter submits that, even if that is their political reality, they may continue to suggest something more. With this push away from the home and into the marketplace, tax credits do not increase the value which society places on the act of parenting, and given that women continue to bear the bulk of parenting obligations, women's 'work' itself will continue to be devalued. Indeed, tax credits only compensate parenting when it is performed by someone *other* than the mother. Tax credits will be judged on the extent to which they assist families living in poverty, but they also will be considered for the success (or not) of the hype within which they are packaged. The significant role that tax plays in fashioning the subject of family law may not be, thus, and in this context particularly, a positive one, until the gendered assumptions underlying tax, family and the state[146] are addressed.

References

Adler, M (2004) 'Combining welfare to work measures with tax credits in the United Kingdom', 57 *International Social Security Review* 87

Alstott, A (1996) 'Tax policy and feminism: Competing goals and institutional choices', 96 *Columbia Law Review* 2001

Alstott, A (2004) 'What we owe to parents', (April/May) *Boston Review*, http://bostonreview.net/BR29.2/alstott.html

Alvarez, R and McCaffery, E (2000) 'Is there a gender gap in fiscal political

---

145 Davis (1988), p 233.
146 *Per* Sainsbury (1999), n 1.

preferences?', USC Research Paper Series, http://papers.ssrn.com/paper.taf? abstract_id=240502

Andrews, J (1991) 'Discriminatory treatment in the taxation of married couples', 16(2) *European Law Review* 167

Andrews, J (2001) 'Finance Act notes: Credit where it's due? Sections 50–53', 5 *British Tax Review* 306

BBC News Online (2004) 'Families launch tax credit please', (10 November), http://news.bbc.co.uk

Becker, M (1999) 'Patriarchy and inequality: Towards a substantive feminism' [1999] *University of Chicago Legal Forum* 21

Bennett, F (2002) 'Gender implications of current social security reforms', 23(4) *Fiscal Studies* 559

Blumberg, G (1972) 'Sexism in the Code: A comparative study of income taxation of working wives and mothers', 21 *Buffalo Law Review* 49

Blundell, R (2004) 'Labour market policy and welfare reform: Meeting distribution and efficiency objectives', 152(2) *De Economist* 233

Blundell, R and Meghir, C (2002) *Active Labour Market Policy vs Employment Tax Credits: Lessons from Recent UK Reforms*, IFAU Working Paper 2002:1, Institute for Labour Market Policy Evaluation

Board of Inland Revenue (1998) *Annual Report for the Year Ending 31st March 1998*, www.inlandrevenue.gov.uk/pdfs/report98.pdf

Brewer, M (2002) 'Not the Finance Act – tax credits', 4 *British Tax Review* 245

Cahn, NR (2001) 'The coin of the realm: Poverty and the commodification of gendered labor', 5 *J of Gender, Race & Justice* 1

Davis, LA (1988) 'A feminist justification for the adoption of an individual filing system', 62 *Southern California Law Review* 197

Dennis, J (1993) 'The lessons of comparable worth: A feminist vision of law and economic theory', 4 *UCLA Women's Law J* 1

Eskridge, WN, Jr (1995) 'The many faces of sexual consent', 23 *William & Mary Law Review* 47

Feenberg, D and Rosen, H (1980) *Alternative Tax Treatment of the Family: Simulation Methodology and Results*, Working Paper No 497, Cambridge, MA: National Bureau of Economic Research

Fineman, M (1991) 'Images of mothers in poverty discourses', *Duke LJ* 274

Fredman, S (2004) 'Women at work: The broken promise of flexicurity', 33 *Industrial LJ* 299

Gerfin, M and Leu, R (2003) *The Impact of In-Work Benefits on Poverty and Household Labour Supply: A Simulation Study for Switzerland*, Discussion

Paper No 762, IZA Discussion Paper Series, Bonn, Germany: Institute for the Study of Labor (IZA)

Graglia, C (1995) 'The housewife as pariah', 18 *Harvard J of Law and Public Policy* 509

Greenwood, J, Guner, N and Knowles, J (2000) *A Macroeconomic Analysis of Marriage, Fertility, and the Distribution of Income*, PIER Working Paper 01–038, Penn Institute for Economic Research, Department of Economics, University of Pennsylvania

Hakim, C (2004) *Key Issues in Women's Work: Female Diversity and the Polarisation of Women's Employment*, Glasshouse Press: London

Howard, M (2004) Speech on child care, 11 November, http://news.bbc.co.uk/

Jones, C (1994) 'Dollars and selves: Women's tax criticism and resistance in the 1870s', 1994 *University of Illinois Law Review* 265

Kilkey, M and Bradshaw, J (1999) 'Lone mothers, economic well-being and policies', in Sainsbury, D (ed) *Gender and Welfare State Regimes*, Oxford: Oxford University Press

Kornhauser, M (1993) 'Love, money and the IRS: Family, income-sharing, and the joint income tax return', 45 *Hastings LJ* 63

Kornhauser, M (1997) 'What do women want: Feminism and the progressive income tax', 47 *American University Law Review* 151

Lardy, H (2004) 'Is there a right not to vote?', 24 *Oxford J of Legal Studies* 303

Leigh, A (2003) 'Who benefits from the earned income tax credit? Incidence among recipients, co-workers and firms', http://ssrn.com/abstract=473445

Leigh, A (2004) 'Optimal design of earned income tax credits: Evidence from a British natural experiment', http://ssrn.com/abstract=547302

Livingston, M (1998) 'Radical scholars, conservative field: Putting "critical tax scholarship" in perspective', 76 *North Carolina Law Review* 1791

Matthaei, J and Brandt, B (2001) *From Hierarchical Dualism to Integrative Liberation: Thoughts on a Possible Non-Racist Non-Classist Feminist Future*, Wellesley College Working Paper 2001–03

Minow, M (1998) 'Keeping students awake: Feminist theory and legal education', 50 *Maine Law Review* 337

Mumford, A (2001) 'Marketing working mothers: Contextualizing earned income tax credits within feminist cultural theory', 23(4) *J of Social Welfare and Family Law* 411

O'Donnell, G (2004) *Financing Britain's Future – Review of the Revenue Departments*, March, HM Treasury (cm 6163)

Oberst, M (1988) 'The passive activity provision – a tax policy blooper', 40 *University of Florida Law Review* 641

Ochel, W (2001) *Financial Incentives to Work – Conceptions and Results in Great Britain, Ireland and Canada*, CESifo Working Paper No 627, Munich, Germany: Center for Economic Studies & Ifo Institute for Economic Research

Orloff, A (2002) 'Expanding US welfare reform: Power, gender, race and the US policy legacy', 22(1) *Critical Social Policy* 98

Sainsbury, D (1999) *Gender and Welfare State Régimes*, New York: Oxford University Press

Staudt, N (1997) 'Taxing women: Thought on a gendered economy – taxation and gendered citizenship', 6 *Southern California Review of Law and Women's Studies* 550

Wikeley, N (2004) 'The new tax credits and appeals', 12(1) *Benefits* 21

Women's Budget Group (2001) *Response to Inland Revenue Consultation Document, New Tax Credits: Supporting Families, Making Work Pay and Tackling Poverty*, www.wbg.org.uk/pdf/New%20Tax%20Credits.pdf

Women's Budget Group (2003) *Women's Budget Group Submission to HM Treasury: 2004 Spending Review/Childcare Review*, www.wbg.org.uk/documents/WBGInitialSubmissionto2004ChildcareReview.pdf

Chapter 11

'The Branch on Which We Sit': Multiculturalism, Minority Women and Family Law

Maleiha Malik

Feminism's outstanding contribution as an ideology and a political movement has been its insistence that theory and practice are intimately connected. Theory matters: not only because it can influence the way women are treated but also – and crucially – because it can influence women's self-understanding. Yet, at the same time, thoughtful feminist scholars have recognised that when faced with stubborn empirical facts – the sincere claims of individual women – theory must align itself to practice.

Multiculturalism and the politics of difference

One aspect of our contemporary reality to which feminists must now respond is multiculturalism. Increasingly, our societies are comprised of a great diversity of races, cultures and religions. This 'factual multiculturalism' is undisputed. What is more controversial is the normative claim that such diversity is a good thing and, more significantly, the demand that these groups must be accommodated within our public sphere. Multiculturalism has put a considerable strain on feminism. Increasingly, groups claim that the liberal democratic state should grant them autonomy in decision making that affects their individual members; they claim distinct rights even where these are, in many cases, inimical to the interests of women. These issues require feminism to go back to basics: what happens to categories such as 'women', 'women's interests', and 'feminist critique' when they are restructured in conjunction with pressing categories such as race, culture and religion. This is an important question for politics because the most urgent demands for social and political equality are no longer exclusively or predominantly the preserve of feminism. It is also an important question for law because the legal regulation of equality has now moved beyond the traditional categories of race and sex and now extends to religion and some of its cultural manifestations.[1]

Multiculturalism gives minorities in liberal democracies an unprecedented opportunity to live as equal citizens without suffering the worst excesses of forced assimilation. It is not, however, a panacea. It carries within it risks: the prospect of fragmentation of our political communities; and the risk of harm to vulnerable individuals within minority communities.

---

1 See, for example, The Employment Equality Directive 2000/78/EC, implemented in Britain via the Employment Equality (Religion or Belief) Regulations SI 1660/2003 (introduced/presented 26 June 2003; in force 2 December 2003).

Multiculturalism is a wide term that requires some explanation.[2] At a normative level, it includes the claim that different groups – defined along categories such as race, religion, gender and sexual orientation – can make legitimate claims for public accommodation of some of their practices. In this way, it challenges the classic liberal settlement of keeping the public sphere as a neutral space where citizens come together as equal citizens with recognized political rights. Of course, this classic liberal approach allowed minorities to flourish through guaranteeing individual civil and political rights, such as free speech, free association and free exercise of religion, but also provided an overarching framework that allowed minorities to pursue their way of life in the private sphere.

It is worth reiterating that multiculturalism is not only a normative claim but it is also a social and political fact. There has been a significant change in the form and content of the political claims made by minority groups in recent times. Many no longer ask for the 'same' rights as the majority. Some of the most compelling demands of minorities now take the form of calls for the accommodation of 'difference' in the public sphere. This social change is especially problematic for liberal multiculturalism. Claims for accommodation vary greatly: the categories range from race, culture and religion through to gender and sexual orientation and disability. Legal regulation – at the domestic, EU and constitutional level – covers all of these various grounds. I want to narrow the discussion by limiting my analysis to claims made by traditional groups whose claims may be framed in terms of racial, cultural or religious criteria. As I argue below, public accommodation of traditional groups raises a distinct set of problems for feminists and family law. Moreover, claims by traditional religious groups – for the public accommodation of their private religious identity – cause special difficulties. They challenge the most fundamental beliefs of secular liberals, for whom the public–private dichotomy is almost an article of faith: these traditional liberals will vigorously defend an individual right to religion in the private sphere whilst at the same time vigilantly guarding the public sphere as a neutral religion-free zone.

Minorities are no longer willing for their differences to be a matter of 'tolerance' in the private realm: they now demand political rights and accommodation in the public sphere. Feminists recognise this move immediately. Yet, at the same time, they also immediately recognise the way in which this challenge to the private–public dichotomy, especially by traditional cultures, is a threat to women, because processes of multicultural accommodation are likely to create specific risks to vulnerable group members. This is especially true where there is accommodation of traditional racial, cultural or religious practices which often and predominantly harm women.[3] This is partly why the confrontation between feminism and multiculturalism is so painful.[4] Feminism reflecting on multiculturalism often sees its own mirror image. Feminists are acutely aware that they have laid

---

2 See Malik (2000a).
3 Okin (1998).
4 See, for example, Baroness Hale's opinion in the case of R *(on the application of Begum) v Headteacher and Governors of Denbigh High School* [2006] UKHL 15.

the foundations for a wider identity politics. However – as the 'Is multiculturalism bad for women?' debate confirms – despite this intimate connection, at the level of theory, the two movements are also often incompatible. In their most pessimistic moments, as they notice multiculturalism mutating into a threat, feminists have good reason to wonder if they have in fact created a monster.

'Is multiculturalism bad for women?' The challenge for feminism and family law

This chapter does not try to answer the question 'Is multiculturalism bad for women?' Instead, it explores the implications of this debate for feminist theory and family law. Recent developments confirm that feminists working in the area of family law need to take this issue seriously. Legal problems arise in areas such as divorce and the protection of children which force us to ask questions about how law should respond to claims of cultures and religions. The 'Sexual and Cultural' Research Project at the London School of Economics sets out the considerable number of British cases where there is a conflict between sexual and cultural, racial or religious equality.[5] A review of this database of cases confirms that this issue has considerable implications for family law. For example, a number of the cases and policy initiatives relate to forced marriage. The cases on forced marriages arise not only in criminal law proceedings but also in wardship proceedings in the family courts and petitions for the annulment of marriages. Other cases relate to divorce or the dissolution of marriages. Problems about the status and suitability of traditional norms have arisen in cases where the parties (often members of religious minorities) have chosen to submit to foreign jurisdictions in preference to English law in the regulation of divorce. These conflicts can also arise in those cases where there are two types of marriage: first, an English civil marriage and a second, cultural or religious ceremony. Subsequently, some minority women have resorted to forum shopping, challenging inequitable foreign divorce rules in favour of English law relating to divorce.

Difficult questions also arise in cases involving the upbringing of children where the child or the parents are from a traditional culture or religion. The possibility that traditional practices may cause harm to young girls makes this a particularly important issue for law and policy relating to children. Young girls are vulnerable to harmful traditional practices within their cultures for two reasons: because of their sex and because of their age.[6] Of course, parents are rightly concerned about the environment in which their children are raised, but can they impose practices on their young female family members that may cause these children harm? John Eekelaar has recently discussed this issue and concluded:

> Perhaps we should acknowledge that, at least normally, (that is outside cases of persecution), communities may have no specific interests *as communities*. Their

---

5   See 'Women and Cultural Diversity: A Digest of Cases' at http://webdb.lse.uk/gender (accessed on 20 May 2005).

6   Susan Moller Okin (2002; 1998) makes the point that leaving young girls to be raised in a culture which does not respect their autonomy can cause them harm even – and especially – where these young girls internalise the values of the culture.

individual members most certainly do, and this includes the interest in passing on their culture to their children. But that interest is limited, and it is limited first and foremost by the interests of the communities' own children.[7]

As well as resorting to family courts within the mainstream legal system, minorities are also making claims for separate family law tribunals that can govern civil law disputes for minorities. The recent experience of Canada is a good example of the way in which claims of traditional minorities have moved beyond abstract political demands to become a legal reality. Ontario's Arbitration Act 1991 allows the use of alternative dispute resolution procedures to resolve personal disputes in areas as diverse as wills, inheritance, marriage, remarriage, and spousal support.[8] This legislation allows individuals to resolve civil disputes within their own faith community, providing all affected parties give their consent to the process and the outcomes respect Canadian law and human rights codes. The use of separate tribunals is a real rather than a theoretical possibility in Ontario, where groups from religious minorities such as Jews and Muslims have indicated their preference for resort to traditional religious justice to resolve family law disputes.[9]

It is understandable why traditional minorities will choose to focus on family law when they make claims for accommodation. Family law governs some of the most private and intimate aspects of who we are, and it relates to our personal identity in the most profound way. It therefore seems appropriate to allow citizens in a liberal democracy to reach an agreement about the rules that will govern these aspects of their life. The problem for feminists becomes most acute when there are claims by not only men but also women from traditional cultures that they prefer traditional legal rules to govern their private disputes. If all persons, and women, freely choose to be governed by a traditional justice system – the argument goes – then there seem to be no conclusive reasons why the state should not respect these choices. This is – at first sight – an attractive argument. However, feminist theory has taught us to be vigilant about the automatic acceptance of claims of the 'free choice of women' without asking further questions about context: 'which women'; 'when'; 'how'; 'under what personal, social, economic or political conditions?' Once we undertake this more detailed analysis it becomes clear that the argument moves too swiftly from 'free choice of minority women' to a separate system of family law. Most significantly, such a quick analysis pays insufficient attention to the myriad ways in which granting control over family law to a

---

7 See Eekelaar (2004), p 191.
8 For a summary of relevant primary and secondary sources, see the bibliography at www.attorneygeneral.jus.gov.on.ca/english/about/pubs/boyd/bibliography.pdf.
9 See report in *The Forward*, 14 January 2004: 'In a move that is angering Jewish feminists, B'nai Brith Canada is supporting the demands of conservative Muslims in the province of Ontario who wish to have the right to use private arbitration based on Islamic law for the resolution of their marital, custody and inheritance disputes. A report prepared for the Ontario Ministry of the Attorney General recommended last month that family arbitration based on Islamic law be permitted, but regulated, under the province's Arbitration Act. But both Muslim women's groups and Jewish feminists are opposed, fearing that vulnerable female immigrants will be coerced into submitting to Islamic arbitration.' Cited in The Pluralism Project. See www.pluralism.org/news/.

traditional culture or religion has the potential for causing harm to vulnerable group members such as women.

Feminist theory also encourages us to undertake a deeper analysis of social practices to reveal the distinct impact that they have on women. This should immediately alert us to the more subtle reasons why family law and women have become a focus – sometimes an obsession – for traditional groups concerned with the preservation and transmission of their culture or religion. Women are always at the forefront of attempts to re-create collective identity because they reproduce and socialise future members of the group. Therefore, controlling with whom and on what terms they should undertake their child-bearing and child-rearing functions becomes an issue not only for individual women, their partners and families but also for the wider community. From this perspective, it becomes a critical matter that women should enter into their most intimate relationships and functions in a way that preserves the membership boundaries and identity of the whole community. For all these reasons, the control of women – especially in areas such as sexuality, marriage, divorce and in relation to their children – is a recurring feature of traditional cultural and religious communities. Women are also often given the status of passing on the particular collective history of the tradition and its social, cultural and religious norms to the next generation. Women become a public symbol of the group as a whole. This explains why traditional communities focus on family law when they demand accommodation. These groups draw on multiculturalism in support of their political claims: they insist that they, rather than the liberal state, should have exclusive jurisdiction in these key areas.

Simply citing multiculturalism in defence of these claims by traditional groups cannot be the end of the matter. One of the most powerful arguments for multiculturalism is that there are power hierarchies between minority groups, majorities and the state that should be re-negotiated. However, this recognition of external hierarchies should not blind us to the fact that there are also power hierarchies within groups. These internal inequalities of power may cause vulnerable individuals, such as women and children, to bear a disproportionate burden of any policy of accommodation of cultural or religious practices.[10] The resulting costs can include entering into a marriage without the right to divorce; inadequate financial compensation in the case of divorce; giving up the right to custody over children; restriction on the right to education, employment or participation in the public sphere; giving up the right to control over their bodies and reproduction.

It is often argued that many women choose to remain members of a group despite the fact that traditional rules and practices undermine their interests. 'They have a right to exit but they freely choose to remain' is the response to any challenge.[11] But this 'right to exit' argument is not a realistic solution to the problem of oppression within groups. It offers an *ad hoc* and extreme option to what is often a systematic and structural problem within traditional cultures and

---

10 Baroness Hale discusses this issue in the *Begum* case, n 4 above.
11 The right to exit argument is defended by Kukathas (1995). For the opposite view, see Green (1995). See also an application of this argument in Shachar (2001).

religions. It puts the burden of resolving these conflicts on individual women and relieves the state (which has conceded jurisdiction in this area to the group) of responsibility for the protection of the fundamental rights of its citizens. Most significantly, the right to exit argument suggests that an individual woman at risk from a harmful practice should be the one to abandon her group membership, her family and community.[12] The complexity of the choices that women face in these circumstances makes it more likely that they will continue to consent to practices despite the fact that they experience harm. This internalisation of harmful practices is exactly what exacerbates women's vulnerability in these contexts, and we owe feminist theory a great debt for revealing that women can develop a false understanding of their own best interests, and that consciousness raising is an important task for those concerned with the defence of the rights of women.[13] In the 'multiculturalism and minority women' debate, the stark fact is that emotional attachment, economic circumstances and sometimes religious commitment makes the 'right to exit' not only an unrealistic but also a tragic choice for many women from minority communities.[14]

There will be significant diversity in the responses of minority women who are faced with harmful practices within their own communities. In this context, it is worth remembering that not only are 'minority women' not a monolithic group, but also that there is variety *within* the category 'women'. This insight is more likely to ensure that our analysis does not distort the choices of minority women. Theory must also be alert to the fact that although women's membership of a cultural or religious group may provide a useful marker of their preferences, it cannot be allowed to pre-determine the complex possibilities for belief and action available to them. In the face of oppressive practices within their group some women will choose to leave altogether. Of course, they should be assisted if they make this decision and exercise their 'right to exit'. These are not, however, the hard cases. It is much more difficult to know how to respond to those women (probably the majority) who choose to remain 'insiders' within cultures and religions which do not always give them power, safeguard their interests or allow them full participation as equals. This is perhaps one of the most perplexing aspects of the behaviour of minority women that confuses contemporary feminists.

---

12 Shachar (2001), ch 3. For a critique of the right to exit argument in the specific context of minority women see Okin (2002).

13 For a discussion of the case for, and some scepticism about, consciousness raising in feminist theory see Smart (1989), p 80. A classic exposition of consciousness raising is to be found in the work of the late Andrea Dworkin: see, for example, *Pornography: Men Possessing Women* (1983). Feminist theory that draws on methods from psychoanalysis understandably gives great status to consciousness raising as a useful method for theory and practice. Luce Irigaray and Julia Kristeva's work are examples of this; see Duchen (1986).

14 The LSE Gender Institute's Project Grant Report on the Nuffield *Sexual and Cultural Equality: Conflicts and Tensions* states in the context of forced marriage: 'The UK initiatives have focused very heavily on exit, and more specifically, on assisting individuals forced into marriage with an overseas partner . . . our research suggests that exit only works up to a point. It leaves to many individuals with what they perceive as no choice, for when the choice is between rejecting an unwanted marriage partner or being rejected by one's family (and as many experience it, then having to abandon one's cultural identity), the costs are set impossibly high.'

There is rarely one right answer to such complicated personal choices. Some women may choose to remain silent despite the injustice in their communities. Others may seek to challenge the dominance of certain 'interpretations' of their traditions that are a source of their oppression. For example, certain traditions within Islamic and Jewish family law give men the right to unilateral divorce but make the right to a divorce for a woman conditional on the consent of her husband. One consequence of this is that, where the husband refuses to grant a divorce, Muslim and Jewish women have to obtain an annulment from traditional religious authorities: called *khula* (in Arabic) for Muslim women; *get* (in Hebrew) for Jewish women. Rather than bypassing the traditional religious rules altogether and seeking dissolution of the marriage via secular legal authorities, some Muslim and Jewish women may choose to continue to seek redress using traditional forms of justice whilst at the same time pressing for a change in the way in which their religion interprets the rights to divorce. As Shachar argues, the state can assist these women in this struggle by providing incentives and safeguards for individual rights.[15]

Of course, all women will immediately recognise that collective units such as the family can often oppress women. Feminists are familiar with the argument that vesting rights in the family does not safeguard the interests of women and that the grant of individual civil and political rights to women has been an invaluable strategy in challenging the oppression of women.[16] Yet, at the same time, there is considerable agreement that the understandable status of individual rights needs to be offset against the importance of group membership (in a family and wider community) for minority women, which is a critical aspect of their self-definition.[17] However, this analysis need not collapse into a zero-sum game between individual and group rights. One of the great errors of some forms of multiculturalism, just like familism, is the assumption of essentialism of groups: the claim that it is possible to identify one fixed definition of a tradition or culture, or religion or family. Any complex group contains not just one but a plurality of ideas and arguments. Some of these voices are backed by existing power structures whilst others are relatively silent and do not have access to public space.[18] It should not surprise us to learn that very often those who purport to speak on behalf of traditional cultures or families do not represent the interests of women.

This conflict is not just a quarrel between minority women and their communities. It is also of vital concern for the state and for outsiders who are not members of these communities. Most pointedly, feminists must give this issue priority. Questions about how minority women should respond to harmful

---

15 Shachar (2001), pp 132–45. In England and Wales, see s 10A Matrimonial Causes Act 1973.

16 See, for example, Susan Moller Okin's comment (1979), p 282 that: 'In spite of the supposedly individual premises of the liberal tradition, JS Mill was the first of its members to assert that the interests of women were by no means automatically upheld by the male heads of the families to which they belonged, and that therefore women, as individuals, should have independent political and legal rights.'

17 See Kymlicka (1995), p 7. See also Malik (2000b).

18 For a discussion of some of these issues, see Nussbaum (1999), especially pp 8–10.

practices within their own groups, and how other women can support them in this struggle, should be of critical concern to feminism. If complex traditional groups contain within them a plurality of ideas and arguments, then women who are insiders within these groups have some space for resistance against the dominant interpretations of the groups' practices. This struggle bypasses the tragic choices involved in 'exit' from the group. It is also exactly the sphere in which minority women can and should expect support – intellectual, political and practical – from other women. A sensitive understanding of the concerns of minority women can assist in this delicate task of political advocacy. Once we move beyond the assumption that 'exit' is the only legitimate response of minority women who face injustice within their communities, then it becomes clear that the challenge is to strike a balance between showing solidarity for minority women whilst at the same time maintaining a critical perspective. This less extreme response would accept that partial recognition of a traditional group does not require the wholesale uncritical acceptance of all its practices.

In the concluding comments in this chapter, I will suggest that we need to reach some consensus on the foundations for feminist theory. At this point, I want to stress that clarity and articulacy about these foundations are invaluable assets for minority women themselves. In fact, one of the most significant contributions that outsiders can make is to 'hold the line' by using key principles such as autonomy as the basis for a detailed and constructive critique of traditional communities and their family practices. Insiders, minority women, can turn to this critique as a precious source of information and ideas to inform their tradition, which often contains within it the resources to allow them to challenge injustice and oppression within their own communities and families. Similarly, insiders will also be able to appropriate legitimate arguments from outside their own tradition and use the experience and ideas of Western feminism and other political movements to make demands for dignity and justice. Western feminism has made an outstanding contribution towards securing dignity for women. It also has an understandable and healthy scepticism about traditional group practices, particularly in the family context. It is therefore lamentable when this constructive analysis collapses into the view that minority women must shed all their group affiliations before they can be considered legitimate partners in feminist, or indeed any, intellectual and political movements. This is a significant barrier to minority women establishing alliances – feminist alliances – that would assist them in the Herculean task of challenging the power of men within their own communities.

There are other arguments against an 'all or nothing' approach. Insisting that all traditional groups are misogynistic and patriarchal – whether or not this is true – will cause us to miss those areas in which there is internal resistance to the oppression of women. This is likely to put minority women on the defensive by reintroducing the stark dilemma of 'your rights or your culture'. Multiculturalism draws its strength from the idea that membership and public recognition of a cultural or religious group can be a source of individual well-being.[19] In addition

---

19 Taylor (1992).

to this point of principle, there is also a strategic argument against such a wholesale rejection of traditional practices. Vehement and indiscriminate attacks on traditional practices may make a community group defensive, thereby weakening the position of minority women in their attempts to launch an internal challenge to harmful practices. It is essential that minority women are given an opportunity to formulate a criticism of their practices from within their own tradition. Minority women have the potential to be the most effective and devastating social critics of the traditional practices that harm them. Their knowledge and experience – and ability to speak the language of the group – give them an authority that cannot be replicated by outsiders. Taken together with the previous argument that 'outsiders' can offer an invaluable critique of social practices, this analysis supports the view that there is a need for alliances – feminist alliances – between all women. It also reinforces the point that feminist theory and practice must give priority to understanding and accommodating minority women. The real challenge is to be able to find a place for the experience of minority women within 'traditional' feminist theory: 'Experience is, in this approach, not the origin of our explanation, but that which we want to explain.'[20]

Feminist theory and minority women

How should feminism respond to those women within a particular group – the *insiders* – who freely choose to be governed by traditional systems of justice that contain rules that are likely to harm them? My main argument is that it is possible for feminism to respond to this challenge at the levels of theory and practice. However, this requires us to revise the usual methods that we employ in understanding the lives and choices of women.[21]

'How can we start to understand the beliefs and conduct of minority women who are insiders within groups?' is obviously not a question that is unique for us. There is a vast array of theoretical writing about methodology in the human and social sciences. Feminism is sometimes suspicious of grand theories that may, by making universal claims, crowd out the reality of differences between men and women. Theory, it is argued, needs to give greater priority to individual experience and practice. At one level, this position displays an understandable scepticism about the very status of 'grand theory' as a useful tool for analysis.[22] Feminist critique of traditional methods of analysis in the human and social sciences takes a variety of forms, but one recurring theme is the call for a focus on practice as a way of revealing the reality of women's oppression. This connection between

---

20 Scott (1992), p 40.

21 For a discussion of the importance of theory see Crosby (1992).

22 Smart writes (in the context of feminist jurisprudence, but the arguments have a more general relevance to feminist theory): 'It sets up a specific feminist theory as superior to other versions, not on the basis of a set of political values, but on the basis that radical feminism is the Truth and its truth is established through the validity of method and epistemology. This is scientific feminism; it attempts to proclaim its unique truth above all other feminisms and other systems of thought. It turns experience into objective truth because it has taken on the mantle of a positivism which assumes that there must be an ultimate standard of objectivity.' (1989, p 68.)

theory and practice in feminist theory is widely acknowledged. MacKinnon, for example, recognises the importance of individual experience to theory. In her early work, feminism – 'Unmodified' – is presented as a method that uses practical experience as the point of entry into a more universal theoretical project.[23] Carol Smart has noticed the way in which this method takes on the mantle of empiricism and a 'scientific feminism'.[24] More recently, Drucilla Cornell has made a similar criticism of this feminist method. She writes:

> Of course, there are examples of moralising which purportedly divide the righteous feminists from those women who have fallen prey to false consciousness and who disagree on a given position enunciated by a self-defined feminist. One glaring example is Catharine MacKinnon's accusation that feminists who disagree with her position on pornography are collaborators.[25]

Smart points out that theorising within law seems to be especially vulnerable to encouraging this tendency: 'It is unfortunate that working within the discourse of law seems to produce such tendencies – it is as if law's claim to truth is so legitimate that feminists can only challenge it and maintain credibility within law by positing an equally positive alternative.'[26] Smart does not argue against theory altogether but rather seeks to challenge a particular method that 'wants to claim that its truth is better than other truths. I would prefer that it sought to deconstruct truth and the need for such truths and dogmatic certainties, rather than adding to the existing hierarchies of knowledge'.[27] She concludes that: 'This is not an argument against theorizing, however, but a specific critique of grand theorizing.'[28]

Smart and Cornell's critique of MacKinnon also provides us with a prescient insight into the perils of automatically applying these traditional feminist methods to minority women. Extrapolating from personal experience to grand theory, and then presenting this as the 'scientific' or 'positive' truth about women as a group, is a risky strategy when we move beyond a heterogeneous group of women and start to accommodate differences based on factors such as race, culture or religion. What seems to be the neutral truth will often ignore or marginalise the experiences of minority women. In these circumstances, collapsing back into a position that gives overwhelming authority to the personal experience of these 'different women' will not provide a solution either. As Segal notes,

> if we rely on personal experience alone we cannot explore how that experience is itself shaped by the frameworks of thought of those immediately around us. These frameworks are not static or inflexible; there is conflict and disagreement within

---

23 MacKinnon (1987). See also a passage from MacKinnon's earlier work on feminist method by Smart (1989, p 70): 'Radical feminism is feminism . . . Because its method emerges from the concrete conditions of all women as a sex, it dissolves the individualist, naturalist, idealist, moralist structures of liberalism, the politics of which science is the epistemology. Quoted from MacKinnon (1983).'
24 See Smart (1989), p 71.
25 Cornell (1995).
26 Smart (1989), p 71.
27 *Ibid.*
28 *Ibid.*

the groups we are born into over ways of living and relating to others, ways of interpreting and experiencing the world. We cannot, however, easily step outside our own specific culture.[29]

So how should feminism – more specifically, feminist method – respond to difference in the category 'women'? There is a fine balance to be struck between the recognition of difference in our definition of 'women' and exaggeration of its relevance and importance. The move in feminist theory in the 1980s against essentialism ensured that 'difference between women' became almost as important an issue as the 'difference between men and women'.[30] An important contribution in this field is the work of Elizabeth Spelman.[31] She argues that: 'There are startling parallels between what feminists find disappointing and insulting in Western philosophical thought and what many women have found troubling in much of Western feminism.'[32] This is especially damning for feminists because it turns their critique of the exclusionary tendencies of mainstream political thought – that it marginalises and excludes women – on themselves. The accusation is that traditional feminism marginalises women who are differentiated along categories of race, culture, religion or class. This critique is now well established. Mainstream feminist thought is comfortable with the idea that theory and practice can sometimes exclude or marginalise women who do not fit comfortably into the majority category because of their race, culture, religion or class.

Being vigilant about differences between women on grounds such as race, culture or religion does not, however, necessarily mean that gender must be wholly determined by these other categories for analysis. It is possible to argue that there is something specific about oppression where it is based on gender without necessarily collapsing into the position that oppression based on other grounds is irrelevant. What we need is a more sophisticated analysis: one in which gender is restructured along with these other pressing categories such as race, culture, religion and class. This does not mean that gender is no longer a distinct category or that it should be subsumed within these other grounds. Instead, this increasing complexity in the subject matter means that we need more sophisticated methods that are sensitive to differences between women in those cases where difference is both present and relevant to analysis. We have to be aware of the danger of abstracting from personal experience (which is given such high status in feminist theory) to universal claims and then to conclusions that these are the truth about all women. It also means that, in some cases, we may want to insist that there are similarities that allow us to talk meaningfully about 'women' as a coherent category. This approach is more likely to achieve a workable balance between the need to make some generalisations about the form of oppression experienced by all women without marginalising important differences.[33]

---

29 See Segal quoted in Smart (1989), p 79.
30 See, for example, Hooks (1984).
31 Spelman (1988).
32 *Ibid*, p 6.
33 For a general discussion of these issues and a critique of Spelman, see Okin (1979).

One consequence of this delicate balance between essentialism and the recognition of valid difference is uncertainty about how we define fundamental categories and objectives within feminist theory. Recent feminist theory influenced by postmodernism confirms some of these insights. Feminists who draw on these ideas usefully reveal the way in which power is not a concept that can reveal male oppression; it also infuses the way in which we undertake theoretical analysis. For Judith Butler, key questions for feminism include the following: 'Through what exclusions has the feminist subject been constructed, and how do these excluded domains return to haunt the "integrity" and "unity" of the feminist "we"?'[34] Smart, Spelman and Segal's insights are also illuminating because they point us towards some tentative conclusions about how to capture and understand the experience of minority women. Smart and Segal affirm the importance of theory but eschew the traditional positive feminist claims that there is one grand theory – to use Smart's terms, a 'scientific truth' – for analysing all women. We must also be alert to difference within the category 'minority women'. Just as there is a risk of distortion if we treat the category 'women' as a monolithic concept, so there are also dangers in a method that uses 'minority women' as an undifferentiated term. Such a crude approach cannot hope to capture the subtle variety and important nuances in the responses, beliefs and actions of these women. Of course, this concern with capturing difference renders the subject matter 'women' or 'minority women' complicated and unstable. One consequence may be that our choice of method does not yield the usual degree of certainty and predictability with which we are familiar. Feminist theory and practice, as I argue below, may need to accept this as an inevitable by-product of deepening its analysis of women's oppression. It will have to open itself up to a degree of uncertainty in the realms of concepts and ideas; objectives and policies.

Smart and Segal both acknowledge this risk and they are critical of a method that is in constant search for certainty.[35] Segal concludes her analysis of the challenge posed to feminist theory with a salutary reminder of the challenge facing any feminist theorist seeking to accommodate minority women: 'We cannot, however, easily step outside our own specific culture.'[36] It is difficult enough to develop a method that can do justice to differences between women that arise from categories such as class or sexuality. A method that seeks to capture difference among women will always give rise to problems of uncertainty and mutability. Race, and especially culture and religion, provide us with yet more intractable problems. As Clifford Gertz has noted, the study of cultures and religions is difficult because analysis must constantly balance grasp of detail, the perspective of insiders and objective analysis. There is a danger of reification on the one hand and reductionism on the other.[37] Yet, at the same time, these criteria – race, culture

---

34 See Nicholson (1995), p 5.

35 Smart writes, 'I hope to show below why we need to theorize women's oppression and why we cannot simply rely on experience as if it were a concrete reality which merely needs to be exposed thereby circumventing the problems and difficulties of intellectual work.' (1989, p 72.)

36 See Segal quoted in Smart (1989), p 79.

37 Gertz (1993).

and religion – are some of the most crucial determinants of personal identity and well-being. Membership of a racial, cultural or religious group is a secure form of personal identity: it is a based on belonging rather than accomplishment.[38] Hence, the conundrum for feminism: we are being asked to accommodate theory to a subject matter that is intrinsically – and notoriously – difficult to theorise. Moreover, to add to the dilemma, there is no realistic prospect that analysis can bypass the cultural and religious affiliations for minority women. Participation in a group provides women with meaningful choices about how to live their lives; it affects how others in society perceive and respond to them and therefore goes to the heart of a concern with 'self-identity' and 'self-respect'. It is this tension – between the fact that race, culture and religion are so resistant to our analysis whilst simultaneously being critical aspects of the personal identity of women – that raises a significant challenge for feminist theory. So we return to the question at the start of this analysis: 'How can we understand the beliefs and conduct of minority women who are insiders within groups?'

Theorising difference: *'From their own perspective . . . '*

One alternative to traditional approaches in feminist theory is what we can loosely label post-modern feminist theory.[39] Post-modern feminism is especially useful in any attempts to accommodate the claims of minority women because it challenges assumptions about the definition and status of the subject 'woman', therefore providing room for alternative definitions and analysis. It also makes clear that definitions of identity – such as women, race or religion – are never merely descriptive; they are also normative categories that need to be challenged and reconstructed ('resignified' in Butler's terms). In the present discussion about feminist theory, post-modern feminism's insights into the way in which power (and politics) influences our choice of theory are particularly pertinent.[40] The methods and conclusion of post-modern feminism confirm the earlier criticism of 'scientific feminism' by acknowledging the uncertainty in basic categories such as 'women' and 'their interests' and 'tradition' and 'culture'. In all these ways, post-modern feminism is invaluable to any attempt to analyse and accommodate the claims of minority women.

In the discussion that follows, many of the insights about theory are influenced by post-modern feminism. However, rather than explicitly making a choice between alternative ways of 'doing' feminist theory, I want to take a different approach. I do not want to set myself the impossible challenge of providing a conclusive answer on how we should theorise difference. Instead, I want to make a tentative gesture towards examining whether there are methods that can assist us in capturing the beliefs and experiences of minority women without distortion and misrepresentation. One way of making this issue more manageable is to

---

38 See Kymlicka (1995). See also Malik (2000b).
39 See discussion in Collier, Chapter 12 in this volume. For a challenge to the definition and use of the term post-modernism see Butler (1995a; 1995b).
40 Butler (1995a; 1995b).

reduce the methodological choices that we face to two contrasting models. Of course, such a reductive choice is vulnerable to the criticism that it is a caricature. At the same time, presenting the arguments in this way has a number of advantages. I hope that this contrast will make clear not only what, but more importantly just how much, is at stake in the initial choice of method. In addition, the reduction of complex positions to their simple end results will allow us to see that each of the models reflects ideas, presuppositions and debates which will be immediately familiar. The aim of this analysis, therefore, is neither to resolve the issue between post-modern feminism and its critics nor to provide one overarching theoretical approach. Rather, it is a more modest task of retrieval: what modifications do we need to make to the usual methods of feminist analysis so that we can better understand – and accommodate – minority women?

The first cluster of ideas, which I have loosely called 'scientism',[41] is similar in some respects to the 'scientific feminism' of approaches that have been criticised by Smart and Cornell. It has as its central presupposition the belief that the study of human practices can model themselves on the natural and physical sciences. It is partly summarised in the approach of certain writers such as AJ Ayer: 'Just as I must define material things . . . in terms of their empirical manifestations, so I must define other people in terms of their empirical manifestations – that is, in terms of the behaviour of their bodies.'[42] There are a number of aspects of this approach which are important for an analysis of gender and minority women. The first is the belief that there must be a strict separation between fact and value: description of a social practice is one thing; its evaluation is something quite different. The second is the *priority of the right over the good*: the belief that human agency is about the capacity to create an identity through the exercise of radical choice, rather than about participating in any prior conception of the individual or common good.[43] Third, the subject is abstracted from the context of decision making such as language, community and culture; identity tends to be interpreted as a 'monological' process. Thus, there is an atomistic treatment of human conduct: complex human actions are analysed in terms of their simple components. This ahistorical analysis emphasises the basic action as the proper temporal unit for the study.[44] The importance of the intentions, motivation and inner states of consciousness of the human agent is ignored, or at the very least marginalised.[45]

The techniques for analysis which this model advocates are description and observation. The theorist is encouraged to neutralise her own perspective and evaluative criteria before studying the subject matter. In this way, the subject

---

41 For an example of the use of this term see the work of Schumacher: eg, Schumacher (1973).

42 1971, p 171.

43 Examples include leading works such as John Rawls (1971), *A Theory of Justice* and, more recently, his *Political Liberalism* (1993); also Ronald Dworkin (1986), *Law's Empire*.

44 See, for example, Oakeshott (1975).

45 This idea is captured by AJ Ayer's famous statement that: 'Just as I must define material things . . . in terms of their empirical manifestations, so I must define other people in terms of their manifestations – that is, in terms of the behaviour of their bodies, and ultimately in terms of sense-contents.' (1971, p 171.)

matter is made more manageable: the focus is on qualities which are absolute and can be stated with precision; the theorist is necessarily forced to concentrate on the outward rather than inner dimensions of human conduct. A particular practice is described using accurate, certain and definite concepts, and in an all-or-nothing way. Finally, this positivist model is consistent with an understanding of language as an instrument for 'designating' existing subject matter and reality which exists 'out there'.

I think it will be clear from the way in which I have presented the model that I do not consider it an attractive way to proceed, and nor do I find its assumptions concerning human agency convincing. Moreover, this method is inappropriate to address the central challenge of understanding minority women because it does not have the appropriate resources to allow description of, and qualitative distinctions relating to, inner states. These inner states – motivations, feelings and desires – cannot be stated with scientific accuracy or tested by the empirical tools of scientism.

Most importantly, this approach ignores the need for feminist theory to move beyond claims that it has access to one absolute truth and to accommodate the complexity of difference in the lives of women. Recognition of difference means that the focus of our enquiry – the lives and practices of women – is no longer homogenous or stable. Both Smart and Segal argue for a method that is willing to sacrifice some certainty and objectivity in favour of greater responsiveness to difference. Their approach comes closer to what I term a 'human sciences' approach that lies in contrast to the scientific feminism I described above. I do not want to undertake a point-by-point comparison of 'scientific feminism' and a 'human sciences' approach to feminism, but some contrast between the two is illuminating because it reveals the specific ways in which we need to modify feminist analysis to accommodate minority women in a way that takes experience and difference seriously.

The key distinction between the two models is that the human sciences approach takes as an essential principle the fact that human agency raises unique issues for method and analysis. This has a number of consequences for theory. First, this alternative approach challenges not only the validity but also the possibility of describing human conduct without first undertaking the difficult task of evaluation: that is, we cannot understand human action without first understanding the purpose pursuant to which that action was undertaken. Therefore, understanding the point, value and significance of conduct as conceived by the people who performed those actions – and which are reflected in their discourse, actions, and institutions – is a key task for the theorist.[46] Second, any study of individual human conduct must also attend to the communal context of actions: for instance, language, community and culture, which mediates and is mediated by family, including affective ties and emotional, physical and economic hierarchies and dependencies. This means that individuals cannot be understood in an atomistic, all-or-nothing way; the exercise of freedom and choice by an individual must be

---

46 Weber (1978).

understood in this wider context. Third, this different approach is less resistant to shifting the focus of analysis from the outward manifestation of human conduct towards inner states of consciousness. It is consistent with the view that an essential rather than contingent feature of human agency is that agents not only make choices about what they want, but also undertake a process of reflection about these choices, by ranking them against evaluative criteria. They undertake a process of self-interpretation to judge certain inner states as belonging to an integrated, and therefore more valuable, mode of life; and others as unworthy.[47] Purpose, intent, motivations and inner states necessarily require us to place these features within the context of the agent's history, and social practices become intelligible only when understood as part of an ongoing tradition. The basic action gives way to a different temporal unit for analysing human conduct. Human action therefore needs to be analysed not as a static one-off event, but as part of a dynamic process. To paraphrase Alisdair Macintyre's observations: human agency is 'a quest – a narrative – a progression towards purpose and unity'.[48] Like post-modern feminism, this approach takes seriously the need to 'situate' women in a wider context for analysis.

These modifications will allow a greater focus on the purposes, intentions, motives of subjects. They will also take seriously the way in which historical and social contexts are important to the self-definition of women, their feelings and their choices. In this way, it is more likely that the experiences of minority women can be better articulated, understood and accommodated.

This alternative approach has important implications for our choice of method, concepts and language. Observation and description remain important devices, but the theorist has to start by undertaking the difficult task of identifying the good, point, value and significance which the subjects feel they are pursuing. Rather than mere description of outer action, this method gives a better understanding of the subject *from her own perspective*. In this sense, it is an inter-subjective understanding rather than an objective description that is being forced from the outside.[49] However, this move from neutral universal description to inter-subjective understanding raises some intractable problems. How can an outsider to the tradition (race, culture or religion) accurately understand purpose and inner motivations? Are there any evaluative criteria by which we can judge these purposes and inner motivations as being better or worse; beneficial or harmful to women? There will be a wide variety of purposes and inner states of consciousness which will vary between minority women and within the individual lives of minority women. How can a method capture such unstable subject matter?

---

47 This is the idea of 'strong evaluations' that we find in the work of Charles Taylor and the idea of second-order desires and reflexivity in Harry Frankfurt discussions of the mind–body problem. The idea is that motivations, intention and inner states of consciousness should be a central focus for the study of human conduct. See, for example, Taylor (1985a); Frankfurt (1971).
48 Macintyre (1985), ch 15.
49 For a full discussion of inter-subjective interpretations, see Taylor (1985b). See also Malik (2000b).

A non-distorted understanding of a tradition might come from women who are themselves able to recognise, appreciate and accurately describe the inner motivations of subjects, but at all times, analysis must align itself with the lived experiences of minority women, as they understand them. In a less formal sense, this idea is reflected in Iris Murdoch's philosophical and fiction writing, which is a passionate call for our theorising to connect with essential features of our human experiences.[50] In the present context, paying attention to texts that have authority in the lives of minority women, and their own writing and literature, will be an essential task for any theorist who sets herself the task of making minority women's inner lives more intelligible.

There remain more fundamental problems of 'uncertainty' which arise because attention to point, motivation and inner states of consciousness complicates the subject matter. These features vary between different persons and contexts; they can also vary considerably within the life of the same person over a period of time. Taking them into account makes the lives of women less amenable to study using descriptive and 'all or nothing' concepts. Conceptual devices such as the identification of the focal meaning or the ideal type of a traditional practice, which are then used as the basis for evaluation and analysing how and in what ways the current practice has become corrupted, become more useful.[51]

Other acute problems of uncertainty will arise in evaluating the lives of minority women. Recent post-modern scholarship tells us that this problem of 'ethno-centrism' arises whenever we seek to understand a tradition as outsiders by applying evaluative criteria which are external to that tradition. Feminist theory has taken both sets of issues seriously. Critics have argued that these approaches risk eliminating 'normative philosophy' from feminist theory. Benhabib, for example, argues that to move away from universal claims about the importance of equality as a universal value underpinning feminism is to throw away crucial foundations that are 'the branch on which we sit'.[52] Butler replies that there is a need to challenge these foundations because power precedes theory, but argues that the resulting uncertainty need not collapse into nihilism.[53]

Their disagreement reflects the longstanding debate between post-modern feminism and its critics. Post-modern theory provides two interrelated ways of treating the problem of applying evaluative criteria by 'outsiders' to the practices of 'different insiders'. First, there are those – often relying on the work of Nietzsche and Foucault – who suggest that all criteria are ultimately a matter of

---

50 See Murdoch (1997).

51 Max Weber states, in relation to ideal types: 'The sociologist seeks also to comprehend such irrational phenomena as mysticism, prophecy, inspiration and emotional states by theoretical concepts which are adequate on the level of meaning. In all cases, rational and irrational alike, he abstracts himself from reality and advances our knowledge of it by elucidating the degree of approximation to which a particular historical phenomenon can be classified in terms of one or more of these concepts . . . In order that these terms should have clear meaning, the sociologist must for his part formulate "pure" or "ideal" types of systems of the relevant kind which exhibit the internal coherence and unity which belongs to the most complete possible adequacy at the level of meaning.' (1978, p 23).

52 Benhabib (1995).

53 Butler (1995a).

'power' and therefore refuse to use any standards for evaluation. Second, there are others who emphasise 'diversity' and suggest that the application of judgments is to do 'violence' – a term which Jacques Derrida uses – to the other, and shows a failure to respect the 'difference' of the other. In the present context of understanding minority women, it is unlikely that refusal to apply evaluative criteria, for whatever reason, will be helpful. For minority women, especially for those who rely on traditional cultural and religious norms, it is of critical importance that they believe these norms to be objectively true criteria for making value judgments. Therefore, a proper understanding of these norms and their status in the life of minority women must take this fact seriously. In these circumstances, it is tempting to fall back on a descriptive method that is 'neutral' between truth claims. At least observation – and adopting a neutral 'point from nowhere' – has advantages because it allows us to bypass difficult questions of the choice of evaluative criteria. However, this model – as suggested above – is not ideal. The evaluation becomes obscure, but that does not mean that it is not operating.[54] In particular, this method will miss altogether purpose, motive, intention and sentiment, which are essential features for a non-distorted understanding of the other tradition. Therefore, a seemingly innocuous description results in distortion and misunderstanding.

This dilemma may be resolved – in part – by remaining committed to, rather than abandoning, the central requirements of the human sciences model. Hans Gadamer's work reminds us that, in these contexts, we come to understand through an act of comparison which allows us to 'place' the different practice against a similar or analogous home practice. Attention to the purpose, intention and motivation which is necessary for us to make sense of our own practice also provides the basic modular frame within which the different practice is accommodated and made more intelligible. Gadamer states: 'Only the support of the familiar and common understanding makes possible the venture into the alien, the lifting out something out of the alien, and thus the broadening and enrichment of our own experience of the world.'[55]

The introduction of a method that makes comparison between the familiar 'home' understanding of a practice and the new 'alien' practice has a number of significant consequences for those involved in theorising difference. For observers, this requires moving beyond the dominant idea that 'understanding' is about reaching agreement on foundational arguments, which is an epistemology which is particularly attractive for scientific modes of thought. Once we start to move away from the assumptions of that model, we can start to see the way in which the idea of 'understanding' needs to be recast as a hermeneutic and relational process. On this analysis, the act of comparison of the practices and experiences of minority women with our home understanding carries within it the seeds of its own success.

---

54 Iris Murdoch (1992), p 204 states: 'Theories which endeavour to show that all evaluation (ascription of value) is subjective, relative, historically determined, psychologically determined, often do so in aid of other differently described or covert value systems, whether political or aesthetic.'

55 Gadamer (1986).

Whereas previously the other practice may have been viewed as merely different, undertaking comparison in a self-conscious and formal context can be illuminating; placing the different practice against an analogous 'home' practice which has point, value and significance within the life of the observer may allow a shift – albeit modest – in understanding.

The use of hermeneutic methods, in a comparative context of a theorist seeking to make the practice of minority women more intelligible, may also have some transformative potential in two important respects. First, most obviously, it can allow the 'outsider' theorist to gain a more accurate appreciation of the value of the practice and beliefs of minority women as they themselves experience them. Second, more subtly, it presents a formidable and intimate challenge to the theorist's own perspective. This alternative approach uses a 'home' understanding rather than a neutral point from nowhere as the essential starting point for understanding. It follows that success in this method will require the theorist to have a more accurate understanding of her own 'home' perspective: that is, she will need to review and re-examine her own commitments as a (possibly minority) feminist. Self-understanding and the ability to analyse these pre-existing commitments will be as important as objective observation and description. The theorist will need to remain open to the possibility of transformation: the study of minority women may lead to a change and shift in the fundamental criteria which are the starting point of her analysis.

There will also be important limits to this method. Most importantly, it could lead to the problem of the 'hermeneutical circle' into which all women cannot enter, because they are not able to share the 'home' understanding of the particular theorist, and which cannot be broken because we have jettisoned the appeal to objective and neutral criteria. The method will work well in those cases where, despite difference, there remains a sufficient basis for some shared goals, attributes and experiences. It will not work as well where these criteria start to diverge significantly and it may fail altogether where there is a substantial chasm or binary opposition between the two world views: that of the theorist and that of the 'different' subject. Therefore, in some cases, the tradition or practice of minority women may be so alien and irrational that there is no possibility of any advance in understanding. One example of this may be the clash between a commitment to autonomy in the home understanding of the theorist and a minority woman's insistence on adhering to a practice that causes her substantial harm. There are many practical examples of exactly these types of conflict: ranging from the extreme case of consent to female circumcision through to other examples such as voluntary veiling or gender segregation. In the family context, the Islamic and Jewish law practice of making a right to divorce conditional on the consent of the husband is an obvious example. When faced with these fact situations, the immediate response of the outside observer may be: 'Why did she consent?' In these cases, comparison between the theorist's pre-existing commitments and values and the claims of minority women may not be illuminating. The 'home' understanding in these cases may be an absolute barrier to understanding. These practices will remain irrational and inexplicable to the theorist, as well as being accompanied by a judgment (using the home understanding as evaluative criteria) that they are wrong. Therefore, it could be argued that this approach will fail in exactly those situations where there is the most need to make the practices of minority women more intelligible.

This last problem sheds light on the limits inherent in attempts to move away from neutral objectivity as the preferred method for analysis. My argument suggests that the term 'woman' needs to be subjected to analysis to allow greater accommodation for minority women. The methods I advocate do not resolve all the issues, but they do provide one way of gaining a more accurate understanding of the claims of minority women from their own perspective. Further work needs to be done that allows us to delineate the issues with greater precision. Is difference always relevant? If not, what are the circumstances in which we need to be specially vigilant about differences caused by race, culture and religion? We also need to ask ourselves about the status of traditional values in the lives of women and the limits of consent.[56] Is there a floor of individual rights which minority women cannot negotiate away?[57] Out of these enquiries we can start to develop a better theoretical understanding of the priorities – emotions, desires and choices – of minority women and whether, and if so how, feminist theory and family law can accommodate these aspects.

Feminism already contains considerable resources that allow us to develop an intelligent and sensitive response to many of these questions. For example, sophisticated concepts such as 'autonomy', 'power', 'hierarchy' and 'false consciousness' can be used, carefully, to analyse the position of minority women within their own communities. The starting point must be a better understanding of the choices, experiences and feelings of these women from their own perspective. With this knowledge in place, it becomes easier to imagine the way in which sustained and rigorous analysis can inform discussions about why minority women may consent to harmful practices. Feminism and multiculturalism both also require a more nuanced and sophisticated definition of social and political equality: one in which gender is aligned with categories of identity such as race, culture and religion. Clearly, we must reconsider dominant constructions of 'woman' to take into account these criteria and accept multiculturalism's charge that the misrecognition of private identity is a serious injury. Yet, at the same time, we should also acknowledge that misrecognition and the forced assimilation of a minority are not the only harms that should preoccupy feminists. Analysis needs to move on

---

56 Many of the cases that arise where there is a conflict between women's rights and traditional cultural and religious practices raise issues of consent. More specifically, many of these cases relate to the apparent consent of young women to marriage which they later repudiate. See, for example, *Sohrab v Khan* [2002] SCLR 663, Outer House (Scotland), and *P v R* [2003] Fam Law 162, Family Div. See also Baroness Hale's comments in the *Begum* case above, n 4.

57 One possible source for establishing limits on consent to harmful practices is international human rights law: see McGoldrick (2005). An example of existing limits on consent to harmful practices is female circumcision. The Female Genital Mutilation Act 2003 repealed and re-enacted the Prohibition of Female Circumcision Act 1985. It makes it an offence for UK nationals or permanent UK residents to carry out female genital mutilation abroad, or to aid, abet, counsel or procure the carrying out of female genital mutilation abroad, even in countries where the practice is legal. The 2003 Act also increases the maximum penalty from five to 14 years' imprisonment.

to delineate the nature and limits of valid consent. There are other injustices – violence, poverty and social exclusion – that remain urgent issues for feminists. Can we find a common basis for a 'home' understanding of feminist theory around these wider sets of concerns? Is it possible to challenge dominant constructions of 'woman' without collapsing into nihilism?[58] Is it unrealistic to hope that autonomy remains a fundamental and transformative organising principle for feminism? What is the 'branch' upon which feminists sit? Before we can understand and accommodate the needs of minority women, we will need to achieve some consensus – or, at the very least, reach a *modus vivendi* – on these essential questions. Until then, multiculturalism will continue to trouble feminism and family law.

Acknowledgments

I would like to thank Professor Anne Phillips, The Gender Institute, London School of Economics, for her patient assistance with this work.

References

Ayer, A (1971) *Language, Truth and Logic*, Harmondsworth: Penguin

Benhabib, S (1995) 'Subjectivity, historiography and politics', in Benhabib, S, Butler, J, Cornell, D and Fraser, N (eds) *Feminist Contentions: A Philosophical Exchange*, London: Routledge

Butler, J (1995a) 'Contingent foundations', in Benhabib, S, Butler, J, Cornell, D and Fraser, N (eds) *Feminist Contentions: A Philosophical Exchange*, London: Routledge

Butler, J (1995b) 'For a close reading', in Benhabib, S, Butler, J, Cornell, D and Fraser, N (eds) *Feminist Contentions: A Philosophical Exchange*, London: Routledge

Cornell, D (1995) 'What is ethical feminism', in Benhabib, S, Butler, J, Cornell, D and Fraser, N (eds) *Feminist Contentions: A Philosophical Exchange*, London: Routledge

Crosby, C (1992) 'Dealing with differences', in Butler, J and Scott, J (eds) *Feminists Theorise the Politics*, London: Routledge

Dworkin, A (1983) *Pornography: Men Possessing Women*, London: The Women's Press

Dworkin, R (1986) *Law's Empire*, London: Fontana Press

Duchen, C (1986) *Feminism in France*, London: Routledge & Kegan Paul

---

58 One response to this challenge is Drucilla Cornell's call that definitions of the concept 'woman' require feminism to take seriously issues of 'ethics' and define what we mean by the 'feminine'. In the context of the discussion on minority women this raises particular problems: how do we define the 'ethical' and 'feminine' in the face of deep differences between women? Cornell (1995).

Eekelaar, J (2004) 'Children between cultures', 18 *International J of Law, Policy and the Family* 178

Frankfurt, H (1971) 'Freedom of the will and the concept of a person', 67(1) *J of Philosophy* 5

Gadamer, H (1986) 'The universality of the hermeneutic problem', in Linge, D (ed) *Philosophical Hermeneutics*, Berkeley, CA: University of California Press

Gertz, C (1993) *The Interpretation of Cultures*, London: Fontana Press

Green, L (1995) 'Internal minorities and their rights', in Kymlicka, W (ed) *The Rights of Minority Cultures*, Oxford: Oxford University Press

Hooks, B (1984) *Feminist Theory: From Margin to Center*, Boston: South End Press

Kukathas, C (1995) 'Are there any cultural rights', in Kymlicka, W (ed) *The Rights of Minority Cultures*, Oxford: Oxford University Press

Kymlicka, W (1995) 'Introduction', in Kymlicka, W (ed) *The Rights of Minority Cultures*, Oxford: Oxford University Press

LSE Gender Institute (2005) *Sexual and Cultural Equality: Conflicts and Tensions*, The Nuffield Foundation: Project Grant Report, www.lse.ac.uk/collections/genderInstitute/pdf/finalnuffield.pdf

Macintyre, A (1985) *After Virtue*, London: Duckworth

MacKinnon, C (1983) 'Feminism, Marxism, Method and the State: An agenda for theory', 8(2) *Signs* 635

MacKinnon, C (1987) *Feminism Unmodified: Discourses on Life and Law*, Cambridge, MA: Harvard University Press

Malik, M (2000a) 'Minorities and human rights', in Campbell, T, Ewing, K and Tomkins, A (eds) *Sceptical Approaches to Human Rights*, Oxford: Oxford University Press

Malik, M (2000b) 'Faith and the state of jurisprudence', in Douglas-Scott, S, Oliver, P and Tadros, V (eds) *Faith in Law: Essays in Legal Theory*, Oxford: Hart Publishing

McGoldrick, D (2005) 'Multiculturalism and its discontents', 5(1) *Human Rights Law Review* 27

Murdoch, I (1992) *Metaphysics as a Guide to Morals*, Harmondsworth: Penguin

Murdoch, I (1997) *Existentialists and Mystics: Writings on Philosophy and Literature*, London: Random House, Chatto and Windus

Nicholson, L (1995) 'Introduction', in Benhabib, S, Butler, J, Cornell, D and Fraser, N (eds) *Feminist Contentions: A Philosophical Exchange*, London: Routledge

Nussbaum, M (1999) *Sex and Social Justice*, Oxford: Oxford University Press

Oakeshott, M (1975) *On Human Conduct*, Oxford: Clarendon Press

Okin, S (1979) *Women in Western Political Thought*, Princeton, NJ: Princeton University Press

Okin, S (1998) 'Feminism and Multiculturalism', 108 *Ethics* 661

Okin, S (2002) ' "Mistresses of their own destiny": Group rights, gender, and realistic rights of exit', 112 *Ethics* 205

Rawls, J (1971) *A Theory of Justice*, Cambridge, MA: Harvard University Press

Rawls, J (1993) *Political Liberalism*, New York: Columbia University Press

Schumacher, E (1973) *Small Is Beautiful: Economics as if People Mattered*, New York: Harper and Row

Scott, J (1992) 'Experience', in Butler, J and Scott, J (eds) *Feminists Theorise the Political*, London: Routledge

Shachar, A (2001) *Multicultural Jurisdictions: Cultural Differences and Women's Rights*, Cambridge: Cambridge University Press

Smart, C (1989) *Feminism and the Power of Law*, London: Routledge

Spelman, E (1998) *Inessential Woman: Problems of Exclusion in Feminist Thought*, Boston: Beacon

Taylor, C (1985a) *What is Human Agency*, Philosophical Papers, Vol I, Cambridge: Cambridge University Press

Taylor, C (1985b) *Interpretation and the Sciences of Man*, Philosophical Papers, Vol II, Cambridge: Cambridge University Press

Taylor, C (1992) *Multiculturalism and the Politics of Recognition*, Princeton, NJ: Princeton University Press

Weber, M (1978) 'The nature of social action', in Runciman, W (ed), Matthews, E (trans) *Selections in Translation*, Cambridge: Cambridge University Press

Chapter 12
Feminist Legal Studies and the Subject(s) of Men: Questions of Text, Terrain and Context in the Politics of Family Law and Gender
Richard Collier

Introduction

Within feminist legal scholarship in the field of family law, a critical engagement with the gender of men approached via recourse to the concept of masculinity/ies is a now well-established theme.[1] In recent years, in particular, it has become commonplace within literary and hermeneutic projects informed by the 'post-modern frame'[2] to find discussion of how law has been involved in the constructing, embodying or reproduction of various ideas about men, women and (hetero-normative) 'family life' approached via reference to the concept of masculinity. This work has sought to unpack, reveal or, more precisely, deconstruct the presence of the 'hegemonic masculine' in law (see below) as part of developing an under-standing of the hidden gender[3] of (family) law. A recurring assumption in this work has been that there is a political, analytic and policy gain to be made for feminism by 'taking masculinity seriously'.[4] It is an assumption certain aspects of which I wish to question. What follows presents, in short, a re-reading of the male subject of feminist scholarship within the field of family law.[5] I wish to explore the limitations, ambiguities and confusions which, I will suggest, have come to surround the concept in this area of legal study. I will argue that there are pressing reasons to reconsider what an engagement with masculinity – in particular one approached via the analysis of legal texts – can bring to feminist legal scholarship at the present political moment.

Family law, as a sub-field of legal studies, has in many respects been at the forefront of the study of masculinity within legal scholarship; it is family law, I will argue, which has come to exemplify and illustrate some of the conceptual and political limitations of masculinity for feminism more generally, resulting from a number of political and theoretical developments over the past decade. A rethinking of the male (gendered) subject in family law is a project linked to – indeed, I want to suggest, it is inseparable from – a growing debate taking place

---

1   On the analytic shift towards an engagement with the plural term masculinities see further Morgan (1992). The broader interrogation of the relationship between masculinities and law has been, regardless of the political orientation, methodology or underlying epistemological presuppositions of the work in question, a longstanding and significant presence within feminist legal studies.
2   Thornton (2004), p 10.
3   Graycar and Morgan (1990).
4   Compare in the field of criminology the argument of Newburn and Stanko (1994).
5   Family law is, of course, a conceptually unclear, ambiguous and profoundly contested sub-field of legal study: see further, and generally, Diduck (2003; 2001); O'Donovan (1993; 1986).

about the future direction and politics of feminist scholarship within legal studies. It has been suggested that 'feminist legal theorists are in disarray';[6] a situation engendered significantly (although by no means exclusively) by the twin impacts of neo-liberal market imperatives on the academy and the impact of post-modernism on feminist legal theory. This debate is embracing concerns about the relation between 'high theory' and (feminist) practice, questions of audience and accessibility; of the relationship of men to legal feminism;[7] and, my concern here, about what it means to speak at the present moment, in the context of a growing debate centred around what has been termed the new 'male victimhood' in the field of family justice, of there being an interconnection between men, masculinity and family law.

Family, law and feminism: Putting masculinity on the agenda

The study of men and masculinities in the field of family law has occurred at a nexus of developments which, although linked, draw on distinct political and intellectual trajectories in terms of how the central relationship between law and the power of men has been conceptualised. A number of authors associated with the critical study or new sociology of men and masculinities have figured, with varying degrees of prominence, in this work. The most significant influence on the analysis of masculinity within family law has, however, undoubtedly been that of feminism.[8] The very project of feminist legal studies is, of course, contentious, not least in terms of an epistemological foundation around the unified subject 'Woman'.[9] It is nonetheless, for heuristic purposes, possible to identify a number of distinctive 'phases' or approaches within feminist scholarship in family law, each of which have conceptualised men and masculinity in some very different ways.[10]

Institutions, practices and the (hidden) gender of family law

Within what has been termed 'first phase' liberal-progressivist feminist scholarship,[11] through to the work of those writers who later sought to engage with what

---

6 Thornton (2004).

7 See, for example, the debates between: Bottomley (2004); Naffine (2004; 2002); and Barron (2000); Goodrich (2001). Note, generally, the arguments of Drakopoulou (2000); Conaghan (2000); Sandland (1998a; 1998b; 1995). An excellent account of the relationship between men and legal feminism can be found in Halewood (1995).

8 The broader sociological study of masculinities within the academy has itself largely, although by no means exclusively, emerged as part of an attempt to develop a self-identified 'pro-feminist' politics.

9 See, for example, in addition to the works cited above, n 7, Smart (1989); Lacey (1998).

10 This approach is, I recognise, problematic, not least in the way in which it tends to categorise together a vast body of work and assume a linear narrative underscoring what is, in fact, a far more complex history. Equally, it is important not to assume a conceptual 'clean break' with earlier (pre-feminist) sociogenic sex role accounts of masculinity: see further Carrigan *et al* (1985). Contrast, generally, the approach of Naffine (1990), ch 1.

11 Naffine (1990), pp 3–6.

was seen as the inherent 'maleness' of patriarchal legal systems, methods and reasoning (below), the concept of masculinity has been linked in diverse ways to ideas about law and the power of men. Masculinity has been deployed extensively in studies of institutions and practices relating to aspects of law and legal regulation concerning families; in accounts, for example, of the work of solicitors, barristers and judges; the administration of criminal and civil justice; and in studies of legal education, the law school and the legal curricula. Within earlier feminist work, the presence of the distinctive masculine culture (or cultures) of law was singled out as particularly problematic for women, a hetero-normative definition of family life historically enmeshed with a range of gendered, sexualised, sexist beliefs. This 'masculinism'[12] of legal institutions and practices was identified in such phenomena as the sexualisation (the rendered 'Other') of women's bodies; in the denial of women's corporeality;[13] in the prevalence of homosocial and homophobic behaviour;[14] and, encapsulating each of the above, in what has been seen as a persistent benchmarking and assessment of women against a normative, ideal 'benchmark' figure[15] – an individual understood (somewhat paradoxically) to be both gendered (male/masculine: authoritative, rational, competent, unemotional and so on);[16] and, equally, gender neutral, in particular with regard to those commitments and 'inevitable dependencies' seen as relating to the private familial domain.[17]

Within much of this work, and perhaps in particular in studies framed by what Harding[18] has termed a form of feminist empiricism, the maleness, masculinity or masculinism of law was seen as in some way distorting the gaze of an otherwise neutral observer. Thus, in accounts of family law and practice during the 1970s and 1980s, we find an identification of the 'sexism' of family law enmeshed with the critique of the benchmark 'man of law': a gendered subject(ivity) who embodied, it was suggested, a particular *kind* of masculinity. Discussions of equality of opportunity, motherhood, marriage, violence and 'breadwinners and homemakers' in Atkins and Hoggett's influential 1984 text *Women and the Law* perhaps illustrate this kind of approach.[19] If such work tended to engage with studies of case law, statute and the gendered cultures of legal practice, however, a body of feminist jurisprudential thought was seeking to develop a rather different critique of the masculine nature of law: one based, in contrast, on a critique of the masculine nature of legal methods and legal reasoning itself.

Within later standpoint (or 'second phase') feminist scholarship, there occurred

---

12 Brittan (1989), p 4.
13 An excellent account of which can be found in Thornton (1996).
14 See, for example, Bell (1995).
15 This idea has itself been a recurring issue within legal feminism and links to a theme within the critical study of masculinity concerning the tendency for men to claim reason as taken-for-granted, a positionality regarded as final authority and arbiter of social Truth: see, for example, Seidler (1989).
16 See Thornton (1998).
17 Fineman (1995).
18 Harding (1987; 1986).
19 Atkins and Hoggett (1984). Note also Sachs and Wilson (1978).

a shift in how men, masculinity and the power of law are conceptualised. Drawing on a forceful critique of the earlier liberal-progressivist position, classic tenets of liberal legalism (for example, individualism, autonomy and so forth) were refigured as quintessentially 'masculine' values.[20] Family law, not least in relation to a construction/reproduction of a public–private dualism,[21] was seen as profoundly implicated in a historical effacing of the distinctive social experiences of women. In one strand of this work, in particular, a direct link is made between law's status as an androcentric, positivist discipline and the masculine nature of law's governance, institutions and jurisprudence. Here, law, implicated with other phallocentric, totalising and oppressive knowledge formations, did not just equate with the power of men; law could be seen, in some accounts at least, to constitute, in its purest form, that power. Oft quoted, but summarising neatly: 'The state is male in the feminist sense. The law sees and treats women the way men see and treat women.'[22] Family law's purported neutrality would thus itself appear to be simply a mask for the '*masculinity of its judgements*'.[23]

Towards the 'post-modern frame': Discourse, text and the 'man of (family) law'

By the mid/late 1980s, in work which, by 1990, Naffine felt able to describe as itself constituting a 'third phase' of feminist scholarship,[24] a far-reaching critique had taken place of the limits of each of the above two approaches. Yet, once again, a conceptualisation of masculinity appeared central to how the relationship between law, the family and the power of men was understood within feminist legal scholarship. A key criticism of the second phase work, as above, had been that it ascribed to the category 'woman' an essentialist ontological status; in so doing, it negated the discursive construction of the (feminist) subject 'Woman', the diverse positionality within/between women's lives. It was also recognised, however, that much of the earlier feminist work had itself often tended to conceive of men as, in some way, a homogenous group, and law then as the (unproblematic) embodiment of the social power *of* men. Seen by those writers increasingly informed by post-modernism and post-structuralism as an approach which was, ultimately, as androcentric as the theories it purportedly sought to supersede, singled out for particular criticism was an underlying essentialism (something which resulted in 'a paradoxical mix of debilitating pessimism and unfathomable optimism');[25] and, related to this, an embrace of an apparently all-encompassing notion of the 'masculinity of law' (and, with it, of male (hetero)sexuality),[26] which

---

20 See, for example, West (1988).
21 Itself a central theme in feminist scholarship: note, for example, although from a different perspective, the argument of O'Donovan, (1985); *cf* Rose (1987).
22 MacKinnon (1983), p 644; also MacKinnon (1987).
23 MacKinnon (1983), p 658.
24 Naffine (1990).
25 Jackson (1993), p 211.
26 On which see, more generally, Segal (1994), p 46.

served, it was suggested, to efface the complexity and diversity in the lives both of men *and* women.

It is not difficult to see, in retrospect, why a transition should have taken place within feminist work at this time, and, in turn, why feminists and pro-feminist scholars should have sought to turn 'their attention to men and masculinity in a discursive attempt to stop the depiction of women as "the problem", as well as to resist the on-going objectification of women'.[27] The shift is perhaps encapsulated in the work of the British scholar Carol Smart, whose 1989 book *Feminism and the Power of Law*[28] illustrates themes subsequently taken up in the study of masculinity and family law during the 1990s. Within her earlier work in family law, such as *The Ties that Bind: Law, Marriage and the Reproduction of Patriarchal Relations* (1984),[29] Smart had sought to question whether there might be a distinction between what she termed 'legal regulation' and 'male control'; whether the fact particular legal agents may be understood as 'subscribing to sexist attitudes to protect their material interests' necessarily rendered law itself, as a whole, 'sexist *or somehow masculine in nature*'.[30] Such questions had similarly informed the 1985 text *Women in Law: Explorations in Law, Family and Sexuality*, co-edited by Julia Brophy and Carol Smart,[31] in which it was argued that law

> is not in fact a unity, organised with the specific purpose of oppressing women, although clearly this is how it may be experienced . . . the law [is not] . . . a homogenous unit with a unitary purpose. It is possible to find contractions both in law and legal practice, and between legal agents, *which cast doubt upon the existence of a male, legal conspiracy.*[32]

Building on a growing concern in feminist work to address the nature of the gendered subject in family law, and drawing on the broadly Foucauldian understanding of the relation between law and power which was developing within (as well as, of course, beyond) feminist scholarship at the time, Smart's analysis in 1989 begins, in contrast, with a belief that although law may be '*constituted as masculine* on both empirical and cultural grounds' (that, at the very least, 'doing law' and being identified as 'masculine' can be congruous), this is not because of any straightforward biological imperative. Rather, what is at issue are the 'significant overlaps' or 'mutual resonances' between how 'both law and masculinity are constituted *in discourse*'.[33] Thus:

> Law is not rational because men are rational . . . law is constituted as rational as are men, *and men as the subjects of a discourse of masculinity* come to experience themselves as rational – hence suited to a career in law. In attempting to transform

---

27 Thornton (2004), p 12.
28 Smart (1989). Contrast Sandland (1995), p 3.
29 Smart (1984); also O'Donovan (1985).
30 Smart (1984), p 17, my emphasis.
31 Brophy and Smart (1985).
32 Smart and Brophy (1985), p 17, my emphasis.
33 Smart (1989), p 86, my emphasis.

law, feminists are not simply challenging legal discourse *but also naturalistic assumptions about masculinity.*[34]

This argument continues to fuse a challenge to dominant notions of masculinity with a feminist critique of law. It is, after all, 'assumptions' about masculinity which are to be challenged and questioned as part of developing a feminist politics of law.[35] Yet what is significant here is the notion of men 'as the subjects of a discourse of masculinity': a theme which opens out to analysis of the plurality and contingency of those discourses which speak not only of 'Woman'/'women', but also of 'men and masculinity' across diverse institutional and cultural contexts. There is (albeit implicitly) an acceptance that all men do not have equal access to cultural, symbolic or economic capital; that there might, at the very least, be a need to engage with the plural (discursively encoded *as*) 'familial' masculini*ties*. In turning critical attention to the construction of the Woman of legal (and, indeed, of feminist) discourse,[36] what was (inescapably) brought into the critical frame is the nature of the 'Man' of law – and, one might add, the 'man' of legal feminism itself.

'Deflecting the gaze?' Textual analysis and the critical study of the 'family man' in law

Deflection of the objectifying gaze from women and Indigenous people to benchmark masculinity and heterosexuality, as well as 'whiteness', represents an attempt to disrupt the conventional orderings of modernity within legal texts.[37]

It was in an attempt to explore the above concerns that a range of studies developed in family law during the 1990s concerned explicitly with addressing issues around men and masculinities. In turning attention to men, and 'in a discursive attempt to stop the depiction of women as "the problem" ',[38] this work sought to engage, in particular, with the 'social construction' of the 'man', 'men' or 'masculinities' within, or of, legal discourse. My own book, *Masculinity, Law and the Family*,[39] published in 1995, illustrates aspects of this approach in its attempt to unearth or reveal the 'hidden' masculinities of law, the assumptions about men contained within a range of family law texts and practices. At the same time, and across diverse areas of legal study,[40] a growing feminist and pro-feminist

---

34 Smart (1989), pp 86–7, my emphasis.
35 Note, for example, the depiction of the 'phallogocentrism' of legal discourse as the fusing of a *masculine*, heterosexual imperative and the fixing of sign/signifier within a patriarchal structure of power/knowledge relation (Smart (1989), p 86); also 'the needs of the masculine imperative which receive a cultural response' (O'Donovan (1993), p 5).
36 Contrast Smart (1992).
37 Thornton (2004), p 15. See further Middleton (1992), p 159.
38 Thornton (2004), p 12; see also Thornton (1989).
39 Collier (1995).
40 As simply an illustration of this body of work note, for example, Bibbings (2000); Berger *et al* (1995); Carver (1996); Collier (2000); Liddle (1996); Naffine (1994); Thomas (1995); Heins (1995); Williams (1995). On law, crime and criminal justice see Newburn and Stanko (1994); Goodey (1997); Jefferson and Carlen (1996); Collier (1998); Groombridge (1998).

literature has sought to unpack the diverse ways in which ideas about men as gendered subjects have been constructed or depicted at particular historical moments in laws relating to the family.[41] This work has involved the analysis of cases, statutes, legal utterances and cultural representations of law; what has emerged is what has since become a complex, rich picture of what might be termed 'the (family) man of law'.

This masculine subject in family law has been seen, in a number of respects, as a distinctively 'embodied' being.[42] Thus, in relation to laws around marriage and divorce, for example, it has been argued that whilst the penis frequently appears within law as somehow subject to a man's rational thought and control, the vagina, in contrast, has been presented as a space, as an always-searchable absence.[43] Related assumptions have been noted around the idea of there being a natural (hetero)sexual 'fit' between the bodies of women and men, with notions of male (hetero)sexual activity and female passivity informing the legal determination, historically, of what does, and does not, constitute a valid marriage[44] (as well as, indeed, a legally valid exit from any such marriage). In accounts of how paid employment can inform ideas of men as 'respectable' (and socially safe) familial subjects, meanwhile, an ideal of the liberal rational individual had been deployed in such a way as to depict a sexed, autonomous masculine subject as, in marked contrast to women, a peculiarly *dis*embodied being; a figure bounded, constituted as *male*, in ways ever dependent on a separation from other men and, crucially, on a hierarchical difference from women.[45] Such dissociation appears particularly marked, it is argued, in relation to ideas of care, caring and vulnerability commonly associated with the private sphere and 'family life'.

In keeping with the broader corporeal turn in legal scholarship during the 1990s, later work on masculinities has noted the way in which, whilst women's bodies in law often appeared as incomprehensible, fluid, *un*bounded, defined by 'openings and absences', the bodies of men, Sheldon suggests, all too often appear to be marked by ideas of bodily absence and physical disengagement rather than any sense of presence.[46] For Sheldon, men's 'safe', stable and bounded bodies signify a somewhat tangential and contingent relation to gestation, fertility and reproduction in families; one which, certainly, stands in marked contrast to women. In the work of Bibbings, similarly, although working more in the field of criminal law, the bodies of men are positioned in particular ways in relation to ideas about masculinity, not least a cultural condoning of intra-male violence.[47] In my own work,[48] men's subjectivity has appeared, across a number of contexts, as related to historically specific ideas about heterosexuality, parenthood and 'family

---

41 As earlier examples of this kind of study note, for example, O'Donovan (1993), ch 5; Moran (1990); Collier (1992).
42 See Hyde (1997). Contrast Bridgeman and Millns (1995).
43 Hyde (1997), p 172.
44 In addition to work cited above, see also Waldby (1995).
45 Naffine (1994).
46 Sheldon (1999); also (2001).
47 Bibbings (2000).
48 Collier (2002b; 2001; 2000; 1999a; 1999b). See also Coltrane (1996).

practices';[49] and, once again, on some (in fact questionable) assumptions about the nature of men's physical and emotional relationship to children, child care and ideas of dependency.

The engagement with masculinity in feminist and pro-feminist scholarship in family law cannot be confined to such analyses of legal texts. There has also occurred a broader political and cultural debate focused around the notion of 'masculine crisis' or 'crisis of masculinity',[50] which has itself informed a range of issues concerning policy and practice relating to law and the family. Across diverse cultural artefacts, recurring concerns and anxieties around the meaning of social, economic, cultural and political change have served to redraw the parameters of what is deemed to constitute a normal/normative (hetero)sexual family; in so doing, struggles around what has (or has not) been happening *to* men and 'their' masculinity/ies is an issue which has assumed an emblematic status, a powerful, symbolic significance – a cipher for broader transitions and tensions around shifting relations between men and women (as well as, importantly, children).[51]

This latter development has a number of dimensions. In some contexts, for example at the interface of family and employment law, there has emerged an agenda concerned with promoting (gender) equity by, explicitly, challenging ideas of masculinity which, it is argued, have become increasingly anachronistic. The aim here has been to engage with law reform in such a way as to encourage and/or reinforce certain kinds of behaviour on the part of men.[52] Thus, whether it be in relation to securing a satisfactory balance between the commitments of 'work and home', in the promotion of 'good enough' post-divorce/separation parenting on the part of men[53] or in securing the provision of child support,[54] we find a concern with changing men's practices and attitudes bound up within this debate about what is happening to contemporary masculinity. In other contexts, however, such questions of gender equity, law and law reform have been placed centre stage in some rather different – and far more contentious – ways. Nowhere, perhaps, have these issues and concerns been clearer – or more publicly and politically visible – than in relation to what has become, internationally, an increasingly high-profile debate about the gender politics of family law reform; a debate in which, it has been suggested – significantly for feminist legal studies – it is, in relation to the area of contract law in particular, *men*, and not women, who have now become the 'new victims' of family law.[55]

Where does my argument thus far leave us? Masculinity, I have suggested, has been deployed in a number of different ways within feminist legal scholarship at

---

49 Morgan (1999), p 13. Also Morgan (1996).
50 See further Brittan (1989), pp 25–36; Hearn (1987), pp 16–31; Connell (1987), pp 183–6; Carrigan *et al* (1985), p 598. Compare Clare (2000); Faludi (1999).
51 See further Beck and Beck-Gernsheim (1995); Giddens (1992).
52 Collier (1999a).
53 See further Smart (1999); Smart and Neale (1999a; 1999b).
54 Diduck (1995); Wallbank (1997).
55 See Smart, Chapter 7, and Kaganas, Chapter 8, both in this volume. On the 'zero-sum' conception of power implicit in such a view see Collier (1999b).

different historical moments. If there has been no one model of masculinity in this work, however, it is possible to identify the contours of a distinctive masculine subject of family law which has emerged within feminist and pro-feminist legal studies: a man or male figure who has embodied a certain *kind* of masculinity. At the same time, we have seen, masculinity has been politicised more generally, an issue which has had far-reaching implications for questions of policy and reform across diverse areas of law relating to the family.

In the remainder of this chapter, I do not wish, in any way, to downplay the insights and value of the work undertaken to date in family law on the subject of men and masculinity. In suggesting that this work can itself be seen as the product of a particular cultural and political moment – a distinctive 'episteme' of feminist legal theory – I do, however, wish to unpack a number of unanswered questions in this area; questions which, in a context of formal equality and the rise of the 'male victimhood' referred to above, lead one to believe that masculinity may well have become an increasingly double-edged concept for feminist legal studies developing a critique of the gendered politics of family law. Why is this so?

(Re)conceptualising the male subject in family law

Recent empirical and theoretical scholarship concerned with exploring the gendered discourses of family law has sought, in a number of ways, to explore the masculine subjects of family law. Whether it be in relation to studies of divorce law and practice, contact law reform, marriage, parenthood or men's relation to employment, for example, it is possible to see in family law the concept of masculinity being deployed in a number of ways.[56] There has occurred a questioning of the way in which ideas about masculinity have mediated men's and women's experiences of the family justice process, with research speaking of the emergence of a distinctive 'masculinised discourse' of divorce; of men adopting 'masculine' subject positions within the processes of separation;[57] of ideas of a normative masculinity correlating, broadly, with the tendency of men to relate to, and appeal in their engagement with the legal process in terms of, a rights-based framework.[58] Elsewhere, a sense of challenged masculinity has been evoked in such a way as to link aspects of male identity either to an embrace of or (more frequently) resistance *to* changes seen as taking place in the (nuclear) family unit.[59] The latter theme has been particularly evident in recent studies of fathers' rights groups and, more generally, in work focused on the interventions of the men's movement in the field

---

56 See, for example, Brown and Day Sclater (1999); Day Sclater (1999a; 1999b); Day Sclater and Yates (1999).

57 Day Sclater (1999a); Arendell (1995).

58 Compare Dewar (1998), who suggests that the concerns about justice expressed by fathers' rights groups appear to be shared by many who have expressed a growing dissatisfaction with the perceived limits of a broad discretionary system in the family law field.

59 An appeal to a normative familial masculinity has been directly linked to a defence of a 'traditional' (heterosexual) family; a family premised on broadly clear-cut sexual divisions of labour and male economic authority: see below.

of family law.[60] Far from seeing women as the real or potential victims of family law reform and/or practice – a position which has, arguably, informed debates about family law at various points in the past – a powerful discourse has emerged which suggests that a range of ostensibly liberalising reforms may have, in fact, rendered men the real 'losers' in the field of family justice. It is against this background that feminist scholars have suggested that what is in fact taking place in this area is, internationally, something akin to, if not a 'backlash project', then a resistance *to* 'feminist inspired' legal and social changes; a development which reflects the disproportionate influence of fathers' rights groups in managing to set reform agendas in the field of family law.[61]

In much of the textual-based study of law discussed above, however, it is possible to identify a rather different object of analysis; it is in relation to these kinds of study that, I would suggest, the problems with masculinity can appear particularly marked. It has been a recurring theme within the study of masculinity in legal studies that law has been involved in the reproduction and/or embodiment of a form of 'hegemonic masculinity'. This is an idea closely associated with the structured model of gender power[62] developed in the work of RW Connell.[63] Repeatedly, this hegemonic masculinity has appeared as something which is to be unpacked, deconstructed or uncovered in law. Certainly, such work engages with the contested nature of law, the ever-present possibility of resistance, in ways that are in keeping with themes developed in feminist legal scholarship during the 1980s around the 'open-ended' nature of law. However, it does leave certain questions unanswered. It is unclear, in particular, how the model of hegemonic masculinity seen to be embodied in law relates to the actual lives and gendered practices of men and women. Thus, whilst textual readings can provide a wealth of information about how law constructs, sees or produces particular *ideas* about men and gender in the context of family law (although see further below), what we do not find is any account of how this relates to what individuals *do*. Why, for example, should it be the case that, whilst some men might 'turn to' or invest in particular (hegemonic) masculine subject positions (let us say, within a post-divorce separation context), others do not? Men encounter a diverse range of circumstances which frame their individual experiences of 'family life'. If it is to be argued that a distinctive kind of familial masculinity is 'offered up' for all men within a particular socio-cultural, structural location, why do individual men choose one, and not another, masculine identity? (And who, in any case, is doing this 'offering up'?)[64] There is clear evidence that men might identify with a diverse range of resources to 'accomplish' their masculinity in this sense. This does not, in itself, argue against the proposition that men are 'doing' hegemonic masculinity in the process of 'doing' family practices. However, it remains unclear how

---

60 Kaye and Tolmie (1998a; 1998b); Collier (1996); Arditti and Allen (1993); Berotia and Drakich (1993); Berotia (1998); Smart, Chapter 7, and Kaganas, Chapter 8, both in this volume.
61 Boyd (2003); Boyd and Young (2002); Graycar (2000).
62 See further Whitehead (2002), pp 84–99, 103.
63 Connell (1987; 1995; 2000). See further Whitehead (1999); Hall (2002).
64 Walklate (1995), p 180.

questions of individual life-history and biography impact on any such choice. How adequate, in short, is this kind of theorisation in seeking to account for the subjectivity of individual men? And what is the process by which these distinctive 'masculinities' are then constituted?

In this kind of deployment of a normative hegemonic masculine subject within critical scholarship, there does appear to be a certain rigidity in terms of how men are understood to be accomplishing or aspiring to the attributes of a dominant form of masculinity. Indeed, a model of gendered power would appear to hold in place a normative masculine gender as the object of (feminist) critique; one to which is then assigned a range of (broadly undesirable/negative) characteristics. Yet, at the same time, it appears to impose 'an a priori theoretical/conceptual frame on the psychological complexity of men's behaviour'.[65] What this means is that masculinity can all too easily appear, at once, as both a primary and under- lying cause (or source) of a range of social effects (of what men do); and, simul- taneously, as something which results from certain social actions. This is, at the very least, a tautologous proposition.[66] There is a sense in which social structure would appear to constrain men's practice. Yet a vast body of empirical, historical and autobiographical research on men suggests that there can be a richness, tex- ture and subtlety to the 'gendered lives' of men, which this kind of deployment of hegemonic masculinity – and the associated (selective) focus on what are seen to be the negative connotations of the hegemonic masculine – cannot by itself account for.[67]

Underscoring these problems is another issue: how the masculine social subject has itself been theorised. There has emerged in recent years, within the sociology of masculinity, an attempt to build on the above critique of the structured action model and to seek, in contrast, to take the psychic dimensions of (masculine) subjectivity seriously. This is a perspective which has begun to inform studies of family law and practice in a number of ways.[68] It is not possible to do justice here to the complexity of the substantive analyses which have been produced in this area; nor the complex groundings of strands of this work within contemporary psychoanalysis.[69] It is, however, possible to trace elements of this development in terms of what it might have to say about developing understandings of the male subject in family law.

This psycho-social perspective, as it has been termed, tends to draw on the concept of discourse[70] rather than that of social structure. It has evolved, as it were, from the 'third stage' thinking as outlined above. In one strand of this work, what is placed centre stage is an attempt to engage with the presentational forms of masculine performances, identities, corporeal enactments and so forth.[71] In

---

65 Collier (1995).
66 Walklate (1995), p 181.
67 See Wetherell and Edley (1999).
68 As above, for example, in relation to accounts of post-divorce family life; also, on interventions aimed at addressing men's violence in families, see Gadd (2000; 2002).
69 Adams (1996).
70 Compare Pease (2000); Jefferson (1994).
71 Contrast Butler (1993; 1990).

rejecting, in suitably post-modern fashion, the idea of a unitary rational male subject, the aim has been, rather, to develop a social understanding of the masculine psyche; one which might, it is argued, shed light on men's behaviour across diverse areas of law and legal practice. Allied to the insights of queer theory (a body of work, arguably, strangely absent within the field of family law), the masculine subject has appeared as a 'performative construction' naturalised through repetition; contingent, unstable, nothing more (or less) than (at most) a temporary association with a particular desire and/or social identity; a manifestation of a gendered self conceptualised in terms of a series of constantly shifting practices and techniques.

This approach does offer up a way of prising open the possibility of making sense of the contradictions and difficulties that particular men may experience in becoming masculine. For example, by seeking to integrate questions of individual biography and life history, it is argued that a handle is given on the important question, noted above, of why some men do, and others do not, invest or engage in certain kinds of behaviour or subject positions. Importantly for feminist legal studies, questions of social power do remain. However, the focus of analysis shifts to how a (non-unitary) 'inherently contradictory' social subject comes to invest, whether consciously or unconsciously, in what are then seen at particular historical moments as socially empowering discourses around masculinity.

This approach has a rich potential for feminist scholarship in the field of family law, as has been evident in relation to studies of the fluid, evolutionary nature of post-divorce family life. It offers a great advance politically on the (always, already) empowered subject implicit within both the structured model of gender power, as above, as well as strands of feminist and pro-feminist thought. It would also appear to reject any 'reductive view of men as oppressors . . . [one] that [has] not endeared feminism to those men who might otherwise have been sympathetic'.[72] However, criticisms can also be made of this approach. Leaving aside the issue of whether the more explicitly psychoanalytically informed strand of this recent work on masculinity might itself be premised on an unduly mechanistic model of personality formation, an argument remains: although what we have here can offer a rich story for describing the effects of discourses of masculinity within particular contexts relating to families, they remain, at the end of the day, just that – stories. It is difficult to see how readings produced about the 'taking up' of a masculine subjectivity can ever be tested or proven in any meaningful way.[73] It is also unclear whether we are reduced, ultimately, to an 'all is discourse' position, an issue which links to the broader critique of post-modernism within and beyond feminist scholarship. In disavowing any outer reality, is one left with a wholly semiotic account in which, as Connell himself observes, 'with so much emphasis on the signifier, the signified tends to vanish?'[74] As John Hood-Williams has noted,[75] is it not difficult to maintain that there are many 'discourses of

---

72 Thornton (2004), p 10.
73 See Frosh (1997; 1994).
74 Connell (1995), pp 50–1.
75 Hood-Williams (2001), p 37.

subjectivication' whereby masculine identities become attached to individuals and, at the same time, maintain (as some do) that the claims this approach is making are grounded in real, historically specific and irreducible psychological processes?

What, ultimately, is meant by the term masculinity in this context? 'Is it a discourse, a power structure, a psychic economy, a history, an ideology, an identity, a behaviour, a value system, an aesthetic even?' Or is it 'all these and also their mutual separation, the magnetic force of repulsion which keeps them apart . . . a centrifugal dispersal of what are maintained as discrete fields of psychic and social structure'?[76] Masculinity has encompassed within feminist legal studies such diverse attributes as the psychological characteristics of men, a range of gendered (as masculine) experiences and identities, psychoanalytic readings of social practices (as above), as well as analyses of men's gendered behaviour within specific institutional settings.[77] To speak legitimately in this work of a 'discourse of masculinity', however, entails showing that 'a particular set of usages was located structurally within a clearly defined institution with its own methods, objects and practices'.[78] It is possible one could argue this in relation to law, although the heterogeneity and diversity of the issues discussed above would suggest otherwise. Yet if that is the case, references to 'discourses of masculinity' are themselves simply references to 'repeated patterns of linguistic usage'.[79] Whilst masculinity may be produced within some discourses, most examples 'of "masculine" utterances' are not necessarily discourses. At the very least, I have argued elsewhere,[80] masculinity is not a fixed, homogenous or unchanging concept; it encompasses a complex range of ideas and debates about the connections between a multiplicity of parallel worlds: of, for example, workplace, family, friendships, body regimes, sexual practices and relationships.[81]

Practice, politics and the limits of masculinity

The above concerns point to the conceptual limits of masculinity in relation to family law. I wish to draw this discussion to a close by considering an issue central to feminist legal scholarship – the way in which such analytical imprecision[82] renders the concept potentially fraught with *political* dangers for feminism at the present moment.

The project of 'revealing' the presence of the hegemonic masculine in law – the common tactic, I have suggested, within much critical work in the field of family

---

76 Middleton (1992), p 152.
77 Note the argument of Hearn (1996), p 203.
78 Middleton (1992), p 142.
79 *Ibid.*
80 Collier (1998).
81 Hearn (1996), p 202; contrast Connell (2002).
82 It is possible, Hearn suggests, that masculinity might in many respects be 'an ethnocentric or even a Eurocentric notion', a product of a particular historical moment which is, in some cultural contexts at least, at best 'irrelevant or misleading' (1996, p 209).

law to date – rests on a number of assumptions. There is a tendency here for social theory and the practices, texts and institutions of law to appear linked in what is, in effect, a systematic unity of shared assumptions, each embodiments of 'the masculinity of law'. Depicting law as contingently, essentially or otherwise irredeemably masculine in nature, however, fails to address 'the theories or institutions [of law] as such . . . the significance of . . . statements within their specific discursive contexts'.[83] The depiction of law as masculine or masculinist can conflate, by reference to preconstituted definitions of ideological or cultural meanings of masculinity, certain culturally specific beliefs about practices, identities, value systems and so forth.[84] And such a model of analysis – ironically, given its progressive political intent – can also be seen to result in a systematic *de*politicisation of issues of power and material interest.

Why is this so? We return to a familiar question – what is left *after* the 'deconstructive moment'?[85] There is a level of abstraction involved in the above kind of engagements with masculinity which can easily slide into something else – an effacing of broader questions about the development of a political, economic and materialist analysis of gendered labour.[86] Far from focusing attention on men's practices – what men do – the focus of analysis has all too often been the gender category masculinity. What is left open to question in such a line of thinking is the extent to which men's gender then itself appears as 'a reification . . . of men's practices (and, of course, the practices of women that support them) . . . [a] reification [which] is then employed to explain these same practices'.[87] What fades from view, that is, are questions about social power – the very issues raised by the feminist scholarship during the 1970s and 1980s in the first place. It is this issue which, at the present moment, would then appear to have far-reaching implications for feminist legal scholarship in the context of a politico-economic episteme framed, not just by neo-liberalism and post-modernism, as Margaret Thornton has recently indicated,[88] but also by a general acceptance and embrace of formal gender neutrality across many areas of law. It is this latter point which, I would suggest, further calls into question the use of masculinity within feminist legal studies in family law at the present moment.

The political limitations of masculinity for feminism are not simply a matter of the way in which the open-ended nature of the term means it can be (and has been) deployed as much by explicitly anti-feminist social movements[89] (notably when allied to the idea of masculine crisis, as above) as it has by feminists and pro-feminist men. It relates, rather, to the way in which a public debate on masculinities has, across a diverse range of cultural artefacts, rested upon what is in effect an

---

83 Brown (1990), p 48. It is important to consider in this regard the diversity and conceptual ambiguity of 'family law' as a field of study.
84 *Ibid.*
85 Does an account such as this suggest, for example, a return to the (inevitability) of establishing some kind of normative foundation of the human subject?
86 See McMahon (1999).
87 McMahon (1993), p 689.
88 Thornton (2004).
89 See Messner (1997).

individualising of a politics of gender. Instead of questioning whether men should change their behaviour, or else looking to broader questions about materialist analyses of labour and political economy, a debate has effectively been constructed around ideas of men 'wrestling with the meaning of masculinity'. Such a political and cultural project itself in many respects appears disconnected from any appreciation of the many insights of feminist scholarship around the gendered nature and material realities of issues around care and caring.

Concluding remarks

Writing in the *Australian Feminist Law Journal*, Margaret Thornton has recently spoken of her wish to begin 'a conversation which I hope others will join so that we might discursively constitute a new *episteme* of feminist legal theory that is linked to the political'.[90] In exploring whether 'the conjunction of postmodernism and neoliberalism' might add up 'to post-feminism',[91] Thornton questions whether the 'institutional base' of feminist legal scholarship may well be 'disappearing beneath our feet' in the context of the rapidly changing political economy[92] in which feminist research into law is now undertaken within and beyond universities.[93] What is necessary, she suggests, is a return to 'political engagement, rather than introspection', a discouraging of 'an exclusive focus upon the individual and micropolitical sites ... disconnected from *the broader political picture*'.[94]

This chapter has sought to contribute to this new episteme of feminist legal theory by re-examining how the male subject has been conceptualised in critical family law scholarship to date. Thornton has suggested that 'clinging to the universals of the past [cannot] save legal academic feminism'.[95] Rather, she argues, what is necessary is to locate *both* feminist legal studies and post-modernism in the context of 'a particular politico-historical moment'.[96] This is a moment which is, I have suggested, marked by an embrace of formal gender neutrality and the twin pincers of neo-liberalism and post-modernism. In such a context, it has become a paradox of gender and law scholarship that the development of the academic study of masculinity has itself, in so many ways, concentrated on the individual and micropolitical sites, on issues of text and discourse, rather than these wider questions about terrain, political engagement and social power referred to by Thornton. Indeed, there is a sense in which the very model(s) of masculinity central to much feminist legal scholarship must themselves now be

90 Thornton (2004), p 22, my emphasis, following Drakopoulou (2000).
91 Thornton (2004), p 21.
92 Contrast Hillyard and Sim (1997).
93 The wider literature on this subject is itself now voluminous. See, for example, Brooks and Mackinnon (2001); Currie and Newson (1998); Slaughter and Leslie (1997); Currie *et al* (2002); Thornton (2001). See also Collier (2002a).
94 Thornton (2004), p 9.
95 *Ibid.*
96 *Ibid.*

seen as, in fact, the product of a particular 'episteme' – one whose time is, if not past, then at least now open to question in some far-reaching ways.

It is in such a context that these questions about masculinity take on a particular significance. There is growing reason to believe that, in many respects, the study of masculinity and law is at an important juncture. Increasingly, the concept central to so many feminist engagements with law and gender – the gender of men, termed, variously, masculinities, masculinism, masculinity – has been subjected to critique. This chapter has questioned the implications for family law of the growing call for researchers in this area to rethink actively both their *categories of analysis* and *focus of enquiries* in relation to the study of men and masculinity;[97] to question, for example, the overarching epistemic frame of sex/gender which has informed so much of the studies to date;[98] to rethink the dualism between hetero-homosexuality;[99] and, in particular, to re-appraise the place of materialist analyses of labour in developing an understanding of the politics of law. The latter issue assumes a particular significance in the light of the potentially 'corrosive impact' of neo-liberalism and marketisation on feminist legal scholarship within the academy more generally.[100] As Whitehead argues, it is only through a much more egalitarian material sexual division of labour that it will be possible to explore the 'freeing up' of gender identities advocated within so much of the work on masculinities and law; or, at the very least, to do so without the suspicion and recrimination about motive which appears to mark so many interventions in this area.[101] Tackling material inequalities in the relative position of women and men is more likely to bring about change than attempts pitched solely at the level of textual/deconstructive reforming men's 'selves', personalities or identities, or else aimed at 'subverting' dominant discourses around masculinity.[102]

Ultimately, it is important to remember, as Connell himself has long argued, that as a material practice, gender cannot be detached from what are increasingly *global(ised)* struggles around power and material interest.[103] 'Changing men', as a political end, cannot be reduced to questions of individual or collective projects of self-actualisation. The approach outlined in this chapter has sought to appreciate the undoubted strengths and insights of those analyses which have sought to develop understandings of masculinity in the field of family law. Yet it is through a recognition of the limitations of these approaches that it becomes possible to see what the ultimate problem in this area of scholarship may be: not one of the limits of deconstructive analysis *per se* but the analytic and political limitations of a model of structured action which has rested on outmoded and essentialist notions of masculine identity. At the same time, and in recognising the force of perspectives originating from within a broadly post-modern frame, it is equally imperative

97 Whitehead (2002).
98 See, for example, Daly (1997).
99 Edwards (1994).
100 Thornton (2004), p 1.
101 Whitehead (2002).
102 MacInnes (1998).
103 Connell (1998).

that questions of power, interest and political economy are not overlooked. What is as intriguing as it is worrying about recent developments is the way in which, whilst a range of cultural discourses have certainly problematised the relationship between men and family law in far-reaching ways, they are doing so in such a way that, behind a purportedly progressive rhetoric of gender equity, questions of power and material interest continue to be systematically marginalised and depoliticised. The current debate about contact law reform in the UK can itself be seen to serve as a case in point in this regard.

Family law has a particular significance in these debates. Indeed, it can be seen to exemplify the effects of a depoliticising of gender, an issue which has a worrying significance for feminism. Across a number of areas of family law and policy, gender-neutral norms and assumptions about gender neutrality are being applied to what remain, in many cases, profoundly gender*ed* areas of social life.[104] What is so revealing about present struggles in this area is how, alongside a downplaying of questions of the wider political economy in which knowledge of 'masculinity' is produced, much of the rhetoric in conversations about men and the changing family then takes the form of attempts to bolster and re-affirm traditional social relations in the face of the challenges posed by economic and cultural change. If that is where the study of masculinity and law has led us then there is, perhaps, good reason to take up the call by Thornton to seek to 'discursively constitute a new *episteme* of feminist legal theory'.[105] For all the seeming heterogeneity of the 'new ways of being a man' foregrounded in so much of the literature on masculinities, what tend to be side-stepped are questions of the material basis of what research suggests are still-entrenched sexual divisions of labour;[106] still-pertinent questions about the autonomy of men to 'opt out' of caring relations; and, importantly, still-unanswered questions about what all of this might tell us about the way contemporary advanced capitalist neo-liberal societies value social care and intimacy.

Acknowledgments

This chapter is based in part on an address delivered at the opening Colloquium ('Text and Terrain: Legal Studies in Gender and Sexuality') of the AHRB Research Centre in Law, Gender & Sexuality at the University of Kent, Canterbury, UK, September 2004. I would like to acknowledge the support of an AHRB Research Leave Scheme award (Ref: AN 8065/APN 16739) in funding the leave period in which research for this paper was conducted.

References

Adams, P (1996) *The Emptiness of the Image: Psychoanalysis and Sexual Differences*, London: Routledge

---

104 Note, for example, the arguments of Boyd (2003; 2001; 1991); Rhoades and Boyd (2004); Kaganas (1999); Kaganas and Day Sclater (2004); Fineman (1995; 1991).
105 Thornton (2004), p 22, original emphasis.
106 McMahon (1993), p 689; see also Duncombe and Marsden (1999).

Arditti, J and Allen, K (1993) 'Distressed fathers' perceptions of legal and relational inequities post-divorce', 31 *Family and Conciliation Courts Review* 461

Arendell, T (1995) *Fathers and Divorce*, London: Sage

Atkins, S and Hoggett, B (1984) *Women and the Law*, Oxford: Blackwell

Barron, A (2000) 'Feminism, aestheticism and the limits of law', 8 *Feminist Legal Studies* 25

Beck, U and Beck-Gernsheim, E (1995) *The Normal Chaos of Love*, Cambridge: Polity

Bell, C (1995) 'All I really need to know I learned in kindergarten (playing soccer): A feminist parable of legal academia', 7 *Yale J of Law and Feminism* 133

Berger, M, Wallis, B and Watson, S (eds) (1995) *Constructing Masculinity*, New York: Routledge

Berotia, C (1998) 'An interpretative analysis of the mediation rhetoric of fathers' rightists: Privatisation versus personalisation', 16(1) *Mediation Quarterly* 15

Berotia, C and Drakich, J (1993) 'The fathers' rights movement: Contradictions in rhetoric and practice', 14(4) *J of Family Issues* 592

Bibbings, L (2000) 'Boys will be boys: Masculinity and offences against the person', in Bridgman, J and Monk, D (eds) *Feminist Perspectives on Criminal Law*, London: Cavendish

Bottomley, A (2004) 'Shock to thought: An encounter (of a third kind) with legal feminism', 12 *Feminist Legal Studies* 29

Boyd, S (1991) 'Some postmodernist challenges to feminist analyses of law, family and State: Ideology and discourse in child custody law', 10 *Canadian J of Law and Society* 39

Boyd, S (2001) 'Backlash and the construction of legal knowledge: The case of child custody law', 20 *Windsor Yearbook of Access to Justice* 141

Boyd, S (2003) *Child Custody, Law and Women's Work*, Oxford: Oxford University Press

Boyd, S and Young, C (2002) 'Who influences family law reform? Discourses on motherhood and fatherhood in legislative reform debates in Canada', *Studies in Law Politics and Society* 26

Bridgeman, J and Millns, S (eds) (1995) *Law and Body Politics: Regulating the Female Body*, Aldershot: Ashgate

Brittan, A (1989) *Masculinity and Power*, Oxford: Blackwell

Brooks, A and Mackinnon, A (eds) (2001) *Gender and the Restructured University*, Buckingham: SRHE/Open University Press

Brophy, J and Smart, C (eds) (1985) *Women in Law: Explorations in Law, Family and Sexuality*, London: Routledge and Kegan Paul

Brown, B (1990) 'Reassessing the critique of biologism', in Gelsthorpe, L and Morris, A (eds) *Feminist Perspectives in Criminology*, Milton Keynes: Open University Press

Brown, J and Day Sclater, S (1999) 'Divorce: A psychodynamic perspective', in Day Sclater, S and Piper, C (eds) *Undercurrents of Divorce*, Aldershot: Ashgate

Butler, J (1990) *Gender Trouble: Feminism and the Subversion of Identity*, London: Routledge

Butler, J (1993) *Bodies That Matter: On the Discursive Limits of Sex*, London: Routledge

Carrigan, T, Connell, R and Lee, J (1985) 'Towards a new sociology of masculinity', 14 *Theory and Society* 551

Carver, T (1996) ' "Public Man" and the critique of masculinities', 24 *Political Theory* 673

Clare, A (2000) *On Men: Masculinity in Crisis*, London: Chatto and Windus

Collier, R (1992) ' "The art of living the married life": Representations of male heterosexuality in law', 1 *Social and Legal Studies* 543

Collier, R (1995) *Masculinity, Law and the Family*, London and New York: Routledge

Collier, R (1996) ' "Coming together?": Post-heterosexuality, masculine crisis and the new men's movement', 4 *Feminist Legal Studies* 3

Collier, R (1998) *Masculinities, Crime and Criminology*, London: Sage

Collier, R (1999b) 'From women's emancipation to sex war? Men, heterosexuality and the politics of divorce', in Day Sclater, S and Piper, C (eds) *Undercurrents of Divorce*, Aldershot: Ashgate

Collier, R (1999a) 'Feminising the workplace? (Re)constructing the "good parent" in employment law and family policy', in Morris, A and O'Donnell, T (eds) *Feminist Perspectives on Employment Law*, London: Cavendish

Collier, R (2000) 'Straight families, queer lives', in Stychin, C and Herman, D (eds) *Sexuality in the Legal Arena*, London: Athlone

Collier, R (2001) 'A hard time to be a father?: Law, policy and family practices', 28 *J of Law and Society* 520

Collier, R (2002a) 'The changing university and the (legal) academic career – rethinking the relationship between women, men and the "private life" of the law school', 22 *Legal Studies* 1

Collier, R (2002b) 'Male bodies, family practices', in Bainham, A, Sclater, S and Richards, M (eds) *Body Lore and Laws*, Oxford: Hart

Coltrane, S (1996) *Family Man: Fatherhood, Housework and Gender Equity*, Oxford: Oxford University Press

Conaghan, J (2000) 'Reassessing the feminist theoretical project in law', 27 *J of Law and Society* 351

Connell, R (1987) *Gender and Power*, Cambridge: Polity

Connell, R (1995) *Masculinities*, Cambridge: Polity

Connell, R (1998) 'Masculinity and globalization', 1 *Men and Masculinities* 3

Connell, R (2000) *The Men and the Boys*, Cambridge: Polity Press

Connell, R (2002) 'On hegemonic masculinity and violence: A response to Jefferson and Hall', 6 *Theoretical Criminology* 89

Currie, J and Newson, J (eds) (1998) *Universities and Globalization*, London: Sage

Currie, J, Thiele, B and Harris, P (2002) *Gendered Universities in Globalized Economies: Power, Careers and Sacrifices*, Maryland: Lexington

Daly, K (1997) 'Different ways of conceptualising sex/gender in feminist theory and their implications for criminology', 1 *Theoretical Criminology* 25

Day Sclater, S (1999a) *Divorce: A Psycho-Social Study*, Ashgate: Aldershot

Day Sclater, S (1999b) 'Experiences of divorce', in Day Sclater, S and Piper, C (eds) *Undercurrents of Divorce*, Aldershot: Ashgate

Day Sclater, S and Yates, C (1999) 'The psycho-politics of post-divorce parenting', in Bainham, A, Day Sclater, S and Richards, M (eds) *What is A Parent? A Socio-Legal Analysis*, Oxford: Hart

Dewar, J (1998) 'The normal chaos of family law', 61 *Modern Law Review* 467

Diduck, A (1995) 'The unmodified family: The Child Support Act and the construction of legal subjects', 22 *J of Law and Society* 527

Diduck, A (2001) 'A Family by any other name . . . or Starbucks comes to England', 28(2) *J of Law and Society* 290

Diduck, A (2003) *Law's Families*, London: Butterworths

Drakopoulou, M (2000) 'Women's resolutions of laws reconsidered: Epistemic shifts and the emergence of feminist legal discourse', 11 *Law and Critique* 47

Duncombe, J and Marsden, D (1999) 'Love and intimacy: The gender division of emotion and "emotion work" ', 27(2) *Sociology* 221

Edwards, T (1994) *Erotics and Politics: Gay Male Sexuality, Masculinity and Feminism*, London: Routledge

Faludi, S (1999) *Stiffed: The Betrayal of Modern Man*, London: Chatto and Windus

Fineman, M (1991) *The Illusion of Equality: The Rhetoric and Reality of Divorce Reform*, Chicago: University of Chicago Press

Fineman, M (1995) *The Neutered Mother, The Sexual Family and Other Twentieth Century Tragedies*, New York: Routledge

Frosh, S (1994) *Sexual Difference: Masculinity and Psychoanalysis*, London: Routledge

Frosh, S (1997) *For and Against Psychoanalysis*, London: Routledge

Gadd, D (2000) 'Masculinities, violence and defended psycho-social subjects', 4 *Theoretical Criminology* 429

Gadd, D (2002) 'Masculinities and violence against female partners', 11 *Social and Legal Studies* 61

Giddens, A (1992) *The Transformations of Intimacy*, Cambridge: Polity

Goodey, J (1997) 'Boys don't crime: Masculinities, fear of crime and fearlessness', 37 *British J of Criminology* 401

Goodrich, P (2001) 'Barron's complaint: A response to "Feminism, aestheticism and the limits of law" ', 9 *Feminist Legal Studies* 149

Graycar, R (2000) 'Law reform by frozen chook: family law reform for the new millennium', 24 *Melbourne University Law Review* 737

Graycar, R and Morgan, J (1990) *The Hidden Gender of Law*, Sydney Federation Press

Groombridge, N (1998) 'Masculinities and crimes against the environment', 2 *Theoretical Criminology* 248

Halewood, P (1995) 'White men can't jump: Critical epistemologies, embodiment, and the praxis of legal scholarship', 7 *Yale J of Law and Feminism* 1

Hall, S (2002) 'Daubing the drudges of fury: Men, violence and the piety of the "hegemonic masculinity" thesis', 6 *Theoretical Criminology* 35

Harding, S (1986) *The Science Question in Feminism*, Milton Keynes: Open University Press

Harding, S (ed) (1987) *Feminism and Methodology*, Milton Keynes: Open University Press

Hearn, J (1987) *The Gender of Oppression*, Brighton: Harvester Wheatsheaf

Hearn, J (1996) 'Is masculinity dead? A critique of the concept of masculinity', in Mac an Ghaill, M (ed) *Understanding Masculinities*, Buckingham: Open University Press

Heins, M (1995) 'Masculinity, sexism and censorship law', in Berger, M, Wallis, B and Watson, S (eds) *Constructing Masculinity*, New York: Routledge

Hillyard, P and Sim, J (1997) 'The political economy of socio-legal research', in Thomas, P (ed) *Socio-Legal Studies*, Aldershot: Dartmouth

Hood-Williams, J (2001) 'Gender, masculinities and crime: From structures to psyches', 5 *Theoretical Criminology* 37

Hyde, A (1997) *Bodies of Law*, Princeton, NJ: Princeton University Press

Jackson, E (1993) 'Catherine MacKinnon and feminist jurisprudence: A critical reappraisal', 19 *J of Law and Society* 195

Jefferson, T (1994) 'Theorizing masculine subjectivity', in Newburn, T and Stanko, E (eds) *Just Boys Doing Business?* London: Routledge

Jefferson, T and Carlen, P (eds) (1996) 36(3) *British J of Criminology* 337–444

Kaganas, F (1999) 'Contact, conflict and risk', in Day Sclater, S and Piper, C (eds) *Undercurrents of Divorce*, Aldershot: Ashgate

Kaganas, F and Day Sclater, S (2004) 'Contact disputes: Narrative constructions of "good" parents', 12(1) *Feminist Legal Studies* 1

Kaye, M and Tolmie, J (1998a) 'Discoursing dads: The rhetorical devices of fathers' rights groups', 22 *Melbourne University Law Review* 162

Kaye, M and Tolmie, J (1998b) 'Fathers' rights groups in Australia and their engagement with issues in family law', 12 *Australian J of Family Law* 12

Lacey, N (1998) *Unspeakable Subjects: Feminist Essays in Legal and Social Theory*, Oxford: Hart

Liddle, M (1996) 'State, masculinity and law: Some comments on English gender and English State formation', 36 *British J of Criminology* 361

MacInnes, J (1998) *The End of Masculinity*, Buckingham: Open University Press

MacKinnon, C (1983) 'Feminism, Marxism, method and the State: An agenda for theory', 8 *Signs* 635

MacKinnon, C (1987) *Feminism Unmodified: Discourses on Life and Law*, Cambridge, MA: Harvard University Press

McMahon, A (1993) 'Male readings of feminist theory: The psychologization of sexual politics in the masculinity literature', 22 *Theory and Society* 675

McMahon, A (1999) *Taking Care of Men*, Cambridge: Cambridge University Press

Messner, M (1997) *The Politics of Masculinities: Men in Movements*, London: Sage

Middleton, P (1992) *The Inward Gaze: Masculinity and Subjectivity in Modern Culture*, London: Routledge

Moran, L (1990) 'A study of the history of male sexuality in law: Non-consummation', 1 *Law and Critique* 155

Morgan, D (1992) *Discovering Men*, London: Routledge

Morgan, D (1996) *Family Connections: An Introduction to Family Studies*, Oxford: Blackwell

Morgan, D (1999) 'Risk and family practices: Accounting for change and fluidity in family life', in Silva, E and Smart, C (eds) *The 'New' Family?* London: Sage

Naffine, N (1990) *Law and the Sexes: Explorations in Feminist Jurisprudence*, Sydney: Allen and Unwin

Naffine, N (1994) 'Possession: Erotic love in the law of rape', 57 *Modern Law Review* 10

Naffine, N (2002) 'In praise of legal feminism', 22 *Legal Studies* 71

Naffine, N (2004) 'Shocking thoughts: A reply to Anne Bottomley', 12 *Feminist Legal Studies* 175

Newburn, T and Stanko, E (1994) *Just Boys Doing Business?* London: Routledge

O'Donovan, K (1985) *Sexual Divisions in Law*, London: Weidenfeld

O'Donovan, K (1986) 'Family law and legal theory', in Twining, W (ed) *Legal Theory and Common Law*, Oxford: Blackwell

O'Donovan, K (1993) *Family Law Matters*, London: Pluto

Pease, B (2000) *Recreating Men: Postmodern Masculinity Politics*, London: Sage

Rhoades, H and Boyd, S (2004) 'Reforming custody laws: A comparative study', 18 *International J of Law, Policy and the Family* 119

Rose, N (1987) 'Beyond the public/private division: Law, power and the family', 14 *J of Law and Society* 61

Sachs, A and Wilson, J (1978) *Sexism and the Law: A Study of Male Beliefs and Judicial Bias*, Oxford: Martin Robertson

Sandland, R (1995) 'Between "truth" and "difference": Poststructuralism, law and the power of feminism', 3 *Feminist Legal Studies* 3

Sandland, R (1998a) 'Seeing double? Or why "to be or not to be" is (not) the question for feminist legal studies', 7(3) *Social and Legal Studies* 307

Sandland, R (1998b) 'The mirror and the veil: Reading the imaginary domain', 6 *Feminist Legal Studies* 33

Segal, L (1994) *Straight Sex: the Politics of Pleasure*, London: Virago

Seidler, V (1989) *Rediscovering Masculinity: Reason, Language and Sexuality*, London: Routledge

Sheldon, S (1999) 'Preconceiving masculinity: Imagining men's reproductive bodies in law', 26 *J of Law and Society* 129

Sheldon, S (2001) 'Sperm bandits: Birth control fraud and the battle of the sexes', 21 *Legal Studies* 460

Slaughter, S and Leslie, L (1997) *Academic Capitalism: Politics, Policies and the Entrepreneurial University*, Baltimore: John Hopkins University Press

Smart, C (1984) *The Ties that Bind: Law, Marriage and the Reproduction of Patriarchal Relations*, London: Routledge and Kegan Paul

Smart, C (1989) *Feminism and the Power of Law*, London: Routledge

Smart, C (1992) 'The woman of legal discourse', 1 *Social and Legal Studies* 29

Smart, C (1999) 'The "new" parenthood: Fathers and mothers after divorce', in Silva, E and Smart, C (eds) *The 'New' Family?* London: Sage

Smart, C and Brophy, J (1985) 'Locating law: A discussion of the place of law in feminist politics', in Brophy, J and Smart, C (eds) *Women in Law: Explorations in Law, Family and Sexuality*, London: Routledge and Kegan Paul

Smart, C and Neale, B (1999a) *Family Fragments*, Cambridge: Polity

Smart, C and Neale, B (1999b) ' "I hadn't really thought about it": New identities/new fatherhoods', in Seymour, J and Bagguley, P (eds) *Relating Intimacies: Power and Resistance*, Basingstoke

Thomas, K (1995) ' "Masculinity", "the rule of law" and other legal fictions', in Berger, M, Wallis, B and Watson, S (eds) *Constructing Masculinity*, New York: Routledge

Thornton, M (1989) 'Hegemonic masculinity and the academy', 17 *International J of the Sociology of Law* 115

Thornton, M (1996) *Dissonance and Distrust: Women in the Legal Profession*, Melbourne: Oxford University Press

Thornton, M (1998) 'Authority and corporeality: The conundrum for women in law', 6 *Feminist Legal Studies* 147

Thornton, M (2001) 'The demise of diversity in legal education: Globalisation and the new knowledge economy', 8(1) *International J of the Legal Profession* 37

Thornton, M (2004) 'Neoliberal melancholia: The case of feminist legal scholarship', 20 *Australian Feminist LJ* 7

Waldby, C (1995) 'Destruction: Boundary erotics and refigurations of the heterosexual male body', in Grosz, E and Probyn, E (eds) *Sexy Bodies: The Strange Carnalities of Feminism*, London: Routledge

Walklate, S (1995) *Gender and Crime: An Introduction*, Hemel Hempstead: Prentice Hall/Harvester Wheatsheaf

Wallbank, J (1997) 'The campaign for change of the Child Support Act 1991: Reconstituting the "absent" father', 6 *Social and Legal Studies* 191

West, R (1988) 'Jurisprudence and gender', 55 *University of Chicago Law Review* 1

Wetherell, M and Edley, N (1999) 'Negotiating hegemonic masculinity: Imaginary positions and psycho-discursive practices', 9 *Feminism and Psychology* 335

Whitehead, S (1999) 'Hegemonic masculinity revisited', 6 *Gender, Work and Organization* 58

Whitehead, S (2002) *Men and Masculinities: Key Themes and New Directions*, Cambridge: Polity

Williams, P (1995) 'Meditations on masculinity', in Berger, M, Wallis, B and Watson, S (eds) *Constructing Masculinity*, New York: Routledge